Adventure Guide

Nicaragua

Erica Rounsefell

HUNTER

HUNTER PUBLISHING, INC.
130 Campus Drive, Edison, NJ 08818
☎ 732-225-1900; 800-255-0343; fax 732-417-1744
www.hunterpublishing.com

Ulysses Travel Publications
4176 Saint-Denis, Montréal, Québec
Canada H2W 2M5
☎ 514-843-9882, ext. 2232; fax 514-843-9448

The Roundhouse Group
Millstone, Limers Lane, Northam
Devon, EX39 2RG England
☎ 01237-474474; fax 01237-474774

ISBN-13: 978-1-58843-632-0

© 2008 Hunter Publishing, Inc.

*This and other Hunter travel guides are also available as
e-books through Amazon.com, NetLibrary.com and other
digital partners. For information, e-mail us at
comments@hunterpublishing.com.*

Cover photo: Cyclist in Granada
© Margie Politzer/LonelyPlanetImages.com
Interior images provided by the author and various other
sources as noted.
Maps © Hunter Publishing, Inc. 2007
Index by Inge Wiesen

4   3   2   1

ABOUT THE AUTHOR

Erica Rounsefell is a free-lance writer in Washington, DC. Originally from Stayton, Oregon (population 6,000), Erica has traveled, studied, and worked in more than 70 countries, including a year-long stint as a Fulbright Scholar in South Korea. She first went to Nicaragua to volunteer at a home for street children. Erica has a BA in Government and International Relations and a MA in International Develop-  ment from Clark University in Worcester, MA. She welcomes readers' stories and suggestions and can be reached at ericanico@gmail.com.

ACKNOWLEDGMENTS

Gracias enormes go to the guys at Quinta Los Chavalos in Granada, including Juan Carlos, Julio, Mario, Moises, Ismael, and Ezequiel, for introducing me to *la vida granadina* on my first visits to Nicaragua. Billy Bob Matuz Sequeira showed me the best Juigalpa has to offer. Donna Tabor, *el juigalpino* Mike Knowles, and Rafael Praslin were also instrumental in my research. Thanks to the Peace Corps Volunteers taking the Foreign Service Exam at the U.S. Embassy in Managua for tips about their regions. Marissa Davies was always up for adventures in Bluefields, the Corn Islands, and Granada. Thanks also to *mi hermano* Chris for killing cockroaches and exploring the Northern Highlands with me.

Contents

■ MAPS

■ USING THIS BOOK

Phone numbers, email addresses, websites, and even business locations change rapidly in Nicaragua; if you're planning a detour to visit a specific attraction, restaurant, or hotel, it's worth getting in touch in advance to confirm its continued existence. Some hotels and restaurants and hotels, especially in smaller towns, do not have phones. Hotel and restaurant listings are loosely listed in this book in the order of value for the money; generally, hotels and restaurants that are unclean or have some other quality that renders them not worthy of a recommendation are eliminated from the listings. However, in some isolated locations there are few accommodation and dining options; be prepared for the occasional cockroach, and you'll have great stories to tell your friends when you get home!

Introduction

Nicaragua is the largest Central American country yet also one of the least visited. It does not have the archaeological ruins or the national parks that attract visitors to other parts of Central America; rather, its strongest assets are its vibrant, unpretentious way of life

and its natural beauty that remains largely untouched. This is not to say that Nicaragua is without its attractions: the country lays claim to Central America's largest lake, Lago de Nicaragua, and the oldest Spanish city in the continental Americas, Granada. Nicaragua also offers nature reserves brimming with **wildlife**, uncrowded **beaches**, well-preserved colonial **architecture**, and a growing number of excellent **ecotourism** opportunities.

Until the late 1990s, Nicaragua received few visitors beyond foreign workers. Lingering visions of recent revolution and civil war kept travelers away, but the country has emerged from decades of political instability to transform itself into a peaceful nation with an eye on the future while retaining its passion for traditional culture. The tourism industry in Nicaragua is still in its infancy, and limited infrastructure and little promotion abroad mean that Nicaragua remains largely off the radar for tourists. And this is precisely the reason to go there. Though Nicaragua continues to be a sought-after destination for adventurous travelers eager to experi-

*Guardabarranco (*Eumomota superciliosa*), national bird of Nicaragua*

ence adrenaline-filled water sports and land-based outdoors activities, upscale hotels and resorts are becoming increasingly common, attracting visitors looking for relaxation. More and more visitors are becoming aware of Nicaragua's opportunities to get away from it all by relaxing on Pacific **beaches** or secluded private **islands** and experiencing nature through **boating** or **birdwatching**.

Shoppers find that the markets offer quality **crafts**, and it is often possible to meet the artisans themselves. Visitors can improve their Spanish through a **language course** and homestay, or they can **volunteer** in a local community to get an inside look at the country and its people.

With ample biodiversity and cultural offerings, Nicaragua is unlikely to remain off the tourism map for long. For now, however, many travelers are inclined to keep the secrets of its picturesque lakes, lush rainforests, secluded beaches, and vibrant cultures to themselves.

Isla Olmetepe.

THE PEOPLE

Nicaraguans, who often refer to themselves as "**Nicas**," are renowned for their friendly and welcoming nature. Visitors are still a curiosity in many parts of the country, and most tourists feel warmly received. Local **markets** and **festivals** offer glimpses into traditional rural life, while Managua boasts all of the trappings of a large urban area.

Five and a half-million people call Nicaragua home, with one-fourth of the country's population residing in Managua, the nation's sprawling capital of over one million. The country's two other main cities, **León** and **Granada**, retain the relaxed air of large towns and are favorites with visitors for their colonial architecture and numerous sites of cultural and historical distinction.

Street in Granada.

© José Cuadra

Nicaragua is multiethnic and multicultural. The majority of the population is Mestizo (mixed indigenous and white. This group is associated with much of Nicaragua's vibrant folklore, music, dance, and religious tradition. On the Atlantic Coast there is a strong African influence, particularly evident

in local food and music, which stems from black workers brought in by the British to work on plantations. A trickle of immigration from the Caribbean, particularly Jamaica, continues to diversify the sparsely-settled Caribbean region. Small populations of indigenous peoples, who live primarily along the Caribbean coast, include the Miskito, Sumu, and Rama. The population is 69% Mestizo, 17% white, 9% black and 5% indigenous.

Nicaragua has the smallest population in Central America, but it is also the fastest-growing country in the region. Many Nicaraguans have moved abroad seeking economic opportunity; the most common destinations are Costa Rica, with an estimated 700,000 Nicaraguans, and the US, with a half-million.

■ RELIGION

Roman Catholic 72.9%, Evangelical 15.1%, Moravian 1.5%, Episcopalian 0.1%, other 1.9%, none 8.5%. Though most Nicaraguans identify themselves as Catholics, many are non-practicing. Evangelical Protestant groups are growing rapidly, especially in rural areas. Nicaragua has no official religion. Many Nicaraguans enjoy discussing religion, both theirs and yours, and will express surprise and confusion if you profess to have no religion.

Many private homes display elements of their religious devotion, including this image, which can be seen on the exterior of a home in Granada.

Introduction

■ LANGUAGE

Spanish is the official language of Nicaragua, and it is spoken by 97% of the population. English and indigenous languages, including Miskito, are spoken on the Caribbean coast. The English of the Caribbean coast has developed a unique regional personality, though locals will often use a more standard form of English when speaking with foreigners. The country's literacy rate is 67% for both men and women.

THE ARTS

■ MUSIC & DANCE

Nicaraguans are enthusiastic musicians and dancers, and you are likely to be encouraged to get up and join in the fun. Nicaragua's national instrument is the **marimba**, which is made from strips of wood attached to bamboo or metal tubes of vary-

© R Andrew Lepley

Marimba keys are usually made from rosewood.

ing lengths. The instrument is played with soft hammers and is usually accompanied by guitars and drums. Music in the Atlantic region has a strong Afro-Caribbean influence, and reggae music is common. An excellent occasion to experience the sensual regional music and dance of the Caribbean Coast is at the **Palo de Mayo** (Maypole) Festival in Bluefields throughout late May.

Though Nicaraguans listen to music from throughout Latin America and beyond (young Nicas are particularly fond of pop, and many Atlantic Coast residents have a penchant for American country music), local singers are well-regarded by Nicaraguans.

> **TIP:** *For an excellent introduction to traditional and contemporary Nicaraguan music, you can download free music clips from the website of the Nicaragua Ministry of Tourism, www.intur.gob.ni/english/musica/musica.html.*

One of the country's most prominent singers is **Carlos Mejía Godoy**, whose songs are inspired by life in Nicaragua. Mejía Godoy and his brother, composer **Luís Enrique**, showcase their work at La Casa de los Mejía Godoy (The House of the Mejía Godoys) in Managua. Other prominent Nicaraguan performers include **Lia Barrios**, **Camilo Zapata**, **Salvador** and **Katia Cardenal**, and the band **Dimensión Costeña**.

Carlos Mejía Godoy

■ THEATER

Though performances can be a challenge to find, Nicaragua has a theatrical heritage stemming from the country's indigenous ancestors. Many works are performed during festivals and can also be experienced at the **Teatro Nacional Rubén Darío** in Managua or the **Casa de los Tres Mundos** in Granada. Look for **Los Caballeros Elegantes del Toro Guaco** (The Elegant Gentlemen of the Guaco Bull) and **El**

Casa de los Tres Mundos

Drama Epico del Gigante (The Epic Drama of the Giant). Try www.vianica.com/thisweek.php for weekly performance listings countrywide.

■ TRADITIONAL ARTS & CRAFTS

Nicaragua's tradition of arts and crafts isn't as prolific as that of some other areas of Central America, though this is hard to believe if you pay a visit to Masaya's bustling **markets**, the destina-

tion of much of the country's *artesanía*. Nonetheless, artisan communities can be visited in several places around the country, and Nicaragua is known in particular for its unique **pottery** produced in the Pueblos Blancos (p 195) and the Northern Highlands, quality **hammocks** from Masaya (p 134), and Primitivist **paintings** and balsa wood **carvings from Solentiname** (see box).

Hammock workshop, Masaya

SOLENTINAME'S PRIMITIVIST PAINTERS

Many of Nicaragua's finest painters hail from Solentiname, a group of more than 30 remote islands in the southern part of Lago de Nicaragua. The artistic tradition began in 1966 when a sculptor and poet from Granada, Ernesto Cardenal, arrived in Solentiname. He was so impressed by the natural talent displayed by many of the islands' inhabitants for carving balsa wood and dried fruit that he invited a friend, Pérez de la Rocha, to the island. Together, they founded the Primitivist art school in Solentiname and trained many local residents to paint the natural beauty of the archipelago. Today, many of Nicaragua's finest painters, most of whom continue to work in fishing and agriculture in addition to painting, reside in Solentiname.

Primitivist art is typically rendered with oil on canvas and is characterized by its naiveté, bright colors, and theme of everyday life. Solentiname's paintings are inspired largely by the lush flora of the area. Animals such as birds, reptiles, mammals, and fish are often depicted, and the backgrounds usually feature mountains or volcanoes. Though the paintings portray typical village life, the style is not realistic. Little shadowing or perspective is used and the size of the subject with respect to the surroundings is rarely authentic.

The Primitivist style of painting is passed down from generation to generation; the art is taught by parents to children and grandchildren. Visitors can see local paintings at the Musas Museum, but a stroll along island paths often leads to impromptu encounters with locals at work. Paintings from the archipelago can be viewed at museums and galleries in Managua and Granada.

HISTORY

Six thousand year old human (Paleo-Indian) footprints preserved in volcanic mud near the lake in Managua, Nicaragua.

© DR d12

■ PRE-COLONIAL LIFE

When the Aztec city of Teotihuacán met its demise in 1000 AD, displaced peoples headed south to find a new homeland. Guided by a **prophecy** to settle when they saw two volcanoes, they remained in what is now Nicaragua when the twin peaks of the volcanoes on the island of Ometepe came into view. Two cultural groups settled in the area, the

Ometepe's twin peaks

Chorotegas and the **Nahuas**. The two groups intertwined and were ruled by **Chief Nicarao**, who was dubbed Chief Nicaragua by the Spanish, which gave rise to the present-day name of the area. Nicarao formed relations with the Spanish and many of the chief's subjects were baptized **Catholic**.

While the peoples of the Pacific Lowlands came from what is now central Mexico, the residents of the Northwest Highlands, called **Chontales, Matagalpas** and **Populucas,** belonged to a different group that stemmed from the Maya. These groups were not as friendly with the Spanish as were Chief Nicarao and his subjects. The Chontales, Matagalpas, and Populucas communities, failing to submit to the changes brought on by the Spanish, were eventually eradicated.

Introduction

The peoples of the Atlantic Coast region were culturally and linguistically distinct and separated from their neighbors in the west by dense foliage and unforgiving heat and humidity. The pre-Miskito **Sumu** and **Rama** constituted the area's indigenous population. Due to its proximity to the islands of the Caribbean, this region had significant contact with people from the islands, and the peoples mixed with the freed or escaped Afro-Caribbean slaves from the British West Indies.

■ THE COLONIAL ERA

Spain became aware of the area that is now Nicaragua in the early 1500s, but it was not until 1522 that a group of Spanish explorers penetrated the interior by sailing up the Río San Juan and arrived in Lago de Nicaragua. Two years later **Francisco Fernandez de Córdoba** (featured here on a 1924 postage stamp) founded the region's first cities, **Granada** and **León**, after suppressing local indigenous groups. The subsequent extraction of resources, subjection of indigenous people as slave labor, and introduction of European **diseases** to which the pre-Columbian peoples had no immunity wreaked havoc on the population. On the Atlantic Coast, where the Europeans did not settle, diseases did not so significantly ravage the indigenous groups living there. The Spanish government paid little attention to Nicaragua and did not do much exploring or building in the region throughout the colonial period. Spain was much more attentive to Peru and Mexico, in which the most significant riches were being discovered. Labor was required to extract the gold, and many indigenous Nicaraguans were sent as **slaves** to work in the mines of Peru. The focus on faraway lands meant that by the end of the 1500s León and Granada remained the first and only Spanish settlements. The rest of Nicaragua languished in poverty and continued to be largely ignored by the Crown.

■ GAINING INDEPENDENCE

Spain's grip on power in the area began slipping by the beginning of the 1800s. As in other colonies in the Americas, in Nicaragua only men born in Spain could hold powerful political and economic positions. This contributed to the frustrations of the local-born **elite**, who were fueled by an uprising in 1811 in El Salvador related to the same situation. In 1821, Nicaragua, along with the other countries of Central America, gained **independence** from Spain. The Central American countries formed the Central American Federation. Nicaragua subsequently became an independent country in 1838. At the time, the US, prompted by the California Gold Rush, was seeking a route in Central America to ship goods and people between the Atlantic and the Pacific. The location of Río San Juan and Lago de Nicaragua made Nicaragua a prime candidate for the location of a new place to rapidly and economically cross the isthmus. American Cornelius Vanderbilt collaborated with the Nicaraguan government to found the **Accessory Transit Company** in 1849, which subsequently provided steamboats to transport passengers and supplies. Though the canal that would ultimately transect the isthmus was ultimately built in Panama, the shipping industry did provide Nicaragua with an infusion of cash, increasing the country's prosperity.

■ WILLIAM WALKER

Tennessee-born **William Walker** came to Nicaragua in 1855 with political ambitions and a request from the Liberal city of León to take over Conservative Granada, the center of the country's power. With just 60 soldiers, Walker managed to appropriate the city. Nicaragua's neighbor to the south, Costa Rica, did not take this situation lightly, considering Granada's proximity to the Costa Rican border. In 1856, Costa Rica declared **war**

Portrait of William Walker by Mathew Brady

on Walker, but the invasion was quickly curtailed when a bout of cholera struck the Costa Ricans. Walker's hunger for power wasn't fulfilled with Granada, however. A few months after taking over the city, Walker managed a rigged election that installed him as President of Nicaragua. His policies of legalized slavery and making English the country's official language did not endear him to Nicaraguans. Nicaragua's Central American neighbors were fearful of the situation and its implications for potentially stirring up something similar in their own territories, thus Guatemala and Costa Rica banded with local Nicaraguans to oust the rogue American from power. The number of Nicaraguan lives lost was substantial, but Walker was ousted from Granada, though at the end he ordered the city of Granada to be burned. The fighting continued in the nearby city of Rivas from 1856-57. The battles became known as the **National War** and were quelled only when the US military detained Walker and shipped him back to the US. Walker's ambitions were not yet satisfied, and he ventured again to Central America. Tired of his antics, the British detained him and gave custody to Honduras. He was executed in Trujillo, Honduras, in 1860.

■ THE US INVADES

Following the departure of William Walker, relative stability returned to the region. **Coffee** was becoming an increasingly fashionable drink in Europe and North America, and Nicaragua's Northern Highlands region became the center of a burgeoning coffee industry. Foreign companies wanted a hand in the profitable enter-

Coffee was an important industry.

prises, and they aligned with Nicaragua's wealthy landowning families to share production.

During this time, a route through Central America was still being sought. Nicaragua's strategic location kept it as a forerunner in the competition, but in 1904 the US selected Panama as the recipient of the **canal**. An irritated President José Santos Zelaya offered the opportunity to build a competing canal across Nicaragua to Germany and Japan. Though this canal never came to fruition, it increased tensions between Nicaragua and the US, causing a civil war to erupt in late 1909, pitting the pro-US Conservatives against the nationalistic Liberals. The US intervened in the situation by sending 400 **troops** to Nicaragua's Caribbean Coast, prompting Santos Zelaya to resign soon after. The troops remained from 1912 until 1933, which contributed to the Conservatives' ability to maintain power. The presence of the US marines also inspired Nicaraguans' love for baseball, which continues today. Though the political situation appeared to be relatively calm during this time, unrest was brewing. Socialist **Augusto César Sandino**

Augusto César Sandino

created a militia of poor laborers and partnered with the Liberals to wage guerilla war on the Conservatives and their US backers. The US responded by taking control of Nicaragua's military in the early 1930s and supplementing it with a **Nicaraguan National Guard**, ostensibly to protect peace. The Guard was under the control of **Anastasio Somozo García**, whose power had just begun to grow.

■ THE SOMOZA GOVERNMENT

General Somozo's took control of the country's future in 1934. As the head of the Nicaraguan National Guard, **General Somoza García** issued an order for the assassination of Augusto César Sandino, who had become the favored Liberal candidate for the upcoming Presidential elections. Sandino's death cleared the way for Somoza to rig the national elections and become President of Nicaragua in 1937. Improving the lives of

General Somoza García

Nicaraguans was not in his agenda, unless they happened to be those of his family and closest political cronies. He molded the Nicaraguan National Guard into his own personal military and gave it far-reaching powers, including control of the media. Throughout the 1940s Somoza accumulated power, profit, and land, the traditional symbol of wealth in Central America. The end of his term did not mean Somoza exited political and economic life, however. He went to extremes to maintain power, even amending the constitution's term limits to retain his office. Not surprisingly, many Nicaraguans were unhappy about the situation. In 1956 Somoza was assassinated in Leon by a young poet, **Rigoberto López Perez**, who in turn was immediately shot by the Nicaraguan National Guard. Growing discontent with the Somoza rule was not sufficient to quell his family's power, however. Somoza's son, **Luís Somoza Debayle**, who, like his father, was educated in the US, became President. Another son, **Anastasio Somoza Debayle**, took charge of the Nicaraguan National Guard. Under their tutelage, the status quo of repression and election rigging continued.

Discontent with the political situation and the Somoza's penchant for torture and appropriation led the Conservatives and Christian Social Party to join together in 1967 to form the **National Opposition Union**. Despite the growing solidarity against Somoza rule, the family's corruption and intimidation prevailed yet again, and Luis Somoza Debayle became President. His rule didn't last long, however; he had a heart attack soon after the election and Anastasio Somoza Debayle consolidated his power by becoming President while maintaining his position as the head of the Nicaraguan National Guard.

■ THE TIDE TURNS

The 1972 **earthquake**, which killed more than 10,000 Nicaraguans, caused widespread destruction. Even as Somoza's family maintained their fortune (padded even more by interception of reconstruction aid from abroad), tens of thousands of Nicaraguans lost everything. This situation angered Nicaraguans, even friends of Somoza, sufficiently, that dissidence became widespread. By the early 1970s the FSLN (Frente Sandinista Liberación Nacional) and its Marxist-Leninist ideology garnered widespread support, especially among peasants. In December 1974, guerillas from the FSLN invaded a government official's home, taking several members of the Somoza family hostage. The US government provided a $1 million ransom for the release of the hostages, and the Somoza family's ensuing increase of repression stifled the FSLN movement at least temporarily. The Somoza regime continued to receive support from the US, but, with the election of President Jimmy Carter in 1977, oversight increased and military assistance to Nicaragua was tied to improving the human rights situation. At this point, the FSLN was still loosely formed, but in October 1977 a group of intellectuals from Nicaragua had a covert meeting in Costa Rica. From this reunion an anti-Somoza organization would emerge. A few months later, one of the opposition leaders, **Pedro Joaquín Chamorro**, who was also editor of a national newspaper, was gunned down by the Nicaraguan National Guard. This incited thousands of Nicaraguans to demonstrate against the government. The US condemned the assassination and cut off military aid to Nicaragua. The loss of aid combined with a strike led to further economic problems, raising unemployment and causing unrest. This situation culminated in August 1978, when the FSLN attacked the National Palace and took 200 members of Congress hostage. After two days with no sign of the FSLN backing down, a humiliated President Somoza had to acquiesce to the FSLN's demands. As the 1970s came to a close, widespread discontent had solidified and isolated violent skirmishes took place around the country.

■ THE REVOLUTION BEGINS

Despite Somoza's setbacks, in 1979 he declared that he would retain the presidency for two more years regardless of the approaching conclusion of his term. This announcement sparked further violent outbreaks, and other Marxist sympathizers, including Cuba, provided aid to the FSLN. In May 1979, the FSLN, dubbed the **Sandinistas**, had grown more consolidated and organized and demonstrated their force with attacks in Estelí and Jinotega. The following month, a **government-in-exile** was formed in Costa Rica. Its five figures included FSLN leaders and **Violeta Barrios de Chamorro**, the widow of the editor assassinated by Somoza's forces. Though Managua remained under the control of Somoza and his National Guard, within a few weeks the Sandinistas controlled much of the country. Somoza, realizing he had few options, resigned and moved to Miami. Just days later the Revolution was over, and the FSLN came into power officially on July 19, 1979. Somoza was assassinated in 1980 by leftist guerrillas in Paraguay.

THE SANDINISTAS & THE CONTRA WAR

The Sandinistas inherited what was essentially the failure of several hundred years of a feudal system, and upon the ascent of the FSLN, the economy was in shambles. Nonetheless, Nicaraguans were optimistic about their future and rebuilding began rapidly. Twenty percent of Nicaragua's farmland had been owned by the Somozas, and this was **expropriated** by the new government. Literacy programs were established to reach out to the 66% of the country that was illiterate. The Sandinistas also restructured the government and created a new military, the **Sandinista People's Army** (EPS). A unique feature of the new military was that it allowed women to join the forces. The Sandinistas also organized workers into unions and associations. Despite these bright spots, the economy was still in trouble due to astronomical spending on the recent war. To fill these gaps, *internacionalistas*, or workers from abroad, many of whom served as volunteers, arrived to provide basic education, healthcare, and other humanitarian services to Nicaraguans.

In 1984 the Sandinistas held the first elections since the new government had come into power, which were also the first elections since 1928 that weren't overseen by the US. **Daniel Ortega** won, receiving 67% of the vote. The primary dissenters were the residents of the Atlantic Coast, many of whom had resisted forced relocations of indigenous people at the hands of the Sandinistas.

The US, under the tutelage of newly-elected President Reagan, became increasingly apprehensive about Nicaragua's shift to the left (particularly since the Sandinista People's Army was receiving training from Cuba and the Soviet Union). Ever nervous about the spread of **Communist** tendencies, the administration cut off aid to Nicaragua in 1981, thereby heightening tensions between the US government and the Sandinistas and spurring **The Contra War**. The US supplied the Contras (*Contrarevolucionarios* or Counterrevolutionaries), who were primarily former National Guard soldiers under Somoza, with training in Honduras and unofficial bases both there and in Costa Rica. These were supplemented with Miskito indigenous people from the Atlantic Coast, who were irate about Sandinista pressure to embrace leftist ideology. Regardless of their views of the Sandinistas, the former National Guard troops were universally reviled, which was a major cause of Nicaraguans opposition to the Contra movement. The Sandinistas, revoked many of the freedoms that had been the basis for the Revolution, including freedom of the press. They also turned Nicaragua into an official one-party state, squelching legal political opposition. The US responded by imposing a trade embargo that lasted five years and weakened the Sandinista rule. The US found itself in the spotlight of a scandal, dubbed **Irangate**, involving illegal sales by the CIA of weapons to Iran in order to fund the Contras, much of which was orchestrated by **Oliver North**.

Though the government of Costa Rica had been largely silent as the Contra War was waged, **Oscar Arias**

Sánchez, the Costa Rican President, initiated the Arias Plan. The Arias Plan laid out a roadmap for peace in Central America that was signed by the presidents of the countries of Central America and the US in 1987. The plan also led the way for the Contras and the Sandinistas to sign a peace agreement in March 1988.

THE CHAMORRO GOVERNMENT

The February 1990 presidential elections saw a multi-party system restored once again in Nicaragua. No fewer than 14 political parties were running against the Sandinistas.

The opposition parties formed a coalition, the **National Opposition Union** (UNO), and gained the support of the US. The UNO established Violeta Barrios de Chamorro, who had become editor of *La Prensa* newspaper in the wake of her editor husband's death, as their presidential candidate.
Doña Violeta, as she was known, was a formidable opponent for the Sandinista incumbent candidate Daniel Ortega. Despite the loose organization of the UNO, on February 25, 1990, Violeta Barrios de Chamorro became President of Nicaragua with 55% of the vote. The Nicaraguan people had signaled their desire for peace and a new beginning. The US, pleased with the choice of a moderate leader, withdrew its support for the Contras and lifted the five-year embargo. The World Bank and the IMF agreed to reduce Nicaragua's international **debt** based

Violeta Barrios de Chamorro

on an agreement of economic restructuring, a plan that ultimately did little to improve the country's economic situation. Continued astronomical inflation and other economic woes caused strikes by workers, many of whom remained loyal to the Sandinistas. President

Chamorro's cabinet collaborated with the Sandinista leadership to alleviate the strikes.

The presidential elections of 1996 saw Violeta Chamorro facing the former Mayor of Managua, **Arnoldo Alemán**, whose political party was affiliated with that of the larger National Liberal Party (PLN), the party of Anastasio Somoza. Squabbles within the PLN caused it to splinter and thereby effectively handed the election to Alemán.

■ ALEMÁN & THE RETURN OF ORTEGA

© American Society of States

Arnoldo Alemán

Arnoldo Alemán formed another coalition government focused on cementing good relations with the US and the Catholic Church as well as the eradication of Sandinismo. Many leftist Nicaraguans saw this shift as a resurrection of the policies of the Somozas. The leftists were dealt a blow in 1998 when FSLN leader Daniel Ortega was accused by his stepdaughter of rape. The charges were left unproven, and Ortega returned to the public eye and continued his leadership in the FSLN. During this scandal, President Alemán was also dealing with accusations of corruption that became increasingly public. Amidst the continuing political problems, in October 1998 **Hurricane Mitch** devastated much of the infrastructure of central and northern Nicaragua and killed 2,500 people, with thousands more left homeless. The Alemán government was accused of financial mishandlings related to foreign contributions for hurricane reconstruction. Two years later, Nicaragua was again hit hard, this time by an **earthquake**, and in 2000 by **Hurricane Keith**.

As the 2001 presidential elections neared, support for the Sandinistas remained strong, largely due to little more than the Alemán government's failings. Nonetheless, Daniel Ortega, the FSLN candidate, lost to Liberal Party (PLC) candidate Enrique Bolaños, who was tasked with rebuilding not only the economy of Nicaragua but also his people's trust, with a strong focus on combating corruption. After years of discussions, Nicaragua signed on to CAFTA (the Central America Free Trade Agreement) in August 2004. CAFTA is designed to remove barriers to trade with and investment in the region and further regional economic integration while implementing economic reforms. It remains to be seen how CAFTA and the November 2006 election of Daniel Ortega as the new president of Nicaragua will affect Nicaragua's economic situation.

THE LAND

Nicaragua, geographically the largest country in Central America, occupies approximately the same amount of land as the state of New York. Bordered by the Pacific Ocean on the west and the Caribbean Sea on the east, Nicaragua is home to Lago de Nicaragua and Lago de Managua, two of Central America's largest lakes. Nicaragua is bordered on the north by Honduras and on the south by Costa Rica. The country is divided into three distinct geographic regions: the Pacific Lowlands in the southwest part of the

country, the Northwest Highlands, and the Atlantic Coast in the east. The **Pacific Lowlands** region, which includes the cities of Managua, León, Granada, and San Juan del Sur, is the most-visited area of the country. This region consists of expansive plains dotted with some 40 volcanoes. The **Northwest Highlands** region, which includes the cities of Estelí and Matagalpa, are largely hilly and forested. Much of the land is covered with coffee plantations. **Boaco** and **Chontales** are hilly and primarily covered with ranches and farms. In the isolated southeast area of the country **Río San Juan** is carpeted with dense jungle, and the islands of **Solentiname** in Lago de Nicaragua are forested and hilly. The **Caribbean Coast** (sometimes referred to as the Atlantic Coast) borders the Caribbean Sea and consists of low-lying land with dense vegetation. This region also includes the coral-fringed Corn Islands (shown below), which are located off the coast of the city of Bluefields. The Caribbean Coast region is sparsely populated and receives few visitors.

■ FLORA

Nicaragua is home to almost 10,000 species of plants, and you'll be amazed at how quickly the natural environment changes as you climb in elevation or travel from one region to another within the country. In the **Pacific Lowlands**, much of the land is covered by **tropical dry forest**. This type of foliage is equipped to handle long periods without rain, and for much of the dry season the plants and trees in this region appear dry and brittle; their leaves are shed almost entirely near the middle of the season. In May when the rains begin, the forest seems to spring to life, and the foliage becomes lush.

In the **Northern Highlands** the mountains are largely forested. The trees are nourished by the cool temperatures of the higher altitudes, and the conditions are ideal for **coffee** growing, specifically in the areas around Matagalpa and Jinotega, which are home to large plantations. Some areas of the Northern Highlands are covered by **pine**, particularly in the northernmost part of the region near the border of Honduras.

The **Caribbean Coast** and **Río San Juan** are largely flat and densely forested with tropical canopies. The flora in these regions are fortified by frequent showers and high humidity, and the regions are crisscrossed by rivers. These regions receive more rain than anywhere else in the country; the forest is lush and green year-round.

■ FAUNA

Nicaragua is also replete with fauna, and many visitors are dazzled by the array of wildlife they see during their adventures. In total, almost 200 mammal species have been identified in Nicaragua. However, keep in mind that they are wild animals, and you are never guaranteed a showing, especially by some of the country's more elusive species, such as the **jaguar**, which is endangered and virtually never spotted by tourists. Many of Nicaragua's mammals are a more common sight,

however, including **white-faced capuchin monkeys**, **spider monkeys**, and **howler monkeys** – the three types of monkeys that live in Nicaragua. Some of the easiest places to see (and hear!) monkeys are Laguna de Apoyo, Charco Verde on Isla Ometepe, and on Volcán Mombacho.

Nicaragua is home to almost 700 **bird** species, including the **quetzal**, one of the most sought-after sights in Central America. The quetzal is most likely to be seen in the Northern Highlands, though bird life is plentiful throughout the country and particularly prevalent on Isla Ometepe, Río San Juan, and in Las Isletas near Granada. **Reptiles** (almost 200 species at last count) are also a fairly common sight, including **caimans** and **turtles**. Endangered **Paslama sea turtles** can be

Resplendent Quetzal (Pharomachrus mocinno)

seen nesting in La Flor and Chacocente on the Pacific Coast, a sight not to be missed if you visit Nicaragua between July and late January. The most commonly seen creatures are perhaps the country's **insects** (you may get a personalized viewing right in your bungalow!). Nicaragua is home to more than 200,000 insect species. The **butterflies** are particularly beautiful.

> **TIP:** *Nicaragua's flora and fauna have been subject to a smaller amount of scientific research than any other country in Central America. Write yourself a grant, and come on down!*

▨ PRESERVATION

Before 1988, Nicaragua had little protection for its unique flora and fauna. In more recent years, the Min-

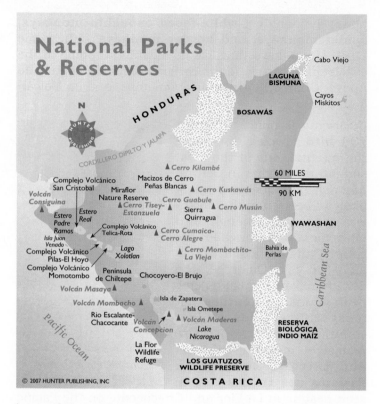

National Parks & Reserves

Cabo Viejo

LAGUNA BISMUNA

Cayos Miskitos

HONDURAS

BOSAWÁS

CORDILLERO DIPILTO Y JALAPA

▲ Cerro Kilambé

60 MILES

90 KM

Complejo Volcánico San Cristobal
Miraflor Nature Reserve
Macizos de Cerro Peñas Blancas ▲ Cerro Kuskawás

Volcán Consiguina ▲

▲ Cerro Tisey-Estanzuela
Cerro Guabule
▲ Cerro Musún

Estero Padre Ramos
Estero Real
Sierra Quirragua

Isla Juan Venado
Complejo Volcánico Telica-Rota
▲ Cerro Cumaica-Cerro Alegre

WAWASHAN

Complejo Volcánico Pilas-El Hoyo

Lago Xolotlan
▲ Cerro Mombachito-La Vieja
Bahia de Perlas

Complejo Volcánico Momotombo
Península de Chiltepe
Chocoyero-El Brujo

Volcán Masaya ▲

Volcán Mombacho ▲
Isla de Zapatera

Isla Ometepe

Río Escalante-Chacocante
Volcán Concepcion ▲
▲ Volcán Maderas
Lake Nicaragua

RESERVA BIOLÓGICA INDIO MAÍZ

Pacific Ocean

Caribbean Sea

La Flor Wildlife Refuge

LOS GUATUZOS WILDLIFE PRESERVE

© 2007 HUNTER PUBLISHING, INC

COSTA RICA

istry of Natural Resources and the Environment, along with the help of international partners like USAID, has established 73 **nature reserves** countrywide that encompass approximately 17% of the Nicaragua's territory. Further, a fledgling **ecotourism** industry is making visiting remote areas, including Río San Juan (p 401), a feasible option for travelers eager to see some of the country's unique flora and fauna. For visitors with limited time, many nature reserves are accessible by day-trips from the country's main cities. To see some of Nicaragua's unique species, consider an excursion to **Volcán Mombacho** (p 191) from Granada or **Selva Negra** (p 363) from Matagalpa, or **Chocoyero-El Brujo** from Managua. For a more comprehensive nature experience, try a stay at one of the country's growing number of **eco-lodges**; see *Ecotourism* (p 73) for information.

CLIMATE

Nicaragua's climate is tropical, though variations in temperature occur according to altitude. Like most tropical countries, Nicaragua has two distinct seasons, a **dry season** (November through May; also referred to as summer), and a **wet season** (called winter) when it rains frequently from May through Oct. The Pacific Lowlands in the southwest are hot and receive less rainfall than other regions of the country. During the dry season (the summer), the area can become dusty, particularly during February and March, when winds sweep in, relieving the heat. In the Northwest Highlands it is considerably cooler than in the Pacific Lowlands, and the rain here is sporadic throughout the year though it's concentrated more in the wet season. The Caribbean Coast region is steamy throughout the year, with high **humidity** and plentiful rains. Even the short dry season in this area (March through May) often sees downpours. Some roads in the region become impassable during the wet season. Despite these climactic variations, temperatures do not fluctuate significantly, and most of Nicaragua is pleasant to visit throughout the year.

POLITICS

Nicaraguans are ardent about engaging in political discourse, and, if your Spanish is up to it, most people are eager to discuss politics. Parties reflected in the **National Assembly** (*Asemblea Nacional*), in which members are elected by proportional representation, include the Liberal Alliance parties, the Sandinista party, and the PLC. Sandinista **Daniel Ortega** was elected president in the Novem-

The FSLN remains wildly popular in the northwest.

ber 2006 elections, an outcome that will weigh heavily on Nicaragua's political and economic future, though the effects of the new presidency have yet to play out. For more on Nicaragua's political history, see the *History* section p 9-21.

GOVERNMENT

Nicaragua gained independence from Spain in 1821 and formed a republic. The Nicaraguan government is a **constitutional democracy** with executive, legislative, judicial branches of government. Executive power is vested in the President, who serves a term of six years and is assisted by a Vice President and an appointed cabinet, the Council of Ministers. The current President of Nicaragua is Daniel Ortega.

The legislative branch is made up of a unicameral National Assembly (*Asamblea Nacional*), which consists of 92 elected members who serve a five-year term plus one additional seat for a previous President. The judicial system is based on civil law and is presided over by the Supreme Court (*Corte Suprema*) consisting of 16 judges who are elected for five-year terms by the National Assembly.

Nicaragua has a national **military**, which has been involved with several minor border skirmishes with Honduras and Costa Rica in recent years. The Chamorro government reduced the size of the Army from 80,000 to 15,000 and the draft was ended. Attempts are currently being made to reduce the military's power by placing it under civilian control.

Geographically, Nicaragua is divided into 15 ***departamentos*** (provinces or departments). The **Pacific Zone** includes Nueva Segovia, Rio San Juan, Madriz, Estelí, León, Chinandega, Managua, Masaya, Granada, Carazo, Rivas, Boaco, Chontales, Matagalpa and Jinotega. The **Atlantic Zone** consists of two ***regiones autonomistas*** (autonomous regions): North Atlantic (RAAN) and South Atlantic (RAAS).

THE ECONOMY

Nicaragua's economy has been traditionally based on **agriculture**, focusing on coffee, bananas, and tobacco. Political challenges and natural disasters have greatly contributed to the country's ongoing economic woes. Nicaragua is currently the second-poorest country in the hemisphere (after Haiti). It faces a low per capita income, high unemployment and underemployment, and staggering external debt. As of 2003, 52.2% of employed Nicaraguans worked in services, 30.5% in agriculture, and 17.3% in industry. Some 50% of the population remains below the poverty line.

Many rural residents, called campesinos, come to town to sell agricultural products from their land.

Though Nicaragua qualified for $4 billion in foreign debt reduction in 2004 under the Heavily Indebted Poor Countries initiative, debt burdens are still debilitating. Many Nicaraguans see the burgeoning **tourism** industry as a bright spot; foreign tourism increased 16.9% between 2003 and 2004 and continues to grow, with ongoing political stability, improving tourist infrastructure, and an overflow of visitors from Costa Rica.

Travel Information

ENTRY REQUIREMENTS

isitors to Nicaragua must have a **passport** that is valid for at least six months from the date of entry into the country. Most visitors, including citizens of the US, the UK, and Canada, can enter Nicaragua for up to 90 days. A US $5 **tourist card** (the money goes to INTUR) must be purchased at the airport or the point of entry and is required to enter Nicaragua. If entering Nicaragua overland, you must purchase a tourist card and pay an additional entry fee (the cost varies by location and time of day, but

should be less than $10). Most visitors wishing to extend their visit beyond 30 days spend a couple of days in Costa Rica or Honduras before their tourist card expires and re-enter Nicaragua on a new tourist card. Alternatively, though with more red tape and potential delays, you can request an extension at the Immigration Office in Managua. Departure fees vary by exit point; to leave from the airport in Managua the fee is $34 in US dollars only. Regulations do change, so reconfirm entry requirements prior to departure.

EMBASSIES

Nicaraguan embassies can provide details about entry requirements as well as tourism information.

■ NICARAGUAN EMBASSIES

Embassy of Nicaragua
407-130 Albert St.
Ottawa, ON Canada
☎ 613-238-7677

Embassy of Nicaragua
Suite 31, Vicarage House
58-60 Kensington Church Street
London W8 4DP United Kingdom
☎ 020-7938-2373

Embassy of Nicaragua
1627 New Hampshire Avenue NW
Washington, DC 20009 USA
☎ 202-939-6570

Consulates are also in Houston, Los Angeles, Miami, New York, and San Francisco. Visit www.travel.state. gov for details.

■ FOREIGN EMBASSIES IN NICARAGUA

CANADA
Street Address:
Costado Oriental de la Casa Nazareth,
una cuadra arriba, Calle El Nogal
Managua, Nicaragua
Mailing address:
Apartado Postal 25
Managua, Nicaragua
☎ 505-268-0433

UNITED KINGDOM
Plaza Churchill
Reparto los Robles
Managua, Nicaragua
☎ 505-278-0014

UNITED STATES
Street Address:
Kilometer 4.5 Carretera Sur
Managua, Nicaragua
Mailing address:
APO AA 34021
Managua, Nicaragua
☎ 505-266-6010
http://managua.usembassy.gov

Travel Information

LANGUAGE

Spanish is the official language, although you can often find residents with at least a basic grasp of English in areas that see a number of foreigners, such as Managua, Granada, León, and San Juan del Sur . Learning a few basic Spanish phrases before you go will help you get around and also facilitates meeting Nicaraguans, many of whom are eager to get to know visitors. If you plan to travel in rural areas, a basic command of Spanish is indispensable.

ELECTRICAL CURRENT

Electrical appliances from the US and Canada are compatible with Nicaragua's 110 Volts, 60 Hz. There are frequent power outages in Nicaragua, but they usually don't last more than an hour or so. In more isolated areas many hotels and guesthouses rely on generators and may only have nighttime electricity. If you plan to travel outside of major towns, consider bringing along a surge protector for expensive electronics.

MEASUREMENTS

Nicaragua uses the **metric system**, though gallons are used for gasoline.

Going Metric

To make your travels in this region easier, we have provided the following chart that shows metric equivalents for the measurements you are familiar with.

GENERAL MEASUREMENTS

1 kilometer = .6124 miles

1 mile = 1.6093 kilometers

1 foot = .304 meters

1 inch = 2.54 centimeters

1 square mile = 2.59 square kilometers

1 pound = .4536 kilograms

1 ounce = 28.35 grams

1 imperial gallon = 4.5459 liters

1 US gallon = 3.7854 liters

1 quart = .94635 liters

TEMPERATURES

For Fahrenheit: Multiply Centigrade figure by 1.8 and add 32.
For Centigrade: Subtract 32 from Fahrenheit figure and divide by 1.8.

Centigrade	Fahrenheit
40°	104°
35°	95°
30°	86°
25°	77°
20°	64°
15°	59°
10°	50°

WHAT TO PACK

Most visitors bring enough **toiletries** with them to last the for duration of their trip, though many basics are available at pharmacies (*farmacias*) throughout the country and at larger supermarkets (primarily in Managua, Granada, and Leon). If you have preferred brands for items such as shampoo or toothpaste, bring them with you as they may not be available locally. At a minimum, bring **sturdy shoes**, **mosquito repellent** designed for camping (weaker versions don't seem to faze the perpetually hungry Nicaraguan mosquitoes), **sunscreen** with an SPF of at least 30, a **day pack** (like a small backpack), a **money belt**, a compact umbrella or **rain gear**, a **clothesline**, a rubber **sink stopper**, and a basic **first aid kit**. Dental floss and deodorant can be found in major towns only. Baby wipes and a small bottle of waterless **antibacterial hand gel** (sold at pharmacies throughout the US and Canada) can be indispensable for keeping hands clean. Condoms are widely available; be sure to check expiration dates. Most areas of Nicaragua are steamy year-round, so light,

Many basic items are sold in shops like this one on Little Corn Island.

breathable clothing that can be layered is a good choice. Evenings can be cool, especially at higher elevations, so bring a sweater.

Most dining and nightlife spots in Nicaragua are very casual, so it is advisable to choose comfort over style when packing. Many towns in Nicaragua have unpaved or cobblestone roads, so you may want to consider bringing a backpack instead of a suitcase. Eagle Creek, North Face, Columbia, Victorinox, Samsonite, and High Sierra make quality backpacks designed for travel, some of them with wheels. Before selecting a backpack, do some walking with the pack fully loaded to ensure it is comfortable.

FOOD & DRINK

Many visitors find that eating and drinking in Nicaragua is one of the highlights of their trip.

TRADITIONAL DISHES

The staple of Nicaraguan *comida típica* (local or traditional food) is ***gallo pinto***, or beans and rice, which sometimes comes with a dollop of cream on top. As a result, **vegetarians** (*vegetarianos*) will have little trouble in Nicaragua; eggs and cheese are plentiful, as are fresh fruits and veggies. *Comida típica* includes meat, rice, beans, salad, and tortillas. Lunch is the main meal of the day, and many businesses close between noon and 2 pm as long lunches are enjoyed. Nicaraguan food is generally very mild, though spicy sauces are available, particularly along the Atlantic coast. Most Nicaraguan dishes are fried; even rice is made by frying uncooked rice in oil with a bit of garlic, onion, tomato,

Comida típica *is good value; this meal costs less than $2.*

or mild red pepper before it is boiled. Be sure to try **vigorones** (beans, rice, cabbage salad, and pork skin, all steamed in a banana leaf), **maduros** (sweet fried plantains), and **tamales**, steamed cornmeal that comes filled with a variety of meat and vegetarian fillings.

THE VERSATILE PLANTAIN

There are few foods in Nicaragua that are served in so many ways. When ripe, plantains (*plátanos*) can be eaten like a banana (*banano*), though they have a slightly more bitter taste. More commonly, ripe plantains are sliced lengthwise and fried to produce the beloved **maduros**. Green plantains are sliced razor-thin lengthwise, then fried to produce **tajadas**, which have a taste and texture similar to potato chips. A similar effect is produced by slicing the green plantain to produce **tostones**, thin rounds that are fried and smashed, then

Tostones *served in a coconut shell.*

served with ketchup (*salsa de tomate*) or a white cheese similar to feta (*cuajada*).

Seafood is widely available in coastal areas, while chicken, pork, and beef feature prominently inland. You can buy excellent **fruit**, including mangos, passionfruit, guavas, and papayas very inexpensively at markets and roadside stands. A favorite of young Nicaraguans is the *jocote*, a small round fruit that is often eaten while still green.

© Ian Maguire

Jocote

Many foods on the Caribbean Coast contain fresh coconut.

Afro-Caribbean influences are reflected in the cuisine of Nicaragua's Caribbean Coast. While *gallo pinto* remains a staple dish, coconut becomes a prominent feature in many foods in this region. Try the **coco bread** (*pan de coco*), a local favorite available everywhere. Seafood is also plentiful and fresh in towns along the coast.

■ BEVERAGES

The warm climate means particular attention should be given to staying hydrated. In most parts of Nicaragua, visitors should stick to purified **bottled water** (*agua purificada*), which is sold either flat (*sin gas*) or with bubbles (*con gas*) at most shops and supermarkets for less than $1. Boiled water is also fine and is what is used in most drinks at restaurants. Take care to avoid ice cubes, which may be made with tap water. Bottled soft drinks are ubiquitous.

Pozol is a thick traditional drink made from cooked corn and sugarcane paste. On the Caribbean Coast, **coconut milk** is a popular thirst-quencher. **Flor de Caña rum** (shown at right), produced in Chichigalpa near Chinandega, is often considered one of the best in the world. **Toña** and **Victoria** are the most popular types of **beer** in Nicaragua; **Premium** and **Brahva** are also produced domestically. Bottles of rum, which cost less than $10, make excellent gifts.

Delicious fresh-squeezed **juice** (*jugo*) is sometimes available at restaurants and cafés, though more common are **refrescos**, sold at local markets, cafés, and in parks These drinks, also known as **frescos**, contain varying mixtures of fruit, seeds, milk, sugar, and water. Below is a bilingual cheat sheet of *refresco* flavors.

REFRESCO FLAVORS

Many visitors gain an instant addiction to the delicious *refrescos* (juice and water mixed with lots of sugar) available in Nicaragua, but sometimes it's difficult to know what you're ordering.

cantaloupe . . . . melon
lime . . . . limón
coconut . . . . coco
orange . . . . naranja
watermelon . . . . sandía
papaya . . . . papaya
tamarind . . . . tamarindo
starfruit . . . . melocotón
Other common refrescos
thick, pink, with bubblegum flavor . . . sébaco
milky yellow with large seeds . . . . . granadilla
ground chocolate beans with milk . . . . cacao
tart, very sweet, pink with tiny seeds . . . . chía

Excellent **coffee** is produced in the north of Nicaragua, though inexplicably you will often be served instant coffee in restaurants.

> **TIP:** *If you miss Nicaraguan coffee once you return home, Nicaraguan Fair Trade coffee can be purchased at* **Whole Foods** *(www.wholefoods.com) and* **Trader Joe's** *(www.traderjoes. com) stores.*

COMMUNICATIONS

TELEPHONES

Nicaragua's **country code** is 505. All **phone numbers** in Nicaragua consist of seven digits. Making calls from hotels can be astronomically expensive. Instead, make domestic and international calls at **Enitel** offices, which have phones in private booths. Enitel can be found in virtually every town large or small. Enitel charges a set fee per minute based on the destination of your call. International rates are usually posted in the booth. To make a call, let the attendant know and she will show you to a booth. Pay the attendant when you are finished making your call. An even better, and increasingly popular, option for making international calls is by using **Internet telephony**, available at most Internet cafés. An alternative for making domestic calls is to purchase a local **phone card** at most pharmacies and supermarkets for use in public phones. Insert the card into the phone to place your call.

INTERNET

Keeping in touch by email is becoming increasingly easy. **Internet** cafés are popping up all over the country and are particularly plentiful in Managua, Granada, León, and San Juan del Sur. Even many smaller towns have at least one Internet café. Prices are very reasonable; connections generally cost $1 or less per hour. If you don't already have a free web-based email account, sign up for one at www.gmail.com or www.yahoo.com.

FAXES & SNAIL MAIL

Fax machines are easiest to find in Managua's large hotels; many Internet cafés and some copy shops also offer this service in major towns. **Post offices** (*Correos de Nicaragua*) are in even the smallest towns. Be sure to specify that you want your letters or postcards sent by

air mail (otherwise they won't arrive for several months, if at all). Mail generally arrives overseas within a few weeks. For packages, a parcel service, such as **DSL**, is a significantly more reliable, if more expensive, option. Letters cost about 60¢ to the US and 70¢ to Europe. The mail system is fairly reliable and most items make it to North America within a week, slightly more to Europe. Letters often have more luck arriving than postcards, the latter of which may be too tempting as home décor for a small-town postal worker. Packages are more likely to reach their destination through a service like **DHL**, which charges significantly more. Post offices are generally open Mon-Fri until late afternoon and Sat morning.

MONEY

The national currency of Nicaragua is the ***córdoba***, often referred to by travelers as "cords" and written with a C preceding the amount (for example, an item that costs 12 *córdobas* would be marked C12). *Córdobas* come in bills of 10, 20, 50, 100, and 500, and coins come in denominations of one and five *córdobas*. Less common are coins of 10 and 50 *centavos*, or cents. US dollars are very commonly

accepted in Nicaragua at slightly lower exchange rates, though other forms of currency, such as euros or Canadian dollars, will be very difficult to unload except at banks.

Prices listed in this book are calculated at 17.3 *córdobas* per US dollar. Check www.xe.com for current exchange rates.

> **TIP:** *Shopkeepers in Nicaragua are usually hesitant to accept any bills of C100 or above. A C500 note will often inspire despair and protests. Whenever possible, carry small notes and when exchanging money ask for your cords in small denominations. A good place to unload your large bills is at a fixed-price supermarket.*

■ BARGAINING

Bargaining in Nicaragua isn't done with the diehard fervor that travelers may experience in other countries. Usually the exchange will go back and forth no more than twice. Beyond that point, don't embarrass yourself or the vendor by continuing to haggle, and if you agree to a price, stick to it. If you're not convinced that the vendor has offered a good price, keep looking and go back if you don't find something better. A good rule of thumb is to browse in fixed-price shops a bit to get a sense of what prices are like for the type of item you are looking for, then go one-fourth to one-half lower in the markets.

■ TIPPING

Tipping is generally not expected, though it is becoming increasingly common in upscale restaurants and on tours. Guides and baggage handlers in particular often expect a small token of appreciation. Taxi drivers need not be tipped.

Many Nicaraguans live a subsistence lifestyle and even a small amount of generosity can make a difference in their lives; nonetheless, large tips can create unrealistic expectations and a dependency on foreign tourists. Use your discretion.

■ ATMs

ATMs are becoming increasingly common in Nicaragua. ATMs can be found in major cities as well as regional centers. Be discreet when withdrawing cash. If your PIN number is based on letters, be sure to memorize the corresponding numbers before departure; some ATM buttons have numbers only.

ATMs are usually indicated by a large sign like this one.

> **NOTE:** *Many machines accept only* ***Visa*** *cards. While ATMs are the most convenient way to access cash, be sure to have a backup, including cash and a credit card, in case of emergency. ATM locations are listed in the Money section of each city chapter.*

■ CREDIT CARDS

The Nicaraguan economy is mainly cash-based, and this is particularly true outside the main cities. Though many upscale hotels and restaurants now take credit cards, especially in Managua, acceptance is limited or nonexistent in smaller towns and at budget establishments. Many businesses in Nicaragua add a surcharge for credit card use, often up to 7% of your purchase. Be sure to ask about **fees** before making a purchase. Carrying a credit card is strongly recommended in case there is an emergency, but keep some cash on hand as a backup.

Carrying valuables, including cash, credit cards, passport, and plane tickets, in a **money belt** or **neck pouch** is strongly recommended. Exchange a credit card with a travel companion; if the worst-case scenario occurs, you'll have a backup.

Travel Information

■ CURRENCY EXCHANGE, TRAVELER'S CHECKS

There are banks in all main cities and most towns. Banking **hours** are generally Mon-Fri 8:30 am-4 pm and Sat 8:30 am-noon. **Banks** usually change dollars for a small commission. **Traveler's checks** are rarely accepted and, when they are, the commission is usually sky high. Only a few banks will change traveler's checks, so a better idea is to arm yourself with cash and plastic. Other than banks, the main form of currency exchange is through **money changers** on the street. Though technically illegal, you'll often see police officers themselves unloading their dollars and, in general, money changers are fairly accepted. Rates available from money changers are usually slightly better than at banks, but count your cash carefully, several times, in front of the money changer. The best idea is to stick to banks or ATMs whenever possible.

TIME ZONE

Nicaragua is six hours behind Greenwich Mean Time. Daylight savings time is instituted in April and reverts back in October; the government announces the day it will occur just a few weeks in advance, so ask around if your visit falls during this period. Daylight savings is a new concept in Nicaragua, and for weeks after the time change many clocks throughout the country will display the old time; in rural areas the change may be disregarded entirely. Double-check the time if you have a flight to catch!

SHOPPING

Nicaragua is well known for its sprawling markets, which offer quality crafts, textiles, and furniture at bargain prices. Particularly good buys include beautiful and durable **hammocks**, **pottery**, Primitivist **paintings** from Solentiname, and **rocking chairs** (which can

Street-side stalls, such as this one in Juigalpa, offer a colorful range of handicrafts.

be purchased packed in a flat box in pieces to be reassembled at home). Other shopping options include visits to **artisans' workshops** in Solentiname (p 430) or Masaya (p 134) and small gift shops at museums. Overall, the markets of **Masaya** are generally the best place to shop in Nicaragua.

RESTROOMS

Finding public restrooms (ones you'd want to use) can be a challenge. Returning to your hotel is usually the best option if you're in a small city or town, or stop for a drink or snack at a restaurant and use the restroom there. Public restrooms are usually available at markets, but they are frequently unclean and are often squat toilets. Carry **toilet paper** with you as it may or may not be available in restrooms. Do not throw toilet paper into the toilet: there will be a trash can next to the toilet for paper. Nicaraguan sanitation systems are unequipped to handle paper and tossing it in the toilet can wreak havoc, sometimes resulting in a very wet floor. Bring waterless anti-bacterial hand gel with you from home, as **soap** is rarely available in public restrooms.

ETIQUETTE

Nicaraguans are generally very welcoming to foreign visitors, and a smile is often all it takes to strike up a conversation. Learning a few Spanish phrases before you go is useful and helps you connect to local people.

While Nicaragua is a culturally diverse country, certain trends transcend regional differences. Nicaraguans place great importance on **family**, and visitors often find that new Nica friends will inquire about the health or wellbeing of family members, even if they've never met them. Elders are well respected and usually live among their children and grandchildren. Nicaraguans have a great respect for a well-kept appearance, even in the countryside. *Campesinos* that own only a few pieces of clothing will nonetheless do their best to ensure they are freshly-shaved with their shirt tucked in. Travelers wearing comfortable but clean, neat clothing will be well-received.

An invitation to accompany Nicaraguans to an event is a great opportunity to experience local culture. In Nicaragua, the person who extends the invitation is expected to pay, even if it involves a large group. Exceptions sometimes take place in middle-class Managua and among people who are accustomed to the foreigner paying no matter who offers the invitation. Solo women should be advised that single males rarely have friendship in mind if they invite new acquaintances to a social event or meal. Nicaraguans are renowned for their friendliness, and many visitors are pleasantly surprised how easy it is to meet people.

Nicaraguans love to socialize, and family gatherings are often an excuse for a party. A theme that runs throughout many social events, including religious festivals, is **alcohol**. Men, especially, generally drink copious amounts of rum and see it as a sign of their manliness to be able to consume until they are falling-down drunk. Driving while under the influence is a serious problem, and motorists should exercise extreme caution on the road, especially during holidays. Non-drinkers may be able to avoid imbibing by claiming an allergy to alcohol; women are usually not pressured, but men may have a more difficult time avoiding it.

Local residents are usually very gracious about giving **directions** when requested. However, out of politeness and an effort to be helpful, many people tend to give directions even if they are uncertain where something is located. It can be a good idea to ask two or three people about your destination before setting off, especially since businesses pop up and disappear at a rapid pace.

The concept of **time** in Nicaragua is vastly different than what most visitors are used to. "Ahora," the word for "now," is commonly interpreted as meaning "sometime" or "later." It is polite to arrive at social events at least a half-hour late; in fact, if you show up at the appointed time, the hosts will likely be unprepared. Businesspeople often experience something similar, with meetings beginning late or being rescheduled at the last minute with little explanation. Visitors retain their sanity by maintaining an attitude of "it will happen when it happens."

HEALTH & SAFETY

Overall, Nicaragua is a peaceful, safe country, and many visitors find that they feel safer in Nicaragua than at home. Most visitors never experience problems with safety during their stay, and violent crime is very rare. However, as at home, it pays to be vigilant, particularly in Managua. Pickpocketing is the most common crime in Nicaragua; remaining aware of your surroundings and leaving valuables at home are your best defense. When traveling within the country, keep your bags with you at all times. Locking your valuables in a safe at your hotel and carrying only small amounts of cash in a money belt can help protect yourself against theft. Wearing flashy jewelry or expensive watches can attract thieves, so it's best to leave them at home. When going out at night try to travel in a group and take an official taxi to your destination. Individual chapters list local numbers for the **police** and give recommendations about local conditions and neighborhoods that are best avoided. The US State Department issues a consular information sheet that keeps travelers apprised of local security conditions at www.travel.state.gov.

> **Warning:** Insurance companies require a police report before they will reimburse victims of theft for their losses, so be sure to secure one at the police station; obtaining one after the fact is practically impossible.

■ WOMEN TRAVELERS

Many solo women travel safely and enjoyably in Nicaragua, but it is prudent to take normal precautions. Familiarize yourself with the city layout by examining maps before heading out. It's also smart to avoid walking alone at night. Women travelers should keep in mind that *machismo* is alive and well in Nicaragua, and catcalls and overly friendly would-be suitors are not uncommon. Ignoring advances is the best solution. Persistent Romeos can often be repelled by enlisting the help of a nearby elderly local woman. Hostels can be great places to meet other travelers with whom to explore or enjoy nightlife, and after dark going out with a group is smart. Alternatively, go for drinks and conversation at the bar or restaurant in your hotel or hostel.

Women are wise to bring sanitary products from home, though pharmacies usually supply local and some foreign brands of sanitary napkins and, occasionally, tampons.

■ SPECIAL CONCERNS

TRAVELING WITH CHILDREN

Children are well-loved in Nicaragua, and most visitors traveling with children report having excellent experiences. Advance planning is key to a positive experience. If children are old enough, involve them in the planning process. In general, sticking to a few destinations minimizes time spent on the road and maximizes time to enjoy cultural and natural adventures. Day trips are a great option. Few hotels outside of Managua have special facilities for children, but staff is generally accommodating if you have a special request. Bringing some favorite items from home, such as small, washable toys, as well as some familiar non-perishable snacks, like granola bars or cereal, to enjoy during your stay can go a long way to help children adapt to their new surroundings. For more information about traveling with children, try www.babygoes2.com and *Travel With Children* on Lonely Planet's Thorn Tree (www.lonelyplanet.com). Also see *Further Reading* on page 500 for a list of **children's literature** about Nicaragua.

PHYSICALLY CHALLENGED TRAVELERS

Nicaragua is a challenging place to travel for visitors with disabilities. Potholes, cobblestones, and a lack of sidewalks in many places make navigating local streets difficult. Many facilities are not accessible to travelers with disabilities. Planning ahead will greatly enhance your visit and give you peace of mind. Contact hotels to find out about facilities and accessibility, and reconfirm any special arrangements just before arrival. Arrange private transport that meets your needs; public buses are usually crowded and unequipped to accommodate travelers with special requirements. Joining a group eliminates the need for intensive planning: **Go With Wheelchairs** (www.gowithwheelchairs.com) has adventurous packages to Nicaragua for travelers with special needs.

OLDER TRAVELERS

Elders are respected in Nicaraguan society, and older travelers are generally warmly received. In fact, Baby Boomers are one of the fastest-growing groups of visitors to Nicaragua. Though few businesses cater specifically to older travelers, and you'll rarely find senior citizen discounts, almost all older travelers find that they are well-received in Nicaragua.

PREDEPARTURE HEALTH

There are no mandatory vaccinations required to enter Nicaragua unless you are arriving from a yellow fever endemic area in which case a certificate showing a yellow fever vaccination is required. Current information on recommended vaccinations and other health precautions is available from the **Centers for Disease Control and Prevention**'s hotline for international travelers at ☎ 877-394-8747 or www.cdc.gov. See your doctor before you go for any recommended vaccinations. It is much more convenient to obtain vaccinations prior to leaving your home country, and be sure to bring a sufficient supply of prescription medicine for the duration of your trip as well as a copy of the prescription. Vaccinations against **typhoid** and **hepatitis A** are suggested (as well as hepatitis B for longer stays). **Malaria** prophylaxes may be prescribed, particularly for travelers visiting Rio San Juan and the Caribbean Coast. Though malaria is present in urban areas as well, it's less of a risk. **Chloroquine** is generally the weapon of choice against malaria in Nicaragua. You should begin to take malaria pills two weeks before you

depart and continue them for four weeks after returning home.

■ STAYING HEALTHY

Getting a sufficient amount of rest and eating properly
can go a long way toward keeping yourself healthy.
Wash your hands often, stay hydrated, and stay out of
the sun during the hottest times of the day. If you become dehydrated or severely sunburned, purchase
packets of *suero* (rehydration salts) at any pharmacy
and mix it with water. Be sure to stick with **bottled water**. Avoid ice cubes and veggies washed in tap water,
including salads.

Restaurants and food stalls with many customers are
less likely to have their food sitting out for long periods
of time. Peruse your options before choosing a place,
especially at markets or other places with lower levels of
sanitation; if the cleanliness looks suspect, move on.

Street stalls, such as
this *quesillo* vendor in
Granada, offer some
of the country's most
economical and
authentic traditional
food. Don't miss out,
but take a look before
buying to get a
sense of the standard
of hygiene.

If you do get **diarrhea** during your visit, most likely it
will only last a day or two. Longer bouts put you at risk
for dehydration, so see a doctor if it persists. While
over-the-counter meds like Immodium may tempo-
rarily relieve symptoms they keep the bacteria or virus
in your body and should be avoided if possible.

In addition to taking care with your eating and drinking habits, **mosquitoes** pose health threats in Nicaragua. Protect yourself by wearing **repellent** (bring it from home), wearing long pants and long-sleeved shirts in the evenings, and using a mosquito net (*mosquitero*) at night if you don't have screened windows. Mosquitoes can carry dengue fever and malaria, neither of which will contribute to the enjoyment of your vacation. **Dengue fever** (*dengue*) is transmitted by daytime-biting mosquitoes. It's often referred to as "bone-break fever" with good reason; victims experience intense joint pains, headaches, and a high fever. Many people also develop a rash within several days of contracting dengue. There is no vaccine, nor is there any treatment beyond hydration and rest, but if you experience these symptoms, get a blood test; low platelets can mean that you have contracted dengue. **Malaria** (*malaria*) is another concern in many parts of the country. Consult your doctor before departure to obtain a prescription for malaria prophylaxes. Symptoms include fever, exhaustion, and chills that often recur every 24 hours. Malaria is treatable, but see a doctor immediately if you experience these symptoms. **Chagas disease** is present, though it is one that short-term visitors are unlikely to contract. Chagas bugs, also called kissing bugs, have triangular-shaped noses and live in low-income thatch and adobe dwellings, primarily in rural areas. They prefer to bite victims on the face. If a victim contracts the disease a fever usually occurs a week after the bite. The disease is potentially fatal. Use those mosquito nets!

AIDS (*la Sida*) is not yet prominent in Nicaragua, but the number of cases is growing. Condoms are widely available at supermarkets and pharmacies even in small towns.

Medical care is limited, particularly outside Managua. Basic medical services are available in Managua, Leon, and Granada. More serious injuries often require airlifting. Hospitals require immediate payment in Nicaragua. Be sure to get receipts to submit to your insurance company.

INFORMATION SOURCES

MEDIA

The most interesting publication for travelers, and Nicaragua's only English-language magazine, is **Between the Waves**, which includes up-to-date tourist information and articles aimed at visitors. It can be a good source of information about upcoming cultural events. This publication is available at tourist offices and many larger hotels, or you can pick up a copy in the immigration area at the airport upon arrival. Foreign newspapers and magazines are almost nonexistent in the country, though you'll likely have the most luck at the international hotels in Managua. Nicaragua has two major newspapers, both of which are published only in Spanish and are widely available throughout the country: **La Prensa** (www.laprensa.com.ni) and **El Nuevo Diario** (www.elnuevodiario.com.ni). Nicaraguans are accustomed to graphic photos accompanying their news stories (think death and dismemberment).

Online sources include **Bolsa de Noticias** (www.bolsadenoticias.com.ni), which has a news roundup of current stories, including a brief section on tourism. **Estrella de Nicaragua** (www.estrelladenicaragua.com) is published by the Nicaraguan expat community in Miami in Spanish. Nicaraguan **television** offers six free channels, the most popular of which are **Televicentro** (Channel Two) and **Telenica** (Channel Eight). There is also a 24-hour news station. *Telenovelas*, or soap operas, most of which come from Mexico and Colombia, are outrageously popular, with the whole family often joining in to follow the saga. Most hotels and many local families take advantage of widely available cable TV, which includes a host of stations from the US. There are several private and government

radio stations, most of which belt out bouncy pop music from Nicaragua and abroad.

■ WEBSITES

Nicaragua Ministry of Tourism Visitors: www.visitnicaragua.com.

ViaNica is an English-language site with perhaps the most comprehensive listings of sights, accommodations, and practical information for travelers: www.vianica.com.

Nicatour has an overview of each area of Nicaragua with useful information for visitors: www.nicatour.net.

The **University of Texas** has an extensive list of links to all things Nicaraguan, many in Spanish: www1.lanic.utexas.edu/la/ca/nicaragua.

Maps, activities and tourism information in English: www.guideofnicaragua.com.

The US **CIA**'s statistical information on Nicaraguan demographics: www.cia.gov/factbook.

NicaNet, a left-leaning project of the Alliance for Global Justice, reports on social and environmental justice issues: www.nicanet.org.

Amigos de Nicaragua, published by and for Peace Corps Volunteers, lists insider information about services and things to do in each region of Nicaragua: www.amigosdenicaragua.

Trip Planning

WHEN TO VISIT

Nicaragua is warm year-found and can be comfortably visited throughout the year. Its cultural and religious **celebrations** are often a highlight of visitors' trips and some, particularly **Semana Santa**, are worth arranging a trip around. See *Major Festivals* on page 58 for information on when celebrations take place in Nicaragua.

Temperature and **rainfall** are also considerations when planning your trip. Patterns are similar throughout the country, but they do vary somewhat by region and altitude. During the **rainy season** (called *el invierno*, or winter, by Nicaraguans), daily downpours occur throughout the country. They are particularly frequent and heavy in the **Caribbean Coast** region, and streets, particularly unpaved roads in rural areas, can become impassable. On the upside, the rainy season leaves Nicaragua's **landscape** lush and green, boat travel time is shortened, **wildlife viewing** is at its finest, and prices are often reduced. The **dry season** (*el verano*, or summer) is characterized by infrequent rainfall, higher temperatures, and a dry landscape. The dry season is a better time for **hiking**, **horseback riding**, **cycling**, and spending time at the **beach**.

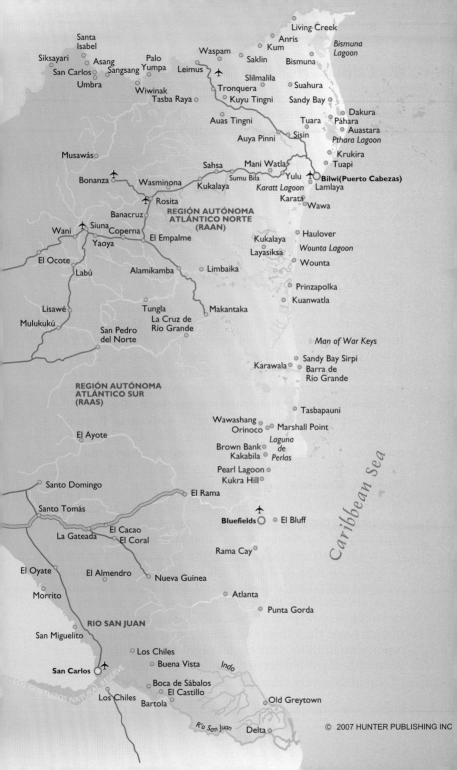

■ PUBLIC HOLIDAYS

All offices and many private businesses are closed on public holidays. In addition to national public holidays, many towns observe their own holidays.

January 1 . . . . New Year's Day
A week in March or April . . . . Semana Santa
May 1 . . . . Labor Day
July 19 . . . . Revolution of 1979
September 14 . . . . .Battle of San Jacinto
September 15 . . . . Independence Day
November 2 . . . . All Souls Day (Día de los Muertos)
December 25 . . . . .Christmas Day

■ MAJOR FESTIVALS

Each town and region has its own festivals, and some are particularly colorful. The **Palo de Mayo** festival (now billed by the tourism powers that be as **Mayo Ya**), takes place in **Bluefields** during the last weekend of May. The festival is characterized by dancing and music that last all night and copious amounts of Caribbean-tinged food. **Esteli** is home to a **mariachi festival** the same weekend. **Masaya** puts on a **Folkloric Festival** replete with traditional costumes, dance, and handicrafts on the last Sunday in November. **Purísima** (the Immaculate Conception) is celebrated in **Managua**, **Masaya**, **Granada**, and **León** in December.

In addition to these celebrations, each town in Nicaragua has its own patron saint. These saints are honored annually with celebrations called *fiestas patronales*. While the purpose is religious, the focus is on drinking, dancing, and socializing. Even in the smallest villages, *fiestas patronales* are celebrated with vigor. The party lasts several days to more than a week depending on the town. Young girls parade around in their best attire, horses wear their finest saddles, parades wind through town, and families stay up all night celebrating. *Fiestas patronales* are an experience not to be missed if you are in the area where they are taking place.

Semana Santa is one of Nicaragua's (and Latin America's) favorite celebrations. Semana Santa takes place annually during the week leading up to Easter. **Processions** take place, businesses close, and seemingly everyone heads to the **beach**. Semana Santa is celebrated with variable amounts of enthusiasm in each town, though **León** is often considered one of the best places in the country to experience the traditional aspects of Semana Santa. If you're more inclined to join the partying masses, the action centers around **San Juan del Sur**, though virtually every beach in the country is packed during the week of Semana Santa.

Semana Santa is one of Nicaragua's most entrancing celebrations. If you are here during that time, be sure to enjoy the festivities. *Pasos*, or religious statues, like this one in León, feature prominently in processions.

GETTING HERE

BY PLANE

The gateway to Nicaragua is **Managua International Airport** (MGA), a few miles west of Managua. The newly-renovated airport is small and easily navigable and a variety of services are available, including an **Intur** tourism desk, several restaurants, car rental, and a **bank**. The bank's hours are Mon-Sat 8:45 am-5:45 pm and Sun 8:45 am-3:45 pm, rendering it useless to the many passengers arriving on evening flights. There is an **ATM** next to the bank, but for some inane reason it only dispenses dollars. All taxis will accept dollars. There is a **VIP lounge** that charges a pricey $30 for three drinks, a plate of snacks, and express check-in.

For more information about Managua International Airport, see *Getting Here* in the Managua chapter, p 88.

International Airlines Serving Managua

Aero Caribbean (www.aero-caribbean) to Havana

Air Transat (www.airtransat.com) to Montreal

American Airlines (www.aa.com) to Miami

Continental Airlines (www.continental.com) to Houston-Intercontinental

Copa Airlines (www.copa.com) to Guatemala City, Panama City, San José (CR), San Juan, and San Salvador

Delta Air Lines (www.delta.com) to Atlanta

TACA (www.taca.com) to Los Angeles, Miami, San José (CR), and San Salvador

Iberia (www.iberia.com) to Madrid and Miami

Another option, particularly attractive to visitors headed to southern Nicaragua, including San Juan del Sur, is flying into **Costa Rica**, which often costs up to $100 less than a flight to Managua. **San José**'s **Juan Santamaria International Aiport** (SJO) is serviced by Lacsa/Taca, America West, Delta, American, US Airways, KLM, British Airways, Mexicana, and Iberia. From the airport it's only a half-hour by taxi to the terminals of **Ticabus** (www.ticabus.com) and **Transnica** (www.transnica.com), which have multiple daily departures and Nicaraguan destinations. It takes about six hours to reach the border by bus from San José.

You can also fly to Costa Rica's **Liberia**'s **Daniel Oduber International Airport**, in the Guanacaste region six miles outside of Liberia. Liberia has international flights on American, Delta, United, and Continental.

Additionally, **Nature Air** (www.natureair.com) flies to Granada, Nicaragua. From the airport, it's a 45-minute drive by taxi or a bit more by bus to the Nicaraguan border. Once you reach the border, **taxis** are available, as are buses to Rivas with connections continuing on to San Juan del Sur, Granada, Masaya, and Managua. For more info on crossing the border at Peñas Blancas, see page 215.

■ BY CAR

Driving in Nicaragua can be a hair-raising experience, but if you want to get off the beaten path and really explore, it is an option. A 4WD vehicle is necessary for many destinations within the country. Drivers can enter Nicaragua from Costa Rica in the south at Peñas Blancas or from the north from Honduras at El Guasale, El Espino, or Las Manos. Note that cars rented in Honduras and Costa Rica cannot be brought into Nicaragua. If you come by private vehicle be sure to have a valid **driver's license**, the **car's title**, and $10 for a temporary (30-day) license.

■ BY BUS

International **luxury coach** services are a good option for travelers that want to travel to several countries in Central America. **Ticabus** (www.ticabus.com) and **Transnica** (www.transnica.com) both offer multiple daily departures and comfortable buses. Ticabus services southern **Mexico**, **Guatemala**, **El Salvador**, **Honduras**, **Costa Rica**, and **Panama**. Multiple cities in Nicaragua are serviced by these companies, including **Esteli**, **León**, **Managua**, **Granada**, and **Rivas**. See individual city chapters for local office contact details. Note that tickets must be purchased in person at a Ticabus or Transnica office at least one day before departure, and no credit cards are accepted.

Another (slower and less expensive) option is to take a **local bus** from Costa Rica or Honduras, walk across the border, and take a connecting Nicaraguan bus to your destination. This method allows more flexible travel and buses depart more frequently, but the journey is often more time-consuming and is not recommended unless you have a basic command of Spanish.

■ BY SHIP

Cruising is an increasingly viable option for visitors who would like a brief taste of Nicaragua, though the only ports of call currently available are San Juan del Sur and Corinto. Excursions are available to nearby destinations within Nicaragua. The following cruise lines call at San Juan del Sur, and their US phone numbers are shown.

CRUISE LINES	
Holland America	☎ 877-724-5425; www.hollandamerica.com
Orient	☎ 800-333-7300; www.orientlines.com
Princess	☎ 800-774-6237, www.princess.com
Seabourn	☎ 800-929-9391, www.seabourn.com
Silversea	☎ 877-760-9052, www.silversea.com
Windstar	☎ 800-258-7245. www.windstarcruises.com

Holland America has 17- to 23-night cruises, while Silversea and Seabourn have luxury ships with 14- to 28-night itineraries that include San Juan del Sur. Windstar offers intimate small-ship, week-long cruises that stop at San Juan del Sur. Princess has a 19-night itinerary that calls at Corinto.

TICKETS & TOURS

Shop online for the best prices on **plane tickets**. With fuel prices rising substantially, you'll want to shop around for the best prices. In general, the most expensive times to fly are around Christmas, New Year's, and

Easter. Prices tend to be at their lowest during October and November. Search discount websites like **Sidestep** (www.sidestep.com), **Kayak** (www.kayak.com), and **Orbitz** (www.orbitz.com). Be sure to read the fine print about date changes and other details before purchasing. Don't neglect the airlines' own websites, which often match the prices offered by discounters.

Finally, consider saving money by flying to an alternative airport in Costa Rica (see details, p 60) instead of to Managua.

Tours run by companies based outside of Nicaragua often cost substantially more than tours arranged locally, but if you have a limited amount of time and want peace of mind, try **GAP Adventures** (☎ 800-676-4941 in the US or www.gapadventures.com) or **Latin American Escapes** (☎ 800-510-5999 in the US or www.latin americanescapes.com).

Within Nicaragua there are a number of professional tour operators with English-speaking operations managers and guides and many years of experience:

- ■ **Careli Tours**, ☎ 505-278-6919, www.carel itours.com

- ■ **Tours Nicaragua**, ☎ 505-270-8417, www. toursnicaragua.com

- ■ **Munditour Tours**, ☎ 505-278-5716, www. munditur.com.ni

- ■ **Nicaragua Adventures**, ☎ 505-276-1125, www.nica-adventures.com

- ■ **Grayline Tours** (☎ 505-883-6994, www.gray linenicaragua.com) offers **one-day tours** of the main cities and sights.

Additionally, tours can easily be arranged in most cities and towns; each destination chapter has details.

■ TRAVEL INSURANCE

Travel insurance can protect you in case of unforeseen medical emergencies or travel disruptions. Benefits vary by company and insurance plan; be sure to read the fine print carefully before purchase and carry the details with you on your trip. Insurance providers include **Travelguard** (www.travelguard.com) and **STA Travel** (www.statravel.com).

GETTING AROUND

■ BY AIR

Nicaragua has two domestic airlines, both of which have good safety records, though planes are small and the ride is often bumpy. **La Costeña** (☎ 263-2142, fax 263-1281, jcaballero@lacostena.com.ni) has the country's most extensive air network and services **Managua**, **San Carlos**, **Siuna/Rosita/Bonanza**, **Puerto Cabezas**, **Bluefields**, **Corn Island**, and **Waspám**. The airline currently has no website, but this should change in 2007. **Atlantic Airlines** (☎ 222-3030, fax 228-5614, www. atlanticairlines.com.ni reservaciones@atlanticairlines. com.ni) flies to **Bluefields** and **Corn Island** from **Managua** and also serves **Guatemala**, **Honduras**, **El Salvador**, and **Costa Rica**. Reservations for both airlines can be made by phone (when you show up for the flight you can pay then), at the airport, or through a travel agent. See the chapter of your destination for flight information and prices.

Neither domestic airline is part of an international carrier network, so if you fly in from another country you will need to clear customs and recheck your baggage before connecting to a domestic flight.

■ BY BUS

Often nicknamed "chicken buses" for their propensity to transport the occasional farm animal along with passengers, Nicaragua's buses will become familiar to virtually every traveler. Most travelers do the vast majority of travel around the country by bus, usually a refurbished American school bus. Nicaragua has a well-con-

Ordinario *buses go to almost every corner of the country to deliver passengers and their parcels.*

nected network of buses, departures are frequent, and fares are very inexpensive. *Ordinario* buses are slow, stuffed with people and produce, and stop at even the tiniest of villages. Larger towns and cities are served by **express** buses. Express buses are sometimes school bus-type vehicles, but if you have a choice or a need for speed, opt for the express **minibuses**, which hold a dozen people and are much speedier and only slightly more expensive than their hulking cousins. If you have a lot of **luggage**, you may have to purchase an additional seat for your bags if there is no luggage rack on top. On large buses you may be permitted to keep your bags with you, or they will go under the bus or be strapped to the top. Most visitors don't experience any trouble, but keep an eye on your bags, especially when the bus stops. Keep valuables with you and try to put anything of value toward the center of your larger bag that wayward fingers might want to prod; passengers sometimes ride on the roof with the luggage if the bus is full. Each bus has an **ayudante** that will stow your luggage and, after the bus has departed, collect your fare. Change is usually available, and don't worry if the *ayudante* says he will come back with your change. He will, but just be sure it's the correct amount.

■ BY CAR

Though driving in Nicaragua is only recommended for motorists with experience driving in developing countries, renting a car to explore the country does have its merits. Car rental is available in the country's urban areas, including Managua, Masaya, Granada, León, Chinandega, and Estelí. Prices average $60 per day, expensive considering the low cost of bus fares. Most ferries (including many that serve Isla Ometepe) transport cars.

Drivers need to be vigilant. Road travel after dark is hazardous as many roads are in poor repair, narrow, and potholed. Many roads were damaged by Hurricane Mitch in October 1998 and have not been fully repaired. Horses, abandoned vehicles, and pedestrians are frequently encountered even on main thoroughfares. Vehicles involved in accidents should not be moved until authorized by a police officer. Drivers who violate this policy may be held legally liable for the accident.

■ BY TAXI

Taxis in Nicaragua are ubiquitous and inexpensive. Be sure to agree on a fare before departing. Many taxi prices are per person; be sure to confirm the total price with the driver if you are with a group. Taxis are usually a collective experience; if others are headed in your direction your driver will pick them up. For a higher fee you can request that the driver not pick up additional passengers, worthwhile in Managua at night and when you are in a hurry. Travel times can be significant if there are other passengers to drop off. Most taxi drivers do not speak English, so it's a good idea to have a hotel staffer write down directions to your destination.

ACCOMMODATIONS

RATES

Rates are usually similar year-round with the exception of **Semana Santa** (which falls at Easter), **Christmas**, and **New Year's**, when prices often double at beach locales and accommodation is booked far in advance. At other times of the year, accommodation is generally not full (in fact, you may have the place to yourself in small towns and rural areas), and reservations are usually unnecessary. Arriving without prior notice is generally not a problem and often results in lower prices. However, if you have your heart set on a particular hotel, be sure to make a reservation. Reservations are recommended in Managua, Granada, Río San Juan, and Solentiname.

HOTEL PRICE CHART	
Cost per night for two people, before tax	
$	Up to $15
$$	$16-$30
$$$	$31-$60
$$$$	Over $60

> **NOTE:** *Mid-range and upscale hotels and restaurants usually charge 15% tax. Inexpensive guesthouses, restaurants, and food stands generally don't charge tax. Ask if you're not sure whether tax is included in listed prices.*

HOW TO BOOK

Phone bookings are the most common way to reserve accommodation in Nicaragua. An increasing number of hotels are creating **websites** and **email** addresses, though in some places Internet access isn't widely available and hotel owners may not reply immediately. Websites and email addresses change with remarkable speed in Nicaragua. If you don't receive a response via email, be sure to call. While booking online can be a convenient way to make a reservation, keep in mind that this type of technology is a new development in Nicaragua and things can go wrong. It's a good idea to reconfirm your booking by phone or email, and to check with the hotel again just prior to departure. Some hotels and guesthouses do not accept reservations; in this case arriving early in the day can enhance your chances of getting a spot.

■ TYPES OF ACCOMMODATION

HOTELS

Hotels with international standards, including those affiliated with foreign chains, are available in the main tourist destinations. Managua, Granada, and San Juan del Sur offer some of the country's most upscale accommodation. Smaller hotels, including many housed in historic homes in Managua, Granada, and Leon, often offer more personalized service. Hotels commonly have amenities such as an on-site restaurant, Internet access, air-conditioning, and private parking. The standard of **service** at some hotels is sometimes not equal to that of more developed countries.

HOSTELS

Hostels are popular options for the young and young at heart and can be a good option for solo travelers. Hostels aren't only for travelers willing to share a large dorm room: most offer private rooms, and many hostels offer amenities that are not typically associated with budget stays, including copious freebies. Complimentary international calls, Internet, coffee, and more are often available. Hostelling is a new concept in Nicaragua, and hostels are only available in a few destinations, including **Granada**, **León**, **San Juan del Sur**, and **Isla Ometepe**. Hostels can be searched and booked through www.hostels.com.

GUESTHOUSES

Guesthouses (known as *hospedajes* or *hostales*) are the most common type of accommodation in Nicaragua. Ranging from rustic to plush, guesthouses can be found in even the smallest towns. Many guesthouses are family-run, giving visitors insight into local culture. Many guesthouses do not have phones, but they are rarely full; if possible, check out a couple of places before making a commitment.

Guesthouses are often simple and friendly.

CAMPING

Camping is formally available in some places, but many travelers choosing this option simply ask locals for permission to pitch a tent on private property. Established **campgrounds** are usually open spaces managed by adjacent guesthouses, which provide use of restrooms and sometimes other facilities. In general, unless you have a particular affinity for camping, carrying equipment isn't worth the hassle, especially with the low price of accommodation in rural Nicaragua.

Travel Information

> **Caution:** *Autohoteles* exist throughout Nicaragua. Tourists should steer clear. These places, which take measures to protect guests' privacy, exist as clandestine locales for affairs and meeting spots for young couples away from the watchful eye of relatives. They are most often located along highways, marked by an *"Autohotel"* sign and parking that shields cars from view.

LONG-TERM ACCOMMODATION

Real estate agencies, including **Coldwell Banker** (www.cbnicaragua.com), **Century 21** (www.century21 granada.com), and **ReMax** (www.nicaraguaproperty.com), all have rental listings, though website offerings are usually not up to date. Contact them for currently-available properties.

> **TIP:** *After arriving in Nicaragua, **notice boards** in hostels are a good source of information about rental apartments and houses at all price ranges.*

Many **hotels** and **guesthouses** will negotiate significantly lower rates for long-term stays, and some have kitchens available. Another option is to rent a room from a local family.

SPECIAL INTEREST VACATIONS

■ SPECTATOR SPORTS

While most countries in Central America are soccer fanatics, the US Marine presence in Nicaragua at the beginning of the 20th century instead instilled a passion for baseball (*el beísbol* or, more commonly, simply *beís*). Spectators can view professional baseball games in the country's main cities, and many neighborhoods have popular informal baseball diamonds. Neighborhood basketball is popular in some towns, and visitors with some degree of skill will often be welcome to participate. In rural areas visitors can see sports such as cockfights and bullfights, neither of which are for the faint of heart.

■ ACTIVE VACATIONS

CYCLING

Many guesthouses and hotels rent bicycles for independent exploration. Equipment is sometimes not well-maintained, so check your rental thoroughly before setting out. **Professional Nicaragua Adventures** (www.nica-adventures.com) organizes customized cycling tours for around $900 per week, including meals and accommodation.

CANOPY TOURS

Canopy tours have become one of Nicaragua's most popular activities for visitors, and it's easy to see why: attached securely to a harness, participants zip along on cables above the forest canopy. Ostensibly, canopy tours allow up-close and personal wildlife viewing, but most people are having too much fun to focus on anything but the sensation of flying. Canopy tours are a particular favorite for children.

Try it for yourself in Managua (p 107) or near Granada (p 172) or San Juan del Sur (p 253).

DIVING & SNORKELING

The Caribbean Sea offers Nicaragua's premiere scuba diving and snorkeling opportunities.

Corn Island (p 472, shown below) and **Little Corn Island** (p 484) offer the country's best underwater activities, and PADI certification courses are available. Diving and snorkeling are also available at **Laguna de Apoyo**'s crater lake (p 145), and **San Juan del Sur** (p 252) has certification courses.

Corn Island

ECOTOURISM

© Storkk

White-faced capuchin monkey
(Cebus capucinas)

Nicaragua is an ecotourist's paradise. While finding unspoiled natural environments that are not inundated with tourists is difficult in Costa Rica, most of Nicaragua is still pristine. Nicaragua is dotted with **national parks**, **national reserves**, and **private reserves** that offer a variety of different activities and environments. Nicaragua also has a growing number of eco-lodges that promote sustainability and exploration of natural surroundings. Some of Nicaragua's finest include **Selva Negra** (p 363), **Finca Esperanza Verde** (p 361), and **Morgan's Rock** (p 268), all of which offer plenty of adventure opportunities coupled with relaxation.

FISHING

Fishing is a popular activity in coastal areas, particularly near **San Juan del Sur**, and on the **Rio San Juan**. On the Pacific Coast near San Juan del Sur, the main big game fish are marlin, sailfish, dorado, rooster, and tuna. Tarpon, snook, and drum are the focus at Rio San Juan. Kingfish, barracuda, and snapper make their way from the waters near the

© Surfari Charters

Corn Islands onto your dinner plate. See the **San Juan del Sur** (p 251), **Río San Juan** (p 419), **Corn Island** (p 472), and **Little Corn Island** (p 484) chapters for information on arranging customized fishing trips.

HIKING

You'll find plenty of opportunities to hike in Nicaragua. The best time of year to hike in most areas is during the **dry season** from late November to early May. During

Hiking Cerro Negra Volcano.

© Tours Nicaragua

the rainy season, paths are often muddy and are sometimes inaccessible. On the upside, the rainy season is when Nicaragua's forests are at their finest, so beautiful views sometimes compensate for inconvenience caused by rain. Regardless of the time of year, be sure to bring plenty of **water**, **sunscreen**, and **mosquito repellent**. While you will be tempted to wear shorts in this tropical climate, layer loose, breathable pants whenever possible to lower the risk of scratches and, less likely, snake bites. It's never a good idea to hike alone, and let someone know where you're going before you set out. Hiring a local **guide** is inexpensive and you'll often be amazed by the variety of wildlife guides can spot and explain. While hiking is popular throughout the country, Nicaragua's **volcanoes** provide some of the most unique hiking experiences.

VOLCANO GUIDE

Nicaragua's history and culture are intricately tied with its volcanoes, and in rural areas you can still hear stories about the volcanoes' spiritual significance. Perhaps of most interest to travelers is that the volcanoes also offer excellent **hiking** opportunities. The **Los Maribios** range is popular for hiking and stretches from Honduras to Isla Ometepe. Several volcanoes in this range are easily accessible from **León**, including Cerro Negro and Telica. **Cerro Negro** also offers the unique opportunity to go **volcano boarding** on the loose black sand. Day or overnight tours can be arranged in town. **Telica** has a double crater and rises 1,061 meters above the villages of Telica and San Jacinto, the latter of which is home to the **Hervideros de San Jacinto**, bubbling pools of mud created by gases emitting from beneath the earth's surface. Neighboring **Volcán San Cristobal**, just outside **Chinandega**, is the tallest volcano in Nicaragua at 1,745 meters; check locally for conditions before hiking here as early 2006 saw increased evidence of activity. Hikes at **Mombotombo** (1,258 m) and its offspring, **Mombotombito** (389 m, shown below), offer great views of Lago de Nicaragua. The two volcanoes can be visited by tour from **León** or **Managua**. Heading farther south,

© Frédéric Eveno

Volcán Masaya is within easy reach of the city of Masaya. This volcano is the home of Nicaragua's first national park. The volcano is crisscrossed by several hiking trails. The volcano is unique in that it emits large amounts of suphuric gases and has a lagoon, Laguna de Masaya, at its base. Just south of Masaya you'll find **Laguna de Apoyo**, another lagoon situated in an extinct volcano that last erupted more than 20,000 years ago. It is possible to hike or drive from the Carretera Masaya highway down to the lagoon, which is between Masaya and Granada. **Swimming** in the lagoon is a popular activity, and there are a variety of tourist facilities, including hotels, in the crater. Just south of Granada is **Mombacho**, one of Nicaragua's most lush volcanoes. Topped by a cloud forest, Mombacho has two hiking trails and easy access by bus or tour from **Granada**. Hopping over to **Isla Ometepe** by boat from Granada or San Jorge, you'll find **Volcán Concepción** and **Volcán Maderas**, twin volcanoes that are each a challenge to hike. Maderas houses a lagoon, and on a clear day both volcanoes offer spectacular views of Lago de Nicaragua and the island.

While Nicaragua's volcanoes offer excellent hiking opportunities, be sure to take safety precautions, especially on active volcanoes. Hiking with a **guide** is recommended, and bring plenty of water and sunscreen.

DID YOU KNOW? There are nine active volcanoes in Nicaragua.

HORSEBACK RIDING

Horseback riding is a popular activity in Nicaragua, and outside of urban areas horses can usually be fetched from the fields and rented for around $5 per hour including a guide.

SURFING

The beaches north of San Juan del Sur offer the most popular surfing in the country. See the **San Juan del Sur** (p 252) and **The Tola Beaches** (p 269) for details about **surf camps**, **board rentals**, and **transport** to the hottest surf spots.

© L Paul Mann

■ LEARNING VACATIONS

Nicaragua is a great place to **study Spanish**: prices are affordable and classes are flexible. Language schools are widely available as are **private tutors**. Combining Spanish study at a language school with **volunteering** or **cultural excursions** is also an option with most programs. The most popular locales for Spanish study are **Granada** and **San Juan del Sur**, but consider towns with fewer foreigners, such as **Matagalpa** or **León**, if you want a complete immersion experience. See the Managua (p 109), Granada (p 173), San Juan del Sur (p 253), León (p 290), Estelí (p 328), and Matagalpa (p 353) chapters for language school listings.

More formal programs, some of which facilitate college credit, are available for higher fees. **The School for International Training** (www.sit.edu) offers a semester-long course in Managua focusing on development. **Augsburg College** (www.augsburg.edu) sponsors a semester-long, three-country study trip that includes Nicaragua. **Costa Rica Rainforest Outward Bound School** (www.crrobs.com) offers a month-long Tri-

Country Experience that explores Nicaragua. **Travel Alive** (www.travelalive.com) offers short- and long-term programs that combine language study with community involvement. **Ometepe Biological Field Station** (www.lasuerte.org) on Isla Ometepe has short-term and semester-long classes ranging from photography to dance to tropical ecology.

For high school students, the **Spanish Through Leadership** month-long summer program (www.nicaragua-studyabroad.org) combines language and cultural studies. **Cloud Forest Adventures** (www.cloudforest adventures.com) has a similar program.

EMPLOYMENT OPPORTUNITIES

■ WORKING

Nicaragua has a high rate of unemployment, and finding work locally is a challenge. For **jobs** or **internships** in the fields of development or social services, try **Action Without Borders** (www.idealist.org) or **DevNetJobs** (www.devnetjobs.org). **Transitions Abroad Magazine** (www.transitionsabroad.com) has comprehensive information about working overseas. **Teaching English** to Nicaraguan students is an option, though salaries are very low. Professional teachers may find possibilities at Managua's international schools; contracts are usually for two years. Some **guesthouses** and **hostels** offer accommodation and a small salary in exchange for short-term work (try The Bearded Monkey in Granada or Bigfoot Hostel in León). Unless you're looking for a long-term career, arranging a job after arriving in Nicaragua is usually more feasible than finding something in advance.

■ VOLUNTEERING

A more realistic option for working in Nicaragua can be serving in a volunteer capacity. Long-term commitments often provide accommodation or meals. **Volun-**

teer Abroad (www.volunteerabroad.com/nicaragua.cfm) lists a variety of positions throughout the country. **Habitat for Humanity** (www.habitat.org) accepts volunteers to assist with building houses for low-income families. The **Peace Corps** sends volunteers to work on a variety of development projects (two-year commitment and American citizenship required). **Locally-based opportunities** to volunteer, most of which do not charge any volunteer fees, are detailed in city chapters.

NATIONAL SYMBOLS

Nicaraguans are proud of their national symbols and you'll frequently see them prominently displayed, on t-shirts and elsewhere.

National Flower . . . . Sacuanjoche
National Tree . . . . Madroño
National Bird . . . . Guardabarranco
National Flag . Blue and white with the coat of arms in the center. The current flag was adopted in 1971.

Nicaragua's flag flies proudly over El Castillo's fortress.

Top Picks

TOP 20 THINGS TO DO

1. Watch the sun set over Granada from the bell tower of Iglesia La Merced (p 166).

2. Explore the wildlife of Las Isletas by kayak (p 170-172, 190).

3. Hike in the cloud forests of Volcán Mombacho.

4. Shop for handmade hammocks and crafts in the markets of Masaya.

5. Swim in the crater lake of Laguna de Apoyo.

6. Sample Nicaragua's best market food in San Juan del Sur (p 248). Don't miss the freshly-caught fish!

7. Surf with the locals at Playa Maderas.

8. Visit the churches of León, including the oldest church in Central America.

9. Feel the adrenaline rush of volcano boarding at Volcán Cerro Negro.

10. Study Spanish at one of Nicaragua's many language institutes.

11. Learn about coffee production and sustainable development at Selva Negra (p 363) or Finca Esperanza Verde (p 361).

12. Experience vibrant Semana Santa festivities, notably in León or San Juan del Sur.

13. Enjoy the beaches of Charco Verde (p 228) or Playa Santo Domingo (p 237) on Isla Ometepe.

14. Zip through the forest on a canopy tour.

15. Fish for tarpon in the Río San Juan.

16. Take a boat trip from Lago de Nicaragua to the Caribbean Sea.

17. Practice your Spanish while volunteering with a local community organization.

18. Shop for crafts and paintings in Solentiname Archipelago.

19. Scuba dive or snorkel in the waters of the Caribbean.

20. Swim at Little Corn Island's secluded, palm-fringed beaches.

SUGGESTED ITINERARIES

A limited time to travel means you'll want narrow the scope of your trip to match your interests. The minimum amount of time needed to complete each itinerary is indicated for the following trip planning ideas.

■ COUNTRY OVERVIEW (ONE WEEK)

> ❑ MANAGUA
> ❑ GRANADA
> ❑ ISLA OMETEPE
> ❑ SAN JUAN DEL SUR
> ❑ MASAYA

Begin your journey by taking a half-day tour of **Managua** to see the city's historical highlights. Continue to **Granada** and spend the next couple of days taking in the town's colonial architecture and museums. Be sure to spend a morning touring **Las Isletas** by boat or kayak. Take the ferry to **Isla Ometepe** and soak up the sun at **Charco Verde** or **Playa Santo Domingo**. Explore the island on horseback, or put on your hiking boots and climb one of the island's volcanoes. Take a ferry to San Jorge and connect by bus or taxi to the beach town of **San Juan del Sur**. Indulge in fresh seafood, take a canopy tour, or relax on the beach. Spend your final day shopping for hammocks or handicrafts in the markets of **Masaya**.

■ ECO-NICARAGUA (THREE WEEKS)

❑ GRANADA
❑ MASAYA
❑ LAGUNA DE APOYO
❑ ISLA OMETEPE
❑ REFUGIO DE VIDA SILVESTRE LA FLOR/CHACOCENTE
❑ MORGAN'S ROCK
❑ RÍO SAN JUAN
❑ RÍO INDIO LODGE
❑ SELVA NEGRA/FINCA ESPERANZA VERDE

Begin your exploration of Nicaragua's natural wonders by spending at least three nights in Granada. While here, take a **canopy tour**, explore **Volcán Mombacho**, and kayak through **Las Isletas**. Take a day-trip to **Masaya**, where you can shop for handicrafts in town before exploring adjacent **Volcán Masaya**. Spend an afternoon swimming or diving in the clear waters of nearby **Laguna de Apoyo**. You can overnight at the lake, or return to Granada. Take the ferry from Granada to verdant **Isla Ometepe**. Climb one of the volcanoes here, and swim and hike at **Charco Verde**. Take a ferry from Isla Ometepe to San Jorge and transfer to **Morgan's Rock**, Nicaragua's premiere ecolodge, where you can learn about sustainability, swim on the nearby beach, or take nature-based excursions. If it's turtle season, see endangered turtles nesting or hatching at **Refugio de Vida Silvestre La Flor** or **Chacocente**. Transfer to Managua for a quick flight to San Carlos, the jumping-off point for the **Río San Juan**. Spend a few days exploring the river; don't miss the ruins of **El Castillo** or the wildlife viewing in the secluded **Reserva Natural Indio Maíz**. End your trip down the river at **Río Indio Lodge**, one of Nicaragua's finest and most remote accommodations. Go fishing, canoeing, or birding before returning to San Carlos for your return flight to Managua. If you have a couple of days remaining before your departure, from here spend at least one night at **Selva Negra** or **Finca Esperanza Verde**, where you can enjoy your time hiking, horseback riding, and learning about the area's sustainable coffee production.

■ BEACHES & ISLANDS OF NICARAGUA (1½ WEEKS)

☐ SAN JUAN DEL SUR
☐ ISLA OMETEPE
☐ GRANADA
☐ CORN ISLANDS

Begin your itinerary by spending a few days surfing, boating, fishing, or swimming in **San Juan del Sur**. Take a water taxi or private boat for a day excursion to some of the area's secluded beaches, such as **Bahía Majagual**, for surfing or sunning. Continue on to **Isla Ometepe** by ferry from San Jorge to enjoy the beach at **Playa Santo Domingo**. Take a ferry from here to **Granada** and explore by boat or kayak some of the more than 300 islands that make up **Las Isletas**. Catch a flight from Managua to the **Corn Islands** to spend your last few days snorkeling, diving, fishing, or relaxing on the spectacular white sand beaches.

NOTE: For this itinerary you may want to fly into Liberia International Airport in Costa Rica near the southern border of Nicaragua and connect by bus or taxi to San Juan del Sur via Rivas. Alternatively, you can fly into Managua and connect by bus or taxi to San Juan del Sur via Rivas.

■ ARTISTIC NICARAGUA (ONE WEEK)

☐ MANAGUA
☐ SOLENTINAME
☐ LEÓN
☐ GRANADA
☐ MASAYA

Begin your artistic travels by spending a day exploring **Managua**'s galleries in the Bolonia neighborhood.

Travel Information

Check to see if there are any art exhibits or performances taking place at Teatro Nacional Rubén Darío during your visit. From Managua, fly to San Carlos and take a boat to **Solentiname** for one night. View artists at work in their homes and shop for paintings and handicrafts at the Casa de Taller. Don't miss a visit to the Musas Museum. Take a return flight to Managua and connect by bus to **León**. Spend two nights in Leon viewing the city's spectacular churches, the art at the Casa de Cultura, the city's political murals, and the modern art at Centro de Arte Ortiz-Guardián. Connect by bus to Granada via Managua. Spend two nights in **Granada** visiting the museum at the Convento San Francisco and admiring the city's colonial architecture. Enjoy your last day in **Masaya** shopping for handicrafts and hammocks before returning to Managua to catch your flight home.

The Pacific Lowlands

Sandwiched between the Pacific Ocean and Lago de Nicaragua, the Pacific Lowlands region of Nicaragua is the country's most populated area. **Managua**, Nicaragua's capital city, has all the usual urban trappings, yet nearby natural attractions, including the beaches of Montelimar and the nature reserves of Chocoyero-El Brujo

and Montibellire are easily accessible. Two ancient volcanoes, Mombacho and Masaya, are situated next to two of the region's largest cities, **Masaya** and **Granada**. Two other volcanoes, Maderas and Concepción, tower above **Isla Ometepe**, while the stark black peak of Cerro Negro is easily accessible from **León**.

The fertile plains of the Pacific Lowlands support agricultural production and are also home to Nicaragua's declining beef industry. More recently, the area has become the center of a fledgling tourism industry, with the vibrant student life of **León**, graceful colonial buildings of **Granada**, and the crafts markets in **Masaya** drawing visitors. The area's volcanoes and **Las Isletas** offer enticing ecological experiences, while **Los Pueblos Blancos** give visitors a taste of local village life. Escape to the waters and wildlife of **Laguna de Apoyo**, in the crater of an ancient volcano. **San Juan del Sur**, until recently a sleepy oceanside hamlet, attracts a growing number of travelers in search of surf and sun.

MANAGUA

DID YOU KNOW? Managua is home to 1.3 million people, more than a quarter of Nicaragua's total population.

This, the capital of Nicaragua, is the country's premiere economic center as well as its largest city. Managua is mindful of its past while looking toward its future as the capital of a country that has experienced a decade of peace. Upscale developments, most notably the neighborhoods around Carretera Masaya, are replete with international restaurant chains and luxury boutiques that serve as the play-grounds of the city's well-heeled residents. Meanwhile, in the *barrios* that edge the city, many families maintain a traditional way of life that is far removed from the hustle and bustle of urban life.

Managua's layout is perplexing to the first-time visitor. A request for a taxi driver to take

Managua before the 1972 earthquake.

you to the city center will likely be met with a blank stare: this big sprawling city has no real downtown. It wasn't always this way. The city was devastated by a severe **earthquake** in 1972 that wiped out more than 600 of the city's blocks, and the growth of infrastructure since then has been haphazard. As a result, exploring Managua in depth in a short amount of time can be a challenge. The decentralized nature of the city means distances can be great, and seemingly innocuous neighborhoods sometimes have unexpectedly substantial crime rates. Further, though Managua has been the capital of Nicaragua since 1857, most of its streets remain unnamed, making navigation difficult.

Despite these challenges, Managua offers many of Nicaragua's most vibrant accommodation, dining, and entertainment options to visitors willing to seek them out.

The Pacific Lowlands

MANAGUA HIGHLIGHTS

- Views from the Tiscapa Canopy Tour.
- Live music at La Casa de Los Mejía Godoy.
- A performance at Teatro Nacional Rubén Darío.
- An excursion to Reserva Natural Chocoyero-El Brujo.

Managua has a handful of worthwhile sights, but it's not one of Nicaragua's more attractive cities. Most visitors prefer to spend their travel time in less congested locales, and a half-day city tour is enough to see the city's highlights (see p 96). If you prefer to move on immediately, it's easy to see Managua on a half- or full-day tour from Masaya, Granada, or León.

INTERNET RESOURCES: The official site of the Mayor's Office in Managua (**www.managua.gob.ni**, Spanish only) has info about city services and some minimal details about local events and festivals.

> **TIP:** *The hottest time of year is March through early May, when the heat combines with the urban grime to render a visit to the city less pleasant than at other times of year. If you can be flexible, October through February has the coolest temperatures. December 7 offers visitors the chance to experience La Purísima celebrations in honor of the Virgin Mary.*

■ GETTING HERE

BY PLANE

The city's **Managua International Airport** (sometimes referred to by its former name, Augusto Sandino International Airport, is compact and easy to navigate. Arriving passengers pay $5 in US cash for a **tourist card** (which goes into the coffers of the Ministry of Tourism); departing passengers pay $32 in US cash, a tax that may or may not already be included in your ticket price. Most visitors are now given a 90-day visit allowance, though a few nationalities still receive only 30 days (the allowable length will be stamped in your passport). Check with your embassy in advance for specifics.

The airport is at Km 11 on Carretera Norte, a 20-minute taxi ride from the city. Taxis are readily available at the airport, as are **rental cars**, including Budget (www.

budget.com.ni), Toyota (www.toyotarentacar.com) Alamo (www.alamo.com), Payless (www.paylesscarrental.com), Hertz (www.hertz.com), and Avis (www.avis.com). Several hotels have **airport shuttles**. Though most people take a taxi to one of Managua's bus stations if they plan to move on to another city, **buses** to **Estelí**, **Matagalpa**, and **Jinotega** stop next to the airport (the last bus passes by in late afternoon). To catch one of these buses, exit the airport, cross the parking lot, and walk north (right) 30 yards.

> **Caution:** Renting a car to explore Managua is not a sound idea unless you know the city well and have experience driving in developing countries. Managua is confusing to navigate, has many roads in poor condition, motorists that seem to moonlight as racecar drivers, and an accident (even if it is the fault of the other driver) can cause serious legal hassles and significant expense. Taxis are an inexpensive way to get around.

The airport also offers **domestic flights**. **La Costeña** (☎ 263-2142, fax 263-1281, jcaballero@lacostena.com.ni) flies from Managua to San Carlos, Siuna/Rosita/Bonanza, Puerto Cabezas, Bluefields, Corn Island, and Waspám. **Atlantic Airlines** (☎ 222-3030, fax 228-5614, www.atlanticairlines.com.ni) flies from Managua to Bluefields and Corn Island and also has flights to Guatemala, Honduras, El Salvador, and Costa Rica. Reservations for both airlines can be made by phone (when you show up for the flight you can pay then), at the airport, or through a travel agent. Check the chapter of your destination for flight times and prices.

BY TAXI

Granada and **Masaya** are common destinations from the airport; pay no more than $38 one-way for up to four passengers. Other destinations include **León** ($65) and **Estelí** ($90).

The Pacific Lowlands

> **TIP:** *If you arrive at the airport and plan to take a taxi, leave the airport, cross the parking lot, and flag down a taxi on the street for a lower price than getting one at the terminal. Before leaving the airport, ask a local how much you should pay to your destination so you'll have a ballpark figure before negotiating the price with the taxi driver.*

BY BUS

International Buses

Ticabus and **Transnica** offer luxury coach service with a/c and restrooms on board. These buses are the most comfortable, efficient way to travel internationally by bus in the region. Each company has its own office in Barrio Martha Quezada where buses depart. Prices are for one-way economy tickets. Make reservations in-person at any of the buses' offices at least one day in advance. **Ticabus** (☎ 222-6094, www.ticabus.com) sends buses to **San José** and **Panama City** at 6, 7 am, noon, and 12:30 (12 hrs/$12.50 for San José, 18 hrs/$37 for Panama); **San Salvador** at 5 am and 12:30 pm (8½ hrs/$28); to **Tegucigalpa** at 6 am (7 hrs/$20); and **San Pedro Sula** (11 hrs/$28). Buses to **Guatemala City** and **Tapachula**, **Mexico**, require an overnight in San Salvador. Buses depart at 5 am, arrive San Salvador at 4 pm, and arrive the following day at **Guatemala City** ($36) at 11 am and **Tapachula** ($51) at 5 pm.

Trip durations and fares are nearly the same on **Transnica** (www.transnica.com), which goes to **San José** at 5:30, 7, 10 am, noon (luxury service), and 3 pm; to **Tegucigalpa** at 2 pm; to **San Salvador** at 5 am and 12:30 pm; and **Choluteca** at 5 am (4 hrs/$12).

> **Caution:** If you have an early morning or evening bus departure, take a taxi even if it's only a few blocks to the station.

Domestic Buses

Managua is the epicenter for bus travel in Nicaragua. Its numerous bus stations are primarily at the city's markets, and each station sends **express** and *ordinario* buses to specific regions of the country. The country's most frequented destinations are also served by **express minibuses**, which usually leave from a different station. Most bus stations in Managua have posted destination and schedule **information**, but this is often

Bus stations are located at the city's markets, which makes it easy to pick up a snack for the trip.

out of date. Reconfirm times at the information booth that is available at most stations, or ask the bus *ayudantes* (helpers who work on the buses).

The Pacific Lowlands

BUS SCHEDULES

To Destinations South: **Masaya**, **Granada**, **Rivas**, **&** **San Juan del Sur**

Buses depart for southern cities from **Mercado Roberto Huembes** (usually just referred to as "Huembes"). *Ordinario* **buses** head to Granada every 15 mins. via the market in **Masaya** and arrive at the terminal west of town on Avenida Elena Arellano (1 hr 20 mins. from Managua/80¢; 35 min./60¢ from Masaya). Daily **express buses** leave for **San Juan del Sur** at 9, 9:30 am and 4 pm (2½ hrs/ $3.50). *Ordinario* **buses** go to **Rivas** (every 30 mins.-1 hr, 3 hrs/$1.50); for San Juan del Sur, take a Rivas-bound bus and change there for a bus to San Juan del Sur (every 45 mins., 50 minutes/50¢).

To Destinations Northwest and Southwest: **León**, **Chinandega**, **Masachapa/Pochomil/ Montelimar** & **Jinotepe**

Buses leave from **Mercado Israel Lewites** (also known as Mercado Boer). León-bound *ordinario* buses leave every half-hour from 4 am-6:30 pm. *Ordinario* buses go to **Chinandega** every 40 mins. from 5 am-7:30 pm (2 hrs 40 mins./$2.20). Buses head to **Masachapa/Pochomil/Montelimar** every half-hour (1½ hrs/$1). **Express** buses to **Jinotepe** leave at 6, 7:30, 8:30, 10:15 am, and noon.

To Destinations North and East: **Estelí**, **Ocotal**, **Somoto**, **Matagalpa**, **Boaco**, **Juigalpa**, **El Rama** & **Siuna**.

From Mercado Mayoreo **express** buses leave for Estelí at 5:45, 8:15, 9:15, 10:45, 11:45 am, 12:20, 1:15, 1:45, 2:45, 3:15, 3:45, and 5:45 pm (2 hrs/$3.50). *Ordinario* buses leave every half-hour from 4 am-5:30 pm (3 hrs/$2). **Express** buses to **Ocotal** take off at 5:10, 6:10, 6:45, 7:45, 8:45, 10:15, 11:15 am, 12:15, 2:15, 2, 4:15, and 5:15 pm. **Somoto**-bound **express** buses leave six times daily (3½ hrs/$4). **Express** buses leave for **Matagalpa** at 3:30, 5:30, 6, 7, 9, 11 am, 12:30, 1:30, 2:30, 3:30, 5 and 6 pm. *Ordinario* buses depart every half-hour from 3:45 am-6:45 pm. *Ordinario* buses leave for **Boaco** (2 hrs/$2) and **Juigalpa** (2½ hrs/$2.50) every 45 minutes. Buses to **El Rama** leave every two hours from 4 am-10 pm (8 hrs/$7.25). **Transporte Aguilar** (☎ 248-3005) leaves Mayoreo at 9 and 10 pm. Bone-cruncher buses to **Siuna** leave at noon and 5 pm (24 hrs/$17.75).

Express minibuses leave from the **La UCA bus lot** near Metrocentro. Buses leave when full (at least once per hour) for **Masaya**, **Granada**, the **Carazo** towns, and **León**.

■ GETTING AROUND

ON FOOT

Managua is not an ideal city for walking. Distances are often vast, street names are usually unmarked, sidewalks are in disrepair or nonexistent, and a notable crime rate in many neighborhoods makes **taxis** a better option in most areas of the city.

> **Caution:** Managua's sidewalks are often riddled with holes. Pay attention to where you are stepping; dangerous grates and open sewers are common.

BY BUS

Managua has an extensive, belching bus fleet that circulates throughout the city. However, schedules often follow the whims of the driver, and route maps are nonexistent. Rides across the city often take more than an hour due to frequent stops and heavy traffic. Don't even consider taking a city bus if you have luggage with you; the buses are perpetually overcrowded and theft can be a problem. Nonetheless, visitors that speak Spanish and have a good sense of the city's layout will find several useful bus routes. Bus 110 goes from **Mercado Huembes** to **Mercado Mayoreo** and **La UCA** every five minutes (exit the Huembes station, take a right, and catch the bus every five minutes on the main road). The trip takes almost an hour. Bus 119's most useful stretch is between **Metrocentro**, **Plaza España**, and **Mercado Huembes**. Bus 109 runs between **Teatro Rubén Darío**, **Plaza Inter**, and **Mercado Huembes**.

The Pacific Lowlands

MANAGUA CITY BUS DO'S & DONT'S

1. Don't take luggage on the bus with you; if you have shopping bags or suitcases, travel by taxi instead.

2. Count out change in advance and pay the driver as you enter the bus (30¢ flat fare). Drivers can make change.

3. If you are unsure about where you should disembark, ask the driver to advise you when to get off (*Me puede decir cuando debo bajar para _____, por favor*). Sit in the front of the bus to get a better view of your surroundings; farther back, the crunch of passengers can make visibility almost nonexistent.

4. Refrain from wearing expensive jewelry or watches and keep valuables in a money belt or neck pouch; theft is a common problem on city buses.

5. Kick back and enjoy the (often lengthy) ride! Managua city buses provide a true slice-of-life look at the city.

> **NOTE:** *Rotonda Metrocentro is also known as Rotonda Rubén DaRío.*

BY TAXI

Managua has ample taxis, on which most visitors (and residents) rely heavily. To hail a taxi, just stick your arm out parallel from your shoulder. Tell the driver through the window your destination and arrange a price before getting in. Official taxis have red license plates, though plenty of entrepreneurs search for passengers using private cars as taxis; avoid the latter. Taxis roaming the streets (*colectivos*) generally charge per passenger, and the driver will cram as many people into the taxi as possible, often stopping to pick up passengers along the way. This means that visitors need to allow ample time to get to their destination as the route will likely not be direct. At night for safety reasons you might want to pay a surcharge to the driver for private service so additional passengers won't be picked up. Approximate daytime fares are C40 (just under $3) to go partway across the city and C60 (around $4) to cross the entire city. Fares to and from the **airport** have risen substantially in recent years; count on at least $12 for up to four passengers to reach any Managua hotel that isn't adjacent to the airport; the return trip should cost around $10. Hotels can call a taxi for you (there will usually be one waiting outside anyway), or, for a surcharge, call a radio taxi:

- Cooperativa Mario Lizano, ☎ 268-7669
- Cooperativa 2 de Agosto, ☎ 263-1512
- Cooperativa 25 de Febrero, ☎ 222-5218

Arrange the price over the phone and reconfirm the price when the taxi arrives.

INSIDE ADVICE ON TAXIS

Though in general taxi drivers (*taxistas*) are friendly and helpful in Managua, unscrupulous drivers often try to price gouge unsuspecting foreigners. Be sure to negotiate the fare before getting into a taxi, and level the playing field to some extent by asking nearby locals what you should pay before entering into negotiations. Spanish speakers will likely do better on prices, but if your Spanish is shaky, write down the price so there isn't any dispute later on. Pay the driver when you reach your destination. If you've had a satisfactory ride and will be staying in town for a few days, it's worthwhile to get the cell phone number of the taxi driver. While calling for a pickup costs a bit more, the security and reliability often outweighs the additional expense.

Most visitors are amazed to find that a city of Managua's size has no street names. When

The Pacific Lowlands

asking directions, keep in mind that many directions are given locally in terms of buildings or landmarks that might no longer exist (*dónde fue....*). Be consoled by the fact that most taxi drivers are adept at finding local hotels, restaurants, and sights; usually giving them no more than the name of your destination is sufficient. If you're headed somewhere obscure, ask your hotel's reception to write the directions down in Spanish and show them to your taxi driver (most taxi drivers can read fairly well, but if your pronunciation is up to it, it can help to give them verbal directions).

BY SHUTTLE

A few Managua hotels, including **Best Western Las Mercedes**, **Camino Real**, and **Holiday Inn**, have airport shuttles ranging from free to $5. This is a particularly good option for passengers with early or late flights.

■ SERVICES

TOURS & INFORMATION: Managua's flagship **Intur** office (☎ 222-3333) is a block south and a block west of Hotel Crowne Plaza. Open Mon-Fri 8 am-noon and 2-5 pm. A small Intur office is also up and running at the **airport**.

Managua boasts the country's largest selection of tour agencies, most of which can arrange accommodation and activities throughout the country. Managua is one of the few places in Nicaragua where taking a city **tour** is highly recommended; the city's main sights are spread throughout the city and finding them can be a challenge. Tour agencies can arrange a half- or full-day tour, or you can hire a **taxi** for a full day of sightseeing within the city for around $50. Hotels and guesthouses can also make arrangements.

Travel agencies that specialize in arranging plane and bus tickets can be found grouped around Plaza España. **Viajes Atlántida** (a block east and a half-block north of Plaza España, ☎ 266-4050) is a professional operation.

MONEY: You'll find that credit cards are more widely accepted in Managua than anywhere else in the country. **Banks**, including **BDF**, **Banic**, and **BAC**, are clustered along Carretera Masaya (the highway that leads to Masaya). There is also a **BDF** at Hotel Intercontinental. Banks in Managua are open Mon-Fri 8 am-4 pm and Sat 8 am-noon. **ATM**s are most conveniently found in malls and at most bank branches.

INTERNET: Most mid- to upscale hotels in Managua have free Internet connections, including wireless. Two Internet cafés can be found in **Plaza Inter** (one on the ground floor and one upstairs next to the food court). The **Metrocentro Mall** also has Internet.

LIBRARIES: Managua is home to most of Nicaragua's major universities, all of which house libraries. Check their websites for details on use policies and services (www.uni.edu.ni, www.uca.edu.ni, www.aum.edu.ni). Nicaragua's national library, **Biblioteca Nacional Rubén Darío**, is at the Palacio Nacional de la Cultura (☎ 222-2722 binanic@tmx.com.ni).

> **TIP:** *Visitors with an in-depth interest in anything Nicaraguan won't want to miss the enormous **Biblioteca Roberto Incer Barquero** (☎ 265-0500) at Km 7 on Carretera Sur. With 67,000 books, free Internet, and an art gallery, you can while away an entire day in air-conditioned bliss. Open Mon-Fri 8:30 am-6 pm and Sat 9 am-1 pm.*

LAUNDRY: Most guesthouses and hotels in Managua have laundry service (usually handwashed at inexpensive guesthouses and machine-washed at mid-range hotels). Better hotels have dry cleaning and alteration

The Pacific Lowlands

services. **Dryclean USA** is at Plaza Bolonia. There are no public laundromats.

MAIL & TELEPHONE: Post offices and Enitel offices are usually next to each other in Managua. Visitors staying in Nicaragua for an extended period of time should consider buying a **cell phone** to use for the duration of their trip, an option that is surprisingly inexpensive. **Enitel** sells cell phones and phone cards and also offers domestic and international calling. There are **Enitel offices** and neighboring **Correos de Nicaragua** (post offices) in the **airport** and at Palacio de Comunicaciones near the Catedral Viejo (Old Cathedral). The Palacio branch also sells a wide variety of Nicaraguan **stamps** for collectors.

RESTROOMS: Public restrooms are virtually nonexistent in Managua. Each of the **markets** has poorly-maintained restrooms; elsewhere, stop for a drink at a restaurant and use the restroom there. Large hotels often allow non-guests use lobby restrooms.

MEDICAL: Nicaragua's best hospital is two-year-old **Hospital Vivian Pellas** (☎ 255-6850), just outside of town at Km 9.5 on Carretera Masaya. **Hospital Bautista** (☎ 249-7070) in Barrio Largaespada and **Hos-**

Vivian Pellas Hospital

pital Militar (☎ 222-2172) next to Laguna de Tiscapa are also decent options.

The **dental** office of **Dr. Martha Montalvan** (☎ 276-1603) is well-regarded and she speaks English. Her office is in Las Colinas shopping center. **Mongalo and Mongalo** (☎ 270-3173, www.implantes.net) has international standards (both dentists are Florida-trained) and modern equipment.

STAYING SAFE: Managua is one of the safest capital cities in Central America. Nonetheless, Managua struggles with crime more than most cities in Nicaragua, and visitors need to stay aware of their surroundings, particularly when on foot. Neighborhoods that are best avoided include **Las Americas**, **San Judas**, **Renee Schick**, **La Fuente**, **Vida Nueva**, **Los Pescadores**, the areas adjacent to **Mercado Oriental** and **Catedral Nueva**, and **Batahola** (which surrounds the US Embassy). Though **Barrio Martha Quezada** is a popular location for accommodation, avoid walking between this neighborhood and Plaza Inter; the distance is short, but there has been a surge in daytime. In general, the south-central part of the city is safest; the areas around **Bolonia**, **San Juan**, **Los Robles**, **Altamira**, and **Metrocentro** enjoy fairly low rates of crime, and they have a variety of accommodation and dining options. Managua has **centralized emergency numbers**: call 115 for the **police**, 118 for the **fire department**, and 128 for the **Cruz Roja** (Red Cross).

> **Caution:** Some Managua neighborhoods that initially appear safe may not be; ask at your guesthouse for current recommendations before venturing out on foot. Reduce risks by taking taxis, leaving valuables at home, and traveling with a companion.

MARKETS: Managua has multiple sprawling markets, some of which also serve as bus stations. Managua's markets offer a vast array of goods, though the most useful to travelers is **Mercado Huembes**, which has the best **handicrafts** selection. Managua's markets are generally open from around 7 am-4:30 pm, though mornings see the most activity and allow shoppers to beat the heat. Keep an eye on your belongings at every market in Managua, and it's best to avoid **Mercado Oriental** altogether; it's notorious for crime.

Managua has three major **supermarket chains** to complement the small neighborhood shops that are spread throughout the city. If you're heading to smaller towns after your stay in Managua, stocking up on toiletries and other basics is smart. **La Colonia** is a clean, comprehensive US-style chain with air-conditioning (!), a good selection of local and foreign products, liquor, inexpensive clothing, and magazines (including a few in English). Each outlet has a **fast food**-style eatery, notable for generally poor service but very inexpensive Nicaraguan dishes, along with mediocre made-to-order sandwiches. **La Union** resembles La Colonia but has a smaller selection. **Palí**, affiliated with Wal-Mart, is a no-frills chain that carries mostly local products at low prices. Below is one of Managua's growing number of malls, Galerias Santo Domingo.

MANAGUA HISTORY 101

Managua today reflects its often tumultuous history. The city, then known as *Mana-huac* (Large Vessel for Water), has its origins as a Nahuatl village. Fiercely independent, the town infuriated the Spanish during the colonial period by refusing to submit to Spanish control, and the town was demolished. It wasn't until the middle of the 19th century that Managua gained prominence when it was declared the capital in a compromise between the Liberals of León to the north and the Conservatives of Granada to the south. The site seemed ideally-located between the two cities until a severe earthquake struck in 1931, killing 1,000 people and giving the small but thriving community a sobering indication that Managua was in fact located on multiple major fault lines. Reconstruction began, only to be eradicated by fire in 1936. The resourceful inhabitants again rebuilt, but in December of 1972 a staggering earthquake virtually leveled the city, killing more than 10,000 people in the process. The arduous task of rebuilding homes and lives was made more difficult by widespread corruption, much of it overseen by Somoza, and little international aid reached those who needed it most.

Tall buildings and high density were not a wise choice, given Managua's likelihood of being struck by earthquakes again. The sprawling nature of Managua today reflects that outlook, though after decades of little economic growth, changes are now happening, spurred to a great extent by Nicaraguans who left for Miami during Sandinista times and are now returning with money and entrepreneurial ideas.

The Pacific Lowlands

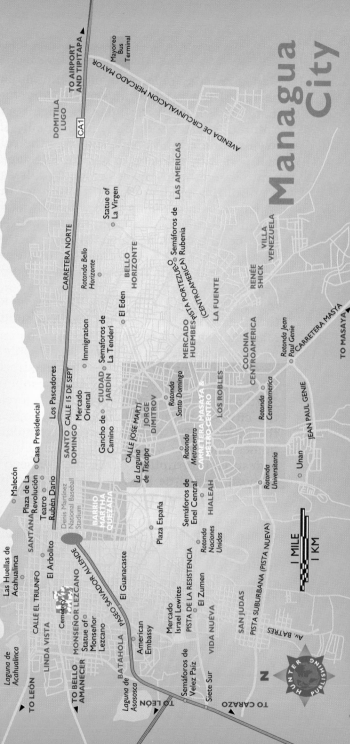

Managua City

Lago Xolotlán

TO AIRPORT AND TIPITAPA

DOMITILA LUGO

CA1

Mayoreo Bus Terminal

AVENIDA DE CIRCUNVALACIÓN MERCADO MAYOR

LAS AMERICAS

Statue of La Virgen

CARRETERA NORTE

Rotonda Bello Horizonte

BELLO HORIZONTE

El Eden

Semáforos de Rubenia

Semáforos de La Tenderi

MERCADO HUEMBES

PISTA PORTEZUELO (CENTROAMERICA)

VILLA VENEZUELA

LA FUENTE

RENÉE SHICK

Immigration

Rotonda Jean Paul Genie

CARRETERA MASYA

TO MASAYA

COLONIA CENTROAMERICA

Rotonda Centroamerica

Gancho de Camino

SANTO CALLE 15 DE SEPT DOMINGO

Mercado Oriental

CIUDAD JARDÍN

CALLE JOSE MARTI

JORGE DIMITROV

Rotonda Santo Domingo

LOS ROBLES

Los Pascadores

Plaza de La Revolución

Casa Presidencial

Malecón

SANTANA

Teatro Rubén Darío

La Laguna de Tiscapa

Rotonda Metrocentro

CARRETERA MASAYA & METRO-CENTRO

JEAN PAUL GENIE

Unan

Rotonda Universitaria

Las Huellas de Acahualinca

CALLE EL TRIUNFO

El Arbolito

BARRIO MARTHA QUEZADA

Denis Martínez National Baseball Stadium

Plaza España

Semáforos de Enel Central

HIALEAH

Rotonda Naciones Unidas

LINDA VISTA

Statue of Monseñor Lezcano

MONSEÑOR LEZCANO

El Guanacaste

PASEOS SALVADOR ALLENDE

BATAHOLA

American Embassy

Mercado Israel Lewites

PISTA DE LA RESISTENCIA

El Zumen

VIDA NUEVA

SAN JUDAS

PISTA SUBURBANA (PISTA NUEVA)

Av. BATRES

Laguna de Acahualinca

TO LEÓN

TO BELLO AMANECER

Cemetery

Laguna de Asososca

Semáforos de Velez Paíz

Siete Sur

TO LEÓN

TO CARAZO

1 MILE

1 KM

N

HUNTER PUBLISHING PUBLISHING

© 2007 HUNTER PUBLISHING, INC.

■ SIGHTSEEING

Every listing in this book is recommended and considered above average in its category. Listings with one star (☆) are highly recommended. Those earning two stars (☆☆) are considered worthy of a detour. A few places have three stars (☆☆☆), which means you should make every effort to see them.

OLD MANAGUA WALKING TOUR

Though it's a tongue twister, you won't want to miss the **Huellas de Acahualinca** ☆☆ (☎ 266-5774), ancient footprints from 6,000 years ago that edge Lago de Nicaragua. The footprints, left by a dozen or so people, were preserved by a volcano eruption when the resulting ash fell on the prints. They weren't discovered until 1874. A small **museum** now displays the prints (shown in this book on page __), along with a few artifacts. The museum is open Mon-Fri 8 am-5 pm and Sat-Sun 9 am-4 pm. Entry costs $2. The site is a challenge to find by car; taking a taxi is an easier option.

Rubén Darío's monument outside the theater that bears his name.

Catch views of Lago de Managua from the Malecón, a spot to be avoided from late afternoon on. Continue east from here to the **Plaza de la Revolución** ☆, the closest thing to a "tourist center" in Managua and surrounded by many of the city's sights. The **Teatro Rubén**

Darío, which resembles Washington's Kennedy Center, was actually designed by the architects who created the Metropolitan Opera house in New York. Facing the theater is **Parque Rubén Darío**, home of a monument to the great poet.

The Old Cathedral is off-limits to visitors.

The modern **Casa Presidencial** (the home of the president), on the lakefront, is hard to miss (check out the bright paint). Next door, the ruins of **Catedral Vieja** ☆, Old Cathedral, are a focal point and a testament to what Managua once looked like. The cathedral was built in the early 20th century, but disaster struck soon afterward in the form of the 1931 earthquake. The church withstood the tremors, but the 1972 earthquake sealed its fate, leaving it too structurally damaged to be used. Take a look at the shell of the building, but visitors are not allowed inside for safety reasons.

The **Palacio Nacional de la Cultura**, built in 1935, is one of Managua's most attractive buildings. Formerly the home of Congress, the building was penetrated by Sandinista Comandante Cero in 1978 in a hostage takeover. Today the building serves as the **Museo Nacional de Nicaragua** ☆☆, which includes a fine pre-

Palacio Nacional

Columbian permanent exhibit, as well as the **National Library** and the **National Archives**. The museum is open Mon-Fri 8 am-5 pm and Sun 9 am-4 pm. Entry costs $3, which includes a 30-minute guided tour; there is an additional fee for taking photos. Next door you'll find the **Centro Cultural de Managua**, an artistic space devoted to the national art and music schools. Performances sometimes take place, and the center hosts an artisan fair with handicrafts for sale the first Sat of every month.

Across the street you'll find two parks, **Parque Velásquez** and **Parque de la Paz**. La Paz serves as a memorial to the end of the Contra War, and numerous weapons are on display. South of Parque Velásquez is the **Asemblea Nacional**, the National Assembly. Guards will likely keep you at a distance, but take a peek from Avenida Bolivar. Continue on Avenida Bolivar to reach the **Arboretum Nacional Juan Bautista Salas** (☎ 222-2558), home to several hundred plant species. Open Mon-Sat 8 am-5 pm. Entry 75¢.

DID YOU KNOW? Even though Managua grows, skyscrapers may not be in its future: there are 14 major seismic faults within city limits.

The Pacific Lowlands

La Luguna de Tiscapa

Bust of José Martí

CALLE JOSÉ MARTÍ

TO PLAZA INTER AND BARRIO MARTHA QUEZADA

N

TO ROTONDA BELO HORIZONTE

JORGE DIMITROV

Catedral Nueva

HUNTER PUBLISHING

Rotonda Santo Domingo

UNI

Rotonda Metro Centro

Metro Centro Mall

Hotel Intercontinental Metro Centro

Academia de La Danza

$

Casa de Los Mejía Godoy

Hispamer

Hotel Casa Real

El Muelle

El Chamán

UCA

Hotel Seminole Plaza

$

La Hora del Taco

The Wok

Hippo's

La Union Supermarket

LOS ROBLES

Gateria de Los Tres Mundos

Hotel Princess

Casa San Juan

Don Pan

Casa San Juan

ALTAMIRA

Pizza Valenti

La Marseillaise

Hotel Los Robles

CARRETERA MASAYA

Lo Stradivari

Casa de Café

Maria Bonita

Pharoah's Casino

Ache

Cocina de Doña Haydee

TO MERCADO HUEMBES

TGI Friday's

Xs

Rotonda Universtaria

Rotanda Centroamerica

Tacos Al Pastor

Carretera Masaya & Metrocentro

TO MASAYA

© 2007 HUNTER PUBLISHING, INC

TO UNAN

Not to Scale

OTHER LOCATIONS

Catedral Nueva. On the northeast side of Rotonda Metrocentro, the New Cathedral's idiosyncratic protruding domes are hard to miss. Constructed from 1991-93, the cathedral has a starkly modern interior that holds 1,500. Though it was designed by Mexican architect Ricardo Legorreta, who was inspired by a temple in the indigenous village of Cholula, Mexico, the cathedral displays mosque-like characteristics. The style serves a purpose as well: the numerous domes offer protection against seismic activity. Jampacked masses are held Sundays at 11 am and 6 pm and Tues-Sat at noon and 6 pm.

© Fréréric Eveno

NOTE: *In the Nahuatl language, the word Managua means "place where there is an extension of water," a reference to the city's proximity to several lakes.*

■ ADVENTURES

IN THE AIR & ON FOOT

Tiscapa Canopy Tour (next to Hotel Crowne Plaza, ☎ 838-7499) has the most affordable zip line adventure in Nicaragua ($14), but that doesn't mean that the views are compromised: you'll take in a panorama of the entire city. The tour consists of three cables stretching .72 mile. The canopy tour is open Tues-Sun, 9 am-4:30 pm. After the tour, explore the surrounding **Parque Nacional Lomas de Tiscapa**, which has **hiking trails** and great views of the city. The top of the hill is

The Pacific Lowlands

home to a statue of Sandino and two military tanks. The park is also home to the **ruins** of the former **presidential palace**, which now hosts local exhibits; former torture chambers can also be seen from above but not entered. Entry to the park costs $2.

> **NOTE:** *While the waters of Laguna de Tiscapa may look appealing from afar, they are polluted and unfit for swimming.*

Recently renovated **Nejapa Golf and Country Club** (www.nejapagolfandcountryclub.com) has an 18-hole golf course, driving range, and practice green. Services include golf carts, caddies, lessons, a pro shop and bag storage. Other facilities include four lighted **tennis courts**, meeting rooms, a nice **swimming pool**, and a locker room. Green fees begin at $18 and a monthly membership for foreigners costs $250. The golf course is at Km 5 of Carretera Sur a half-block from Hotel Mansión Teodolinda.

ON WATER

If Managua's oppressive heat has you dreaming of cool water, head to **Laguna de Xiloá**, 12 miles (30 minutes) northwest of Managua off the highway to León. The water is clean and there is a small earthen beach for relaxing. Grab a bite or a drink at one of the small **bar/restaurants** ($-$$). The laguna is open daily 8 am-9 pm; visitors must enter before 7 pm. **Camping** here is possible, though no rental equipment is available; ask permission at the **Intur** office at the site. Public transportation to the laguna is not really feasible; by car, take the highway toward León and look for the signs to the laguna entrance.

Lake Managua, with Momotombo Volcano and Momotombito Island in the distance.

Dive Oceanica arranges diving excursions to Laguna de Xiloa, home to 14 species of fish as well as turtles. The laguna's geothermal vents are another point of interest. The site's water is a bit murky but clears up from April to November. PADI Open Water courses cost $289. Dive Oceanica is a block north and 1½ blocks west from the Rotonda Universitaria.

CULTURAL ADVENTURES

The comprehensive **Viva Spanish School** (☎ 877-7179, 270-2339, www.vivaspanishschool.com, vivaspanish@btinternet.com) has flexible programs attuned to a variety of needs. Intensive, 20-hour-per-week Spanish classes can be tailored to specific fields, including medical, business, or religious ($125 plus $75 for a homestay). Additional offerings include literature and culture courses. Special classes are available for children, and working expats can take advantage of evening classes, which take place four hours per week. **Academia Europeo** (☎ 278-0829) has similar offerings and experienced instructors just south of Hotel Princess.

Manna Project International (www.mannaproject. org, daniel@mannproject.org) seeks volunteers to work with low-income children and adults for a minimum of two months. Projects range from teaching art to coaching sports.

■ SHOPPING & ART GALLERIES

Young Managuans are mall fanatics, and the slightly sterile **shopping centers** of **Metrocentro** (next to Rotonda Metrocentro) and **Plaza Inter** (next to Hotel Intercontinental) include foreign chain stores, upscale clothing shops, movie theaters, and food courts. In general, prices are equivalent to those in the US, though Plaza Inter is the less expensive of the two malls and focuses more on Asian imports. These shopping centers are the best place to buy hard-to-find, foreign-made items such as business attire, bathing suits, name-

The Pacific Lowlands

brand electronics, contact lens solution, and makeup. **Centro Comercial Managua**, just east of Rotonda Centroamerica, has a good selection of slightly lower quality goods at correspondingly lower prices. **Price Smart** is a warehouse-style store with low prices; it requires a membership, which may be worth it if you're spending a few months in Managua.

You won't find much in the way of gifts to bring home at the malls; instead, hit the markets (*mercados*) for handicrafts and traditional items. **Mama Delfina** (in the neighborhood of Reparto San Juan adjacent to IBW Internet) has a good selection of crafts in an upscale boutique shop. Another excellent option for gift shopping is to explore one of Managua's **art galleries**, most of which are in the Bolonia neighborhood. **Ipikentro Gallery** (☎ 266-5445) faces Plaza El Carmen and has modern paintings and poetry readings. Open Mon-Fri 8 am-5:30 pm and Sat 8 am-1 pm. Two blocks south of here you'll find the excellent **Añil, Galería de Artes Visuales** (☎ 266-5445), which has a wide selection of paintings, photography, and crafts. Open Mon-Fri 1-8 pm and Sat 9 am-6 pm. Next door is the space of renowned sculptor **Miguel Abarca** (☎ 266-3551).

If you're in search of **paintings from Solentiname**, **Galería Solentiname** (☎ 270-1773), owned by a Solentiname native, has a selection of in this gallery that faces Ache restaurant in Altamira. Open Mon-Fri 8 am-5:30 pm and Sat 8 am-4 pm. From there, head across Carretera Masaya to **Galería Casa de los Tres Mundos** (☎ 267-0304), 2½ blocks north of La Marseillaise restaurant. This is the gallery of Ernesto Cardenal and a variety of items from the archipelago are available, including crafts, paintings, and books.

If you need supplies for photography, visit **Kodak** or **AGFA**, which face Price Smart in Bolonia. **Konica** is in Plaza Espana.

■ ENTERTAINMENT

MOVIES

When the heat gets to be too much, escape to one of the Managua's **movie theaters**, which are air-conditioned with Arctic strength. Movies are generally shown in English with subtitles and come out about a month after their US debuts. Tickets average $3.50. **Plaza Inter Mall** houses Cinema Plaza Inter (☎ 222-5090). Take a taxi at night, even if you are staying nearby. **Metrocentero Mall** has a large Cinemark theater (☎ 271-9037). **Alianza Francesa**, just north of the Mexican Embassy, shows free French films every Wed night at 8 pm.

THEATER

Teatro Nacional Rubén Darío ☆☆. Next to the Malecón, ☎ 222-7426, www.tnrubendario.gob.ni, the national theater has been staging performances since 1969. Though performance schedules can be erratic, it

is well worth giving the theater a call to see what will be playing during your visit. Major performances and concerts take place in the Main Hall, which can seat 1,200. The theater also hosts occasional exhibitions and events, so if there are no performances scheduled during your visit you still want to take a peek inside the building.

Teatro Justo Rufino Garay. Next to Parque Las Palmas, ☎ 266-3714, this 25-year-old theater hosts local and international alternative performances in its 150-seat air-conditioned space. Weekly "Wednesdays of Alternative Cinema" take place to highlight international and alternative films. A second theater, **Teatro**

Victor Romeo (☎ 266-6738) has a similar focus and is also next to Parque Las Palmas.

BASEBALL & SOCCER

Nicaragua's largest stadium, **Estadio Denis Martínez**, can hold up to 40,000 frenzied fans. Often referred to as Estadio Nacional, the stadium is just north of Barrio Martha Quezada. Built in 1949, it is near and dear to

 the hearts of Managuans, and attending a game is a true cultural experience. Baseball is by far the most popular sport, and games usually take place five times per week in season, beginning around 6 pm on weekdays, in the early

afternoon on Sat, and at 11 am on Sun. Tickets cost 50¢-$3. It's not necessary to purchase tickets in advance. The stadium also hosts the occasional concert or religious event.

NIGHTLIFE

> **Caution:** Take a taxi to and from the city's nightlife venues to be safe.

One of the best ways to put your finger on the pulse of life in Managua is by exploring its nightlife. Managua's upscale nightlife venues hug the Carretera Masaya between Rotonda Centroamerica and Rotonda Metrocentro. Bars open and close rapidly; ask locally for the current hot spots. **XS** (☎ 277-3086), is the place to see and be seen for dancing. Located at Km 5 of the Carretera Masaya, XS is the city's most famous disco and is particularly popular with 20-somethings who like hip hop and techno. Another good dance option is **Bar Chamán**, which plays Latin and international songs, just behind Hotel Metrocentro Intercontinental. Cover $2.25. For a more laid-back evening and a slightly older crowd, try one of the city's bars. The venerable **La Cavanga** ☆, at the Centro Cultural Managua, has live music on weekends.

If you want to enjoy views along with your drink, **Mirador Tiscapa**, next to Laguna de Tiscapa, has a nice ambience, live music on weekends, and is open daily until 2 am. **La Curva**, behind Hotel Crowne Plaza, serves unique drinks in a relaxed *rancho*. **Bar Shannon** (a block east and a block south of Ticabus in Barrio Martha Quezada) has Guiness and gaggles of international travelers. Additionally, virtually every mid-range and upscale hotel in Managua has at least one bar.

Pharaoh's Casino (☎ 278-3752, www.pharaohsnic aragua.com) has two locations, one at Hotel Camino Real and the other at Km 4.5 on Carretera Masaya.

The Pacific Lowlands

GAY NIGHTLIFE IN MANAGUA

Managua has an increasingly visible gay scene, and several nightlife venues are popular with travelers and locals. Two of the safer, more upscale options are **Tabu**, three blocks north and a block west of Hospital Militar, and the slightly less stylish **Miami**, a block south and a block west of the Estatua de Montoya statue. **Fundación Xochiquetzal** is a local NGO that focuses on gay issues and can be a good resource about upcoming events. Contact them by mail at Apartado #112, Managua or quetzal@ops.org.ni.

■ WHERE TO STAY

Managua's vast size means that visitors rely heavily on taxis, so the location of your accommodation isn't as crucial here as in some other cities. That said, you should avoid hotels in neighborhoods that experience high levels of crime. Refer to *Staying Safe*, p 99, when selecting a hotel. Accommodation is expensive in Managua compared to other cities in Nicaragua. The city also has some of the country's most upscale hotels, so it's a good place for a splurge. This is one city where prices and safety generally correspond. Unless otherwise noted, the following hotels accept credit cards, arrange tours, and have cable TV, a/c, and private baths with hot water.

HOTEL PRICE CHART	
Cost per night for two people, before tax	
$	Up to $15
$$	$16-$30
$$$	$31-$60
$$$$	Over $60

NEAR THE AIRPORT

Many flights arrive in Managua at night and leave at the crack of dawn, so spending the night near the airport is an excellent option. There are no decent budget hotels in this area, but inexpensive hotels are just 15 minutes by taxi from the airport in Barrio Martha Quezada.

Hotel Camino Real ($$$$, half a mile from the airport at Km 9.5 on Carretera Norte, ☎ 255-5901, www. caminoreal.com.ni, descobar@caminoreal.com.ni). The modern Camino Real is immediately recognizable from the highway due to its large casino. The hotel has 116 fairly nice rooms and four suites set among attractively landscaped grounds that include a nice pool and a restaurant. Doubles cost $165. The hotel offers a variety of services, including babysitting, **car rental**, haircuts, and wireless Internet. The hotel also offers a free airport **shuttle**; the airport is just five minutes away.

© Hotel Camino Real

Best Western Las Mercedes ($$$$, facing the airport, ☎ 263-1011). Notable for its prime location directly across from the airport, Las Mercedes is nothing special, but it is very convenient. This hotel is also a good option for visitors with limited mobility as rooms are all on the ground floor and there is a free **airport shuttle** (unnecessary for most guests – just exit the airport, walk across the parking lot and you're at the hotel). Most rooms are identical and include in-room phone and mini-bar, but, before selecting a room, turn the a/c on to ensure it's not annoyingly loud. Doubles cost $72.

The leafy grounds include tennis courts and a large, well-maintained pool where you can cool off. A range of services, including haircuts and **car rental**, is available. A breakfast buffet (good selection, so-so food at the breakfast buffet – lunch and dinner are better) is included in the price; enjoy your meal indoors or on the patio overlooking the pool.

© Best Western Hotels

BARRIO MARTHA QUEZADA

Barrio Martha Quezada is the nearest approximation to a tourist center in Managua. The neighborhood is not heavy on sights, but it does offer a wealth of amenities that are particularly attractive to budget travelers, including inexpensive street food and close proximity to international bus stations. This area has recently experienced an increase in crime; take a taxi.

✰ **Hotel Mansión Teodolinda** ($$$$, a block south and a half-block west of Intur, ☎ 228-1050, www.teo dolinda.com.ni, hotel@teodolinda.com.ni). Teodolinda has a great location and comfortable rooms directed toward business travelers but convenient for tourists as well. The property is more intimate than many of the city's other upscale hotels. There is a nice pool, two good restaurants, and a wide range of business amenities. The 33 rooms come with tile floors and wood accents, a/c, in-room phones and kitchenettes. Singles cost $80, doubles $95, and one apartment is also available for $100 per night. Breakfast is included.

✰ **Hotel El Conquistador** ($$$-$$$$, a block south and a block west of Plaza Inter, ☎ 222-4789, www. hotelelconquistador.com, info@hotelelconquistador. com). This small, modern hotel is the kind of place where the staff knows your name. The 18 rooms are spacious and include mini-bar. Singles cost $57, doubles $58-$81, and triples $87; ask about discounts if you plan to stay for a few days. Breakfast is included. The hotel's services are plentiful, including laundry service, fax, and a free **airport shuttle**. Internet connections are available in the guest rooms, and free computer use is available in the lobby.

Hotel Los Felipe ($$, 1½ blocks west of Ticabus, ☎ 222-6501, www.hotellosfelipe.com, losfelipe@ideay. net.ni). This budget find is a favorite with travelers. Rooms are dowdy but functional, and service is friendly. Each room has cable TV and a hot water private bath (well, somewhat private – the walls are flimsy and many don't reach the ceiling). Singles with fan cost $15, doubles $20, triples $25, quads $25 (all rooms cost $5 more with a/c). Dorm beds cost $7. Services include laundry, Internet, and tour and plane ticket sales.

Hospedaje Jardín de Italia ($$-$$$, a block east and a half-block north of Ticabus, ☎ 222-7967, www. jardindeitalia.com). This friendly budget guesthouse will do in a pinch. The eight tiny and tired rooms have private bath, a/c, thin wooden walls, and furniture that has seen better days. Singles $10, doubles $20 (double the price for a/c). The property has a bar/restaurant and small pool; parking, Internet, fax, laundry service, and airport transport are all available.

© Hospedaje Jardin de Italia

Hotel Crowne Plaza ($$$$, Facing Plaza Inter Mall, ☎ 228-3530, www.crowneplaza.com). The distinctive pyramid shape of this venerable hotel is hard to miss. Renovated in 2000, the hotel has 140 rooms and 30 suites, some with views of the lake. Rooms are decently furnished and have all the amenities you'd expect.

> *DID YOU KNOW? In the early 1980s, the Sandinistas ran the federal government from the building that houses the Hotel Crowne Plaza, then the Hotel Inter. The international press corps also called the hotel home during the Revolution and the Contra War.*

The hotel specializes in business travel with corresponding availability of conference centers and services. The property has three restaurants; if you overindulge, hit the pool, sauna, gym. Singles $145, doubles $155. A free **airport shuttle** is available, and the hotel is conveniently situated.

> **TIP:** *The Crowne Plaza, a landmark often used for giving directions, was formerly the Hotel Inter and may still be referred to as such (or as "el viejo Hotel Inter").*

NEAR METROCENTRO & CARRETERA MASAYA

☆☆ **Hotel Hostal Real** ($$$$, Facing the German Embassy in Bolonia, ☎ 266-8133, www.hostalreal.com.ni, info@hostalreal.com.ni). This cozy place is well-appointed and has attractive common areas. Antique fur-

The Pacific Lowlands

niture and in-room phones are standard features. Singles cost $70, doubles $75. There is a second Hotel Hostal Real in Los Robles that has similar amenities and prices.

☆☆ **Hotel Los Robles** ($$$$, a hundred feet south of La Marseillaise restaurant, ☎ 267-3008, hotellosrobles. com, info@hotellosrobles.com). This cozy bed and breakfast is one of Managua's, and indeed Nicaragua's,

© Hotel Los Robles

finest. With only 14 rooms, guests are guaranteed personal attention. Rooms have small private patios, in-room phones and are beautifully furnished. Singles cost $80 and doubles go for $95. Business services are available, including free wireless Internet.

☆ **Hotel Princess** ($$$$, at Km 4.5 of Carretera Masaya, ☎ 255-5777, www.hoteles princess.com). The Princess gets high marks for stellar service. The common areas are nicely decorated, and the 104 rooms are very attractive. Singles run $120, while doubles cost $139. The property has a host of business and recreational amenities, including a pleasant pool, and a good restaurant and pub.

© Hilton Hotels

☆ **Real Intercontinental Metrocentro** ($$$$, next to Metrocentro Mall, ☎ 278-4545, www.icmanagua. gruporeal.com). This is one of Nicaragua's most luxurious, comprehensive hotels and amenities are what you'd expect. The hotel is also notable for its convenient location and its extensive business facilities, including 11 (!) conference rooms. The 157 rooms cost $161 for a single or double. Breakfast is included.

Hotel Seminole Plaza ($$$$, a block south of Hotel Intercontinental Metrocentro, ☎ 270-0061, www. seminoleplaza.com, res@seminoleplaza.com). The 85 rooms in this modern hotel are nothing extraordinary, but they are comfortable, fairly spacious and come with free Internet, cable TV, and a/c. The common areas are nicely-maintained and attractive. Singles cost $100 and doubles $110. The hotel offers business services, a restaurant and two bars, a pool, and laundry service.

OTHER LOCATIONS

Holiday Inn Select ($$$$, avenida Juan Pablo II, ☎ 270-4515, www.holidayinn.com.ni, ventas@ holidayinn.com.ni). This hotel has 155 rooms and five suites of international quality. The rooms contain all of the amenities you'd expect at this price level, and service is professional. There are a variety of facilities here, including a conference center, restaurant, pool, parking, and Internet. Prices include breakfast. Though the hotel is not centrally-located (it's north-west of the city center), there is a low-cost airport shuttle available ($5 per person). Doubles cost $95 weekdays and $75 weekends; ask about discounts. Showing up in person often yields lower prices than making a reservation in advance and, due to the number of rooms, the hotel is rarely full.

© Holiday Inn

LONG-TERM ACCOMMODATION

The message board at **Alianza Francesa** (the French Alliance), near Metrocentro Mall, has notices about houses and apartments for rent averaging $350-$500 per month; find Alianza Francesa a half-block north of the Embassy of Mexico. **Hotel Mansión Teodolinda** (a block south and a half-block west of Intur, ☎ 228-1050) has one quality apartment available in an excellent location, as does **Hotel Hostal Real** (facing the German Embassy in Bolonia, www.hostalreal.com.ni, info@ hostalreal.com.ni). **Hotel/Apartamentos Los Cisneros** (☎ 222-3535) has mid-range, furnished apartments with fridge and phone. Hotels and guesthouses usually offer negotiable discounts for long-term stays.

■ WHERE TO EAT

Managua's restaurant scene changes swiftly; call ahead to check that your chosen restaurant is still up and running. Taxi drivers are experts on the location of restaurants; usually giving them the name is enough. Managua has the country's largest selection of upscale eateries, and credit cards are accepted unless otherwise noted.

DINING PRICE CHART	
Price per person for an entrée, not including beverage, tax or tip	
$	Up to $3
$$	$3-$6
$$$	$6-$10
$$$$	Over $10

NICARAGUAN

☆☆ **Casa de los Mejía Godoy** ($$-$$$, two blocks east of Metrocentro Mall, ☎ 222-6110). Set in an enormous *rancho* with an outdoor terrace, this restaurant is as much a cultural space as an eatery. It is owned by legendary Nicaraguan musicians Luis Enrique and Carlos Mejía Godoy, and there is live music Thurs-Sat, often performed by the brothers themselves. A variety of Nicaraguan dishes are served. CDs and books are for sale, and credit cards are accepted. Open Tues-Sun 7 am-12:30 am and Mon 7 am-5 pm.

☆ **Marea Alta** ($$$-$$$$, three blocks south of Metrocentro Mall, ☎ 278-2459). This bright, nautical-themed restaurant serves seafood caught just hours before it lands on your plate. Grilled fish, lobster, river shrimp, and crab are all available and well-prepared. Prices run $5.50 to $13. Open daily noon-midnight.

La Cocina de Doña Haydee ($$, behind Pharoah's Casino). This recently renovated, home-style place has traditional food and is a good spot to try local favorites.

Mi Viejo Ranchito ($$, Km 17.5 on Carretera Masaya, ☎ 885-8792). This is a good option for travelers headed south toward Granada or Masaya; the large *rancho*-style restaurant is right off the highway. Traditional Nica favorites are served (*quesillos* are the restaurant's specialty), and a playground is available for kids. There is live music on Fri nights. Open daily 7:30 am-9 pm.

INTERNATIONAL

☆ **Aché** ($$$, in the former La Vicky in Altamira, ☎ 277-3644). This lively Cuban place has nice stonework, good food, a well-stocked bar, and live music on Thurs. nights. The specialty is roaster pork; pair it with a *mojito*. Open daily, noon until the last customer leaves.

☆ **Hippo's Tavern and Grill** ($$$$, 60 yards south of Hotel Seminole near Metrocentro Mall, ☎ 267-1346). This popular spot has an outdoor patio and a lively bar. The menu has a good mix of Nicaraguan and international dishes (including nine varieties of hamburgers). The grilled meats are a favorite, and salads are well-made. Veggie options include garden quesadillas and cheese and sandwiches. Open daily noon-1 am.

☆ **La Marseillaise** ($$$$, faces Hotel Los Robles, ☎ 277-0224). Nicaragua's best French restaurant has good service, an extensive wine list, and a pleasant dining room with French paintings and a/c. Open Mon-Sat noon-3 pm and 6-11 pm.

Lo Stradivari ($$$-$$$$, a block north of Pharoah Casino on the Carretera Masaya, ☎ 277-2277). This Italian standout serves more than 100 sauces to accompany its pasta dishes. All ingredients are imported from Italy, with the exception of American beef. Pizza and fish are also available. Try the tiramisu for dessert. Meals range from $6-$13.50.

La Hora del Taco ($$-$$$, ☎ 277-5074). This kitschy Mexican restaurant serves consistently good food in two large, festive rooms (one with a/c and the other with fan). Live mariachi music livens things up Thurs-Sat evenings. Open daily 11 am-11 pm.

Pizza Valenti ($$-$$$, a block north and a block west of Pharaoh's Casino in Los Robles, ☎ 278-7474). Perpetually popular Valenti serves good, inexpensive pizza to an appreciative crowd. Pasta dishes are also good. The brightly-painted dining room has a/c, or you can sit outdoors. Open 10 am-10 pm. Delivery available.

TGI Friday's ($$$$, Km 5 on Carretera Masaya, ☎ 277-3260). If you've been craving American food, this US-based chain has it covered. Happy Hour specials from the well-stocked bar are popular. This is also a good spot to meet travelers and expats.

El Wok ($$$-$$$$, Near the Monte de los Olivos stoplight in Los Robles, ☎ 278-0932). El Wok serves the best Chinese food in Managua. The restaurant specializes in Peking Duck, but a variety of Chinese and foreign-influenced (Chinese tacos?) dishes are also served. Dining is available inside or in the street-side outdoor eating area. Open Mon-Fri noon-3 pm and 6-9:30 pm and Sat-Sun noon-9:30 pm. Delivery is available.

Mongolia Buffet ($$-$$$$, in Plaza Inter, ☎ 222-2611), serves buffet-style meals ($8) that include sushi, meat dishes, salads, and more. Neighboring **Tokyo Carne** ($$-$$$, ☎ 222-2611), has meats that are grilled table-side as well as seafood.

VEGETARIAN

Kiosko Vegetariano Nutrem Food ($-$$, 150 yards south of the main entrance to La UCA, ☎ 885-9572). This informal veggie place has a good selection of options and is particularly popular at lunch with students from the adjacent university. You'll find main courses based on lentils and soy accompanied by fresh salads and veggies. Good bread is available. Wash it all down with a fruity *licuado*. Open Mon-Fri 7 am-7 pm and Sat 7 am-3 pm.

CAFÉS

Casa de Café ($-$$, Near Pharaoh Casino in Los Robles, ☎ 278-0605). Though the coffee isn't particularly good, the people-watching and relaxed atmosphere are. Baked goods and light meals, such as sandwiches, are available. Open daily 7 am-10 pm.

Don Pan ($-$$, a block north and west of Pharaoh Casino in Los Robles). Good pastries, bread, and snacks make this a worthwhile stop, particularly at breakfast.

Café Van Gogh ($-$$, facing La UCA). If you have some time to kill while you're waiting for your minivan, this student-friendly spot is good for a snack or drink.

■ DAY-TRIPS FROM MANAGUA

RESERVA NATURAL MONTIBELLI

Km 19 of the Ticuantepe-to-La-Concha highway, ☎ 270-4287, www.montibelli.com. Designated Nicaragua's best private nature reserve in 2004, Montibelli is a 453-acre oasis far removed from urban sprawl. Spend the afternoon exploring the **hiking trails**. Guides are available to take groups on **birding** and **butterfly** expeditions. A small **restaurant** hosts occasional barbecues. If you want to stay over, **camping**, including equipment, is available. Reservations are recommended. The reserve can be accessed by taking a **bus** in the direction of La Concha. Disembark at Km 19 and walk 1½ miles west. The easiest way, however, is by taxi or private car; contact the reserve in advance for assistance.

RESERVA NATURAL CHOCOYERO-EL BRUJO

Beyond Montibelli at Km 21 of the Ticuantepe-to-La Concha highway is another verdant reserve, Reserva Natural Chocoyero-El Brujo ☆☆. Its name comes from two waterfalls, El Brujo and El Chocoyero. The latter is the best place to catch glimpses of the park's famous *chocoyos verdes*, or green parakeets (*Aratinga strenua*). Couch potatoes rejoice: the trail to the Chocoyero waterfall is mostly flat and you'll be rewarded with beauti-

El Chocoyero waterfall

ful views of the cascading waters. The parakeets are most easily seen early in the morning or in late afternoon. Also thriving are 116 other bird species, and several trails will take you exploring. Guides are available for $5 per group. Day entry to the reserve costs $3.50, or camp overnight for $4 per person. Tents are available for $11.50. Meals cost $3; reservations are recommended. The reserve is 18 miles from Managua, but the last four miles of the road are dirt; a 4WD is recommended during the rainy season. ☎ 279-9774, cnd@cable net.com.ni.

MASACHAPA & POCHOMIL

These two **beach** towns, just an hour (40 miles) southwest of Managua, are unfortunately not among the Pacific Coast's finer stretches of sand. Further, accommodation lacks value and comfort. If you crave a day on the sand, distance yourself from the main beach at Pochomil, which isn't particularly clean; the beaches a few minutes' walk south are more attractive, and you can catch a glimpse of the president's brightly-painted (not in a good way) beach house. **Horses** can be rented on the beach in Pochomil at $2 for a half-hour. A row of basic **restaurants** ($$-$$$) serve traditional meals similar in quality and price. If you want to stay overnight, a bright spot in

Lighthouse, Masachapa

the rather sad bunch of overpriced hotels is **Hotel Vistamar** ($$$$, ☎ 855-6889, www.vistamarhotel. com), a recommendable oasis of 17 bungalows and rooms that face the ocean at Pochomil. Each room has private bath with hot water, a/c, and nice furnishings. Kitchen access is available for an additional fee. The property itself is beautifully-maintained and has a small pool and hot tub. Doubles cost $85, and package deals, including meals, drinks, and activities, are available; see website for details.

> **Caution:** Some areas of Masachapa and Pochomil have dangerously strong ocean currents; check locally before taking a dip.

It's possible (and advisable during holidays when the area is packed to the brim and hotels double or triple their prices) to take a day-trip to the beaches from Managua; **buses** leave every 30 minutes in each direction, with the last bus returning to Managua's Mercado

The Pacific Lowlands

Israel Lewites at 5 pm. To reach Pochomil by car, take the Carretera Sur (South Highway) from Managua. After 36 miles you will see signs pointing to Pochomil. You will first arrive at the coast at Masachapa; turn left just before entering town. Drive five minutes more and you will see the entrance to Pochomil on your right. Private cars entering Pochomil are charged $1.50.

> **NOTE:** At the time of publishing, Marriott was planning a hotel in the Pochomil area; check back to see if the addition of this hotel has improved standards and prices at other area hotels.

MONTELIMAR

Located just a few miles north of Masachapa on an attractive beach, Montelimar is best known for the **Montelimar Beach Resort** ($$$$, ☎ 269-6769, www.barcelomontelimarbeach.com), the only true large-scale international beach hotel in Nicaragua. The 588-

© Barcelo Hotels

acre, 292-room all-inclusive property has plenty of diversions, including Central America's largest swimming pool, horseback-riding facilities, sports courts, and much, much more (see their website for details). It also has lots of "minis": mini-golf, a mini-zoo, and well-stocked mini-bars.

Though Montelimar provides a luxurious, relaxing experience, it is light on Nicaraguan culture, which is ironic, considering its history. The property was originally a German-owned sugar plantation. The first General Somoza took a liking to the place, expropriated it, and his son proceeded to turn it into his personal summer palace while raking in profits from the sugarcane. When the Sandinistas took control of Nicaragua it was turned into a beach hotel. When the Sandinistas lost the election of 1990, the hotel was purchased by the Spanish hotel chain that continues to manage the property. Resort guests can still dine in the former home of Somoza. Overall, the resort gets good reports, though the food, which consists primarily of buffets, has mixed reviews. The resort is particularly popular with Canadians, who get good deals on packages that include charter flights. They can arrange airport transfers, or the bus from Managua that serves Masachapa also passes by here.

Los Cardones Surf Lodge ($$$$, ☎ 618-7314, www. loscardones.com, info@loscardones.com). This environmentally focused lodge is tucked away near Montelimar in its own natural surroundings. The idyllic setting is good for wildlife viewing, and nesting turtles can be spotted here. Surfing is also an option. The property's five bungalows are simple but comfortable with large beds. Bathrooms are shared; toilets are compost-style and clean. A variety of package deals are available, including options for families. One night including good meals averages $75 per person, more with activities. The lodge is difficult to find on your own, and a 4WD is necessary in

© Los Cardones

Bungalows are set amid tropical plants.

the rainy season; no public transport is available. Contact the owners for driving directions or to arrange private transport. Reservations are a must; expect to wait a week for a response as there is no Internet on the property.

Masaya, Granada & Carazo

MASAYA

Renowned as Nicaragua's shopping mecca, Masaya is a center for handicrafts and is particularly known for its well-made **hammocks**. If shopping's not your style, there are still several worthwhile sights within easy reach of town, including Volcán Masaya, Fortaleza de Coyotepe, and Masaya's churches. Overall, Masaya isn't a particularly attractive city, but there's enough to keep you occupied for an afternoon; serious shoppers should plan on at least one full day.

Masaya, which has a population of 110,000, clings to its history as a working town. Masaya has been supplying the region with **crafts** since at least 1548, when Spain declared that Masaya would produce hammocks; artisans subsequently took on other crafts, including furniture making. Despite its position as a center of commerce, Masaya has traditionally been less prosperous than Granada, which remains true today. Masaya endured an earthquake in 2000, but thanks to the resourcefulness of the townpeople, you'll see little evidence of the destruction today.

Masaya Highlights

- Shopping for hammocks at local workshops
- Views of Laguna de Masaya from the Malecón

■ GETTING HERE

BY CAR

It's a straight shot from Managua to Masaya by car. The drive takes less than 40 minutes.

BY BUS

The **bus station** shares its space with the chaotic **New Market** (Mercado Nuevo); **express minivans** from Managua arrive closer to the center of town at **Parque San Miguel**. It's on the east side of town; if it's a hot day you may want to take a taxi to the center of town. Buses go back and forth to **Granada** every 20 minutes; the ride costs less than $1. There are direct buses down to **Laguna de Apoyo** departing at 5:30, 10:30 am and 3:30 pm and returning to Masaya at 6:30, 11:30 am, and 4:30 pm (40 minutes/75¢). From **Managua**, *ordinario* buses destined for Masaya leave Mercado Huembes. However, any bus heading south towards Granada, Rivas, or Masatepe will drop you off in Masaya. Buses leave for Managua every 15 minutes between 5 am and 9 pm (1 hr/50¢). A faster option is to take an **express minivan** from Managua, which leaves from the La UCA stop. Minivans run every 20 minutes between 6 am and 8 pm (45 minutes/75¢).

■ GETTING AROUND

Masaya is primarily flat, but the city is spread out, so **taxis** are useful. This is particularly true if you've been on a shopping frenzy and have bags. Taxis congregate in the market areas. **Horse carriages** are also a common form of local transport; find them near the Old Market and Parque Central.

■ SERVICES

TOURS & INFORMATION: There is an **Intur** branch in the Old Market (☎ 522-7615 masaya@intur.gob.ni). Hotels can usually arrange transport to nearby points of interest, including Fortaleza Coyotepe or Volcán Masaya.

MONEY: If you find yourself with more shopping bags than cash, don't despair: **Banpro** is conveniently located on the south side of the Old Market; there is an **ATM** out front. There is a Bancentro on the west side of the park and a **BDF** on the south side of the park with an **ATM**. Most of the vendors in the Old Market accept **credit cards**, as do many hammock workshops; most craftspeople in the New Market accept cash only.

INTERNET: The most convenient place to check your email is at one of the numerous cafés that edge the park. For Internet information on Masaya: www.visitmasaya.com.

MAIL & TELEPHONE: Shoppers rejoice: there is a **post office** in the Old Market. **DHL** is also available in the Old Market, a good, if pricier, way to send your packages that makes them more likely to actually arrive at their destination. **Enitel** is a bit of a hike: it's just south of the old train station in the north part of town.

RESTROOMS: There is a clean **public restroom** in the Old Market (20¢) and a not-so-clean one in the New Market (15¢).

MEDICAL: There is a **hospital** (☎ 522-2778) several miles from town on the Carretera Masaya. Serious conditions should be treated in Managua. **Farmacia La Salud** (☎ 522-2357) faces the southwest corner of the Old Market.

STAYING SAFE: Masaya is fairly safe, but watch your belongings in the New Market. The **police station** (☎ 522-4222) is a half-block north of the Old Market.

MARKETS: Pali is on the west edge of Parque Central. The New Market has every type of produce imaginable and a lot more. See *Shopping*, p 134, for more information about Masaya's markets.

■ SIGHTSEEING

A WALKING TOUR

If you've seen enough trinkets to last you a lifetime, get out and see the town. The layout of the city's sights makes for a convenient **walking tour**. Begin at the sad **Parque Central**, which is in major need of refurbishment (note the, ahem, plastic flowers). The park is officially named **Parque 17 de Octubre**, for October 17, 1977, memorializing Sandinista attacks against Somoza outposts throughout the country. The adjacent Baroque **cathedral**, **La Parroquia La Asuncion**, was seriously damaged in the earthquake of 2000. The church has three interior naves and an image of the Virgin Asuncion lies within a large dome. The decorative interior and exterior stone edging is a characteristic of Baroque architecture.

Masaya's cathedral, built in 1750, towers over Parque Central.

Continue on to the **Galería de Heróes y Mátires** (☎ 522-2977), which is 1½ blocks north of the park in the Mayor's Office on Calle San Jerónimo. The gallery

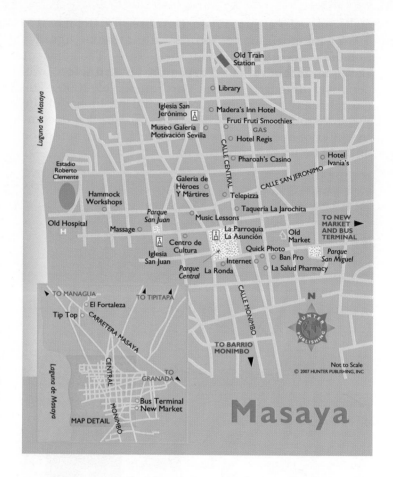

commemorates the local men and women that were killed during the war. The exhibit houses bomb-building materials, a photo display, and weapons. The gallery is open Mon-Fri from 8 am-noon and 1-5 pm. A donation of $1 is suggested.

Retrace your steps back a half-block and turn west (right). Continue down this street (Calle San Jeronimo). After several blocks you'll begin to see **hammock workshops** dotting the sides of the streets. Stop to browse, or continue on to Masaya's **stadium**, **Estadio Roberto Clemente**. Just beyond the stadium you'll be rewarded for all the walking with a panoramic view of **Laguna de**

Laguna de Masaya

Masaya and **Volcán Masaya**. From here, you can return to the center on foot, or take a taxi or horse carriage. As you leave, keep an eye out to the south for the Old Hospital, a hulking white structure.

HISTORIC SITE

Fortaleza El Coyotepe, Km 28 on the Carretera Masaya, has a long and brutal history. In 1893 President Zelaya erected this fortress on a hill edging Masaya to allow his soldiers to see approaching enemy forces consisting of Conservatives from Granada. The fort was also used in 1912 to fight the encroaching US Marines; the effort failed. Later, the fort was used by Somoza as a **prison** that held political detainees, often almost 1,000 at a time, in the dingy underbelly of the structure, which also housed torture cells.

When the Sandinistas took over, the fortress remained in use as a dark, dank prison before (ironically) the Boy Scouts eventually were given control of the structure. The Boy Scouts still manage the fortress today, and it is used for decidedly less sinister purposes, namely as a historical site for visitors. The **views** alone are enough

of a reason to visit; the city of Masaya and the volcanoes of Mombacho and Masaya are all visible from the four towers. The fortress can be reached by private car or taxi (just drive north a few miles toward Managua from Masaya; you'll see the hill and fortress on the east side of the road at Km 28). Alternatively, you can take a bus and hike .9 mile from the highway up the hill. Entry costs $2, plus $2 for a Boy Scout-led tour. Open daily 9 am-4 pm.

> **TIP:** Bring a ***flashlight*** to El Coyotepe if you want to see the basement, which is shrouded in darkness.

■ ADVENTURES

MUSIC CLASSES

If you're staying in town for awhile and want to study **guitar**, **flute**, or **piano**, private teacher **Pepe Duarte** teaches classes a block north and a block west from the northwest corner of the park; look for the sign. Spanish only.

■ SHOPPING

Ahhhh, the renowned shopping capital of Nicaragua beckons credit card holders from far and wide. Masaya's markets are the city's venerable main draw, though their names confuse first-time visitors. The **New Market** (*Mercado Nuevo*) is the sprawling monstrosity next to the bus station. From all outward appearances, this market differs little from other markets in the country, but head inside to the crafts section and you'll find a much better selection of artisan work than in other cities.

The **Old Market** (*Mercado Viejo*) is the newly-re-furbished cas-tle-like market in the center of town. Widely considered the best place to shop in Nicara-gua, the Old Market has

Entrance gate to Masaya's Old Market.

handicrafts from all over the country (though pay atten-tion to what you are buying: Made in China stickers are not unheard of). Prices here are a bit higher than in the New Market, but non-Spanish speakers and visitors looking for high quality will do well here. Though prices are marked on most items, bargaining can often lower the price, especially if you are purchasing multiple items. Credit cards are usually accepted.

> **TIP:** *If you plan to make many pur-chases, browse the Old Market to get a handle on prices, then buy your goods at the New Market (which has a similar selection, unless you want paintings, which are significantly lower quality in the New Market). This is also a conve-nient way to avoid carrying your pur-chases; the bus lot is right next door.*

The Old Market is the best place to shop for **paintings from Solentiname** ☆, though for hammocks consider visiting the workshops of the west side of town for a better selection. This area has more hammock work-shops than anywhere else in Nicaragua. Many double as the artisan's homes and visitors are welcomed (see *Buying Hammocks* below). Little-visited **Barrio Monimbó**, which extends south from Iglesia San Sebastián, has a thriving community of artisans that work out of their homes. You may want to consider hiring a guide to explore the neighborhood; the workshops can be a bit difficult to track down.

BUYING HAMMOCKS

After relaxing in hammocks all over Nicaragua, you'll want to take one home with you. How do you go about tracking down the best quality and price? While both the New and Old Market have a variety of hammocks for sale at similar prices, for the best selection go to the source: the workshops on the western edge of town. To reach the area, walk a block north of the park and turn west; after a few blocks you'll see hammock displays. The workshops extend as far as the Malecón. Proprietors are happy to show you the weaving process and explain the differences in quality and price among their wares. Prices are fairly standard, and many places won't lower their prices. When quibbling over those last few cords, keep in mind that it takes at least two days to weave a hammock. A tight weave will give comfort and durability. Hammocks come either with cane or without; the latter may be preferable if you have space constraints. Typical prices are $22 for a single and $25-$28 for a *matrimonial* (for two people).

Additional good buys include wooden furniture, including **soapstone** (*marmolina*), pottery from the Northern Highlands and locally-made **rocking chairs** ☆ (vendors can break them down and pack them into boxes to take on the airplane for a small fee).

If you need **photography** supplies, **Quick Photo** is on the southwest corner of the Old Market.

■ ENTERTAINMENT & NIGHTLIFE

Most visitors take day-trips to Masaya, thereby missing out on the surprisingly good nightlife in town. Start at

La Ronda on the south side of the park; there's little more than beer to drink, but that certainly doesn't stop the crowds of locals who descend on the place nightly. Tourists flock to **Jueves de Verbena** ☆, a weekly show of live music and traditional dance from all over Nicaragua that takes place Thursday evenings at the Old Market. Things get started at 7:30 pm and wrap up around midnight. The entry price de-

Dancers perform at Jueves de Verbena.

pends on who is performing but never tops $2. If you didn't spend all of your cords shopping, you can dispose of them at **Pharaoh's Casino**, three blocks north of the cathedral. Open daily 11 am-3 am.

During the dry season **baseball games** take place next to the Malecón at **Estadio Roberto Clemente**; the stadium was named after the baseball great, who died in a plane crash en route to Nicaragua to assist with hurricane cleanup.

■ WHERE TO STAY

Most people come to Masaya as a day-trip, but there are a few options if you want to spend the night. If you visit in March or April, splurge for a/c. Many of the places on the highway rent by, er, the hour; avoid them.

HOTEL PRICE CHART	
Cost per night for two people, before tax	
$	Up to $15
$$	$16-$30
$$$	$31-$60
$$$$	Over $60

NOTE: *Few places accept credit cards, so travelers rely primarily on ATMs, which are generally reliable, and involve a minimum of fees.*

Every listing in this book is recommended and considered above average in its category. Listings with one star (☆) are highly recommended, those earning two stars (☆☆) are considered to be exceptional. A few resorts and restaurants rate three stars (☆☆☆), which means they are worthy of a special occasion splurge.

Madera's Inn Hotel ($-$$, 4½ blocks north of the cathedral, ☎ 522-5825). The clean rooms at Madera's vary in amenities, but the cozy common area and friendly service can be enjoyed by all. Rooms range from $12 (for fan and shared bath) to $28 (for a/c and private bath). Internet is available.

Hotel Regis ($, 3½ blocks north of the cathedral, ☎ 522-2300, cmolinapalma@hotmail.com). This family-run guesthouse is a favorite with travelers for its friendly service and low prices. The 16 rooms are clean and adequate, and a good-value breakfast can be enjoyed on the tiny patio ($1.75 for *gallo pinto*, bread, fresh juice, and coffee). Singles cost $3, doubles $6, and family rooms, ranging from $12-$21 can sleep up to seven people.

Hotel Ivania's ($$$, 3½ blocks west of the cathedral, ☎ 522-7632, www.hotelivanias.com, hotelivanias@hotmail.com). This hotel has everything you need for an extended stay in Masaya, though it's overpriced. Ivania's is a good option for families; there's a room that holds up to 10 guests ($160). Room include a/c, private bath with hot water, and cable TV; some offer fridges, coffeemakers, toasters, and microwaves. The hotel is new  and the facilities are in good condition, though many of the rooms are cramped. Singles cost $35, doubles $45-

$50, and triples $50. There is a restaurant, a garden with hammocks, and a billiards table. Excursions, transport, and private parking are available. Credit cards accepted and some English spoken.

■ WHERE TO EAT

☆ **La Ronda** ($$-$$$, facing the south side of Parque Central, ☎ 522-3310). This airy restaurant specializes in grilled meats, but there is also an extensive menu of snacks if you need an excuse to take a break from all the shopping. The

DINING PRICE CHART	
Price per person for an entrée, not including beverage, tax or tip	
$	Up to $3
$$	$3-$6
$$$	$6-$10
$$$$	Over $10

front terrace, which overlooks the park, has some of the best people-watching in town. There is a bar, but only beer is served. Live alternative rock bands play every other week. Meals average $3.50-$8, and credit cards are accepted. Discounts are available for students with ISIC cards. Open Tues-Sun noon-midnight.

☆ **Telepizza** ($-$$, 50 yards north of the cathedral on Avenida San Jerónimo, ☎ 522-0170). This new branch of the longtime popular Granada pizzeria of the same name bills itself as "the best pizza in town," and they may very well be right. In addition to delicious pizza, Telepizza has good salads, pastas, and calzones. Delivery is available.

☆ **Taqueria La Jarochita** ($$$, a block north of the northeast corner of the park). The bright interior, great food, and friendly service make this Mexican restaurant a standout. In addition to authentic Mexican food, Nica favorites are also available. Enjoy the air-conditioning inside, or dine on the small street-side terrace. Meals run $6.50-$9. Open daily 10:30 am-10 pm.

Fruti Fruti Smoothies ($, a block west of the Shell station, ☎ 522-2500). This whimsically-painted place is good for a quick bite, accompanied by a fresh fruit juice or *licuado*. The sandwiches, hamburgers, and baked goods make for a light meal. Open daily 7 am-10 pm.

Tip Top ($$$, Km 27.5 on the Carretera Masaya facing Fortaleza Coyotepe, ☎ 522-2671). Tip Top is usually associated with fast food, but this place is different. A full-fledged restaurant, it specializes in grilled meat, though seafood is also available, including lobster. This restaurant/bar is popular for weddings and the like due to its vast size: there are three dining rooms, including two with a/c. The restaurant is most easily accessed by private car or taxi, though buses running between Masaya and Managua can drop you off here; the restaurant is just a couple of miles north of Masaya. Open 11:30 am-10 pm. Credit cards accepted.

There are a handful of inexpensive eateries within **Parque Central** if you want to stop for a snack or a drink.

> **Caution:** A visit to the national park includes proximity to volcano activity. If you notice any rumbling or shaking of the earth during your visit, evacuate immediately. Visiting the park with a guide is a good safety measure.

■ DAY-TRIPS FROM MASAYA

PARQUE NACIONAL VOLCÁN MASAYA

Volcán Masaya ☆☆ makes an excellent excursion from Masaya, Granada, or Managua, none of which are more than 18 miles distant. The unique nature of the park allows visitors to descend into a volcano crater. The **park entrance** is just four miles northwest of Masaya on the highway to Managua; any **bus** (every 15 minutes) between the two cities can drop you off at the entrance. There is no public transport beyond this point. About 1. 2 miles past the entrance is a **museum** and **visitors center**. From this point it's a steep three miles up a paved road to the rim of the Santiago crater. Once you reach the top you'll have the option of embarking on a hike along some of the area's numerous trails. Conserve your energy for hiking at the top by taking a **tour** from Masaya,

Hikers trekking up Volcán Masaya.

Granada, or Managua. This is particularly smart in March and April, when soaring temperatures make hiking up from the highway an unpleasant experience. The crisscrossing trails and the inherent risk of exploring an active volcano make traveling with a **guide** a very

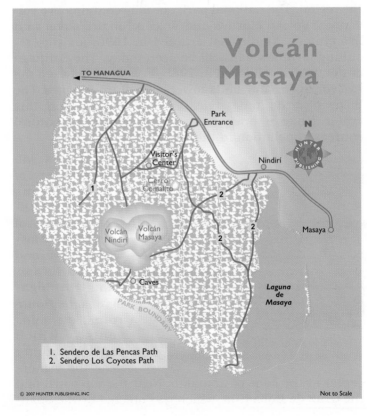

Volcán Masaya

TO MANAGUA

Park Entrance

Visitor's Center

Cerro Comalito

Nindirí

N

1

2

2

Volcán Nindirí

Volcán Masaya

2

2

Masaya

Caves

Laguna de Masaya

PARK BOUNDARY

1. Sendero de Las Pencas Path
2. Sendero Los Coyotes Path

© 2007 HUNTER PUBLISHING, INC

Not to Scale

The Pacific Lowlands

good idea. Tours combining a shopping excursion to Masaya with a visit to the national park are a good way to make the most of your time in the area. The park is open daily from 9 am-4:45 pm. ☎ 522-5415.

The **Chorotega**, the first inhabitants of the Masaya area, were polytheists that believed strongly in witchcraft and the power of worship. They believed that an elderly witch lived in the Masaya volcano. Children were sacrificed to her, and offerings of food were placed on the volcano to ward off evil.

The Spanish first described the volcano at Masaya in 1529. Since then, Masaya has erupted at least 19 times, and it continues to be the most active volcano in the region. The national park actually contains two volcanoes, Volcán Masaya and Volcán Nindirí, along with five craters. Nindirí last erupted in 1690, and the resulting lava flow can still be seen today. The Santiago crater, which collapsed in 1985, is wedged between the two volcanoes and emits towers of sulfurous gases. The billowing toxic fumes released continuously from this crater make it one of the most significant natural sources of pollution in the world.

You'll have to go up the volcano to get a glimpse of its impressive smoking cone.

Adventurers will find a variety of hiking options that take advantage of views of Laguna de Masaya, Masaya, and Lago de Nicaragua. One highlight is the ***fumarolas***, steaming vents, which you'll encounter near the visitors center at the cone of Comalito. Near the top you'll find the **Cruz de Bobadilla**, which was erected by the Spanish in an effort to ward off the devil and the Hell of the lava pool below; it's not currently possible to climb the steps to reach the cross due to concerns about ground stability. It's also possible to hike all the way down to **Laguna de Masaya**.

LAGUNA DE APOYO

Located in the crater of an ancient volcano that last erupted 20,000 years ago, Laguna de Apoyo ☆☆☆ attracts visitors in search of nature and relaxation. At 918 feet deep, Laguna de Apoyo is the deepest geological point in Central America, but the shallow edges of the lake are great for swimming. The waters of the lake are slightly salinated, and snorkelers and divers can spot bubbling *fumerolas*. Underground springs bring warm water into the lake, which has four endemic species of fish found nowhere else in the world. There are 170 documented bird species at the lake, 25 of which are endangered or threatened. Below, Travelers relax on the dock at Crater's Edge (see page 151).

The lake is six miles from Granada, making it a convenient day-trip. However, it's worth an overnight to enjoy the natural beauty and wildlife of the area or to study Spanish at the local language school (p147). Laguna de Apoyo is ostensibly under the protection of a **nature reserve**, but, with only one local official in charge of the entire lake's oversight and the influx of expatriates in the area, it's unlikely to remain pristine for long. Get there now to enjoy an ideal environment for wildlife viewing, water sports, and relaxing with a good book.

Laguna de Apoyo Highlights

- Take a late-night skinny dip in the lake
- Look for howler monkeys near the bottom of the road coming down from the highway
- Walk along the lakefront road toward Norome Resort for great views of the lake.

■ GETTING HERE

Taxis are available from Granada or Masaya to Laguna de Apoyo for around $12 each way.

There is a daily direct **bus** from **Masaya**'s market departing at 5:30, 10:30 am and 3:30 pm, returning to Masaya at 6:30, 11:30 am, and 4:30 pm (75¢). The schedule sometimes varies a bit depending on how many beers the driver has had the night before. There is no direct bus service from Granada. You can also catch a bus (every 20 minutes) from **Granada** that is headed to Masaya and ask the driver to leave you at the entrance to Laguna de Apoyo. From here, you can take a taxi (flag one down on the highway (15 minutes/$5), **hike** (1½ hrs), or try to **hitch** a ride down to the lake. There are rarely taxis available at the lake to return to the top; if you plan to return by taxi, make arrangements with your driver in advance.

A more convenient and reliable option than the public bus is to catch a **shuttle** from Hostel Oasis or The Bearded Monkey hostel in **Granada**. A comfortable van leaves from Hostel Oasis (reservations, ☎ 552-8006) at

10 am and 4 pm daily, returning to Granada at 10:30 am and 4:30 pm ($3 round-trip). A truck leaves from The Bearded Monkey (reservations, ☎ 552-7956) on Mon, Wed, and Fri at 10:30 am, returning to Granada at 6 pm ($1 each way). These shuttles are designed primarily for **day-trips** to **Crater's Edge** and **Monkey Hut** (day use fee $6 at each) at Laguna de Apoyo, where visitors can take advantage of all facilities available to overnight guests (see *Where to Stay* for more information about amenities at the two properties). **La Orquidea** also offers a day-use option for $5 and includes kayaks and snorkels; this is a good option for those who want more privacy. La Orquidea is a bit hard to find; follow the lakefront road for 10 minutes beyond the main village area.

It is also possible to **hike** to Laguna de Apoyo from Granada (two hours each way). Hiking to the lake is tricky, but the staff at the Intur office in Granada will draw you a map. Bring plenty of water and snacks as there are no services at the side of the lake closest to Granada.

Facilities at Laguna de Apoyo are limited and the area largely remains natural, which is precisely the reason to come here.

> NOTE: *Though a Jetski is sometimes available for rent in the village area, keep in mind that motorized water sports are illegal at Laguna de Apoyo and are harmful to local wildlife.*

■ ADVENTURES ON WATER

Laguna de Apoyo is one of the best places to **swim** in Nicaragua: the water is warm, clean, clear, and uncrowded. There are few beaches other than in the main village and near accommodation; most of the lake is edged with vegetation. It's a good idea to wear foot protection as there are stones near the shore. **Snorkelers** should either bring their own equipment or organize a day-trip through one of the local hostels that has equip-

The Pacific Lowlands

ment (see *Where to Stay* below). **Scuba diving** with a focus on monitoring underwater fauna can be arranged for certified divers through the Proyecto Ecológico at the Apoyo Spanish School ($30 for one tank). Commonly seen fish include jaguar cichlids, silversides, and mollies. The project is focused on research, not recreational diving, and no diving classes are available.

Daytrippers at The Monkey Hut or La Orquidea have free access to **kayaks**. Apoyo Spanish School rents kayaks ($5 for four hrs).

Windsurfing lessons ($10 for 45 minutes) are offered through Crater's Edge on Sat mornings; reserve in advance. Windsurfing can also be arranged through Norome Resort.

■ ADVENTURES ON FOOT

There are few paths in this secluded area; ask locals for recommendations. The **hike** up the paved narrow road leading out of the Laguna toward the highway (1.2 miles/two hrs) is very steep and winding but rewards with expansive views of the lake. There are no services along the way; bring water. The most pleasant option for **walking** is to follow the curving lakeside road leading from the village area to Norome Resort. The road is paved, has gradual ascents and descents, and offers great views. You can stop for a drink when you reach the resort to enjoy the views from the lakeside restaurant and bar.

■ ECO ADVENTURES

Guided walks can be arranged through **Apoyo Spanish School** ($4pp, minimum three people) and **Norome Resort**. Keep an eye out for howler monkeys near the bottom of the road leading down from the highway. Birdwatchers visiting Laguna de Apoyo are rewarded with glimpses of squirrel cuckoos, northern orioles, blue-crowned and turquoise-browed motmots, ringed kingfishers, and great kiskadees. There is little in the way of formal paths.

Blue-crowned motmot

■ ADVENTURES ON WHEELS

Apoyo Spanish School (below) rents bikes for $5/day.

■ CULTURAL ADVENTURES

The **Apoyo Spanish School** (☎ 868-0841) provides a peaceful setting for Spanish language study ($210 for five hrs per day including accommodation and meals; $135 for classes only). Transportation is available from the Managua airport ($45), Masaya ($15), or Granada ($15). Nature-lovers take note: this is Nicaragua's only established language school in a rural area. Accommo-

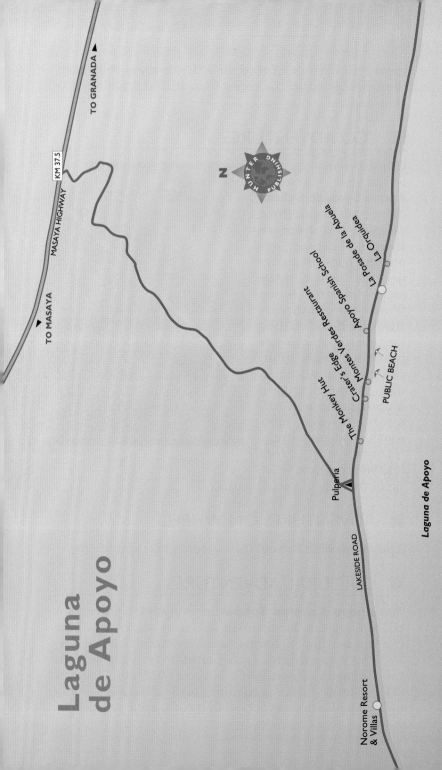

Laguna de Apoyo

Laguna
de Apoyo

TO GRANADA ▲

KM 37.5

MASAYA HIGHWAY

TO MASAYA ▶

N

La Orquídea

La posada de la Abuela

Apoyo Spanish School

Montes Verdes Restaurant

Crater's Edge

The Monkey Hut

PUBLIC BEACH

Pulperia

LAKESIDE ROAD

Laguna de Apoyo

Norome Resort
& Villas

Not to Scale

© 2007 HUNTER PUBLISHING, INC

dation is rustic and is available at both the school or through a homestay; the latter may not include running water or electricity. Alternatively, consider arranging to stay at one of the nearby guesthouses for a higher level of comfort. Classes take place on the pleasant breezy balcony, and volunteer work can be arranged in conjunction with the scientist on staff. Long-term volunteers receive free room and board. Due to the small local population, students will have to make a concerted effort to practice Spanish outside of class.

■ WHERE TO STAY

> **NOTE:** *Few hotels and restaurants accept credit cards, so cash is the norm. Most travelers rely primarily on ATMs , which are popping up even in smaller towns, are generally reliable, and involve a minimum of fees.*

All accommodation at Laguna de Apoyo is lakeside. To reach the area, take the road down from the highway until you reach the lakeside road. There is one hotel down the lakeside road to the right: **Norome Resort and Villas** ☆ ($$$$, ☎ 552-2552, www.noromevillas.com). Norome is the area's most luxurious property. The secluded nine-acre resort offers everything you need for an action-packed lake- side stay: a pool, watersports, nature trails, and local tours. Alternatively, focus on relaxation at

HOTEL PRICE CHART	
Cost per night for two people, before tax	
$	Up to $15
$$	$16-$30
$$$	$31-$60
$$$$	Over $60

© Norome Resort & Villas

The Pacific Lowlands

© Norome Resort & Villas

the spa. If you're loathe to get away from it all, keep in touch with wireless Internet and in-room phones. The resort's 142 rooms are arranged in luxury private casitas sleeping up to 10 (prices range from $65-$199 depending on the room and season; see website for details). Casitas feature a/c, cable TV, private terraces, and large bathtubs. Many of the accommodations are in steep, winding areas, but hotel vehicles can transport you to the various on-site facilities, and the area is good for wildlife viewing. The hotel can arrange a taxi to or from Granada ($15) or Managua ($40).

All other properties are down the road to the left as you reach the lake and are listed in the order that you come to them:

The Monkey Hut ($$, ☎ 552-7956, www.thebearded monkey.com). This sociable place is frequented primarily by young travelers coming from The Bearded Monkey hostel in Granada. It has singles ($16-$18), doubles ($22-$24), and rustic dorms ($10), all with foam mattresses, as well as a brick cabana with a thatched roof that is suitable for two to four guests ($40-$60). The dorm bunks are three tiers high, giving you a place to sleep but little else. For large groups, it is also possible to rent out the whole hostel (starting from $200 per night), which includes the cabana for four, a dorm sleeping six, three private rooms for six, and all

© The Monkey Hut

facilities. The property offers a dock for diving or sunbathing, kayaks, inner tubes, canoes, and snorkels. For those more interested in adventures on land, there is a basketball court, a trampoline, and horseshoes. Relax after a day of activities in the hostel's hammocks or have a barbecue using the on-site outdoor grill and kitchen facilities. There is no restaurant; overnighters should bring provisions that will last for the duration of their stay.

☆ **Crater's Edge** ($$-$$$, ☎ 895-3202, www.craters-edge.com, cratersedge@gmail.com). Crater's Edge has seven clean, comfortable rooms ranging from $20 for a double with fan and shared bath to $40 with two queen beds, a/c, and private bath. There is also a spacious dorm room with 12 beds ($10), lockers, and great lake breezes. Crater's Edge is a new property, with quality beds, free Internet, and good set meals ($$). Friendly Ca-

View from the Crater's Edge terrace.

© Crater's Edge

nadian owner Anne is a good source of information about the area. There is a waterfront *rancho* with hammocks, Adirondack chairs, and a bar. Try the homemade rum balls. A floating dock is popular for sunbathing. A 10% "voluntary" tip is automatically added to your total bill.

La Posada Ecológica la Abuela ($$$, ☎ 880-0368, www.posadaecologicalaabuela.com). La Posada's rooms overlook the water and basic, comfortable cabins

© La Posada la Abuela

are available. Some rooms have a/c and mini-fridges. La Posada has a raised dock area and a mural-filled, thatched roof restaurant overlooking the water. It's a 1.2-mile walk from where the road from the highway intersects with the lakefront road.

La Orquidea ($$$, ☎ 872-1866). La Orquidea (The Orchid) is a new private house with two upstairs rooms, each with a double bed, private bath, a/c, and lake views ($50 per room, $30 without a/c). The spotless house has a kitchen and sitting room with a TV and DVD player, and guests can use the garden hammocks and lakeside swimming area. The American owners live next door and can arrange airport transport ($35 each way). Rates include a breakfast of fruit, cereal, and yogurt, but guests should bring provisions with them for cooking; it's inconvenient to walk into the village at night for meals as there is no lighting on the path. To reach La Orquidea, take a left on the lakefront road and follow the signs; it's just beyond La Posada de la Abuela.

■ WHERE TO EAT

Norome Resort ($$$-$$$$) offers the area's most upscale dining at its lakefront restaurant, featuring Nicaraguan and international cuisine with great views. Its bar occasionally has karaoke and dance contests.

DINING PRICE CHART	
Price per person for an entrée, not including beverage, tax or tip	
$	Up to $3
$$	$3-$6
$$$	$6-$10
$$$$	Over $10

Crater's Edge ($$-$$$) has three good international set meals per day ($4-$7), all served family-style. Make a reservation for a meal if you are staying elsewhere and let them know if you are vegetarian. There is also a bar with a limited selection of snacks and drinks. Don't miss the homemade chocolate rum balls (40¢ each).

Apoyo Spanish School ($$) serves three good set meals ($4) per day; non-students are welcome – let them know in advance that you'll be coming.

There are several rustic **lakefront restaurants** in the main village area with nearly identical menus and prices; all are more popular for drinking than eating. **Montes Verdes** ($$$, ☎ 879-0532), on the right next to the public beach, is recommended over the others as it's the only place that uses well water for cooking (the others use lake water). Meals are standard Nicaraguan fare and the food is good. Beef, chicken, and fish meals cost about $8.

GRANADA

Built in 1524, Granada is the oldest Spanish city in the continental Americas. Situated 28 miles southeast of Managua, the city was founded by Francisco Fernandez de Córdoba, who named Granada after his hometown in Spain. The most attractive city in Nicaragua, Granada beckons visitors with its irresistible combination of colonial architecture, cobblestone streets, and convenient proximity to many of the country's prime sights.

Granada's location also served the city well in colonial times. Situated just 10 miles from the Pacific Ocean, Granada served

Granada's town square.

as an important transit point between Europe and the Americas for shipments of gold and other riches acquired from throughout the Spanish empire. Granada became one of the wealthiest cities in the Americas, which contributed to the city's conservative leanings that continue today.

Granada's wealth and political importance were not without drawbacks, however. Granada's prominent position incited tension with nearby regions, particularly rival city León, northwest of Managua. Ongoing economic and social rivalry between Granada and the more liberal León prompted the leaders of León to encourage American **William Walker's** takeover of Granada in the mid-1800s. His political installment cost many residents of Granada their lives before Walker was finally ousted from Granada in 1856 after two years of rule. However, upon his departure Walker and his cronies inflicted significant damage on Granada by burning parts of the city, including portions of the cathedral. Though Walker was subsequently executed in Honduras, Granada never returned to its former glory.

Despite its tumultuous past, the now-peaceful city of 90,000 still retains much of its graceful colonial beauty. Largely as a result of an increasing number of foreign visitors and residents, Granada is restoring dilapidated historical buildings, and Calle La Calzada is in the process of conversion to a pedestrian-only cobblestone street lined with cafés and shops. Restaurant and entertainment options in all price categories are expanding rapidly to accommodate foreigners and well-heeled Managuans. Beneath the flurry of development, however, Granada remains a welcoming town with a relaxed pace.

Granada Highlights

- The Museum at Convento San Francisco
- A horse-drawn carriage ride down to the waterfront
- People-watching in Parque Central
- Kayaking in Las Isletas
- Exploring Volcán Mombacho

INTERNET RESOURCES: www.granada.com.ni; www.granadanicaragua.net

■ GETTING HERE

BY PLANE

Granada's tiny **airport** is three miles from town at Km 23 on the highway to Mayasa. **Nature Air** (☎ 552-4568 in Nicaragua, 506-299-6000 in Costa Rica or 800-235-9272 in Canada/US, www.natureair.com, reservations@natureair.com) is the only airline that serves Granada. Flights are available to Costa Rica's **San Jose** (55 minutes) and **Liberia** (25 minutes). Flights depart **San Jose** at 7:30 am on Wed, Fri, and Sun ($120 one-way/$240 round-trip). Flights leave **Liberia** at 8:35 am Wed, Fri, and Sun ($140 one-way/$280 round-trip).

Flights return to **San Jose** at 9:25 am on Wed, Fri, and Sun ($120 one-way/$240 round-trip) and to **Liberia** at 9:25 am on Wed, Fri, and Sun ($65 one-way/$130 round-trip). If your trip is flexible, note that it is significantly cheaper to begin your trip in Granada when flying to Liberia rather than vice versa.

BY CAR

It's a straight shot from Managua to Granada through Masaya, though the highway (Carretera Masaya) has been under construction so it may be slow going near Masaya. Granada's **gas stations** are clustered around the corner of Calle Inmaculada and Calle Elena Arellano in the northwest part of town, plus another next to the bus station near the market.

BY TAXI

If you plan to take a taxi to Granada from the Managua airport (45 minutes), it is recommended that you contact your hotel or guesthouse in advance to arrange a pickup ($35 is standard), especially if you are arriving at night. Taxis are also available at the airport. Take only official taxis (look for their red license plates), and agree on a price before departing.

BY BUS OR MINIVAN

Most visitors arrive in Granada by bus. *Ordinario* buses head to Granada every 15 minutes from Mercado Roberto Huembes in **Managua** via the market in **Masaya** and arrive at the terminal west of town on Avenida Elena Arellano (1 hr 20 minutes from Managua/80¢; 35 minute/60¢ from Masaya). You can walk 500 yards from the terminal into the center of town, or taxis are $1. A speedier idea is to take an express **minivan** (45 minute/$1) from the La UCA stop in Managua, arriving just south of Granada's Parque Central. Buses for **Masaya** leave every 20 minutes from their own bus lot a couple of blocks west of the market bus station. Going to León requires a bus change in Managua; take a minibus from next to the park in

Granada to Managua's La UCA, then connect at the same bus lot to one of the frequent **minivans** that continue on to **León** from the La UCA stop. **Tierra Tour** (☎ 552-8723, www.tierratours.com) runs **shuttles** to Restaurante Cocinarte in León on Mon and Fri at 8:30 am. The return to Granada leaves at 4:30 pm ($15 one-way/$25 round-trip).

Ordinario buses also make the trek between Granada and **Rivas** every 45 minutes (1½ hrs/$1.30). Connecting buses to **San Juan del Sur** are available at Rivas. Alternatively, **Tierra Tour** has speedy shuttles from its office in Granada to Big Wave Dave's in **San Juan del Sur** on Wed and Sat at 8:30 am; the return to Granada departs at 4 pm ($15 one-way/$25 round-trip). Buses to **Los Pueblos Blancos** leave every 20 minutes from 6 am-5 pm (40 minutes/50¢).

Ticabus (☎ 552-2899) traverses Central America and international buses depart daily from Granada. Comfortable buses leave **San Jose** for the nine-hour trip to Granada at 3 am ($16), 6 am ($12.50), and 12:30 pm ($12.50). Buses from Granada leave for **Liberia** continuing on to **San Jose** at 6:45, 8 am, 1 pm. **Transnica** (☎ 552-6619) has slightly lower prices and similar service. Buses leave **San Jose** for the northbound journey at 4:30, 5:30 am and 9 am (9 hrs/$12). There is one luxury bus at noon (9 hrs/$20 including a meal). Transnica buses from Granada to **San Jose** leave 6:30, 8 am and 11am; luxury bus at 1 pm). Ticabus and Transnica tickets must be purchased in advance; both offices are just south of the Shell station.

BY BOAT

Boats cross Lago de Nicaragua from **San Carlos** in 12-14 hours, arriving at Granada's pier at 3 pm Wed & Sat. Boats from **Altagracia** on Isla Ometepe arrive at 3 pm on Mon and Thurs and sometimes Sat at noon. Reconfirm schedules, particularly in the dry season.

■ GETTING AROUND

BY TAXI

Taxis ply the streets of Granada, but they are generally unnecessary as the city is compact and easily navigable. The easiest place to find a taxi is generally in front of the Hotel Alhambra, on the west side of the Parque Central.

BY CARRIAGE

Horse-drawn carriages are not just for tourists; they are also a preferred form of transportation for *Granadinos*. Carriages with disturbingly thin horses congregate around the Parque Central; agree on a price before setting off.

■ SERVICES

TOURS & INFORMATION: Granada has some of the country's most professional, experienced tour agencies; arranging your entire trip through one of these companies is feasible and fairly cost-effective. Prices are similar at each company.

Granada's **Intur** office (☎ 552-6858, granada@intur. gob.ni) has a handful of brochures and a fairly unmotivated staff. Their office has moved to new digs on Calle El Arsenal facing Convento San Francisco. Open Mon-Fri 8 am-noon and 2-5 pm. The most comprehensive info board in town is at **The Bearded Monkey** hostel, where you can find fliers for everything from boat tours to apartments for rent.

Tierra Tour (☎ 552-8723, www.tierratour.com, alvaroab@ibw.com.ni) offers a comprehensive set of day-long and multi-day tours. Take a **fishing** trip, tour Managua, visit **Isla Zapatera**, or take advantage of a myriad of other options. Tierra Tour's office is on the north side of Calle La Calzada two blocks east of the park. English and Dutch are spoken.

Oro Travel (☎ 552-4568, www.orotravel.com, information@orotravel.com) arranges well-managed excursions focused on shopping, nature, and history. Oro can also arrange multi-day-trips throughout the country and is the only agent in Granada where you can buy **plane tickets**. Their office is behind Convento San Francisco. English is spoken.

Mombotour (☎ 552-4548, www.mombotour.com, info@mombotour.com) has a variety of adrenaline-pumping adventure tours. Take a **canopy tour** ($35, $25 for students), **kayak** Las Isletas, explore three nearby **volcanoes**, or **mountain bike**. Research your options at their office on Calle La Atravesada in the Hacienda Cutirre building. English is spoken.

Kayaking, Las Isletas

The Pacific Lowlands

MONEY: Every **bank** in town changes dollars. **Banpro** has an **ATM** a block west of Parque Central. **BAC** has another ATM a block north of Banpro. There is no longer an ATM at the Esso station. **Bancentro** (on Calle Atravesada a block west and a block north of the park) changes traveler's checks. **Moneychangers** will hunt you down on the corner of Calle Real Xalteva and Calle Atravesada.

MAIL: Granada's **post office** is across from the movie theater on Calle Atravesada (Mon-Fri 8 am-5 pm, Sat 8 am-noon).

INTERNET: There are a plethora of Internet cafés springing up around town; most are fast and reliable and English is often spoken. Expect to pay approximately 75¢ per hour. Many visitors frequent Cafémail next to Casa de los Tres Mundos, but for more reliable connections try the **Cafémail** on Calle Real Xalteva. Several hostels have free Internet available for guests, and more upscale hotels have free wireless connections (see *Where to Stay* for specifics).

LAUNDRY: Fernanda Laundry Service (two blocks from the park on Calle La Calzada) machine-washes clothes in three hours or less. Up to five pounds of clothing costs $3.50.

TELEPHONE: Enitel is on the northeast corner of the park (open Mon-Fri 8:30 am-5 pm). Granada's Internet cafés do a hopping Internet telephony business as well. There are several **public phones** available roadside in the market area; purchase a phone card at most pharmacies.

RESTROOMS: There is a dearth of public restrooms in Granada. A better option is to have a drink at a restaurant and use the restroom there. It is also often possible to use the restroom (*los servicios*) in one of the larger hotels.

SALONS & HAIRCUTS: Sala de Belleza Hilda (100 yards west of Iglesia Xalteva, ☎ 552-5534) has haircuts, waxing, and manicures. Open Mon-Sat 9 am-7 pm. **Inner Connection Wellness Center** (above Café

Dec Arte on Calle La Calzada, ☎ 552-7954), run by expat Jeannie, offers massage, skin care, aromatherapy, and reflexology. **007**, a half-block west of the park on Calle el Real Xalteva, gives men haircuts and shaves in an atmosphere that hasn't changed for decades (in a good way).

MEDICAL: Pharmacies (*farmacias*) are readily available and have an extensive array of basic necessities. There is a cluster of pharmacies two blocks north of the movie theater. **Farmacia Praga** is a good option 1½ blocks west of the park on Calle Real Xalteva. **Natural remedies** are available at **Farmacia Naturista Barreto** (a half-block south of Banpro, ☎ 552-5829). The **Cruz Roja** (Red Cross) across from Iglesia Guadalupe sees patients with minor injuries or illnesses, and most hotels have **doctors** they can contact if needed. Bilingual **Dr. Blanco** (☎ 552-5989) sees patients at Clinica Piedra Bocona on Calle La Libertad. There are two hospitals just outside of Granada (avoid the public one and opt for **Hospital Privado Cocibolca** (☎ 552-2907), which is on the highway to Masaya). If you have a serious problem, go to Managua by taxi.

STAYING SAFE: Safety in the park after dark has notably increased in recent years due to a more thorough police presence. Nonetheless, when the crowds head home, you should, too. Avoid the **waterfront** at night, and take a taxi home if you go to one of the discos in the area. Contact the **police** at ☎ 552-2929. The **fire department** (☎ 552-4440) is just north of The Bearded Monkey hostel.

MARKETS: Granada has two centrally-located **supermarkets**. **Palí**, situated across from the market on Calle Atrevesada, has a large selection of products at inexpensive prices. It caters largely to local clientele, but quite a few foreign products are available. **Supermercado Lacayo,** ☎ 552-6515), on the left down Calle el Real Xalteva, is smaller, has a/c, and has a larger range of foreign products, including wine and liquor. Though tourists more often frequent Lacayo, check expiration dates and refrigeration requirements

The Pacific Lowlands

carefully (I once saw a package of pasta there that was five years past its expiration date!). **Lacayo** is open Mon-Sat 8 am-8 pm and Sun 8 am-4 pm. The cheapest wine and liquor in town can be purchased at **Licorería Pereira Rocha** (☎ 552-5854) two blocks north of the movie theater. The **market** (*mercado*), just south of the Parque Central, is a sprawling affair that is good for purchasing unique fruits and vegetables (see *Shopping* below for more details).

BEVERAGES: Granada is unique in Nicaragua in that the local **tap water** (*agua del grifo*) is potable. As a result, eating green salads and raw vegetables in restaurants here is generally not a problem as the water used to wash them is safe. Many visitors prefer to drink **bottled water**. You can purchase local or foreign brands inexpensively in supermarkets or corner stores.

■ SIGHTSEEING

IN & AROUND PARQUE CENTRAL

Indisputably the heart of Granada, both physically and in the minds of Granadinos, the bustling **Parque Central** ☆☆☆ should be on every visitor's itinerary. The

You can always catch a carriage at Parque Central.

palm-shaded walkways make for a pleasant stroll while you admire the lush trees, pastel fountains, and carousel. **Craft vendors** ready to cut you a deal set up shop on the north and west sides of the park. Indulge in some people-watching while

The freshly painted cathedral.

you slurp on a *raspado* or ice cream. The park is lined with some of Granada's most impressive colonial buildings, many of which have been painted in the past year, sprucing up the entire area.

Dominating the southeast corner of the Parque Central is **La Catedral**, which is frequently closed to visitors. However, the interior is surprisingly plain and viewing it isn't crucial to appreciate the building. Built in 1712, the imposing structure is undergoing desperately-needed restoration, including a new bright yellow paint job.

Plaza de la Independencia ☆☆☆, on the northeast corner of the park, is usually filled with schoolchildren and serves as an epicenter for life in Granada. It is surrounded by many of Granada's most impressive buildings, including the former home of the Cardinal family, which now serves as an international cultural center known as **Casa de Los Tres Mundos**. The structure was built around 1720, though only the original build-

Plaza de la Independencia

ing's façade remains today. The building was donated to the local government in 1992 by the Foundation of the Casa de Los Tres Mundos (House of the Three Worlds). The building hosts **theater presentations, readings,** and **workshops.** Many of the performances are **free**. Check the bulletin board out front for schedules. There are also books and CDs for sale at the entrance. Open daily 8 am-6 pm.

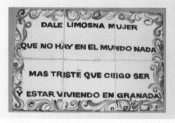

This tile on the east side of Plaza de la Independencia de Los Leónes may be right: "There is nothing in the world that is sadder than to be blind and living in Granada."

One block north and one block east of the Casa de los Tres Mundos is the **Iglesia y Convento San Francisco**, constructed in 1529. The structure has endured a tumultuous history. William Walker occupied it in the 1850s, and some of his men remain buried in the base-

Granada

TO MALACATOYA

Lago Cocibolca

PORT

Malecón

Complejo Turístico Cocibolca

TO LAS ISTETAS AND PUER TO ASESE

Cruz Roja and Spanish School

VISTALAGO WALK

N

HUNTER PUBLISHING

CALLE SANTA LUCIA

CALLE CORRALES

Iglesia y Convento San Francisco

CALLE EL ARSENAL

Intur

CALLE LA LIBERTAD

CALLE LA CALZADA

CALLE EL CAIMITO

CALLE SAN JUAN DEL SUR

.25 MILES

.45 KM

Arroyo Aduana

Parque Sandino

CALLE ATRAVESADA

Pharmacy Row

Kodak

Post Office

AVENIDA BODAN

Plaza de la Indepencia

Parque Central

Iglesia La Merced

Super Lacayo

Express bus to Managua

Market

Main Bus Station

GAS

CALLE CUISCOM

CALLE LA CONCEPCION

CALLE LA CEIBA

Mombotour

Parque Xalteva

Iglesia Xalteva

CALLE REAL XALTEVA

LA HOYADA

CALLE DR. SILVIO CUADRA SAENZ

Old Hospital

Ticabus

Transnica

CALLE LA INMACULADA

Budget GAS

BASEBALL STADIUM

GAS

TO MANAGUA

TO LA POLVORA AND CEMETERY

TO NANDAIME

Arroyo Zacatelique

17   28

20

15

18

25

29

16

21   14

4

31

33

6   5

7

19

13   10   1

9

2

27

8

11

22

23

24   12

32

30

1. Don Daffa
2. El Zaguán
3. Maverick's
4. Licoreriá Pereira Rocha
5. La Casona de Los Estrada
6. Hotel Colonial
7. Hotel Alhambra
8. Posada Don Alfredo
9. La Gran Francia
10. Alcaldía
11. Hotel Oasis
12. Hospedaje La Libertad
13. Cafemail
14. Kathy's Waffle Hut
15. Casa San Martín
16. Casa San Francisco
17. Roadhouse
18. Patio del Malinche
19. Rosticería J3
20. Pizzería Don Luca
21. Telepizza
22. The Bearded Monkey
23. El Club
24. Café Nuit
25. Restaurante Mediterraneo
26. Querubes
27. Nica Buffet
28. Monna Lisa
29. Pali
30. Railroad Museum
31. Movie Theater
32. Don Elba Cigar Factory
33. Sancentro

© 2007 HUNTER PUBLISHING, INC

ment. In 1921 it was invaded by US marines. Somoza occupied it, and it was invaded by the Sandinistas in

*Convento
San Francisco*

1979. Currently, with the help of the Swedish government, the church and convent, now owned by the Nicaraguan government, are being restored. In the **museum** ☆☆☆ adjoining the church, you'll find one of the best museum collections in Nicaragua, including Primitivist **paintings** from the islands of Solentiname and two dozen ancient stone **statues** from Isla Zapatera that continue to puzzle researchers searching for their significance. The museum also houses a gift shop. Open Mon-Fri 8:30 am-5 pm, Sat-Sun 9 am-4 pm. Entry ($2) includes a somewhat bilingual guide.

Iglesia La Merced, two blocks west of the park on Calle Real Xalteva, was severely damaged in 1844 then completely reconstructed in 1895. The church is currently in desperate need of reconditioning.

Continue west along Calle Real Xalteva to reach **Iglesia Xalteva**, another imposing 19th-century church with a somewhat bland interior.

You can get off the beaten path a bit and see two sights often missed by visitors: La Pólvora and the cemetery (*el cementerio*). **La Pólvora**, built in 1748, is a fort and historic gun powder storage facility that were subjected to raids by **pirates** during the 18th century. Though it was restored in 1994-96, the structure is poorly maintained and staffed by an indifferent caretaker who frequently closes the place prior to the official 5 pm closing time (open Mon-Sat). Visitors can climb the rickety, unsteady ladders to reach the top of the towers of La Pólvora, which offer **views** of Granada that are skewed by power lines but still worth a look. If the fort appears to be closed, try knocking at the gate.

Continue down the same street to the **cemetery,** one block west of La Pólvora. It showcases grand tombstones, miniature replicas of churches, and marble statues – testaments to Granada's history of wealth. Some of the cemetery's tombs are 500 years old. There is also a small **chapel** on the premises.

To see the **lakefront** ☆ of Lago de Nicaragua, walk east from the city center on Calle La Calzada for a mile or so; you'll see the port on your left. There is a park area and promenade that is underutilized but has major potential. From here there is a panoramic vista of the lake. It is unsafe to visit this area after dark. To get a closer look at the lake, head south to join the local families congregating on the small grassy beach in front of the **Complejo Turístico** (entry 25¢).

A WALKING TOUR

Granada's major sights are all within easy walking distance from each other, and it is feasible to see them all in one afternoon if you are on a tight schedule. Begin at the center of the city with a stroll through the **Parque Central**. If the **Catedral** is open to visitors, stop in for a look. Walk two blocks north to the **Casa de Los Tres Mundos** and admire the old colonial house that now serves as a cultural center. Next head one block north and one block east of the Casa De Los Leónes to the **Iglesia y Convento San Francisco** and **museum**. You may be surprised by its bright blue façade. After perusing the museum's collection, take a right off of Calle El Arsenal onto Calle Cisnes, which will lead you to Calle La Calzada. Turn left here and walk down to see **Iglesia de Guadalupe**, a church built in 1626 and later used by William Walker. You can continue east down Calle La Calzada to the **waterfront** and **pier** from here if you'd like. Return to the city center on Calle La Calzada, stopping in one of the many restaurants and cafés for refreshments.

Iglesia de Guadalupe

■ ADVENTURES

ADVENTURES ON FOOT

Vistalago Walk

A walk for intrepid travelers interested in seeing local life takes visitors outside of the city center to see what life is like for a majority of Nicaraguans. There are no particular sights or points of interest on this walk; instead, it gives visitors an inside peek at a typical economically-challenged Granada neighborhood, Vistalago.

To begin this walk, take Calle Guzman south from the Parque Central. Local women sell mangoes along this street to local schoolchildren, so stop for a snack if you'd like. When you reach Calle Santa Lucia, turn right. The pavement will end after four blocks; angle left down the unpaved road. After crossing the bridge, you can turn right and walk about 40 feet down to the lakefront. The lakefront here is not an attractive place to stroll; much of the shoreline is littered with trash and is illustrative of the environmental challenges Nicaragua faces.

Continue along the road as long as you'd like; there are several smaller streets heading off to the left, and many of the simple homes there have colorful bougainvillea and poinsettia trees in their yards. Along the way there are a couple of informal convenience stores operated out of the windows of people's homes, where you can purchase a snack or a soda (one is directly across from Quinta Los Chavalos boys' home, which has high white walls and a blue gate). To avoid getting lost, it is easiest to return the way you came; there are no street signs and you are not likely to encounter any English speakers. This walk takes approximately 45 minutes.

No taxis are available in this area, though you can take a taxi or a horse-drawn carriage from the city center to see the area. Though this walk is quite safe during the day, it is not recommended after dark as the roads are unpaved and lack lighting. This walk is also not recom-

The Pacific Lowlands

mended when it is raining as the area's roads sometimes flood and become impassable. Bring water and sunscreen.

ADVENTURES ON WATER

Swimming

The **Complejo Turístico** (Tourist Complex) is a well-maintained park, playground, and beach area that runs along Granada's waterfront. Though the purity of the water in the areas around Granada is questionable at best, if you want to swim near town, this is the place. The modest strip of beach is trash-free (your entry fee at work), and the area is normally quiet, but during holidays the shore is packed with families. There are several restaurants in the complex, all of which offer good Nicaraguan food. To reach the complex from the center of town, walk east on Calle El Caimito until you reach the waterfront, then head south through the faux-castle gates. Entry costs 30¢. Swimmers willing to venture a bit further afield should consider a daytrip to the cleaner **Laguna de Apoyo** (p 143).

Boating

Boating is a pleasant way to explore Lago de Nicaragua and particularly Las Isletas. Las Isletas comprise a string of 350 small islands that were formed from molten chunks spewing out of Volcán Mombacho during an ancient eruption. Boat tours can be arranged to the islands, many of which are uninhabited. To organize a boat trip, head to Puerto Asese (a one-hour walk from the center of town through the Complejo Turístico or a 15-minute taxi ride). Agree on a price for the boat trip before setting off; $15 per person for a one-hour tour is standard. To really experience Las Isletas, a two- to three-hour tour is recommended; bring along a picnic to enjoy on one of the islands if you'd like. Another option is to arrange a **boat tour** ($15 and up) through one of the tour agencies in Granada. Bring plenty of sunscreen, mosquito repellent and water. It is also pos-

Opposite: Vistalago neighbor

sible **spend the night on an island** or to **rent your own private island** (see p 190-191).

Kayaking

Kayaking is an excellent way to explore Lago de Nicaragua. To arrange a guided excursion of **Las Isletas** by

Kayaking is an excellent way to see the flora and fauna of Las Isletas.

kayak, contact **Mombotour** (☎ 552-4548, www.mombotour.com), which offers tours focused on the area's **wildlife**. Mombotour guide Fredder speaks good English and has encyclopedic knowledge about the area's birds.

ADVENTURES ON WHEELS

Cycling

Bicycles are available for rent for $8 per day at **La Posada de Don Alfredo** (two blocks west of the Parque Central on Calle Consulado). **Tierra Tours** also has bikes for rent, but you must leave your passport at the agency and count on a hefty cash deposit. Cycling is a great way to explore the area, but be sure to utilize the lock provided with your rental; bike theft is a problem in Granada.

ADVENTURES IN THE AIR

Canopy Tours

Mombotour takes participants outside of the city to the slopes of Mombacho to fly on zip lines between aerial platforms in the forest canopy. Mombotour's trips include transport along the rough road to the site and are particularly good value for students ($25/$35 for every-

As you explore Granada, take note of the colorful colonial buildings.

one else). The views of the coffee plantation below alone make the experience worthwhile. A second canopy tour, **Mombacho Canopy Tour** (☎ 852-9483) has set up shop on the opposite side of the volcano. The experience is similar, though this tour allows the opportunity to conveniently combine a trip to the hiking trails of Mombacho, which are just up the road from the canopy tour. Both companies have high safety standards and English is spoken. This activity is particularly recommended for families with children.

CULTURAL ADVENTURES

Language Courses

Granada is the most popular place to study Spanish in the country, which brings both benefits and drawbacks. On the plus side, Granada has a variety of schools and plenty of amenities for foreigners. However, students will have to make more of an effort to speak Spanish than they would in a town with fewer travelers. The decision is yours, but there is no denying that there is hardly a prettier place to cram your brain full of grammar. Prices below refer to a week (20 hours) of class plus a homestay. Discounts are available for extended stays.

Students give consistently high marks to **One-on-One Spanish Tutoring Academy** (☎ 552-6771, www. 1on1tutoring.net, oneonone@cablenet.com.ni) on Calle La Calzada, has flexible options and rotating teachers – so students are exposed to a variety of ways of speaking. A week-long program costs $170.

Cocibolca Spanish School (Calle El Caimito, ☎ 889-9375, esc_cocibolca@yahoo.com) has some of Granada's most experienced instructors and costs $200 for a week. Weekend classes are available, as are a huge variety of excursions.

AVE Nicaraguita (at the Cruz Roja, ☎ 552-8538, www. avenicaraguita.com). This new school has received enthusiastic reviews. A week costs $180 and excursions, including farm visits, are available.

APC Spanish Schools (in the Palacio de la Cultura on the west side of the park, ☎ 552-4203, www.apc-spanishschools.com) has the best academic digs in town in a beautiful and historic building right on Parque Central. A week of class costs $200, and excursions and tutoring are available.

Casa Xalteva (103 Calle Real Xalteva, ☎ 552-2436, www.casaxalteva.com). A non-profit school, Casa Xalteva is one of Nicaragua's most established Spanish schools. Classes begin every Mon for a minimum of one week of study ($200 per week). The school offers cultural excursions and assists students seeking volunteer work. The school will pick students up at the Managua airport for $30.

Volunteering

Volunteers interested in **teaching** or **tutoring** should check out **Escuelita Yo Puedo**, which offers excellent opportunities to teach literacy, English, math, or art in a centrally-located school for street children. Volunteers are responsible for their own accommodation, though the project is associated with a volunteer house that has rooms available for $2 per night. Volunteers have ample opportunity to design their own projects. Volunteers are requested to commit for a minimum of two weeks. The project is managed by the tireless Donna Tabor, a former Peace Corps Volunteer in Granada. Contact her at ☎ 552-7113 or donnatabor@ hotmail.com.

La Esperanza Granada (www.la-esperanza-granada. org) encourages volunteers willing to commit at least six weeks to get involved in their education and community development projects in villages around Granada. Rooms at a volunteer house are available for $2 per night.

Volunteer work with La Esperanza Granada.

La Esperanza Housing and Development (www. casas-de-la-esperanza.org, admin@casas-de-la-esperanza.org) seeks volunteers for a minimum of one month to assist with building homes for low-income families on the outskirts of Granada. Volunteers with skills such as carpentry and plumbing knowledge are particularly needed.

GRANADA'S REAL ESTATE BOOM

Expats wax poetic about the days of bargain colonial homes in Granada, but today those structures are a hot commodity, usually commanding at least double what they cost just a few years back. Visitors to Granada frequently return home wistfully wishing for a colonial to call their own, and real estate agencies are popping up all over town to indulge them. **ReMax** (☎ 552-3199, www. nicaraguaproperty.com) and **Coldwell Banker** (☎ 552-2908, www.cbnicaragua.com) both have extensive listings. **Snider's Realty** (☎ 552-4716, www.sniderrealty.com.ni) is next to Hotel Alhambra on the park. **Century 21** (☎ 552-6458, www.gpsnicaragua.com) is next to Café Dec Arte on Calle La Calzada. Agents speak Spanish and English. Before making a move on a property, be certain to hire an attorney; your embassy in Managua can provide listings.

■ SHOPPING

Maverick's (104 Calle El Arsenal, ☎ 552-4120) has handicrafts and Nicaraguan coffee. Enjoy a brownie or smoothie while you shop. Open Tues-Sat 9 am-6 pm and Sun 10 am-midnight. **Sultan Cigars** (near the park on Calle el Caimito, ☎ 552-0275) rolls cigars right in the store and sells them by the box. The museums at the **Convento de San Francisco** and the **Casa de los Tres Mundos** have small gift shops. **Claro Oscuro** is an art gallery on the north side of Iglesia La Merced (☎ 871-0627). **Café Dec Arte** on Calle La Calzada sells locally-made art. For a quick fix, shops catering to visitors line the west side of the Parque Central. For a more local experience, intrepid shoppers head to the **market**, just south of the Parque Central, for the best deals in town on t-shirts and pirated CDs. Serious shoppers should consider taking a day-trip to **Masaya**, where you can find some of Nicaragua's best deals on hammocks, ceramics from the nearby Pueblos Blancos, and paintings from the islands of Solentiname.

■ ENTERTAINMENT & NIGHTLIFE

MOVIES

Granada has one **movie theater**, the **Cine Karawala**, near the Parque Central on Calle Atrevesada. The theater primarily shows American blockbusters. Releases lag several months behind the US, but the convenient location and air-conditioning make it a pleasant rainy day option. The theater shows two films every night; one is in an air-conditioned space (which costs about 50¢ more); the other room has a fan only. Prices for all movies are under $3. Alternatively, **The Bearded Monkey** hostel has an extensive video collection for rent ($1 per movie) and a big-screen television available for guests and non-guests alike. The on-site restaurant offers smoothies and snacks to enjoy during the show. **El Tercer Ojo** (facing the south side of Convento San Francisco on Calle El Arsenal, ☎ 552-6451) shows foreign films on Wed evenings.

CLASSES

Café Dec Arte (a block from the park on Calle La Calzada, ☎ 552-6461) offers **mosaic classes** on Mon and Thurs at 3 pm for $4, including materials.

BASEBALL

Granadinos are baseball aficionados, and the local professional team, the **Tiburones** (Sharks), plays at Granada's stadium (Estadio Roque Tadeo Zavala), northwest of the city center on Calle Inmaculada (take a taxi). Tickets for the games are priced around $2.50 and can be purchased at the stadium. Contact the tourist office for current schedules. Attending a game isn't for the faint of heart, but the crowds, grit, and noise are all part of the experience. Basic snacks and drinks are available at the stadium.

DANCING

On weeknights the streets of Granada are surprisingly quiet, but when the weekend arrives locals and tourists are out in the park and plaza in full force. Granada used to erupt with **live music** and **dancing** every Friday evening as part of the *Noche de Serenata* (Serenade Night), and hopefully by the time you read this the party will be up and running again. The celebration takes place in the Plaza de la Independencia in front of the Casa de los Tres Mundos. Portable stages host local talent (along with the occasional guitar-toting tourist), and dozens of food booths cook up Nicaraguan delicacies. This is an excellent occasion to sample a *vigorón*, a local specialty of rice and beans steamed in a banana leaf, or one the ubiquitous and tasty roasted ears of corn (*elote*).

PARTY BUS

On Sat and Sun evenings a **party bus** (25¢), blasting pop hits, begins on the south side of Parque Central and winds its way down to the waterfront and back; hop on for some silly fun. You can disembark at one of the waterfront clubs or ride back to the park.

Despite the tranquil name, **Café Nuit** ☆☆(northwest of the park on Calle La Libertad, ☎ 552-7658) is the hippest dance spot in town, with live music nightly. The hip, modern **El Club** ☆(on the corner of Calle de la Libertad and Avenida Barricuda) is recommended and attracts a mix of well-heeled Granadinos and visitors. **Roadhouse** (on Calle La Calzada, three long blocks from the waterfront, ☎ 552-8469) serves over 100 varieties of cocktails and attracts a mix of foreigners and locals. Young travelers seeking international company head to the bars at **Hostal Central** and **The Bearded Monkey**.

Gay-friendly **Asia Latina** (a block from the park toward the lake on Calle La Libertad, ☎ 552-4672) is a good place to get a beer. Open daily noon-midnight. A middle-aged, mostly male expat crowd gathers at **Zoom Bar** (☎ 552-8386), three blocks from the park on Calle La Calzada, particularly when there is a game on the big-screen TV.

For **dancing**, the clubs on Granada's lakefront attract a primarily 20-something crowd of locals and tourists on weekends. **Cesar's** is particularly popular. It's also gay-friendly. This area boasts the city's most vivacious nightlife for the young and young at heart, but it's not recommended for solo women. Patrons should take a taxi to and from the area after dark as the area is not well lit.

THEATER

Casa de los Tres Mundos (www.c3mundos.org), on the east side of the Parque Central, hosts both amateur and professional productions. Casa de los Tres Mundos also offers **workshops** (mostly for long-term visitors) and **readings**. Open 8 am-6 pm. Entry 40¢ for foreigners; free for Nicaraguans. The building is attractive and there are paintings on the walls, but, unless you are particularly interested in either one of those aspects, just stop by the entrance to see the posted schedule of upcoming events.

BOOK BINGE

If your adventures leave you ready to spend an evening kicking back with a book, there are several options in town. **Maverick's Reading and Coffee Lounge** (104 Calle El Arsenal near Hotel Colonial, ☎ 552-4120) sells magazines and books and has a relaxed atmosphere popular with expats (the owner herself is

The Pacific Lowlands

Canadian). **El Tercer Ojo** (on the south side of the Convento San Francisco, ☎ 552-6451) has a peaceful atmosphere that makes it easy to relax for a few hours. **Café Don Simon** (on the east side of the park, ☎ 552-4486) has an outdoor terrace, espresso, and bagels. Open daily 7 am-7 pm. Another good reading spot are the plentiful benches at **Parque Central** (if you can fend off the *chicle* or gum sellers). If you run out of reading material, the best book exchange in Granada is at **The Bearded Monkey** hostel. Kept under lock and key (literally), this exchange has a large variety of books in good condition in multiple languages. Show a manager the book you want to trade in and keep your fingers crossed – they are notoriously strict about book quality. **Hostel Oasis** also has a good exchange.

■ WHERE TO STAY

Granada has a wealth of quality accommodation at all prices ranges. Be sure to take advantage of the opportunity to stay in a colonial-style hotel, one of the highlights of a visit to Granada. For visitors arriving without a reservation, a walk down Calle La Calzada is a good way to peruse many of the city's offerings in all price ranges.

HOTEL PRICE CHART	
Cost per night for two people, before tax	
$	Up to $15
$$	$16-$30
$$$	$31-$60
$$$$	Over $60

Every listing in this book is recommended and considered above average in its category. Listings with one star (✰) are highly recommended, those earning two stars (✰✰) are considered to be exceptional. A few resorts and restaurants rate three stars (✰✰✰), which means they are worthy of a special occasion splurge.

> **IMPORTANT:** *Granada has multiple hotels and restaurants accepting credit cards. However, as most of these hotels are independent establishments with limited communications systems, many of which are serviced by generators only and not centralized electricity, traveling without enough cash for a few days' food and hotel is strongly discouraged as sometimes credit card service isn't available even at places that advertise it.*

☆☆ **Casa San Francisco** ($$$, Calle Corrales 207, ☎ 552-8235). Owned by former Peace Corps volunteers from (where else?) San Francisco, this hotel's name is also fitting due to its convenient location near Convento San Francisco. The hotel's colonial building has been lovingly restored, and the small number of rooms lends a cozy feel. Rooms are well-maintained and have private nicely tiled baths with hot water, cable TV, and a/c. There is a small pool, bar, and good restaurant on-site. Prices vary by season and room, but a typical double costs $45.

☆☆ **Hotel El Patio del Malinche** ($$$-$$$$, 2½ blocks toward the lake from the park on Calle El Caimito, ☎ 552-2235, www.patiodelmalinche.com, info@patiodelmalinche.com). Newly opened in mid-2006,

© Hotel El Patio del Malinche

Malinche is housed in a beautifully-restored colonial building. The two attractive patio areas and pool are shared by the 15 rooms. Rooms are fairly small but comfortable and impeccably clean. All have tiled floors, private bath (some with hot water), cable TV, fan or a/c, and free wireless Internet. Some rooms have connecting doors – a good option for families. Doubles cost $55

($63 with a/c). There are nice views of Mombacho from some upper rooms. Breakfast is included in the price, and credit cards are accepted.

☆☆ **Casa San Martin** ($$$, a block toward the lake from the park on Calle La Calzada, ☎ 552-6185). Set in a beautiful colonial house, this hotel has friendly service and new facilities. The attractive garden area is a nice place to relax. The seven rooms have private baths with hot water, a/c, cable TV, and tiled floors. Doubles cost $45 or $50, depending on the size of the room. Credit cards are accepted.

☆☆ **Hotel Colonial** ($$$$, Calle La Libertad, ☎ 552-7581). Though the hotel is housed in what looks like a colonial building, it is actually a new construction. Opened in 2000, this property is one of Granada's most luxurious. The manicured grounds include a pool; some rooms are tucked into small courtyards, lending an air of additional privacy. All rooms have a king-size bed or two queens, private bath, a/c, and cable TV. There is a good restaurant and bar on-site.

Hotel Colonial's bar is decorated with beautiful tile work.

☆ **La Casona De Los Estrada** ($$$$, a few hundred feet west of Convento San Francisco, ☎ 552-7393, lacasona@cablenet.com.ni). This intimate boutique hotel is in an 18th-century colonial building. All rooms have private bath with hot water, a/c, in-room phone, and cable TV. Many rooms are furnished with antiques. Breakfast is included; enjoy it in the cozy dining area. Parking is available, and rental cars and tours can be arranged here.

☆ **La Gran Francia** ($$$$, on the southeast corner of the Parque Central, ☎ 552-6000, www.lagranfrancia. com). The refined La Gran Francia has 21 rooms with private bath in a beautiful colonial building dating from the 1500s. Restored in the 1990s, the hotel offers ice machines, free wireless Internet, cable TV, a pool, an attractive bar, and a restaurant. Each room is unique; bathroom sinks are hand-painted and all rooms have either a balcony or private patio. You'll find real attention to detail here, and the staff is professional. Singles are $80, doubles $95. Rates include a small breakfast.

© La Gran Francia

The Pacific Lowlands

© Hotel El Club

Hotel El Club ($$$$, corner of Calle de la Libertad and Avenida Barricada, ☎ 552-4245, www.elclub-nicaragua. com). This hotel is in a 19th-century former home, but you'd never guess it; rooms are thoroughly modern and decorated in hip Euro style. El Club has 11 rooms with private bath, free wireless Internet, and a/c. A plant-filled restaurant and very popular bar are on-site, the latter of which may be a bonus or a drawback depending on how much you like your sleep. Ellen and Marco, the Dutch owners, speak Spanish, English, German and Dutch.

Hospedaje Cocibolca ($$-$$$, Three blocks from the park toward the lake on Calle La Calzada, ☎ 552-7223, hospedaje@hotelcocibolca.com). The 25 rooms at this friendly family-run guesthouse are nothing special and the mattresses are a bit weak, but they represent good value for the money. Doubles with fan cost $15 (a/c costs double!), and large rooms are available for groups or families. All rooms have private bath. If you're

© Hosedaje Cocibolca

planning to stay in town for awhile, note that the guesthouse offers free kitchen use, and there is a large common room with plenty of rocking chairs. Tours and breakfast are available, and credit cards are accepted.

Hotel Alhambra ($$$, west edge of Parque Central, ☎ 552-4486, hotalam@tmx.com.ni). With a superb location facing the Parque Central, the colonial-style Alhambra has attractive landscaping, a terrace overlooking the park, and a pool. All 60 rooms have private bath, a/c, and TV; the more expensive rooms have excellent views of the park. Ask to see several rooms; some are starting to look dowdy. Give the restaurant a miss.

Hostel Oasis ($$, Calle Estrada near the Corner of Calle Comercial, ☎ 552-8006, www.nicaraguahostel. com). This is the epitome of hostel luxury: guests receive free international calls, free coffee and tea, Internet, a big screen TV with hundreds of DVDs, a swimming pool, and a book exchange, all housed in a beautiful newly-renovated colonial home. While dorms ($8) offer the best value, small private rooms with a/c are available for $22. The staff speaks English but gets mixed reviews for service. Credit cards are accepted.

Dorm beds ($) and **private rooms** ($-$$) are available for just a few dollars at backpacker haunts **Hospedaje La Libertad** (Facing El Club on Calle La Libertad, ☎ 552-4017), **The Bearded Monkey** (Calle 14 de Septiembre, ☎ 552-4028), and **Hostal Central** (Calle La Calzada, ☎ 552-7044). Each of these hostels has a restaurant and free Internet available for guests; La Libertad has free breakfast.

■ WHERE TO EAT

Luckily for the traveler, Granada has an excellent array of restaurants to suit all tastes and budgets. You should keep in mind that most of them close their doors by 10 pm.

DINING PRICE CHART	
Price per person for an entrée, not including beverage, tax or tip	
$	Up to $3
$$	$3-$6
$$$	$6-$10
$$$$	Over $10

NICARAGUAN

✰✰ **El Zaguán** ($$$-$$$$, behind the cathedral, ☎ 552-2522). One of Granada's most upscale Nicaraguan restaurants, El Zaguán specializes in sizzling grilled meat dishes ($6.50-$11). Open noon-3 pm and 6-9:30 pm.

✰✰✰ **Don Daffa** ($, facing the southeast corner of the Parque Central, ☎ 552-5533). This informal buffet restaurant is my favorite budget eatery in town. Popular with locals on lunch break from the Mayor's office next door, this is an excellent place to sample a variety of traditional Nicaraguan specialties, and it is one of the best lunch values in town at less than $3 per meal. Little English is spoken here, but point to what you want and it will be served up with a smile by the friendly staff. Open Mon-Fri 11 am-10 pm and Sat-Sun 6 pm until it empties out.

Tropicana ($-$$, Calle La Calzada). One of the last traditional holdouts on rapidly-gentrifying Calle La Calzada, Tropicana has good-value *comida corriente* and a local clientele. Stop in for an enormous, fruity *licuado* (75¢) and some street-side people-watching.

Querube's ($-$$, on Calle El Comercio next to the market, ☎ 552-7141). Few foreigners have discovered this simple, good-value buffet restaurant. There are several meat options and at least one veggie dish to select from. Point to what you want and bring your tray to one of the checkered tablecloth-clad tables. Open daily 8 am-8 pm.

Rosticería J3 ($-$$, corner of Calle el Xalteva and Calle Comercio, ☎ 552-7376). This secret lunch and dinner spot specializing in roasted chicken is tucked into a shopping pavilion on the right when coming from the park. Food is consistently tasty (the *pollo en salsa* is particularly good) and meals average $3. Open daily 7 am-10 pm.

INTERNATIONAL

Café Dec Arte ($$-$$$, a block from the park on Calle La Calzada, ☎ 552-6461). Dec Arte has Granada's best salads (the Chinese Chicken salad is excellent), but carnivores won't feel slighted. Sandwiches and home-made soups made with organic veggies are popular lunchtime options. This is also a worthwhile stop for dessert; try the cheesecake, apple pie, or chocolate chip cookies with ice cream. There is also a breakfast buffet from 7:30 am-11 am. Open Wed-Sun 7:30 am-10 pm. Free delivery is available.

Lilly's ($$-$$$, Calle Corral 207 near Convento San Francisco, ☎ 552-8235). This cozy spot is tucked into the Casa San Francisco hotel. Lilly's eclectic menu ranges from Mexican to Thai, and all dishes are made with organic produce. Service is friendly, and the staff is likely to remember your name. There is live Nicaraguan music on Saturday evenings and a good Sunday brunch (8 am-1:30 pm). Visa is accepted. Open Mon-Sat 6:30 am-10 pm, Sun 8 am-1:30 pm.

Dona Conchi and Enriqueta moved to Granada from Spain in the early 1990s. The two opened **El Meditteráneo** ($$$$. It's a half-block toward the park from Iglesia Guadalupe on Calle el Caimito, ☎ 882-4924). Then Conchi struck out on her own to open **Doña Conchi's** ($$$$, at Calle El Caimito 413, ☎ 552-7376). Though patrons continue to debate over which of the two restaurants' offerings are superior, both serve quality Mediterranean food in romantic, refined atmospheres. Entrées average around $12 at both restaurants. Both restaurants are recommended for a pleasant evening with attentive, but unobtrusive, service and occasional live music. Open daily except Tues 4-11 pm.

> **NOTE:** *Ask the staff at Doña Conchi's to point out the bullet hole in the wall. Supposedly, American filibuster William Walker was shot at here, but due to his short stature (5 ft 2 inches) the marksman aimed too high and missed him.*

Roadhouse Drinks and Food ($$-$$$, on Calle La Calzada two blocks from the waterfront, ☎ 552-8469). This sports-themed restaurant has jerseys on the walls and good, hearty Nicaraguan food; try the grilled meats. International dishes, including hamburgers and pasta, are also served. There are two dining areas: one has a/c and the other, for smokers, is fan-cooled. The bar here has a good selection of international and local drinks. Open Mon-Fri noon-midnight and Sat-Sun noon-2 am.

The Pacific Lowlands

The Bearded Monkey (Calle 14 de Septiembre, ☎ 552-4028) serves up giant burritos, salads, and smoothies; their burritos come with excellent salsa and are highly recommended. The Monkey is a good place to strike up a conversation with other travelers while admiring the colorful wall murals. Perpetually popular **Hostal Central** ($$, Calle La Calzada) has indoor and street-side seating and similar prices, but the food isn't as good.

Hospedaje El Italiano (on Calle La Calzada behind Iglesia Guadalupe, ☎ 552-7047) has authentic Italian **gelato** and plenty of rocking chairs to relax in while you enjoy your dessert. Open daily except Tues 11 am-9:30 pm.

There is a **Subway** (yes, the real American chain) on Plaza de la Independencia. Don't get your hopes up: the food isn't as good as it is Stateside. Open 10 am-10 pm.

PIZZA

☆☆ **Telepizza** ($, a half-block toward the lake from Plaza de la Independencia on Calle El Arsenal, ☎ 552-4219). Offering some of the best pizza in Granada with excellent prices to boot, Telepizza's calzones are recommended for an inexpensive, filling meal. The pastas, baked potato skins, and salads are also good. Vegetarian options are available, as are a small selection of local desserts. Telepizza is popular with local families and, though it can be crowded in the evening, service is efficient.

Pizzería Don Luca ($$-$$$, two blocks from the park toward the lake on Calle La Libertad, ☎ 552-7822). Don Luca serves wood-fired pizza in a warm, cozy atmosphere. Antipastos and pasta selections are also available. There is a good wine selection. Credit cards are accepted. Open Sun-Thurs noon-2 pm and 6-10 pm.

Monna Lisa ($$-$$$, on Calle La Calzada just before Iglesia Guadalupe, ☎ 552-8187), this new place with a strange spelling serves Granada's most authentic pizza in a refined atmosphere. Pasta is also available, but skip the disappointing salads, which consist mainly of drooping iceberg lettuce. Good cappuccinos and other Italian drinks are available. Open Mon, Tues, Thurs and Fri noon-midnight and Sat and Sun noon-2 pm.

BREAKFAST

Kathy's Waffle House ($$-$$$, facing Convento San Francisco, ☎ 552-7488), Kathy is all about hearty American-style breakfasts. This is the place to come for hefty portions of pancakes, waffles, French toast, omelets, and coffee, served indoors or outdoors on a terrace that overlooks El Convento. Prices range from $3.75-$7. Open daily 7 am-2 pm.

Taza Blanca ($, a few doors east of Hostel Oasis – a block north and a half-block west of the market). Though it's short on atmosphere (think plastic chairs and ragtag posters peeling off the walls), this thoroughly Nica place is good for quick breakfasts (*gallo pinto*, toast, eggs) and low prices. Simple lunches and dinners are served as well. Open Mon-Sat 6 am-9 pm, Sun 6:30 am-2 pm.

Nica Buffet ($-$$, a block south of the west side of the park on Calle Morazan), Granada's oldest breakfast place serves up a morning meal just like your mom used to make, including pancakes, bacon, eggs, and tall glasses of fresh juice. Nica food is also available. This spot is an expat favorite, so it's a good place to meet people while you admire the colorful wall murals. Dutch, English, and Spanish are spoken. Open daily 6 am-noon.

☆☆☆☆ **Café Chavalos** ($$$, ☎ 552-7113) serves as Nicaragua's only culinary school. Started in 2003 to provide job training for underprivileged boys from Quinta Los Chavalos (see *Volunteering* on p 174), this tiny eatery serves a four-course gourmet meal for $8. Diners eat whatever is being served that night; selection changes daily and may include anything from ceviche to sushi. Café Chavalos was closed at the time of printing during a search process for a new head instructor/chef, but do check if it is open when you visit –

it's an experience you won't forget. To reach the restaurant, go down Calle La Calzada toward the lake and turn right on the street after Iglesia Guadalupe. The restaurant is down a half-block on the left; it's painted green and white. Open evenings Tues-Fri (though this may change when the restaurant re-opens).

Boats, Las Isletas

■ DAY-TRIPS FROM GRANADA

LAS ISLETAS

Las Isletas are a tranquil departure from urban life, yet Granada is only a few minutes away by taxi. Learn more about outdoor activities available in the islands by reading *Adventures on Water* on p 170-172. Las Isletas offer unique overnight getaways; how does a private island sound? A short boat ride from Granada whisks you away to your own little corner of paradise on the island of **El Roble** ($$$$, www.nicadescanso.com). Accommodation costs $80 per night for two guests in an upscale house with pool. Excursions, transport, and meals are available for additional fees. An alternative, though you'll have to share the island with others, is a stay on La Ceiba, also one of Las Isletas. **Hotel La Ceiba** ($$$, www.nicaraolake.com.ni) has 10 rooms with a/c and private bath as well as dorm rooms ($14). The hotel will pick you up at Puerto Asese just beyond Granada's Complejo Turístico, for $15.

VOLCÁN MOMBACHO

Volcán Mombacho ☆☆☆ makes an excellent daytrip, and the cool air and lush **cloud forest** of this national reserve area can come as a welcome respite from steamy Granada. To reach Mombacho, take a **bus** (15 minutes) headed south toward Rivas or Nandaime and ask the driver to leave you at the entrance for Mombacho (*"Déjeme en la entrada de Mombacho, por favor."*). There is also a sign on the highway, but it can be difficult to spot. From the highway it's a pleasant, slightly uphill 1.2-mile walk to the visitor center. From

The Eriopsis biloba *Lindley orchid.*

and **grasslands**, rewarding visitors with panoramic **views** of Lago de Nicaragua, Las Isletas, and Granada. Signs point out some of the unique species, including **bromeliads** and 87 types of **orchid**. You can also spot **monkeys** and **reptiles**. The main **trail** is fairly flat and a mile long; a guide isn't necessary. The trail passes two *fumarolas* (natural vents where steam and sulphurous gases escape the earth's depths). A second trail, **Sendero El Puma**, is 2.4 miles of challenging hiking; a guide is required. You can either bring your own, or ask for one at the ranger station.

Though tour agencies in Granada offer guided **tours** to Mombacho, doing the excursion independently is simple and allows for more flexibility. Eco-trucks leave the visitor center for the summit at 8:30, 10 am, 1, and 3 pm and return to the bottom an hour and a half later. Open Thurs-Sun 8 am-5 pm (Tues and Wed for groups of 10 or more only). The $8 entry fee includes the truck ride to the summit.

If you have time to kill waiting for your truck, just south of the ticket window is an **Orquidiario/Mariposario**, which houses **orchids** and **butterflies**. If the kids that staff the place can tear themselves away from their video games long enough to accompany you, a **tour** (Spanish only) is included in the entrance fee. Entry 75¢ for foreigners. Open Tues-Sun 8:30 am-4 pm.

Opposite: Path leading to Volcán Mochambo

> **TIP:** *The truck ride to the top of Mombacho is safe but very steep; don't put anything on the seat next to you, and if you have small children, hold them on your lap.*

View of Las Isletas from Volcán Mombacho.

CLOUD FORESTS REVEALED

Cloud forests, also known as montane forests, are beloved by visitors to Nicaragua as cool, misty oases in an otherwise steamy climate. Cloud forests primarily occur at elevations between 4,000 and 10,000 feet and are distinguishable by their height (the trees are smaller) and by the number of epiphytes (ferns, orchids, and bromeliads), lichens, and mosses that cover the trees. In addition to being beautiful, cloud forests serve an important function in the ecosystem. They prevent erosion and serve as water filters and moisture reservoirs, particularly important during the scorching dry season.

Nature lovers who want to spend more time exploring Mombacho can spend the night at the basic **lodge** ($$, ☎ 552-5858, fcocibol@ibw.com.ni), which has a 10-bed

dorm for $30 per person, including two so-so meals and transport up the volcano, expensive considering the lodge's basic conditions. No private rooms are available. This building also serves as the **ranger station** and **visitor center** and has a small display of information about the flora and fauna. The lodge is a creaky old wooden building with dorm beds that primarily houses scientists and researchers, but tourists are welcome. There is a **cafeteria** ($$) that serves the basics, including a $3.75 *comida corriente*. The trucks from the base of Mombacho drop visitors off right at the lodge.

LOS PUEBLOS BLANCOS

The Pueblos Blancos (The White Towns) offer a pleasant place to spend an afternoon wandering, and the cooler temperatures associated with the hilly environment are a pleasant change from the heat of Granada. This group of villages, which includes **Catarina**, **Diría**, **Diriomo**, **Masatepe**, **Nindirí**, **San Juan de Oriente**, **San Marcos**, and **Niquinohomo**, is known for its **pottery** industry. The villages look quite similar, and even their central parks are nearly indistinguishable. There is not much to do of note other than strolling through the area to see the attractive whitewashed homes and local village life. There is surprisingly little pottery sold here; most artisans work behind closed doors and are difficult to track down. Artisans send the majority of their wares down to the markets in Masaya, so shopping there may be a better option. Of the villages, a visit to **Catarina** is most rewarding. **El Mirador de Catarina** is a viewpoint in the highest area of the village, which has panoramic **views** of Volcán Masaya and the waters of Laguna de Apoyo. You can reach Catarina by **rental car** ($1 entrance to the Mirador), **taxi**, or catch a **bus** (twice hourly) from **Granada**, **Masaya**, or **Managua**'s Mercado Huembes. From Catarina you can walk to the other villages, which makes for a pleasant afternoon excursion from Granada. Though the villages are only a few miles from each other, this is a particularly good excursion to take with a **tour**, which will allow you to spend more time seeing the villages and less time waiting for trans-

The Pacific Lowlands

portation. Tours can be arranged through the operators listed in Granada's *Tours & Info* section, p 158-159.

MARIA COLLEGE OF THE AMERICAS

Tiny San Marcos is home to Ave **Maria College of the Americas**, Nicaragua's most highly-regarded institution of higher learning. The campus, three blocks south of Parque Central, is a sister college of Ave Maria College in Ann Arbor, Michigan. It offers credit and non-credit summer Spanish study courses for foreigners; visit www.avemaria.edu.ni. for details.

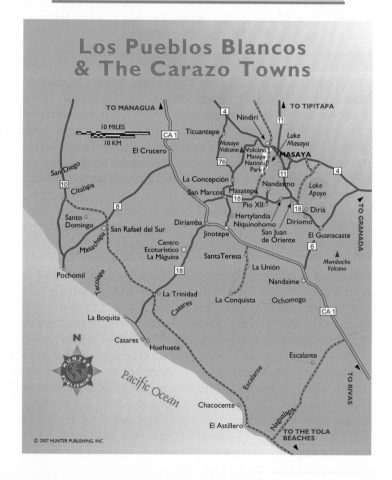

Los Pueblos Blancos & The Carazo Towns

© 2007 HUNTER PUBLISHING, INC

Shopping

Most of the area's craftspeople have workshops within their homes, so shopping is more of a challenge than one would expect in this artisan-rich area. A good place to find locally-made pieces and to see the artists at work is **Cooperativa Quetzal Coatl**, just inside the first entrance to the village of **San Juan de Oriente**. The town is famous for its **pottery** and the quality is high. Browsing the numerous tropical plant-filled **nurseries** along the roads of Los Pueblos Blancos is also pleasureable. Bamboo lamps can be purchased at **Artesanías Pueblos Blancos** (☎ 607-1278), which is a half-mile north of the turnoff to the village of Niquinohomo.

WITCHCRAFT

While Diriomo may outwardly appear to differ little from neighboring villages in Los Pueblos Blancos, the village is known throughout Nicaragua as a center for **witchcraft** and sorcery. Visitors may be approached by *brujos* (witches) offering services ranging from amorous serums to spells, the latter of which may require a down payment (often exorbitant), followed by a supplement "when the spell takes effect."

Where to Eat

☆☆ **Mi Terruño Masatepino** ($$-$$$, south of Masatepe on the east side of the road, ☎ 887-4949). Locals drive from Masaya and Granada to indulge in the traditional food served at this open-air restaurant that specializes in beef and soups (including *sopa de iguana*). Most meals run $5; be sure to pair them with one of the many Nicaraguan drinks served here in gourd cups. There is also good coffee. Open daily 9 am-9 pm. To find the restaurant, look for the sign outside saying "*platos típicos.*"

La Casona Coffee Shop ($$, a block north of Enitel, **San Marcos**). If you're craving a bit of home, you've come to the right spot at this cozy coffee shop. Light meals, including salads and pasta, are complemented by coffee that is roasted on the premises. Tasty pastries are also available; enjoy them as you mingle with students from nearby Ave Maria College.

El Túnel ($$-$$$, on the north side of the Mirador in **Catarina**, ☎ 558-0303). Open daily 7 am-8 pm. Traditional meals are the specialty here. The grilled meats are recommended, but vegetarians will enjoy the cheese, plantains, and salad.

Where to Stay

If you can't tear yourself away from the relaxed village atmosphere, there are a couple of quality places to overnight in Los Pueblos Blancos. Remember to bring cash.

Hotel Casa Blanca ($$$, facing the Baptist Church in **San Marcos**), this pleasant, unpretentious spot is centrally-located and very clean. Rooms have private baths with hot water and fans, and there is a nice patio area.

Hotel y Restaurante Lagos y Volcanes ($$$, 2.4 miles south of **San Marcos**, lagosyvolcanes@hotmail.com). This comfortable place is tucked away behind the Instituto Guillermo Ampie in a grove of citrus trees. The 15 rooms have quality mattresses, private baths with hot water, and cable TV. There is also a pool and restaurant on the property, from which you can enjoy views of Laguna de Masaya.

NANDAIME

Nandaime was once the most important Chorotegan town in the region. An earthquake in 1570 decimated the town, and today it is little more than a laid-back transportation crossroads. Nandaime is generally quiet, but you wouldn't believe it during the last week of July, when the town erupts with a patron saint frenzy that features dancing and a bullfight. There are two attractive churches in town that are worth a look, **La Parroquia** and **El Calvario**.

DOMITILA RESERVA SILVESTRE PRIVADA

Domitila Private Wildlife Reserve (☎ 881-1786, www. domitila.org, info@domitila.org) is 24 miles southwest of Granada on the shores of Lago de Nicaragua. A refuge for endangered species of the dry tropical forest, Domitila boasts 65 species of mammals, including **howler monkeys**. You can go on guided nature **hikes** ($5-$20; available in English, Spanish, or French) that

focus on **birds**, **butterflies**, or **nocturnal** wildlife. Alternatively, see the area on a **horseback riding** trip. Striking out on your own is no problem; the 15 trails are easy to navigate. There are hammocks back at the lodge to relax in after your wilderness adventures. The reserve offers **accommodation** ($$$$) in rustic singles and doubles with private bath ($65 per person including all meals and non-alcoholic drinks). **Dorms** are also available for $45 including meals. If you would like to combine your visit to the reserve with an excursion to **Isla Zapatera** in Lago de Nicaragua, Domitila arranges day-

trips (six-seven hours; $80 per person). If you don't want to overnight at Domitila, you can visit the property for $5 per person; a gourmet lunch is $15.

The Pacific Lowlands

The property is on a dirt road and is accessible year-round by 4WD. There is no public transportation to Domitila; by private car drive south from Granada on the Pan American Highway to the turnoff at Km 71.5. Domitila can provide transportation from Granada ($100), Managua ($150), or the border of Costa Rica ($125).

AGUAS TERMALES LA CALERA

These attractive, toasty **hot springs** are tucked away on a farm next to Lago de Nicaragua. Finding them on your own is tricky; instead, take a trip with **Tierra Tour** in Granada ($20 per person).

ISLA ZAPATERA

Isla Zapatera is one of Nicaragua's most important **archaeological sites**. Large **stone statues** erected by indigenous peoples in pre-Columbian times have been moved to Museo San Francisco in Granada, but it's possible to explore other ancient tombs and structures and enjoy the natural environment. A **tour** is logistically necessary to visit the island; arrange one through one of Granada's tour agencies or through Domitila Reserva Silvestre Privada for around $80 per person.

JINOTEPE

The 30,000 residents of Jinotepe don't see many tourists, but the college students from the local UNAN give the town a youthful air. **Intur** (☎ 412-0298, carazo@ intur.gob.ni) can set you up with maps and info about the region; find it a half-block south of Kodak. Spend your time in Jinotepe soaking up the atmosphere, including its historic buildings, and check out the colorful **mural** three blocks west of Parque Central's northwest corner. The shady park itself is a good place to relax, and take a look at the adjacent **La Iglesia Parroquial de Santiago**, the town cathedral, which was built in 1860 and has stained glass windows imported from Spain.

INTERNET RESOURCE: www.jinotepenicaragua.com.

DID YOU KNOW? Jinotepe has its own radio station, Radio Stereo Romance. Check it out on FM 105.3. You can embarrass your travel companions by dedicating a song to them; request one at www.jinotepenicaragua.com/radio.html.

■ GETTING HERE

Jinotepe can be reached by **bus** from **Managua**; express minivans leave from the La UCA stop, and *ordinarios* leave from Mercado Israel Lewites every 20 minutes from 5:30 am-5:30 pm (1½ hrs/$1.50). Buses leave for **Masaya** every half-hour from 5 am-6 pm (1 hr 20 minutes/$1.25). **Granada** is serviced by express bus at least twice per day at 6:30 am and noon (1½ hrs/$1.35). Buses go to **Rivas** every half-hour from 5:30 am-5 pm (1 hr 45 minutes/$2).

■ VOLUNTEERING

Los Niños del Rey, an orphanage, accepts volunteers interested in working with children. Contact Dr. Kent King for more information at kingkent@hotmail.com.

■ WHERE TO STAY

Hotel Casa Mateo ($$$, 1½ blocks west of the BDF bank, ☎ 532-3284). This blue and white corner hotel has 38 comfortable rooms with cable TV and private bath with hot water. Breakfast is included in the price. Singles and doubles cost $35 ($45 with a/c), and triples ($45), quads ($65), and suites ($50-$65) are available. There is a wide range of services available at the hotel, including conference rooms, tours, car rental and translation services.

■ WHERE TO EAT

☆☆ **Pizzería Colisseo** ($$$, a block north of Bancentro, ☎ 532-2150), Colisseo gets a thumbs up for its great pizza and pleasant atmosphere, with bonus points for a good selection of South American wines. In addition to the pizza, which is often referred to as the best in Nicaragua, there are several other Italian options, most of them made with imported ingredients, adding to the authenticity of the meals. Save room for dessert, such as the sumptuous tiramisu. Open Tues-Sun noon-10 pm.

Bar y Restaurante Sardina ($$$, Km 49.5 on the highway, ☎ 889-4261). This *rancho*-style outdoor restaurant is good for either a meal or a drink. Food is traditional Nicaraguan, and the service is good.

■ DAY-TRIPS FROM JINOTEPE

DIRIAMBA

Diriamba is best known for its **Fiesta de San Sebastián** during the third week of January, when the town erupts in a flurry of dancing, theater, and religious celebrations. During the rest of the year, the town is quiet and there are few diversions beyond the modern, well-maintained **Museo Ecológico de Trópico Seco** (☎ 534-2129), a museum that focuses on geology, endangered animals, and the dry tropical forest of the Carazo region. The museum is painted bright yellow and faces the police station. Open Mon-Fri 8 am-noon and 2-5 pm and Sat 8 am-noon. Entry $1.25.

Getting Here

Buses go back and forth to **Jinotepe** every 15 minutes (30¢). Change buses in Jinotepe for **Granada**, **Masaya**, or **Rivas**. **Managua** is served every 25 minutes from 5:30 am-6 pm (1 hr 20 minutes/$1.50).

Where to Stay

Casa Hotel Quinta Lupita ($$$, Km 42.5 of the Pan American Highway just south of Diriamba, ☎ 534-3399, lupita41@ibw.com.ni). Located in a large, modern white house, Lupita's seven rooms have private bath with hot water and a/c. There are two pools (one for kids and one for adults), private parking, and a dance floor. Singles cost $34.50, doubles $40.25, triples $45, and quads $51.25. Credit cards are accepted.

Where to Eat

☆ **Restaurante Mi Bohío** ($$, a block east of the police station, in **Diriamba**, ☎ 534-2437), this atmospheric spot serves quality Nicaraguan food at good prices. The steak dishes are recommended. On your way out, be sure to check out their selection of **edible gifts**, including traditional candies. Credit cards are accepted. Open daily 9 am-9 pm.

HERTYLANDIA WATER PARK

Though adults may not see the appeal of this dowdy entertainment complex, kids may jump at the chance to cool off in the country's only water park. Just 3.6 miles from Jinotepe at Km 48 on the road to San Marcos, the water park is two decades old and looks its age, but the water slides, mechanical rides, and video games will keep kids occupied for an afternoon. Hertylandia is named for recently deceased Herty Lewites, former Mayor of Managua and Minister of Tourism. Open Wed-Sun 9 am-5:30 pm. Entry costs $5 ($2 without water activities) plus approximately $1.50 for each ride.

The Pacific Lowlands

CENTRO ECOTURÍSTICO LA MAQUINA

At Km 58.5 on the highway from Diriamba to La Boquita, ☎ 887-9141, this 78-acre **nature reserve** makes a nice stopover on the way to the beach, or a convenient excursion from Diriamba, 15 minutes distant. The reserve has a variety of trails that lead into the tropical dry forest. For those with more of an interest in culture than nature, **folkloric performances** occur each Sunday. Even if you don't have time to fully explore the reserve, there is an attractive waterfall just beyond the entrance as well as a **restaurant** ($$). Buses headed to La Boquita can drop you off at the entrance, which has a large sign. Open daily 8 am-6 pm. Entry $1.50. **Camping** is available.

LA BOQUITA & CASARES

These two beach towns see little activity but are suitable for a dip if you're in the area. La Boquita is a better choice for a beach trip; the beach is adequate and there are a handful of rustic *ranchos* serving traditional Nicaraguan meals. Casares also has a wide beach but is more oriented toward local fishermen than beachgoers. If you want to spend the night in the area, opt for La Boquita's comfortable **Hotel Palmas del Mar** ($$$, ☎ 552-8715), which has rooms with private bath, a/c, and cable TV; doubles cost $42. There is a mini-swimming pool, a disco (ask for a room on the opposite side if you're here on a weekend), and a good **restaurant** ($$$$). There is a $1.50 entry fee per car if you come by private vehicle to La Boquita, or take one of the multiple daily **buses** that go back and forth between the two towns and **Jinotepe**.

Rivas & Isla Ometepe

RIVAS

DID YOU KNOW? Rivas was first visited by the Spanish in 1522 and the city still boats some of Nicaragua's oldest colonial buildings.

Though Rivas is unlikely to win any style awards, its usefulness as a travel hub means that most travelers in southwest Nicaragua will end up passing through this town of 42,000 at some point. *"La Ciudad de los Mangos,"* the City of Mangoes, as Rivas is known, has all the trappings needed to accommodate travelers, but with its small population and even smaller number of tourists, it retains a friendly ambience. A couple of hours is enough time to explore the main sights, admire the town's 17th-century architecture, and find the bus to your next destination.

Rivas Highlights

- Museo de Antropología e Historia de Rivas
- Iglesia Parroquial de San Pedro

■ GETTING HERE & AWAY

BY TAXI

Colectivo **taxis** to San Juan del Sur leave when full from 4 am-3 pm and charge $1.30 per person. A **private taxi** to **San Juan del Sur** or the **Costa Rican border** will set you back around $10 for the 20-minute ride.

> TIP: *Taxi drivers have to pay to enter the market area, and they pass the cost along to passengers. Save a few cords by exiting the market area before flagging down a cab.*

Taxis to **San Juan del Sur**, **Playa Gigante**, or the **Costa Rican border** cost approximately $10. Taxis to **San Jorge** (for boats to Isla Ometepe) cost $1 per person.

BY BUS

Ordinario and **express buses** arrive at the lot in the center of the busy market area, while **express minibuses** arrive two blocks south of Parque Central at El Mercadito. At the market bus lot there is no seating available and little shade, but departures are frequent.

Ordinario buses leave for **Managua**'s Mercado Huembes every 20 minutes from 3:30 am-7 pm (2½ hrs/$1.60). **Express** buses leave Mercado Huembes every half-hour from 6 am-7 pm (2 hrs/$2.30). You can also go to the highway to catch a passing express bus to **Managua** that originates in San Juan del Sur (5:30, 6, 7 am, and 4 pm). **Granada**-bound *ordinario* buses depart every 45 minutes (1½ hrs/$1.30), as do buses to **Jinotepe**. Buses leave every half-hour for **Masaya**, **Nandaime**, **Catarina**, **Diriomo**, and **Diría**. *Ordinario* buses go to **San Juan del Sur** every 45 minutes (50 minutes/70¢). Buses head to the **Costa Rican border** every 30-45 minutes (45 minutes/70¢), or buy **Ticabus** (www.ticabus.com) tickets a day in advance at the Supermercado Panamericana next to the Texaco Station. Costa Rica-bound buses pass by here every morning between 7 and 8 am and Managua-bound buses pass between 3 and 4 pm.

Express buses leave **El Mercadito** every hour destined for the Carazo Towns of **Catarina**, **Diriomo**, and **Diria**.

International luxury coaches leave daily for **San José**, **Panama City**, **San Salvador**, **Choluteca**, **Tegucigalpa**, **San Salvador**, **San Pedro Sula**, and **Tapachula**. Contact the local branches of **Transnica** (☎ 898-5195, www.transnica.com) and **Ticabus** (☎ 848-8622) for schedules.

BY BOAT

For boats from San Jorge to Moyogalpa on Isla Ometepe, see p 218.

■ GETTING AROUND

ON FOOT

Rivas is flat and readily walkable, though March-early May brings hot temperatures. Though Rivas is small, the town's layout can be confusing; if you're having difficulty finding your destination, hop in a carriage.

BY CARRIAGE

Horse-drawn carriages take passengers anywhere in the town center for around $1.50.

■ SERVICES

TOURS & INFORMATION: For tours to Isla Ometepe, contact **Ometepe Tours** (☎ 563-4779), which has an office at the dock in San Jorge. The pricier hotels can usually arrange tours.

The **Consulate of Costa Rica** helps with visitor info and immigration questions. Find it two blocks east of the northeast corner of the Parque Central.

MONEY: Plenty of travelers hop over from the beaches simply to hit a bank, and Rivas is well-equipped: **BAC** has an **ATM** and makes advances on credit cards. There is also an ATM at the **Texaco gas station**. **Bancentro** is next to the Biblioteca Pública de Rivas, and **BDF** is one block west of the **Parque Central**. All banks in town are open Mon-Fri 8:30 am-4 pm with an hour break for lunch, and Sat 8:30 am-noon.

INTERNET, MAIL & TELEPHONE: Internet places dot the center of town; connections are fast and cheap (generally 60¢/hr). The most convenient spot is on the northwest corner of Parque Central.

The Pacific Lowlands

The **post office** is open Mon-Fri 7:30 am-4:30 pm and Sat 7:30 am-noon. Find it from the northwest corner of Parque Central by walking one block north and a half-block east.

The **Enitel** office is near the southwest corner of Parque Central. Open daily 7 am-9:30 pm. Fax service is available at the post office.

RESTROOMS: There is a dingy public restroom (10¢) next to the bus lot in the market; ask directions from the shopkeepers.

MEDICAL: The best option for medical care and pharmacy needs is **Laboratorio-Clínica María Inmaculada**, which faces the north side of the Parque Central. The **doctor** is available from 2-4 pm Mon-Fri. The attached pharmacy is well-equipped and is open Mon-Fri 8 am-4:30 pm, Sat 8 am-noon.

MARKETS: The sprawling market surrounds the bus lot; pick up water if you're bus- or boat-bound.

■ SIGHTSEEING

MUSEUM & HISTORIC SITES

Museo de Antropología e Historia de Rivas, ☎ 563-3708, museoderivas@yahoo.es. This museum was founded in 1975, but the history of its structure goes back much farther: it's in one of the oldest colonial farmhouses in Rivas, which was also the site of the successful final battle against filibuster William Walker in his attempt to control Nicaragua. Today the museum is a bit run-down, but it's a worthwhile stop to see the pre-Columbian pottery, mineral samples, and paintings, all of which have descriptions in Spanish and English. Open Mon-Sat 9 am-noon and 2-5 pm. Entry is 60¢ for Nicaraguans, $1 for foreigners.

Iglesia Parroquial de San Pedro. On the east side of Parque Central. Though the cathedral's façade has seen better days, this 18th-century structure is nonetheless imposing and worth a look. Mass takes place daily at 6:15 pm.

Iglesia de San Francisco. Four blocks west of the park. Constructed in 1778, this church was originally a monastery for Franciscan friars. A unique feature is an underground tunnel that leads to the plaza next to Parque Central; there is no consensus on the tunnel's purpose or use.

Though there is nothing to mark its significance, political aficionados can take a peek at the exterior of the **birthplace** of **Violeta Barrios de Chamorro**, who was President of Nicaragua from 1990-1997. The house faces the south side of the Iglesia de San Pedro.

The **Biblioteca Pública de Rivas**, built in the early 1600s, was originally a high school. Today it serves as the city's public library and is worth a look to view one of the oldest buildings in Nicaragua. It's next to Bancentro.

Rivenses, as Rivas residents are known, are proud that American filibuster William Walker was thwarted in his attempt to take over Nicaragua when he was defeated in the Battle of Rivas. This victory led to a commonly-heard local saying: "Nationalism began in Rivas."

The Pacific Lowlands

WALKING TOUR

Rivas is readily walkable and most sights are in close proximity to each other, so there is no better way to see the town than on foot. Late afternoon is good timing for this walk: the heat will have subsided a bit and you'll be able to take advantage of sunset views at the end of the walk. Keep in mind that the museum closes at 5 pm.

Begin by admiring the flocks of **parakeets** that congregate in the trees at the Parque Central. Cross to the east side of the street to see the interior of the **Iglesia Parroquial de San Pedro**. On the south side of the ca-

Rivas

N
HUNTER PUBLISHING

TO MANAGUA

TO SAN JORGE

GAS
GAS
GAS
GAS

PAN-AMERICAN HWY

Baseball Stadium
Restaurante Y Disco el Príncipe

CA 1

TO SAN JUAN DEL SUR, PEÑAS BLANCAS & COSTA RICA

Hospedaje Lidia

Supermercado Panamericana

Monument to Emmanuel Mongalo Y Rubio

Costa Rican Consulate

Restaurante/ Hospendaje el Español

Iglesia Parroquial de San Pedro

Chamorro's Birthplace

Pizza Hot

Post Office

Laboratorio-Clínica María Inmaculada

Internet

Enitel

Central Park

Chop Suey

Pupusas Salvadorenas

El Mercadito (Express Buses)

Hotel Cacique Nicarao

VIP

BDF

Police

Bancentro and Biblioteca Pública

Iglesia de San Francisco

Super Pollo

Museo de Historia y Anthropololae

Bus Terminal and Market

TO CEMETERY AND LA CHOCOLATA

600 FEET
400 METERS

thedral is the **birthplace** of former President **Violeta Barrios de Chamorro**. Walk east 2½ blocks to the **Biblioteca Pública de Rivas**, next to Bancentro, to admire the 17th-century architecture. Continue west for one block to explore the **Iglesia de San Francisco**. Be sure to take a look at the statue in front of the church, which honors the friars that once lived there. Walk 2½ blocks north to the **Museo de Antropología e Historia de Rivas** to see the museum's historic building and collections of artifacts. Finish your city tour by walking south to the hilltop town cemetery to enjoy a view of the sunset.

ENTERTAINMENT & NIGHTLIFE

Rivenses are ardent baseball fans; check out what all the fuss is about on weekends at the stadium on the east side of the highway. The baseball season runs from October to April. After the game, take in the most happening nightlife in town at **Restaurante y Disco El Principe**, next to the baseball stadium. Two blocks west of Parque Central is **VIP**, an attractive bar favored by the Rivas elite. The plaza next to Parque Central hosts **Noches Rivenses** every other Saturday night. These popular see-and-be-seen evenings consist of live music, dancing, and drinking.

WHERE TO STAY

Rivas doesn't have a wide variety of accommodation options. If you're just here to catch a morning ferry, you might also consider staying overnight in San Jorge.

HOTEL PRICE CHART	
Cost per night for two people, before tax	
$	Up to $15
$$	$16-$30
$$$	$31-$60
$$$$	Over $60

The Pacific Lowlands

> **NOTE:** *Few hotels and restaurants accept credit cards, so cash is the norm. Most travelers rely primarily on ATMs , which are popping up even in smaller towns, are generally reliable, and involve a minimum of fees.*

The nicest place in town is **Hotel Cacique Nicarao** ($$$, ☎ 564-3234), conveniently 1½ blocks west of the park. This modern place has comfortable furnishings, private baths, cable TV, a/c or fan, and guarded parking. Doubles cost $50, slightly less without a/c. There is also a good restaurant on-site that serves Nicaraguan food.

A second option is **Restaurante/Hospedaje El Español** ($$, ☎ 563-0006), which is a block east of Parque Central. The four small rooms have fans and share two baths. Doubles cost $19.

Budget travelers' best option in town is **Hospedaje Lidia** ($, ☎ 563-3477), which is just south of the Texaco station. The 12 rooms here are nothing special, but service is friendly. Singles ($5) and doubles ($10) have shared bath, and rooms for three to four guests ($14) have private bath.

Two full-service hotels are near Rivas, and both have guarded parking available:

La Mar Lake Resort ($$$, at Km 123 on the Pan American Highway in La Virgen, ☎ 563-0021, www.lamarlakeresort.com, info@lamarlakeresort.com). Developed by Major League pitcher Dennis Martínez, La Mar is a good choice for families: there are plenty of ac-

© La Mar Lake Resort

© La Mar Lake Resort

tivities to keep active guests entertained: two pools, a game room with billiards and pinball, a playground, a basketball court, and a "Hall of Fame" that displays memorabilia from Martínez's career. There are views of Isla Ometepe from the expansive grounds. Rooms are unremarkable but comfortable and are situated around a grassy courtyard. Each of the 29 rooms costs $65 and includes two double beds, a mini-fridge, cable TV, a/c, and private bath with hot water. Credit cards accepted. La Mar is just off the Pan American Highway through a set of arches. A taxi from Rivas takes less than 10 minutes.

Laredo Restaurant Hotel ($$-$$$, at Km 111 on the Pan American Highway, ☎ 563-0335), this bright pink and white hotel is a good option if you're driving. The modern rooms face a courtyard and have private bath with hot water and TV. Doubles with fan cost $20 ($35

© Laredo Restaurant Hotel

with a/c). Breakfast is included in the room price, and lunch and dinner are also available in the on-site restaurant. Tours can be arranged by the hotel, and laundry service and Internet are available.

■ WHERE TO EAT

Hotel Cacique Nicarao ($$$, 1½ blocks west of the park, ☎ 564-3234). The most upscale restaurant in the town center, Cacique Nicarao offers quality Nicaraguan food in a pleasant atmosphere.

Restaurante Chop Suey ($$-$$$, on the southwest edge of Parque Central, ☎ 563-3235). Opened 45 years ago by a Chinese immigrant, Chop Suey is still managed by the original family's descendants. The restaurant is housed in a pleasant, plant-filled old colonial home. The Chinese food has a distinct Nicaraguan influence, but is tasty nonetheless.

DINING PRICE CHART	
Price per person for an entrée, not including beverage, tax or tip	
$	Up to $3
$$	$3-$6
$$$	$6-$10
$$$$	Over $10

Meals average $6 and credit cards are accepted. Open daily 10 am-10 pm.

Pizza Hot ($-$$, on the northeast corner of Parque Central), this popular spot has a convenient location and surprisingly decent pizza. Indoor and outdoor seating is available. Closed Mon.

Pupusas Salvadoreñas ($, on the northeast corner of El Mercadito), this simple place makes one thing and makes it well: *pupusas*, a Salvadoran specialty that resembles a thick tortilla stuffed with greasy, delicious meat, beans, or cheese. Three *pupusas* served with a tasty cabbage salad cost $2.20. Open for dinner only.

Several good options are available just outside of town:

☆ **La Mar Lake Resort** ($$$, at Km 123 in La Virgen, ☎ 563-0021, www.lamarlakeresort.com). Located just south of Rivas off the Pan American Highway, La Mar is a convenient stopping-off point for lunch or dinner if you're headed south to the border. Dine in one of the indoor eating areas with a/c and lots of windows or, better yet, eat in the outdoor *rancho*, which has great views of Isla Ometepe. Meal options focus on steaks, seafood, and chicken, but vegetarians can be accommodated. Restaurant guests can use the swimming pools free of charge, so bring your bathing suit. There is a full bar available, and credit cards are accepted. Open daily 7 am-10 pm.

☆ **Rancho Coctelera Mariscazo** ($$$$, half a mile south of the baseball stadium). One of the area's best seafood restaurants, Mariscazo has delicious lobster and fish as well as traditional Nicaraguan dishes. Meals average $12.

Laredo Restaurant Hotel ($$-$$$, at Km 111 on the Pan American Highway, ☎ 563-0335), this cheerful restaurant serves all three meals and specializes in Nicaraguan-influenced Mexican food. Parking is available.

■ DAY-TRIPS FROM RIVAS

BORDER CROSSING: PEÑAS BLANCAS

This is the most convenient and most common place to cross the border into Costa Rica. It's generally a fairly simple process to cross the border and usually takes no more than an hour, but try to avoid crossing during holidays, particularly Christmas, New Year's, and Semana Santa, when lines can snake on to eternity. Americans and most Europeans receive 90-day tourist cards for Costa Rica, while Canadians get 30 days.

By the time you visit, the border will be open 24 hrs, though an overtime fee may still be charged early in the morning or late at night (an extra $2). Otherwise, to exit Nicaragua you'll pay $2, and to enter Nicaragua from Costa Rica it's $7. Both fees are payable in dollars only. The town government on the Nicaragua side also charges any foreigner they can spot $1 as a "fee for passing through town." At the border you'll wait in line, have your passport checked, and pay your fee. Be sure to get your **exit stamp** before leaving Nicaragua. After these formalities you'll walk across to the Costa Rican side to have your luggage searched and get your passport stamped.

Reaching the border from Nicaragua is straightforward. **Taxis** from **San Juan del Sur** to the border cost around $25. From Rivas they charge about $10. **Buses** are the most common way to reach the border. **Ticabus** (www.ticabus.com) and **Transnica** (www.transnica.com) are the easiest ways to travel to Costa Rica: an *ayudante* (bus assistant) collects passports and does the waiting in line for you, though if there is anyone on the bus with immigration issues you could be in for a long wait. Ticabus and Transnica tickets need to be purchased at least one day in advance (see their websites for ticket office locations nationwide). Each of these bus lines has several daily departures destined for Costa Rica. **Express buses** leave **Managua**'s Mercado Huembes for Penas Blancas at 5, 8, 9:30 am and 3:30 pm (3 hrs/$3). *Ordinario* buses head from **Rivas** to the **Costa Rican border** every 30-45 minutes (45 minutes/70¢). To get to the border from **San Juan del Sur**, catch a bus headed for Rivas and tell the driver you want to get off at **La Virgen** (20 minutes/60¢). From there, wait for the next southbound bus on the Pan American Highway (every 30-45 minutes).

Driving across the border into Nicaragua is a more trying process than taking a bus, and it's not possible to cross in a rental car. If you do decide to drive your own car across, you'll need to have your passport, the vehicle title, a current tag, and Costa Rican car insurance. If you have everything in order, you'll be presented with a 30-day permit ($10) to drive in Nicaragua. Don't lose the permit – fines are steep.

Buses on the Costa Rican side of the border are waiting to take passengers to points south, including **Liberia** and **San José**. Buy **Transnica** tickets to San Jose (6 hrs/$6) in the booth for daily departures at 5:15, 7:30, 9:30, 10:45 am, noon, 1:30, 3:30, and 6 pm. Each of these also stops in **Liberia**, except for the 1:30 pm bus. *Ordinario* buses also go to **Liberia** until 5:30 pm (2 hrs/$2). Buses usually get pulled over multiple times during your journey southward for passports to be checked.

> **NOTE:** *Trying to cross the border with illegal drugs is a very bad idea. Inspectors and sniffing dogs are plentiful on the Costa Rican side of the border, and penalties for possession are strict. Keep in mind that if you are apprehended, your embassy will do little more than provide you with a list of lawyers.*

SAN JORGE

San Jorge is best known for its bustling port, from which ferries head to Isla Ometepe. Though most travelers breeze right through, San Jorge is a pleasant place in its own right. Nicaraguan families consider San Jorge to be a destination in itself, taking advantage of the lakefront beaches, wide swaths of volcanic sand, and gorgeous views of Isla Ometepe.

Boat heading to Isla Ometepe.

As you enter San Jorge, you'll pass under the **Cruz de España** (Cross of Spain), which marks the spot where Chorotega Chief (*cacique*) Nicarao first met Spanish conquistador Gil Gonzalez Dávila in 1523. Keep an eye out for the accompanying statues of each leader.

Getting Here & Away

By Taxi: Taxis shuffle travelers between **Rivas** and San Jorge for $1 per person; some drivers try to ask unsuspecting tourists for more but, with plenty of competing taxis around, there's no need to give in. As always, agree on the price in advance. You can also negotiate a taxi to **Granada** ($25), **San Juan del Sur** ($10), or the

Costa Rican border ($10). Prices rise substantially at night.

By Bus: Virtually all travelers take a bus to Rivas), followed by a taxi to San Jorge. An alternative is the daily **express bus** from **Managua**'s Mercado Huembes to San Jorge at 9 am. The same bus returns to Managua at 5 pm (2 hrs). There is a local bus that takes passengers to San Jorge, leaving from the traffic circle at the entrance to **Rivas**. However, since they only pass once per hour (at approximately a quarter after the hour), it's not a very convenient option – take a taxi instead unless you're really desperate to save a few cords.

By Boat: The boat schedule is fairly reliable but, if the winds are strong (most likely to occur in the months of March and April), boats occasionally do not depart for days in either direction. The ride takes 40 minutes and costs $1.75 by boat or $2.50 by ferry.

Check in with **Ometepe Tours** to confirm the trans-lake schedule, ☎ 563-4779.

SAN JORGE-MOYOGALPA SCHEDULE	MOYOGALPA-SAN JORGE SCHEDULE
9 am, by boat	5:30 am, by boat
9:30 am, by boat	6 am, by ferry
10:30 am, by ferry	6:30 am, by boat
11:30 am, by boat	6:45 am, by boat
12:30 pm, by boat	7 am, by boat
1:30 pm, by boat	9 am, by boat
2:30 pm, by ferry	11 am, by boat
3:30 pm, by boat	11:30 am, by boat
4:30 pm, by boat	12:30 pm, by ferry
5:30 pm, by ferry	1:30 pm, by boat
-	4 pm, by ferry

> **TIP:** *The waters of Lago de Nicaragua can be fierce, especially during the windy months of March and April. Try to take the **ferry** to Isla Ometepe, rather than a **boat**, which is almost always overcrowded and wet. The ferry is more stable, with spacious seating, and is highly recommended. Vehicles can be transported; make a reservation at the dock in advance.*

Sightseeing & Services

San Jorge is pleasant enough, but there isn't much to see. You may prefer to have a drink at one of the beachside restaurants while you're waiting for your ferry. If you want to take a stroll around town from the dock, walk west until you reach the center of town, then go two blocks south to **Parque Central** and the adjacent **Iglesia de San Jorge**, which exhibits a blend of Muslim and Christian architecture.

If you want to arrange a tour of Isla Ometepe, even for the same day, pay a visit to the well-managed **Ometepe Tours** (☎ 563-4779), which has an office at the dock

> **Caution:** The waterfront is not a safe area at night. If you have dinner in the beach area, take a taxi back to your hotel.

Where to Stay

Hotel Hamacas ($$, 100 yards west and 25 yards south of the dock, ☎ 563-0048). With 11 attractive rooms and lots of light, Hamacas is the best option in town for an overnight. Relax in the hammocks, or take a dip in one of the two pools. Singles ($12) and doubles ($18) come with private bath, cable TV, and fan; a/c costs $8 more. Breakfast is included, and credit cards are accepted.

Hotel Restaurant Azteca ($, ☎ 879-9512). This secure new place is primarily a backpackers' dorm (the 46

The Pacific Lowlands

beds cost $3 each), but a few private rooms are also available. The common area has a pool, Internet, and lockers. To get here from the dock, go two blocks beyond the faux castle, take a right and go two more blocks.

Where to Eat

For the best views in town, hit your choice of the **restaurants** ($-$$$) lining the beach next to the dock. Menus and food don't vary much, relying on Nica staples. **Centro Recreativo Gran Diamante** ($$-$$$, ☎ 886-0384) has good views, a playground, and a party atmosphere that keeps the Flor de Cana (Nicaraguan rum) flowing. The menu focuses on chicken and seafood, but also includes some traditional Nicaraguan options, including five styles of cow tongue. On Saturday nights there is live salsa music. Open daily 11 am-midnight.

If it's raining or the *chayules* (gnats) are in town, eating at the beach won't seem so appetizing. Instead, head to **Hotel Restaurant Azteca** ($), a welcoming hostelry that also serves meals for under $5.

Isla Ometepe

It's easy to spend much longer than you intended on beautiful Isla Ometepe. The relaxed lifestyle is contagious, and there are plenty of scenic adventure activities to participate in as you explore the island. The name "Ometepe" means "two hills," in Nahuatl. The origin of the name is not difficult to discern: the twin volcanoes of **Concepción** and **Maderas** punctuate the landscape and at least one of them is visible from virtually anywhere on the island, a constant reminder of how the island was formed.

Isla Ometepe was central to the settlement of Nicaragua: when the **Nahuatl** people migrated south from what is today Mexico, they were in search of two volcanoes surrounded by a lake that had appeared in a vi-

Isla Ometepe

sion. When Ometepe materialized in the distance, they took it as a sign to settle. To this day, Isla Omeptepe's seclusion is one of the things that keeps it so idyllic: the island is only accessible by **boat** from **San Jorge** near Rivas (arriving at Moyogalpa) or from **Granada** (arriving at Altagracia) and continuing on to **San Carlos**.

Isla Ometepe Highlights

- Wildlife viewing at Charco Verde
- Climbing Volcán Concepción or Volcán Maderas
- Relaxing on the beach at Playa Santo Domingo

MOYOGALPA

Most visitors to Isla Ometepe arrive in Moyogalpa, a small, agreeable port town on the island's northwest side. There isn't anything here that will keep you overnight (except, perhaps, an early morning ferry or volcano climb), but there are a couple of things to do around town if you find yourself with some time to spare. This is also a good place to catch up on errands; there are few services elsewhere on the island.

"Moyogalpa" means "place with the mosquitoes" in Nahuatl. Fortunately for residents and visitors, the mosquitoes here now are minimal.

■ GETTING HERE, AWAY & AROUND

Frequent daily **boat** service connects Moyogalpa with **San Jorge** on the mainland (see p 218 for schedules). Moyogalpa itself is small and walkable, but you'll want to get out of town to explore the island. **Car rental** is a good option if you're short on time. Toyotas can be rented at Hotel Ometepetl (☎ 459-4276). Prices begin at $60/day, slightly less for a half-day. Don't even think about renting anything other than a 4WD during rainy season if you plan to drive anywhere other than the southern route between Moyogalpa and Altagracia. There is only one main road that circles the upper part of the island, so directionally-challenged drivers shouldn't have much trouble. If you're driving from Moyogalpa to Altagracia, take the southern route, as the northern road is in poor condition.

Bus schedules correlate with the boat arrivals, so there will normally be one waiting at the edge of the dock when you arrive. Don't dawdle: the buses are often un-believably full, so hurry to get a seat. Buses run to **Altagracia** Mon-Sat at 5:30, 6:10, 7:30, 9:30, 11:20, 11:45 am, 12:45, 1:45, 5:30, and 6:45 pm. The bus takes an hour and costs $1. Most of these buses pass by **Charco Verde**, but be sure to confirm with the driver (15 minutes/60¢). There is one daily bus to San Ramón at 8:15 am (3 hrs/$2). **Balgüe**-bound buses leave at 10:20 am and 3:45 pm (2 hrs/$1.75). One bus heads daily to **San Ramón** at 8 am, returning to Moyogalpa at 2:30 pm. The **tour agencies** near the dock can give you the latest bus schedules.

Warning: Very few buses service the island on Sundays. If your travel plans fall on a Sunday, organizing a tour or renting a car is highly recommended. If you want to tough it out with the bus, bring a book and be prepared for a long wait.

■ SERVICES

TOURS & INFORMATION: Taking a tour is popular and a convenient way to explore the island, especially if you want to participate in adventure activities. Prices vary according to group size. You can technically visit the island in a single day (set up a **tour** at the dock before leaving San Jorge through Ometepe Tours, and they'll have a vehicle waiting by the time your boat arrives on the island), though you'll probably regret doing so unless you're really on a tight schedule. **Ometepe Tours** (☎ 563-4779) has an office at the dock in San Jorge as well as an outlet in Moyogalpa facing Hotel Ometepetl (ometepeisland@hotmail.com). **Ometepe Ecotours** (☎ 569-4244) is another good option and is just up the road from the dock.

SOLO SOLUTION

Solo travelers can often end up spending significantly more for tours than their couple counterparts. If you'd like to take an island tour and have a flexible schedule, ask the tour companies or freelance guides if there are any groups already signed up for the next few days. Joining a group saves you money and gives you a chance to meet other travelers.

MONEY: There are no banks on Isla Ometepe – bring plenty of cash with you from the mainland. **Hotel Ometepetl** (50 yards above the port on the main street) will change **traveler's checks** with a ridiculously high

The Pacific Lowlands

commission. Most of the island's hotels and tour agencies will accept dollars.

MEDICAL: There is a basic **hospital** in town (☎ 569-4247). For something serious, contact Alvaro through the Ometepe Biological Field Station (☎ 277-4700) or Hotel Hacienda Mérida (☎ 868-8973), who can arrange a helicopter to be sent to Managua for $600.

■ SIGHTSEEING, SHOPPING & ENTERTAINMENT

Moyogalpa is centered around the street that leads from the dock. Head straight up the street to reach the attractive **church** (climb the bell tower for views of town). Also on the main street is **El Museo**, which displays a few **handicrafts**, some of which are for sale, and locally-gathered **pre-Columbian artifacts**. Entry costs $1. The museum has slow **Internet** for $3/hr. You can also see handicrafts (and learn about the island's volcanoes) at **Fundacion Entre Volcanes**, which faces Enitel. If you're ready to relax with a drink after exploring town, try **Rancho Viejo** on the main street.

■ WHERE TO STAY

Moyogalpa doesn't have any particularly recommendable hotels, so you may want to consider moving on to your next destination and securing accommodation there instead. Remember to bring cash.

© Hotel Ometepetl

Hotel Ometepetl ($$-$$$, 50 yards above the port, ☎ 569-4276, ometepetlng@hotmail.com) is the most upscale option in Moyogalpa. It's also a one-stop shop for arranging a tour, a guide, or a rental car (or even a wedding, for that matter). The property also boasts the only swimming pool on Isla Ometepe. Doubles cost $18, or a pricey $30 with a/c, and include fan and private bath with hot water. Rooms are available that sleep up to five guests. Credit cards and travelers' checks are accepted at very poor rates.

Hotelito Restaurante Aly ($-$$, 150 yards above the port, ☎ 569-4196, hotelitoaly@yahoo.com). This sim-

© Hotelito Aly

ple, quiet place gets high marks for its friendly service. There is a large courtyard to relax in, and meals and drinks are served at the bar/restaurant. Double rooms have fan and private bath for $12, but rooms with a/c don't represent good value at $25. Triples, quads, and a family room that sleeps up to six guests are also available.

The youthful crowd at **Hospedaje Central** ($-$$, ☎ 569-4262) keeps things hopping at this colorful and fun hostel two blocks east and one block south of the port. Though many travelers come for the dorm ($3), simple private rooms are also available ($10 with fan, $18 with a/c). Camping in the back garden costs $1 (keep an eye out for the resident deer). The hostel has a movie room, laundry service, a book exchange, and private parking.

■ WHERE TO EAT

The main meal options are at hotels. **Hotel Ometepetl**'s ($$) is the classiest. Opposite is **Ranchón El Chele**, which serves tasty *comida corriente* for $2 in a *rancho*. A notable stand-alone restaurant is **Los Ranchitos** ($$, ☎ 569-4112), in a cozy *rancho* four blocks up the main street from the port and a half-block right. They have a menu loaded with Nica favorites and

The Pacific Lowlands

the best pizza in town (available after noon). Compost toilets are out back. Open daily 7 am-9:30 pm.

■ DAY-TRIPS FROM MOYOGALPA

TOURING TIPS

Isla Ometepe's substantial size and lengthy travel times mean that you'll need to make some decisions about what you'd like to see. Popular choices include Charco Verde, Cascada San Ramón, kayaking Río Istián, beach time at Playa Santo Domingo, and climbing the volcanoes. Trips often include stops at some of the numerous petroglyphs that dot the island. Spend some time browsing through this chapter for ideas, then consult the island's tour operators and freelance guides, who are very knowledgeable about tour options and can arrange custom itineraries based on your interests. They are also a good resource when it comes to planning around seasonal variations (for example, hiking can be a very muddy prospect during the rainy season, and waterfalls can slow to an unimpressive trickle during the dry season). Even if you want to explore independently, stopping in at tour agencies can yield advice, brochures, and updated transportation schedules.

PUNTA JESÚS MARÍA

Punta Jesús María is one of the best places to go for a **swim** near Moyogalpa. It also has great sunsets. During the dry season a long strip of sand reaches out into the lake, but it is submerged during the rainy season. A southbound **bus**, which will take you 2.4 miles from Moyogalpa, plus a 20-minute (one-mile) walk down the unpaved road, or a $10 **taxi** ride, brings you to this relaxed spot. Ostensibly a recreation center, there's not

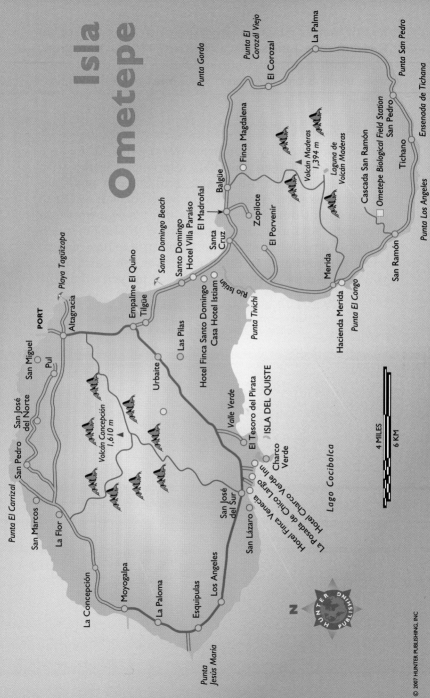

much other than a playground, but there is **Restaurante Linda Vista** (☎ 820-3410), a waterfront place with fish and traditional Nica food that's open from 6 am-8 pm. You can rent a **boat** from the restaurant for $10/hr.

CHARCO VERDE

Fifteen minutes by bus from Moyogalpa is Charco Verde ☆☆☆ (Green Puddle), a private reserve with plenty of wildlife, a nice beach, and copious possibilities for relaxation. You can stop by to check it out or to take a walk through the reserve, but it's well worth an overnight. All three guesthouses have great food, much of it pulled right from the lake, so be sure to have a meal while you're there. Tell the bus driver the guesthouse you're planning to stay in so he will let you off at the

Isla Ometepe has numerous freshwater beaches
that are great for swimming and relaxing,
including this one at Charco Verde.

correct part of the highway. The first path leading into Charco Verde heads to Hotel Finca Venecia and Posada de Chico Largo, while the second path (just another couple of minutes down the highway) goes to Hotel Charco Verde Inn. The reserve is next to Charco Verde Inn, so take that path if you just plan to visit for the day.

To reach any of them from the highway, go south (which is to your right if you are coming from Moyogalpa). Each guesthouse is a 15-minute walk down an unpaved path from the highway so, if you have lots

Look for wildlife on your way to the hotel.

of luggage, you may want to get private transport in Moyogalpa instead of taking the bus (there are rarely taxis available on the highway). The walk through the sugarecane fields to the guesthouses is a pleasant experience in itself, however (try to time your arrival to avoid the midday sun).

Down the first path are neighboring Hotel Finca Venecia and Posada del Chico Largo, both of which have congenial, friendly atmospheres and good food ($$). There isn't much of a beach in front of the guesthouses; walk down the beach to the left to reach a wider beach (in front of Hotel Charco Verde Inn) and the reserve's paths. **Finca Venecia** ☆ ($$-$$$, ☎ 887-0191, fincavenecia@hotmail.com), on the left, is the more attractive and upscale of the two. Rooms cost $10 and cabins are $28-$35. Cabins sleep up to four guests, some have lake views, and one has a fan. Bikes and horses can be rented here, and credit cards are accepted. **Posada del Chico Largo** ($, ☎ 886-4069) is more attuned to backpackers, with a dorm ($4.50) or camping ($2). Buffet meals are available for $3.50, and full moon parties are organized every month. Credit cards are accepted. A bit farther down the highway is

☆☆ **Hotel Charco Verde Inn** ($-$$, ☎ 887-9302, charcoverde22@yahoo.es). Adorable cabins cost $15-$25 and sleep up to three, while a larger cabin sleeps five and costs $50. Rooms in the main building cost $12 for a double with fan and private bath and $5 for a dorm. Rooms in the main building seem to be less prone to housing insects.

Cabins at Hotel Charco Verde Inn.

On-site **Restaurante Charco Verde** ☆☆ ($$-$$$) is very good and serves fish, meat, and veggie dishes in a great open-air atmosphere with good service. Fish with salad, potato wedges, and rice costs $6. Excellent fish soup is $3. Credit cards are accepted. Though it may be hard to tear yourself from the nice beach that fronts the property, the hotel rents **kayaks** and **paddle boats** for $3.25/hr.

The mangrove lagoon at Charco Verde is the source of several legends, all involving a ghostly inhabitant at Chico Largo.

Ask the villagers to recount their interpretation of the tale, which has been passed down for generations.

The **reserve trails** ☆☆ begin from the east side of Hotel Charco Verde Inn (facing the beach, walk to the left). You'll first come to a mangrove lagoon with a plethora of bird life (don't worry, there are no crocodiles: the locals, um, eradicated them when they started getting nervous about the children living nearby). Cross the bridge and continue straight. One path goes to the opposite side of the lagoon (when you reach the other end, return the way you came; there is a maze of barbed wire and private property on the other side). The other trail leads up the hill to the edge of the peninsula, providing great views of Volcán Maderas and Isla de Quiste.

A troop of howler monkeys hangs out along the edges of the lagoon. If you get too close they'll bark and throw things at you. Circle back around through the hotel and go down to the lagoon from the other side to see a variety of trees labeled by species and age. You can hire a guide at any of the hotels to

Resident howler monkey.

show you around, but you don't really need one. You will, however, need a **guide** to climb the volcanoes or to see other parts of the island. Get in touch with **Will** or

Harold through any of the three hotels to arrange a trip. Both are friendly, knowledgeable, and speak good English thanks to time they spent living in the US

Stay on the bus for another couple of minutes beyond Charco Verde to reach the access road for **El Tesoro de la Pirata** ($$, ☎ 832-2429), which has doubles in concrete cabins for $25 with private bath and a/c; dorms cost $3. Camping is also available for $2.50. There is a simple restaurant and a nice swimming beach. To get there from the highway, walk south (to the right if you're coming from Moyogalpa) on the unpaved road for 20 minutes. Taxis are not usually available on the highway.

> **Caution:** Though **Isla de Quiste** looks close to shore, the waters just beyond the beach can become very rough. Limit your kayaking to the calmer waters on the side of the peninsula with the hotels, and ask your driver to hire a boat (around $20) to take you to the island, where you can camp overnight.

Though there isn't anything of note to see there, you can walk to the friendly village of **San José del Sur** (20 minutes) from any of the guesthouses by walking to the highway and heading in the direction of Moyogalpa. There are nice views of the volcano. Travelers are rarely seen here, so expect a few curious stares. There are a few tiny shops selling bread, drinks, and snacks; bottled water is cheaper here than at the hotels. *Fiestas patronales* are celebrated March 19-20.

VOLCÁN CONCEPCIÓN

This 5,280-ft belching cone attracts eager hikers and is one of the main tourist draws on Isla Ometepe, but keep in mind that this is a challenging **nine-hour hike** suitable only for travelers in good condition. It's also necessary to factor in the reality that Concepción is indeed active, and hot gases are perpetually emitted from

The smouldering tip of Volcán Concepción.

The Pacific Lowlands

the volcano (note the cloud cover on top). After several hiking accidents in recent years, it's now required that hikers have a **guide**, available through all hotels or at any of the tour agencies in Moyogalpa for around $20 per group. The exhilaration of completing the hike may have to be enough: the clouds that usually shroud the volcano mean that the island and mainland are usually not visible. Even if it's a hot day, bring layers; it gets downright cold as you climb, and don't forget sunscreen and plenty of water. Confirm that your guide carries emergency supplies like a radio and a first aid kit.

Locals will tell you that in 1957, Volcán Concepción threatened eruption and the islanders were ordered to leave Isla Ometepe for safer ground. Local residents resolutely refused, asserting that they would prefer to die on Ometepe than to live anywhere else.

ALTAGRACIA

Fishermen at dusk.

You would hardly suspect that this tranquil village has a population of 20,000, but relaxed Altagracia is the second-largest town on the Isla Ometepe. Altagracia is pleasant enough to visit, but there isn't much to keep you here. Use it as a springboard for activities farther afield around the island.

■ GETTING HERE & AWAY

By Boat: Altagracia's **port**, called San Antonio, is 1.2 miles from town (30 minutes on foot). Trucks wait to pick up arriving ferry passengers (yep, even in the middle of the night). The ferry goes to **Granada** on Wed and Fri at 1 am (four hrs). **First class** (recommended) costs $3/second class $1.50. The *lancha* goes to **Granada** on Wed and Fri at 11 am. The **ferry** goes from **Granada** to Altagracia at 3 pm on Mon and Thurs. (four hrs/$1.50). The ferry goes to **San Carlos** (arriving 6 am), **Puerto Morrito**, and **San Miguelito** on Mon and Fri at 7 pm. First class costs $4/second class $2. The ferry leaves **San Carlos** for Altagracia on Wed and Fri at 3 pm. Ferry and *lancha* schedules do change. Be sure to confirm departure times at the port.

> **NOTE:** *The ferry might not call at Isla Ometepe if the winds are strong and the waves are high, most commonly in March and April. If you have an international flight, head over to the mainland the day before just in case.*

■ GETTING AROUND

By Taxi: The owner of Hotel Central is a relative of the two main hotels at Playa Santa Domingo and he can provide private transport there, or he can take you to the port to catch a ferry. The other guesthouses can also help with transport arrangements, or stop by the tourist kiosk in the park.

By Bus: The bus schedule changes often; ask at your guesthouse for updates. Few buses run on Sundays. Buses run from **Moyogalpa** to Altagracia Mon-Sat at 8:20, 9:20, 10:20, 11:30 am, 12:30, 1:30, 2:30, 3:30, 4:30, 5:30, and 6:30 pm (one hr/$1). Buses go to **Moyogalpa** at 4:30, 5, 5:35, 7, 8:50, 9:50, 10:50, 11:50 am, 12:30, 1:30, 2, 3, 4:20, and 5 pm. Buses go from Altagracia to **Santo Domingo** at 11:20 am and 3:30, 4:30, and 5:30 pm. **Balgüe**-bound buses leave at 11:20 am and 4:30 pm. Buses go to **Mérida** at 3:30 pm and 5:30 pm (two hrs/$2).

■ SERVICES

The park houses a **tourist kiosk** that can give you updates on transport schedules and hook you up with guides or private transport. Slow, expensive Internet is available at Hotel Castillo (see *Where to Stay*) and **Casa Curál** (on the south side of the park, open Mon-Fri). For basic health services, the **Centro de Salud** (☎ 552-6089) faces the park. There is a hospital in Moyogalpa for anything serious.

■ SIGHTSEEING & ENTERTAINMENT

Museo Ometepe is the place to go if you want to learn more about the island's volcanoes. Open daily 9 am-5 pm. Entry $1. *Fiestas patronales* happen Nov 12-18. Evenings here are quiet, but you can have a drink at one of the guesthouses' bar/restaurants. If you want to explore town by **bike**, rent one at Chido's Pizza for $1/hr.

▪ WHERE TO STAY & EAT

There are three places to stay in Altagracia, and all are centrally located. Accommodation here is rarely full, so take a peek at each before deciding. Each guesthouse has a good restaurant with Nica favorites; letting them know a couple of hours in advance if you plan to eat is a good idea; otherwise, service is slow but friendly. **Chido's Pizza** ($-$$) has decent pies and Nicaraguan dishes and is open 8 am-9 pm. Neighboring **Comedor Nicarao** ($) is a great stop for lunch, offering a filling *comida corriente* for less than $2.

DINING PRICE CHART	
Price per person for an entrée, not including beverage, tax or tip	
$	Up to $3
$$	$3-$6
$$$	$6-$10
$$$$	Over $10

☆ **Hotel Central** ($, two blocks south of the park, ☎ 552-8770). The 25 rooms at this tidy, plant-filled place cost $3 with shared bath, $4 with private bath. Small cabins with private bath are in the pretty garden and cost

HOTEL PRICE CHART	
Cost per night for two people, before tax	
$	Up to $15
$$	$16-$30
$$$	$31-$60
$$$$	Over $60

$7. Laundry service, Internet, and private parking are available, and credit cards are accepted.

Hotel Castillo ($, a block south and a half-block west of the church, ☎ 552-8744). This simple place was the first hotel on Isla Ometepe (1985). The 16 rooms, all of which have private bath, open onto a courtyard. Singles cost $10, doubles $14. Credit cards are accepted. The restaurant serves organic coffee.

Hotel Don Kencho ($, a half-block south of the park, ☎ 832-2594). This hotel has eight rooms housed in a wooden building that has seen better days. **Bikes** and **horses** are available for rent. A double room costs $6 for one bed with private bath, $5 for two beds with shared bath.

PLAYA SANTO DOMINGO

Playa Santo Domingo is the best-known beach on the island, and the attractive beach and upscale accommodation make it a worthwhile place to spend a couple of days. Reserve well in advance if you plan to visit during a holiday. This area of the island can be very windy. A taxi from Moyogalpa will cost you around $15.

■ WHERE TO STAY & EAT

☆☆ **Villa Paraíso** ($$$-$$$$, ☎ 563-4675, ometepe@villaParaíso.com.ni) has beautifully-landscaped grounds and attractive architecture. Doubles are situated in rooms and cute casitas; some casitas have a/c, hot water, TV, and kitchens. Double rooms cost $46, while casitas cost $63. Service gets mixed reviews from guests. Tours and activities are available, including **bike** and

© Villa Paraíso

horse rental. Credit cards are accepted. The upscale **Restaurant Villa Paraíso** ($$-$$$) has carefully-prepared Nicaraguan food and good pancake breakfasts and is worth a stop even if you are just passing through. There is also a bar. Open daily 7 am-9 pm.

Neighboring **Hotel Finca Santo Domingo** ($$, ☎ 552-8787, htstodom@ibw.com.ni) is more rustic, with less attention to detail but with the same beachfront location. Doubles with private bath and a/c cost $25. Credit cards are accepted; meals and tours available.

© Casa Hotel Istiám

Casa Hotel Istiám ($-$$, ☎ 569-4132, ometepetlng@hotmail.com) is 1.2 miles south of Playa Santo Domingo and is across the street from a decent beach. This place is a good option if you want to be in the area but shy away from the higher prices at Santo Domingo. Rooms are decent but plain and cost $8 pp with a/c and private bath/$5 pp with fan, and sleep up to five guests. You can make reservations at Hotel Ometepetl in Moyogalpa.

VOLCÁN MADERAS

At 4,572 ft, Maderas is an easier hike than Concepción but still clocks in at **seven hours**. Guides are required to ascend Maderas; hire one at any of the hotels or at any of the tour agencies in Moyogalpa. The dry season is definitely the preferable time to climb the volcano, but expect mud throughout the year. When you reach the top you'll be rewarded with cloud forests and a beautiful **crater lake**. Descending into the crater requires the use of a rope; be sure your guide has the correct equipment. Views of the island and mainland are hampered by trees and often clouds. There are two departure points for climbing Maderas: one begins at **Mérida** and the other starts at **Finca Magdalena**. If you go the Finca Magdalena route and you're not staying there you'll have to pay a small fee to cross the property. Take layers, a bathing suit if you want to jump in the chilly crater lake, extra socks, and plenty of water.

Maderas Volcano

■ WHERE TO STAY & EAT

Finca Magdalena ($-$$, ☎ 880-2041, www.fincamag dalena.com, info@fincamagdalena.com. This 980-acre organic farm has been a favorite with those on the backpacker trail for decades. The 24 families that live on the farm produce coffee, plantains, vegetables, and milk. Accom-

© Finca Magdalena

modation is available in a range of prices. Bunk up in the dorm ($2) that was built in 1888, or camp for $1.50. Single rooms cost $2.50, doubles $4. Cabins offer more privacy and cost $15 for a double, $10 for each additional guest. The Nica meals made with food from the farm are good value, and you can buy packaged coffee and honey to take home. **Volunteer** opportunities are available on the farm, and **work** of one month or more can be exchanged for accommodation. Tours to learn about coffee-growing and the farm are available, as are volcano hikes and excursions to see the petroglyphs on the property. Expensive Internet is available. Reach Finca Magdalena by taking a Balgüe-bound bus from Moyogalpa or Altagracia. The walk from the highway takes 25 minutes.

At the entrance to the access road to Finca Magdalena there is a guest house with a bit more comfort (and a lot less walking). **Hospedaje y Comedor Maderas** ($, ☎ 882-3535) has basic rooms with fan and shared bath. Doubles cost $5. The restaurant is open 6:30 am-8 pm for Nica standards.

The Pacific Lowlands

MÉRIDA

Tiny Mérida has a population of less than 1,000, but it's becoming increasingly well-known among travelers thanks to **Hotel Hacienda Mérida** ☆ ($, ☎ 868-8973). It's easy to spend more time here than planned, with a myriad of activities and a convivial atmosphere comprised largely of backpackers. Rooms are divided into dorms ($4) and rooms with private bath ($6 pp). Great buffet meals ($3.50) are cooked on a wood fire and eaten family-style every night. Tours and **bike**, **kayak**, and **horse** rental are available, and **Spanish classes** can be arranged. Owner Alvaro is a good source of information and he can help set you up with classes at the Ometepe Biological Field Station (see p 242). **Volunteering** can be done weekday mornings at the Centro Infantil Comunitario, though volunteers are required to purchase breakfast for the women and children that attend this daycare.

A home in a rural area of Isla Ometepe.

■ ADVENTURES

Rio Istían, most easily accessed from Mérida, is secluded and the vegetation is dense, so you need to get there by water. Rent **kayaks** at Hacienda Mérida (above) and paddle the 1 ½ hours along the lake to the mouth of the river. Once you enter the river you'll see monkeys as well as many types of birds. The best times to see wildlife are morning and late afternoon. Bring water and sunscreen and set out early enough to return before it gets dark.

Located just 2.4 miles southeast of Mérida, **Cascada San Ramón** is a popular stop. You can take the bus then hike to the waterfall from the highway, or you can drive part of the way if you have a 4WD, though you'll still have to hike for an hour beyond that point. From the highway it's a two-mile, three-hr steep **hike**. There is one **bus** daily from Moyogalpa at 8 am

San Ramón Falls

returning at 2:30 pm (3 hrs/$3); if you miss it, have the biological station arrange private transport for you. You can **drive** or take a **taxi** the 21 miles from Moyogalpa in an hour and 45 minutes. If you really want to splash out to get here, contact Alvaro at the biological station or Hotel Hacienda Mérida, who will arrange a **private boat** from **San Jorge** to San Ramón for up to 70 people for $600. For the same price, up to three people can take a **helicopter** from Managua.

The Pacific Lowlands

To hike to the waterfall, you'll need to pay the $2 entry fee at the gate (free for biological station guests). A guide is not required for this hike, though with only one daily bus, visiting the waterfall with a tour is easiest.

> **TIP:** *Ask about the status of the waterfall at one of the tour agencies before you embark on the hike to Cascada San Ramón. Though it is impressive during the rainy season, at the peak of dry season it is sometimes reduced to an unimpressive drip.*

Beyond the gate leading to the waterfall you'll find **Ometepe Biological Field Station** (☎ 277-4700, www.lasuerte.org), which offers a variety of short-term and semester-long classes in arts and science. A semester-long course costs $1,600 and includes accommodation at the station and all meals. Tourists can also stay at the station ($$-$$$$), though guests need to be self-sufficient as the staff is occupied with the students. Rooms overlook the water, double with shared bath ($25 for a double with fan up to $105 for a suite with a/c and a Jacuzzi).

■ WHERE TO STAY & EAT

Albergue Ecológico El Porvenir ($, ☎ 552-8770). This secluded spot outside of town is best reached by private transport, or you can walk 40 minutes from the main road that leads to Mérida. Located on the slopes of Volcán Maderas, this simple place gives you a chance to get away from it all. Rooms cost $5pp and have private bath and fan. Meals are served and private transport and tours can be arranged. Credit cards are accepted. Make a reservation at Hotel Villa Paraíso in Playa Santo Domingo or at Hotel Central in Altagracia.

San Juan del Sur & the Tola Beaches

SAN JUAN DEL SUR

Though San Juan del Sur (SJDS) still clings to its village atmosphere, the town's beaches, booming real estate, and proximity to Costa Rica have put it firmly on the map as an international hotspot. In recent years the town has grown to almost 19,000 residents, with expatriates taking advantage of the exquisite views from the hillsides to build dream homes that look straight out of Miami. While the town itself isn't particularly attractive and foreigners often seem to outnumber locals, beaches situated just minutes from San Juan del Sur still offer the chance to have the sand to yourself, though perhaps not for long.

San Juan del Sur Highlights

- Watching the sunset from Pelican Eyes on Piedras y Olas
- Canopy tours at Da Flying Frog
- Surfing at Playa Maderas
- Seeing turtles hatch at La Flor

■ TIMING YOUR TRIP

San Juan del Sur is popular year-round, but holidays and weather considerations may influence your trip timing. Semana Santa, Christmas, and New Year's are peak season in San Juan del Sur; you may find accommodation and activities reserved months in advance and premium prices. The weather in San Juan del Sur is warm year-round with little rainfall even during the wet season. Swimmers hit the beach year-round, though temperatures can be uncomfortably hot during

The Pacific Lowlands

April and early May, and there is little shade in town or on the beach. Boaters and beachgoers may prefer to avoid December-March when winds can be strong. Surfers prefer to hit the waves from April-December. If you want to have the beach to yourself, try May, June, October, and November.

INTERNET RESOURCES: www.sanjuandelsur.org.ni.

■ GETTING HERE & AWAY

BY TAXI

Taxis from the Managua airport charge around $70 to SJDS, or you can arrange one in advance through your hotel for approximately the same price. A taxi to **Granada** or **Masaya** costs around $40. Pricey but reliable **Radio 1 Express** (☎ 568-2489) sends comfortable private vehicles to the **Costa Rican border** for $25 and to the **Managua** airport for $85 for one or two people, $95 for up to four people, and $125 for five or more.

From **Rivas**, *colectivo* **taxis** leave when full from 4 am-3 pm and charge $1.30 per person. A **private taxi** will set you back about $10 for the 20-minute ride.

BY BUS

There are daily farm-animal-free **express buses** from **Managua**'s Mercado Huembes at 9, 9:30 am and 4 pm (2½ hrs/$3.50) – the 9 am bus even has reclining seats. Otherwise, take an *ordinario* bus from Mercado Huembes that picks up passengers in **Rivas** (every 30 minutes-1 hr, 3 hrs/$1.50) and change there for a bus to San Juan del Sur (every 45 minutes, 50 minutes/50¢). Both buses arrive in the center of town next to the market. If you're coming from the **Costa Rican border**, catch the bus headed for Rivas and tell the driver you want to get off at **La Virgen** (20 minutes/60¢). From there, cross the Pan-American Highway and wait for the next bus to San Juan del Sur (every 30-45 minutes). **Express buses** leave SJDS for **Managua** at 5, 5:30, 6:30 am and 3:30 pm. *Ordinario* buses head to Rivas and Managua every half-hour from 5 am-9:30 am, then hourly until 5:15 pm. To reach the **Costa Rican border**, take a Managua- or Rivas-bound bus to La Virgen, cross the highway and catch a connecting southbound bus. Alternatively, take **Ticabus**; book in advance at their office just west of the Texaco station (☎ 834-3425).

BY BOAT

Several cruise lines call at the town's deepwater port. See p 62 for details.

■ GETTING AROUND

SJDS itself is easy to navigate on foot, but for adventures farther afield, take a taxi, bus, or boat.

BY TAXI

Taxis are available for trips to nearby beaches and other points of interest and prices are fixed by the local taxi cooperative. Taxis are available to nearby destinations, including **Bahía Majagual** ($10), **Playa El Yankee** ($10), **La Flor** ($25), **Playa El Coco** ($25) and **El Ostional** ($30). Costs increase significantly at night. The easiest place to find a taxi is in front of the market.

BY BUS

Buses leave from the market. They ply the bumpy dirt road to the beaches south of SJDS as far as **El Ostional** (2 hrs) depart 1, 4, and 5 pm. The bus stops in **Guacalito, La Flor, Brasilito, El Coco, Escameca, El Yankee, Playa Hermosa** and **Tamarindo**. It returns to SJDS from **El Ostional** at 5:30 am and 4 pm and makes the same stops along the way.

BY BOAT

There is a daily **water taxi** to **Bahía Majagual** and **Playa Marsella** that leaves from the beach in front of Hotel Estrella at 11 am, returning at 5 pm ($8 round-trip). Charter a water taxi (☎ 616-5493) for up to eight

The Pacific Lowlands

people for $100 to Bahía Majagual, Playa Maderas, or Playa Marsella, or pay $60 for Playa Remanso.

■ SERVICES

TOURS & INFORMATION: There is no **Intur** office in town, but hotels and the numerous expatriates around town are good sources of information, as are restaurant bulletin boards. Most hotels can arrange day-trips and private transport. From July to January don't miss the opportunity to see nesting **Paslama turtles** just south of SJDS at Playa El Coco (see p 264 for more information). **Casa Oro** hostel has a particularly extensive list of offerings aimed primarily at budget travelers.

Visitors that plan to participate in organized adventure activities should consider a package trip to San Juan del Sur. **Pelican Eyes Piedras y Olas** (☎ in the US 866-350-0555, in Nicaragua ☎ 568-2110, www.piedras yolas.com) offers packages that include accommodation, boating, fishing and some meals. **Superfly Sport Fishing** (☎ 884-8444, www.superflynica.com, bigfish@ superflynica.com) has expensive, professionally-run three-day fishing packages; prices drop substantially if you can pull together a small group.

Surfers should check out budget-minded **Arena Caliente Surf Camp** (www.arenacaliente.com). They arrange packages that include airport transportation, rudimentary lodging, meals, and surfing. Surf veteran **Chelo**, owner of Hotel Colonial, arranges higher-end packages (☎ 568-2539, hotel.colonial@ibw.com.ni).

Even if your chosen hotel does not advertise packages, ask about discounts if you plan to stay more than a few days or if it's low season.

MONEY: A **bank**, **Centro de Finanzas**, has finally made its way to town; it's on the southern end of the beachfront road. Even more useful, there is a new **ATM** next to Hotel Casablanca on the beachfront road. **Casa Oro** hostel and **Casa Internacional Joxi** exchange dollars at poor rates. The higher-end hotels and tour operators in town usually take credit cards, and most guesthouses accept dollars.

MAIL & INTERNET: The **post office** is at the southern end of the beachfront road. San Juan del Sur's Internet is pricier (around $2/hr) and slower than most other locales in Nicaragua. Internet cafés open and close at a rapid rate; try **Cyber Leo** (open daily 8 am-9 pm) or **Hotel Costa Azul** (☎ 568-2294).

LAUNDRY: Most hotels and guesthouses will wash and hang your clothes; allow a couple of days for them to dry during the rainy season. Alternatively, take your dirty duds to **Gaby's Laundromat** (☎ 837-7493), which faces Hospedaje Elizabeth. Open Mon-Sat 8 am-6 pm.

TELEPHONE: Enitel is on the southern end of the beachfront road. Most Internet cafés in town offer inexpensive international calls.

MEDICAL: There is a basic health clinic just west of the Texaco gas station, and there are a few shops in the market area with a limited selection of pharmaceutical supplies. Sunscreen and aloe are expensive in SJDS; if you need to stock up at a pharmacy, consider making a quick trip into Rivas. For anything serious, ask your hotel to arrange private transport to Managua.

MARKETS: There are no supermarkets in town, though you will find plenty of small *pulperias* selling water and snacks. The newly refurbished **market** is a clean, compact affair with green awnings and none of the typical market chaos. It is open until 4 pm Mon-Sat and closed Sun.

STAYING SAFE: The **police station** (☎ 458-2382) faces the beach two blocks south of Calle Central. Make sure the door and windows in your room lock securely. Don't leave belongings unattended at the beach. The beachfront road and beach can be unsafe at night, especially for solo women. There are generally not taxis available in front of the beach bars in the evening – walk with a group.

■ SIGHTSEEING

There isn't much to see in town, but most people are too busy enjoying the beach to notice. Take a few minutes to check out the **Iglesia San Juan Bautista** and the adjacent slightly run-down Parque Central. From the beachfront road, walk up the bluff on the south side of town to see the **lighthouse**, the remains of William Walker's ruined **fort**, and a great view of the town and bay. Even if you aren't staying there, the view from Pelican Eyes Piedras y Olas is worth the climb up the hillside. Catch the sunset and enjoy a drink from their poolside bar.

The beach at San Juan del Sur.

■ SHOPPING

El Gato Negro sells packages of organic **coffee**, including several varieties sold nowhere else. San Juan del Sur's **market** has a few sarongs and sandals. A handful of shops dot the center of town (keep an eye out for "Made in China" stickers), and hopeful adolescents ply bracelets and ceramics along the beachfront road. In general, you're better off waiting to make purchases elsewhere.

Numerous places to exchange used books have popped up around SJDS. Virtually all of them charge for the privilege, and many books are as old as they look, so if you're headed to Granada, hold on to your reading material and trade for higher quality books for free. If you're in immediate need of new tomes, **Marie's Bar**, **Big Wave Dave's**, and **Hospedaje Nina** have exchanges of similar quality. Can't find anything to your liking? Stop in for an excellent selection of new and used books, including Nicaraguan titles, at **El Gato Negro**.

■ ENTERTAINMENT & NIGHTLIFE

SJDS is known for its backpacking revelers, especially during holidays, but more sedate visitors will find plenty of relaxing options as well. Ricardo's Bar, long the most popular nighttime spot in town, closed in late 2006. It remains to be seen who will take over the nightlife scene.

☆☆ **El Gato Negro** (☎ 828-5534, www.elgatonegro nicaragua.com, peace@elgatonegronica.com), an atmospheric bookstore/coffeeshop, is a great place to relax and meet other travelers and expats over espresso, dessert, and English-language books. There is a **game night** for the Scrabble fiend in you on Mondays from 6-9 pm and occasional **yoga classes** ($3); stop by for updated yoga schedules. Meals and snacks that you may not have seen in awhile are also served, including bagels with cream cheese ($1.75) and a tasty hummus plate that comes with organic veggies from a nearby farm ($6). Open Mon 6-9 pm and Wed-Sun 7 am-3 pm.

The upscale bar at **Pelican Eyes Piedras y Olas** (www. piedrasyolas.com) attracts expats and visitors alike,

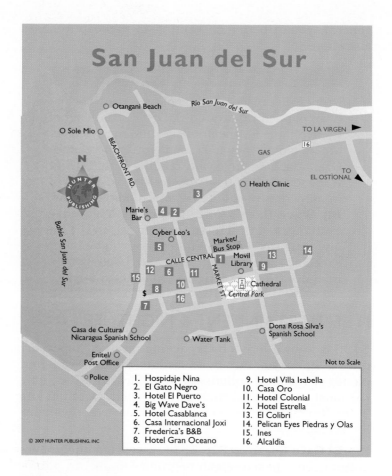

San Juan del Sur

O Otangani Beach

Río San Juan del Sur

O Sole Mio O

TO LA VIRGEN ▶

BEACHFRONT RD

GAS

16

N

TO
EL OSTIONAL ◀

HUNTER PUBLISHING

O Health Clinic

3

Bahía San Juan del Sur

Marie's
Bar O

4 2

Cyber Leo's
O

5

Market/
Bus Stop

CALLE CENTRAL

1 Movil
Library
O

13

14

9

12 6 11

MARKET ST

15

8 10

$

16

Cathedral

Central Park

7

Casa de Cultura/
Nicaragua Spanish School

O

O Water Tank

Dona Rosa Silva's
Spanish School
O

Enitel/
Post Office
O

Not to Scale

o Police

© 2007 HUNTER PUBLISHING, INC

1. Hospidaje Nina
2. El Gato Negro
3. Hotel El Puerto
4. Big Wave Dave's
5. Hotel Casablanca
6. Casa Internacional Joxi
7. Frederica's B&B
8. Hotel Gran Oceano

9. Hotel Villa Isabella
10. Casa Oro
11. Hotel Colonial
12. Hotel Estrella
13. El Colibri
14. Pelican Eyes Piedras y Olas
15. Ines
16. Alcaldia

while the places along the waterfront road, including
Marie's Bar, serve up cold beers and cool breezes
(women should not walk alone there late at night). The
dance clubs in town cater primarily to the fun-loving
backpacker crowd. Try **Otangani Disco**, which gets
started around 11 pm.

If you need something low-key in the daytime while you
nurse your hangover, **Cafetín Cavario**, the local community center, has unlimited billiards and ping pong
for an 8¢ entrance fee – practice your Spanish while
challenging locals kids to a match. Open Mon-Thurs
6 am-6 pm. **Pelican Eyes Piedras y Olas** has **water**

aerobics (free for guests; $3 for non-guests) on Tues and Fri at 10 am. Call in advance to ensure it's still happening.

■ ADVENTURES ON WATER

SWIMMING

Though the water isn't very clear, the swimming is fine in San Juan del Sur and the waves are more manageable than at beaches to the north. It's not advisable to leave anything on the beach while you're in the water due to theft problems. If you prefer a **pool** to the beach, hit Pelican Eyes (**Piedras y Olas**), which has the best pool in town ($3 for non-guests).

© Piedras y Olas

BOATING & FISHING

Each of the following operators has extensive experience and English and Spanish are spoken.

Pelican Eyes Sailing Adventures (☎ US 866-350-0555, Nicaragua ☎ 568-2110, sailing@piedras yolas.com) has trips ranging from $35 pp ($30 pp if staying at Pelican Eyes Piedras y Olas) for a **sunset cruise** to $65 pp ($50 pp for hotel guests) for a full day of **fishing**. Daylong trips include a BBQ lunch, snacks, and open bar. Prices are based on a minimum of 10 people and

© Piedras y Olas

go up steeply unless you have a group.

Superfly Sport Fishing (☎ 884-8444, www.super flynica.com) arranges fly fishing and deep sea fishing as well as multi-day packages.

Roger's Cat Cruises (☎ 845-1043) arranges sailing trips to your choice of beaches and accompanies your trip with Captain Leonardi's Italian cooking ($50 pp with a minimum of six people.

> **TIP:** *If you take a boat trip in April or September, keep an eye out for* **humpback whales***, which migrate during these months.*

SURFING

Playa Maderas, boasting some of the best surfing in Nicaragua, is 20 minutes north of San Juan del Sur. **Arena Caliente** surf shop (☎ 839-7198, www.arena caliente.com), next to the market, provides good-value transport for $7 round-trip from SJDS, leaving around 10 am, returning at 4 pm. Arena Caliente also rents surfboards and boogie boards.

DIVING

Though the water clarity is a disappointment if you're coming from Nicaragua's Caribbean Coast, it is possible to scuba dive around SJDS. **A Bucear** is 50 yards-plus west of the Texaco gas station. PADI open water courses cost $250, and a two-tank wreck dive costs $60. **Dive Nicaragua**, next to Villa Isabella, has similar options.

■ ADVENTURES ON FOOT

Take advantage of panoramic views of the bay and town by taking a **hike** up the hillside to the old **lighthouse** and **fort**. Begin the hike, which takes two hrs round-trip, by taking the beachfront road south until you reach the dock. Go through the gate into the port area, then through the second gate. Take the trail up the hill;

when you the reach the fork, go left to the remnants of the old fort or right to the lighthouse. Costa Rica can be seen to the south.

If you'd like to explore nearby beaches on foot, see *South of San Juan del Sur* p 261.

■ ADVENTURES ON WHEELS

Hotel Colonial and **Hospedaje Elizabeth** rent bikes for $6/day.

■ ADVENTURES IN THE AIR

Great views of the ocean and mountains can be had from the zip lines at **Da Flying Frog Canopy Tour** ☆ (☎ 611-6214, tiguacal@ibw.com.ni), which offers 17 platforms just outside of town on the edge of the mayor's cattle ranch. Canopy tours cost $25. Take a taxi from town (less than 10 minutes), or ask Da Flying Frog to arrange transport, which is free for groups. Closed Mon.

© Da Flying Frog

The Pacific Lowlands

■ ADVENTURES ON HORSEBACK

Da Flying Frog rents horses for $10/hr. Petroglyphs can be found in the area; ask the staff to point you in the right direction. Closed Mon.

■ CULTURAL ADVENTURES

LANGUAGE STUDY

San Juan del Sur is one of the most popular places in Nicaragua to study Spanish. Excursions and airport pickup are available through most schools. The prices listed below include 20 hours of class per week plus homestay and meals. For private tutors, keep an eye out for flyers around town.

Rosa Silva Spanish School, ☎ 621-8905. Students give this school's teachers positive reviews ($160 per week.

San Juan del Sur Spanish School (NSS). A block and a half toward the dock from Hotel Estrella, ☎ 568-2432, www.sjdsspanish.com. As part of the NSS group of schools, students have the option of combining their studies with a stay at another of the school's branches elsewhere in Nicaragua ($195 per week, $365 for two weeks.

Latin American Spanish School, ☎ 820-2252. This new school has experienced, enthusiastic teachers. Homestays include a private bath ($210 per week.

Playas del Sur Spanish School, ☎ 458-2594, is run by a local women's cooperative ($150 per week for one-on-one classes.

VOLUNTEERING

Biblioteca Móvil ☆ (☎ 568-2214, www.sjdsbiblioteca. com). This innovative library project, based in San Juan del Sur, allows the community to check out books and use the cozy library space for studying or organized activities. Twice each week a truck brings books and fun to schools in nearby villages. Volunteers are needed to check out books, teach workshops, and read with students. Contact director Jane Mirandette at janem101@aol.com for more information.

Project Stretch, based in Massachusetts, sends volunteer teams each February and March to provide dental treatment and teach oral hygiene in local villages. Most volunteers are dentists, dental hygienists, and dental students, but other volunteers can sometimes be accommodated. Contact Sheila Clancy at sclancy999@aol.com.

■ WHERE TO STAY

SJDS is one of the best places in Nicaragua to splash out for a nice hotel, and there are plenty to choose from. Accommodation is often booked months in advance during the Semana Santa and Christmas holidays – plan

HOTEL PRICE CHART	
Cost per night for two people, before tax	
$	Up to $15
$$	$16-$30
$$$	$31-$60
$$$$	Over $60

accordingly. At other times, arriving without a reservation is usually not a problem.

> *Every listing in this book is recommended and considered above average in its category. Listings with one star (☆) are highly recommended, those earning two stars (☆☆) are considered to be exceptional. A few resorts and restaurants rate three stars (☆☆☆), which means they are worthy of a special occasion splurge.*

☆☆ **Pelican Eyes Piedras y Olas** ($$$$, 1½ blocks east of the church on the hillside, ☎ US 866-350-0555, Nicaragua 568-2110, www.piedrasyolas.com). San Juan del Sur's most luxurious hotel offers a creative, upscale mix of beautiful rooms and villas carved into the lush hillside. Villas are well maintained and have fully-equipped kitchens; many also have ocean views. Rooms and villas

© Piedras y Olas

can sleep up to six and offer patios, wireless Internet, cable TV, DVD players, and a/c. While privacy prevails throughout most of the resort thanks to lush foliage and careful planning, the pool is the center of the action and overlooks the entire town; a second pool should be open by the time you visit. If you have physical limitations, contact the hotel in advance as many villas are accessed via steps. If you want to spend a lot of time at the beach or in town, Pelican Eyes may not be your best option; the center of town is a 10-minute walk away via a dirt road. Secure parking is available. Rooms range from $100-$130, villas are $160-$180 plus tax, including breakfast. If you plan to visit during Christmas or Easter, note that prices are double and reservations need to be made far in advance.

☆ **Hotel Casablanca** ($$$, on the beachfront road, ☎ 568-2135, casablan@ibw.com.ni). With an ideal location facing the beach, recently-remodeled Casablanca has 14 comfortable and spotless rooms. Each has a private bath with hot water, cable TV, a/c, and a fridge. Mini-suites have private terraces that overlook the beach, but all guests can use the hammock-filled patio. Laundry service, breakfast, kitchen use, and free coffee are available. Singles run $54, doubles $56, triples $64, and suites $80 plus tax. There is also one family room that can sleep up to seven people ($105).

Hotel Villa Isabella ($$$-$$$$, on the north side of the church, ☎ 458-2568, villaisabella@aol.com). This cozy inn has a homey ambience. Videos, books, and games are available in the common room, and there is a small pool. The spotless rooms have tiled floors and lots of

© Hotel Villa Isabella

windows; some have mini-fridges. Singles or doubles with cable TV/ VCR, a/c, and shared bath cost $50 (with private bath $65-$75) plus tax. Mini-suites are also available. Breakfast is included. Note that during Christmas, New Year's, and Semana Santa the rates double. Credit cards are accepted.

Hotel Colonial ($$$, one block west from the market toward the beach then a half-block south, ☎ 568-2539, www.hotel-nicaragua.com, hotel.colonial@ibw.com.ni). Despite the name, the Colonial is thoroughly modern. The hotel's 12 small rooms are thoughtfully decorated and have private bath with hot water, cable TV, and a/c. Rooms range in price from $44 for a single to $75 for a family room that sleeps five. Doubles cost $50. Breakfast is available in mural-clad eating area, and credit cards are accepted.

© Hotel Coloniali

Hotel Gran Océano ($$$, a half-block away from the beach behind the bank, ☎ 568-2219, hgoceano@ibw.com.ni). The modern, comfortable Gran Océano has tidy common areas with plenty of rocking chairs and a good location near the beach. The property has a small pool and parking is available. Singles ($43), doubles ($46), triples ($52), and quads ($57) have private bath with hot water, cable TV, and a/c. Rates include breakfast. Parking is available.

© Hotel Internacional Joxi

Casa Internacional Joxi ($$, 1½ blocks west of the market, ☎ 458-2483, casajoxi@ibw.com.ni). A long-time favorite, funky Joxi has simply-furnished rooms and a convenient location a half-block from the beach. Travelers like to hang out on the second story terrace and watch the action on the street. Norwegian, English, and Spanish are spoken.

Hotel El Puerto ($$, 1½ blocks south of Texaco, ☎ 823-5729, hotel-el-puerto@gmx.net). El Puerto has 10 quiet good-value rooms set back from the street. All have a private bath and face a nondescript garden. Singles cost $18, doubles $23. A relaxing front terrace area features plenty of rocking chairs.

There is a smattering of budget hotels ($-$$) next to the market by the bus stop. Rooms vary substantially; see several before selecting one. Most rooms have seen better days, and some bathrooms are rudimentary. **Hospedaje Elizabeth** is popular, but it's a mystery why: cleanliness is suspect, the wooden floors render downstairs rooms noisy, and prices don't represent good value. Neighboring **Hospedaje Nina** ☆ ($, ☎ 458-2302) is a step above the rest. Offering the best budget deal in town, Nina and her son have spotless tiled-floor double rooms with clean shared baths and good water pressure for $12. Ask for one of the two quiet upstairs rooms, which share a tiled patio with a hammock. The family plans to add additional rooms upstairs in 2007. Nina's son speaks English.

SAN JUAN DEL SUR REAL ESTATE

If you wish you could extend your beach vacation indefinitely, you aren't the only one: at press time there were a remarkable 18 real estate agencies in town, most of which cater to an international clientele. Real estate prices have gone up substantially in San Juan del Sur and nearby areas in recent years, with no signs of slowing down. If you want to get your feet wet in the local real estate craze, do your homework, shop around, and be sure to hire an attorney (your embassy has a list of bilingual lawyers).

■ WHERE TO EAT

If you haven't yet tried Nicaragua's **market** food, San Juan del Sur is the best place in the country to do so. The market eateries are clean and menus are posted; some have explanations in English. They are open for breakfast and lunch only.

☆ **Comedor Itxel** ($, in the market; Open early morning-4pm, Mon-Sat). Popular with locals and visiting surfers alike, this informal spot is an excellent place for a quick meal in the market. Great breakfasts (including pancakes, eggs and fresh fruit) and *refrescos* are served by a friendly, patient staff that speaks some English. A heaping *comida corriente* is a great deal at $2.20; fish is $6. **Comedor Doña Angelita** ($) next door is similar and has a menu in English.

☆ **La Cascada** at Pelican Eyes ($$$-$$$$, 1½ blocks east of the church on the hillside, ☎ 568-2110). La Cascada's quality international and Nicaraguan meals are served in an open-air, upscale *rancho* overlooking the pool, town, and bay. Sample the goods at the plentiful breakfast buffet ($7). Lunch ($6-$10) averages about half the price of

© Piedras y Olas

the dinner options, which include steak, fresh fish, and lobster. Service is professional and there is a full bar. Credit cards are accepted. Open daily 6:30 am-11 pm.

El Colibrí ($$$-$$$$, ☎ 863-8612, marymouse66@yahoo.co.uk). A new restaurant with a great atmosphere, El Colibri combines the eclectic backgrounds of the owners (who are English, Spanish, and Italian) to create a refined, yet relaxed, dining experience. The restaurant specializes in European cuisine. Don't miss the sangria. Meals average $7.

O Sole Mio ($$-$$$, on the northern end of the beachfront road). O Sole Mio serves the best Italian food in San Juan del Sur and the service is attentive. Pizza and a diverse selection of pastas are staples, and if you've been craving salad, you've come to the right place. Vegetarians will find a variety of options. The hours are confusing: open 5:30 pm-9:30 pm weekends only May, June, October and November; the rest of the year, the hours are Tues-Fri, 5:30 pm-9:30 pm, and Sat-Sun, 11:30 am-9:30 pm.

Ines ($$$-$$$$, ☎ 568-2176, on the beachfront road). One of a number of similarly-priced, good restaurants along the waterfront that specialize in seafood, Ines offers shrimp, octopus, and lobster dishes along with Nicaraguan fare in an open-air setting. Open daily, 7 am-9 pm. Credit cards are accepted. For a similar cuisine and experience, neighboring **Restaurante El Buen Gusto**, **El Timón**, and **Brisas del Mar** are also consistently good. Kick back and enjoy the beach views.

Big Wave Dave's ($$, 800 feet south of the Texaco, ☎ 568-2151, bwds@ibw.com.ni). Dave's home cooking is slightly overpriced but popular with expats and surfers, who keep coming back for the chicken pot pies, meatloaf, and fishing tales at the bar. Dave's most popular meal is breakfast, where heaping portions keep surfers and anglers coming back for more. There is a book exchange.

Marie's Bar ($$$, open Tues-Fri, 5:30 pm-late, Sat-Sun, 8:30 am-late). Marie's is a perennial favorite, serving casual international and Nicaraguan food, including sausage, burgers, sandwiches and fries. The food isn't outstanding, but if you miss the taste of home, this is a good choice. Book exchange. German and English spoken.

The Chicken Lady ($, west side of the park). A SJDS institution, this simple one-woman *fritanga* serves up (what else?) roasted chicken and staple side dishes for less than $2. Look for the line of hungry locals, point to what you want, and join the families on the benches in the park to eat. Open evenings only.

There is an **Eskimo** ice cream shop on the beachfront road. Unfortunately, the dingy windows obscure the beach view. Kids can enjoy the indoor playground while they eat their ice cream.

■ DAY-TRIPS FROM SAN JUAN DEL SUR

The beaches south and north of San Juan del Sur are some of Nicaragua's most beautiful and they receive few visitors. Many beaches can be reached by public bus from San Juan del Sur (see *Getting Here & Away*, p 244). The roads are unpaved, and a 4WD vehicle is recommended.

The Pacific Lowlands

> **NOTE:** *During rainy season the roads leading to the beaches south and north of town can be in poor condition or washed out altogether. Check locally for conditions before setting out.*

SOUTH OF TOWN

Many of the **beaches** south of San Juan del Sur are slated for development, so get here while you can. Any of them make a pleasant excursion from SJDS, but during turtle nesting season from July to January, **Refugio de Vida Silvestre La Flor**(page 264) is a must-see for visitors with an interest in wildlife.

Access to the southern beaches is possible by bus, car, or foot. The **bus** from San Juan del Sur to El Ostional (see *Getting Around*, p 245) will drop you off at any of the destinations profiled below; reconfirm the return schedule with the driver. If you're **driving** from San Juan del Sur, reach the beaches by turning south at the bridge at the entrance to town. It is also possible to **walk** to nearby beaches, but bring everything you'll need for the day as there is little in the way of services.

Sleepy **Playa Remanso** today belies what is to come: Remanso Beach Resort is in the development stages, but will contain a yacht club, golf course, hotel, and vacation villas. Playa Remanso is just south of SJDS and is a good beach for **swimming**. There are not yet any services at the beach, but there is a parking area. The walk from SJDS is just a mile or so.

Playa Remanso

A 10-minute drive or a half-hour walk farther south brings you to **Playa Tamarindo**, followed by **Playa Hermosa** (another hour on foot). After Playa Hermosa is **Playa El Yankee** (sometimes spelled El Yanqui), a good spot for surfing. At press time this beach was closed to day-trippers, but follow the signs to the hillside **Cabinas Amaure's** ($$$, no phone) if you want to stay overnight here. Simple doubles run a pricey $50, but meals are included, mitigating the cost.

Playa El Coco

Located 10 miles south of SJDS and just over a mile from La Flor Wildlife Refuge, **Playa El Coco** offers the area's most comfortable accommodation. Though expensive for couples, the bungalows in this area offer good value for families and groups. You're here to enjoy nature, though a few of the bungalows have TV and phone. The beach itself is attractive and secluded, but the surf can be strong, so be careful while swimming.

Coco Cabanas ($$$$, ☎ 278-6045, www.playacococabanas.com, buroj@ibw.com.ni) has four fully-furnished, well-maintained bungalows with a/c, kitchen, and easy access to the beach. Cabins sleep two to five guests and have one ($60) or two ($90) bedrooms with queen-sized beds. Credit cards are accepted, and reservations are strongly encouraged.

© Coco Cabanas

Parque Marítimo el Coco ($$$-$$$$, ☎ 892-0124, www.playaelcoco.com.ni, parquemaritimo@playa elcoco.com.ni) is reminiscent of a summer camp for adults. There is a variety of comfortable house-like bungalows for rent (and for sale) that are located next to the beach. All have private baths and kitchens, and some have a/c. Prices begin at $60; weekends cost sig-

The Pacific Lowlands

nificantly more, and during Semana Santa prices quadruple. Reserve well in advance if you plan to stay during a holiday. **Puesta del Sol**, the on-site restaurant, has good food and specializes in seafood (open daily 8 am-8 pm). A shop carries a small selection of food items at premium prices, but if you plan to cook, bring food with you. Parque Marítimo can arrange **horseback riding** with two days' advance notice and **bikes** are available for rent.

Horseback riding is an option at Parque Marítimo el Coco.

© Parque Marítimo el Coco

The final accessible spot on the road south is the tranquil fishing village of **El Ostional**, which lies beyond La Flor Wildlife Refuge (covered below) at the southern tip of Nicaragua. Though El Ostional is next to the Costa Rican border, it's not legal to cross here. The town is not oriented toward tourism, but you can stop for a meal at **Franco's Bar** and enjoy the beach before making the two-hour bus ride back to San Juan del Sur.

LA FLOR WILDLIFE REFUGE

Located 12 miles south of SJDS just beyond Playa El Coco, La Flor Wildlife Refuge ✩✩✩ is host to a phenomenon seen few other places worldwide: the nesting of endangered **Paslama turtles** (also called Oliver Ridley turtles), which occurs annually July-January at night. The reserve also serves to protect the surrounding tropical dry forest and mangroves (*manglares*), and the wildlife viewing is good. Even if your visit doesn't fall during turtle season, the refuge still makes a worthwhile excursion. The rangers are very knowledgeable about the turtle spawning process, and they are happy to answer questions (Spanish only). Entrance to the reserve costs $10.

Tours to the refuge can be arranged in San Juan del Sur, and this is probably your best bet unless you have your own vehicle. The area is not well developed for tourism (yet), and there is no accommodation in the refuge, but you can **camp** during turtle season for $10 (tents are usually available for rent, and there is an outhouse at the ranger station). Stake your tent beyond the sand in the vegetated area in order not to disturb nesting turtles. Be sure to bring a flashlight for turtle viewing and repellent to combat the hungry swarms of mosquitoes. Paslama turtles generally arrive during rainstorms, so bring a raincoat and sturdy shoes.

Paslama Turtle Nesting

Paslama turtles have migratory habits that induce them to swim large distances between their feeding and spawning habitats, and thousands of the turtles come to La Flor Wildlife Refuge each year to build nests. La Flor is one of the most easily accessible spawning habitats in Nicaragua, and visitors have the unique chance to witness this miracle of nature (the other place to see this occurrence is north of here at Playa Chacocente). The turtles that come to La Flor typically return multiple times during the spawning season.

Each nesting process (called an *arribada* in Spanish) occurs at night and lasts approximately one hour. The turtles begin the process by selecting a nesting site. Each female digs a hole in the sand then proceeds to deposit more than 100 eggs. She covers the eggs, which resemble ping pong balls in shape, color, and size, with sand to protect them from predators. The turtle then

Turtle laying eggs.

returns to the sea, returning once or twice more during the season to repeat the nesting process. The eggs hatch 48 to 52 days after they have been deposited, and visitors delight at seeing the tiny turtles emerge from the next and make their way clumsily to the sea. Only a lucky few make it: the baby turtles are vulnerable on the open sand and are a favorite food of predators, including crabs and birds. Humans are also a threat to sea turtles – the eggs are a coveted food, and rangers at La Flor Wildlife Refuge are vigilant about patrolling the area to ensure that eggs are not poached.

A tiny turtle emerging from its egg in the sand.

The communities that surround the areas where Paslama turtles nest have long relied on the eggs as a source of food and income, however, and an agreement stipulates that 15% of the eggs can be culled for food in an attempt to find a balance between community needs and ecological considerations.

RESPONSIBLE TURTLE VIEWING

The opportunity to see nesting Paslama turtles is a privilege that requires responsible behavior in order to preserve this endangered species.

■ The rangers are knowledgeable about the nesting process; be sure to follow their directions.

■ Don't touch the eggs, turtles, or their nests.

■ Don't use the flash on your camera; it scares turtles and can leave them disoriented.

■ A flashlight can be used to view the turtles, but minimize use whenever possible.

NORTH OF TOWN

To reach the beaches north of SJDS by car, take the road that leads north from next to the Texaco station. The first two beaches aren't accessible from the road, so continue on to **Playa Marsella** – look for the signs on the main road that indicate the access road to the beach, which forks to the left. At press time there was no accommodation available at Marsella, but this may

soon change. The beach isn't the area's most attractive, but it's a nice spot nonetheless; bring snorkel equipment to check out the marine life.

Playa Marsella

Continue along the road to nearby **Playa Maderas**, a popular surf spot. **Camping Matilda** ($-$$$) has spots for camping right on the sand ($3.50 for a site, $4 including tent rental). A dorm bed costs $8. There are also two doubles ($40) and one triple with private bath and

The Pacific Lowlands

fan. Private rooms are not great value, but surfers may consider the proximity to the waves to be worth it. Breakfast is available, but for other meals you'll either need to cook in Matilda's small kitchen or head into town.

Return to the point in the road where you forked left to reach Marsella and Maderas and take the right fork to reach **Bahía Majagual**. This beach, seven miles north of SJDS (taxis cost about $12), is a beautiful spot that is popular with surfers who come to enjoy the fine sands and the **Bahía Majagual Ecolodge** ($$$-$$$$, majagual@ibw.com.ni). The guesthouse is in a rustic

© Bahia Majagual Lodge

setting and is well-loved by backpackers, who come for the dorm ($6 per bed), the beach location, and the myriad activities. Cabins have mismatched décor, fan, private bath, and thin mattresses and can sleep two ($35) to six ($75) guests. Camping is also available. The guesthouse has plenty of rentals available for adventure activities: surfboards, boogie boards, fishing equipment, and snorkels. Horseback riding can also be arranged. There is no phone at the lodge, so get in touch with them by email. Dollars and traveler's checks are accepted; double-check your bill. Ask them about transportation to the guesthouse from the market in SJDS ($4).

Just beyond Bahía Majagual is the exclusive **Morgan's Rock Ecolodge** ☆☆☆ ($$$$, ☎ 296-9442, www.morgans rock.com). A destination in itself, Morgan's Rock sets the standard for eco-

© Morgan's Rock Ecolodge

lodges in Nicaragua and, indeed, Central America. This model of sustainable tourism is a splurge not to be missed. Guests occupy 15 well-appointed bungalows that have private balconies and views of the beach be-

low. Beautiful hardwood is used throughout, including locally-made teak furniture. Each bungalow has a king-sized bed plus a sofa bed. Though you may be tempted to spend

© Morgan's Rock Ecolodge

most of your time on the beach, don't miss the variety of activities that are available, including kayaking and fishing. Some of the most innovative tours focus on the sustainable practices of the hotel, including reforestation and organic food growing. Prices vary significantly based on time of year (see their website for specifics), but average $200 for a double, which includes three delicious meals per day and all domestic drinks. Morgan's Rock does not allow day visitors. Make reservations in advance.

THE TOLA BEACHES

Just beyond Morgan's Rock Ecolodge the road turns inland at the village of Brito. The road leads to Tola and continues on to the half-moons of sand collectively known as the Tola Beaches. The secluded area includes little-visited beaches known for great waves and **Refugio de Vida Silvestre Río Escalante Chacocente** (see page 272). The area is a challenge to access, but intrepid travelers won't be disappointed by the secluded stretches of sand, many of which are slated for imminent development.

The Pacific Lowlands

> **TIP:** *If you take a taxi to one of the Tola Beaches, be sure to arrange a pickup for the return trip; taxis are rarely available in the beach communities.*

Though the stretch of beaches here continues north from Morgan's Rock Ecolodge, the beaches are actually most easily accessed from Rivas, six miles distant. The stretch of road from Rivas to Tola is paved but, beyond Tola and up the coast, a 4WD vehicle is needed, especially during the rainy season. Using your own vehicle (or hiring private transport) is a prerequisite for visiting the beaches in the area; bus travel is not really an option here because the beaches are well away from the bus route.

Playa Gigante

There isn't any reason to linger in the farming village of **Tola**, so continue on to the real reason you came this far: the beaches. **Playa Gigante** is the first beach you come to and it doesn't disappoint. This beautiful stretch of sand is rarely visited by day-trippers, except during Semana Santa, though there are usually a few stalls selling Nica snacks. You can **camp** for free. If you're tempted to catch some waves, you can stay at **Giant's Foot Surf Camp** (www.giantsfoot.com). Guests are housed in one of two adjacent lodges; rooms are serviceable but nothing special and have a/c and private bath. There is plenty of communal space, and guests can use free movies, books, and board games.

© www.giantsfoot.com

Rooms are available for $100 per night including breakfast, and **Spanish classes** are available for $10 per hour. A week-long package including airport transfers, surfing, lodging, and meals costs $1,050.

Though it's not yet overtly obvious, the area north of Playa Gigante is rapidly becoming coveted by the international set, and the first evidence you may see of this is **Playa Iguana**, which may have a golf course by the time you visit, and further north at **Rancho Santana** (www.ranchosantana.com), a new, upscale Florida-style residential project.

Just north of the development's gates are the surfer haunts of **Guasacate** and **Popoyo**. Popoyo is known as one of the best places to surf in Nicaragua, and neighboring Guasacate is home to the upscale, 14-acre **Popoyo Surf Camp** ☆☆ ($$$$, www.surfnicaragua.com). Rooms are situated in well-maintained casitas that have tiled floors, private bath, and a/c, and the property has a pool and manicured grounds. A huge common room has a ping pong table and billiards as well as a big screen TV perpetually showing (what else?) surf videos from the camp's large collection of movies. Meals are served in an enor-

© Popoyo Surf Camp

mous new *rancho.* Packages are available that include accommodation, meals, and activities; check out the camp's website for info and great local surfing photos. Make reservations in advance at this popular spot (credit cards are accepted when booking in advance, but not on-site).

There is also accommodation at the next beach, **Playa Conejo**. **Hotel Punta Teonoste** ☆☆ ($$$, ☎ 884-8777,

The Pacific Lowlands

© Hotel Punta Teonoste

www.puntateonoste.com, info@puntateonoste.com) has nine attractive and up-scale thatched-roof beach-side bungalows with private bath. There's also a nice bar. There are a variety of activities offered through the hotel, including turtle-viewing trips to **Chacocente**. A spa will soon be open. **Surfboards** and **bikes** can be rented. There is a good **restaurant** on-site.

Beat the heat in the nearby village of **Las Salinas** (3.6 miles from Hotel Punta Teonoste), where you can take a dip in the **hot springs** (40¢), which have been encompassed by cement, diminishing their attractiveness. The road is paved from Las Salinas to Managua, a nice change after the area's rough roads. **El Astillero** is the next town you'll reach, and there is a pretty beach here. Good news for independent travelers: El Astillero has **bus** service to and from Managua. **Bar Miramar** is a good stop for cold drinks and great seafood, but at press time there was no accommodation available. It's just a few miles from here to Chacocente Wildlife Refuge.

REFUGIO CHACOCENTE

Chacocente, which along with La Flor Wildlife Refuge (see p 265) is one of the most important nesting areas for endangered **paslama turtles**. The reserve, which consists of tropical dry forest fringed by a beautiful beach, is accessible by 4WD. There is no public transportation available. This is a secluded spot that receives few visitors, and there is no accommodation available at the reserve, though you can camp for free. Bring any supplies you might need as there are no services available. Entry costs $4.50.

León & Chinandega

LEÓN

León is Nicaragua's intellectual capital as well as one of its most attractive cities. Step back in time as you explore the colorful streets lined with colonial buildings. León undeniably has an authenticity that is slowly diminishing in Granada. It has a number of beautiful churches, most notably the impressive cathedral, which is not only a UNESCO heritage site but also Central America's largest church. A number of local cultural sites are also worth visiting, and the city's large number of students gives it a lively atmosphere.

Given the number of cultural and adventure activities here, León sees fewer foreign visitors than you'd expect. Travelers arriving in the searing months of March and April may understand why but, if you time it right, this is also one of the best times of year to visit the city due to some of Nicaragua's most colorful Semana Santa celebrations. At any time of year, plan to spend at least three days exploring the sights and sounds of the city and its surroundings.

León Highlights

- La Catedral
- Semana Santa (in March or April)
- Museo de Tradiciones y Leyendas
- An excursion to Volcán Cerro Negro

■ HISTORY

León has a long history that is intimately intertwined with the history of Nicaragua as a whole. The original city of León was established in 1524 by Francisco Hernandez de Córdoba 18 miles east of the present site. After the devastating 1610 eruption of Volcán Momotombo, just a few miles distant, city residents decided

The Pacific Lowlands

Colorful buildings in Subtiava, a city neighborhood.

to uproot and move to another location to prevent any further loss of life and property to an eruption. The new town was established adjacent to the village of **Subtiava**, and as the towns grew they became increasingly intertwined (Subtiava is now a neighborhood of the city). As León's prominence increased, so did its power, and the city became home of the national government. Ongoing scuffles between the Liberal León and the Conservative Granada led to a compromise that moved the **capital** to Managua in 1852. Though León lost its status as capital, it retained its staunchly leftist leanings through the events of the 20th century.

León was a major thorn in the side of **General Somoza García**, who retaliated by burning parts of the city center and assassinating Liberal hero **Augusto Sandino**. Somoza García himself was executed in León in 1956. *Leónesas* were strong supporters of the **Sandinistas** throughout the next few decades, despite intense discouragement by **Somoza Debayle**, son of Somoza García; his methods included dispatching the National Guard and bombing the city in an effort to quench the Liberals. The Sandinistas retook the city and held it until the Somoza government fell. To this day León retains its Liberal roots and evidence of the city's history can be seen at many local cultural sights.

INTERNET RESOURCES: www.leononline.net

■ GETTING HERE

By Car: The road from Managua to León is in good condition and the drive takes 1½ hours. Car rental is available in León at Hotel El Convento, Hotel Austria, and local travel agencies.

By Taxi: Taxis from Managua cost approximately $65 one-way.

By Bus: León's **main bus terminal** is 1.2 miles northwest of the city center. Trucks waiting at the station serve as buses for a few cords, or take a taxi for C10 (65¢). A second small bus station serving Las Peñitas and Poneloya is at **El Mercadito** in Barrio Subtiava, a long walk or a quick taxi ride (65¢) from the center.

Ordinario buses go back and forth between **Managua**'s Mercado Israel Lewites and León's main terminal every half-hour from 4 am-6:30 pm. **Express** minibuses (recommended) leave **Managua**'s La UCA station every half-hour or when full (1½ hrs/$1.70). The easiest way to get to **Granada** is to take an express minivan to Managua's La UCA station and change there for a second express minivan to Granada (2½ hrs total); there are no direct buses. For

The Pacific Lowlands

Chinandega and **Corinto**, *ordinario* buses leave every 15 minutes from 4:30 am-6 pm (1 hr 15 minutes/70¢); **express** buses also leave frequently. **Express** buses go to **Matagalpa** at 4:25 am and 2:45 pm ($2.50). Express buses leave for **Estelí** at 5:20 am and 3:10 pm ($2.50). One bus leaves daily at 4:45 am for the Honduran border at **El Guasale** (2 hrs/$2.60). For the **El Espino** crossing into Honduras one bus leaves daily at 12:40pm (2 hrs/$2.60).

From **El Mercadito**, buses leave at least once per hour until late afternoon for **Poneloya** and **Las Peñitas** (45 minutes/60¢).

International luxury coaches leave daily from their own stops for **San José**, **Panama City**, **San Salvador**, **Choluteca**, **Tegucigalpa**, **San Salvador**, **San Pedro Sula**, and **Tapachula**. Contact the local branches of **Transnica** (☎ 311-5219, www.transnica.com) and **Ticabus** (☎ 311-6153) for schedules.

■ GETTING AROUND

On Foot: León is primarily flat and pleasant for walking. March and April bring soaring temperatures, making taxis a better option.

By Taxi: Plenty of taxis ply the streets for passengers, a welcome sight when the temperatures are up. Within town, taxis cost C10 (65¢), C15 (90¢) at night. **Radio Taxi** (☎ 311-1043) has on-call taxis available, and they can be rented for day-trips or sightseeing around town.

■ SERVICES

TOURS & INFORMATION: Intur (☎ 341-0058) is 2½ blocks north of Parque Ruben Dario. More convenient is **Cámara de Turismo** (☎ 341-0058), an office just north of the northeast side of the park that is run by tourism students from UNAN. Bus schedules and brochures are available, and basic English is spoken.

Professional **Va Pues Tours** (on the north side of Iglesia El Laborío, ☎ 606-2276, www.vapues.com, info@vapues.com) offers cultural and outdoor trips to nearby cities, cultural sites, and volcanoes. Airport transfers are also available.

Non-profit **Quetzaltrekkers** (☎ 311-6695, 1½ blocks east of Iglesia La Recolección, www.quetzaltrekkers.com) is staffed by international volunteers and runs trips to nearby volcanoes, including volcano boarding,

© Quetzaltrekkers

camping, and full-moon hikes. A hike to Isla Juan Venado, with a night of camping and the opportunity to view nesting turtles in season, costs $37. Even if you don't plan to take a trip, stop by the office for advice on local nightlife and things to do in town.

Buy **plane tickets** at professionally-run **Viajes Mundiales** (☎ 311-5920, rdavila@ibw.com.ni), which you'll find three blocks north and a half-block east of the northeast corner of the park. A second branch is a block south and a block west of Intur.

MONEY: Banks cluster around a corner a block north of the back side of the cathedral. **BAC** has an **ATM** and changes traveler's checks (Viajes Mundiales travel agency does so as well, but at a ridiculously high 10% commission). **Western Union** is two blocks north of the entrance street to Iglesia El Calvario.

INTERNET: The city has perhaps the largest concentration of Internet connections in Nicaragua thanks to the local student population; you'll find one on almost every corner on the east side of the park. Most places charge 60¢/hr; look for one with air-conditioning. One of the city's best is **Cyberfast**, three blocks north of Parque Ruben Dario, which has a/c, **passport photos**, **photocopies**, and **CD burning**. Open Mon-Sat 8 am-9 pm and Sun 8 am-1 pm.

The Pacific Lowlands

MAIL & TELEPHONE: Send off your postcards at the **post office** across from Iglesia La Recolección. You can make international calls from the multitudes of Internet cafés, or head to **Enitel** on the western edge of the park or at the main bus station.

MEDICAL: The so-so **hospital** (☎ 311-6990) couldn't be more convenient: it's a block south of the park. Unless it's a night or weekend emergency, go to a private clinic instead: **Policlinica La Fraternidad** (☎ 311-1403) and **Policlínica Occidental** (☎ 311-2722) face each other and are conveniently-two blocks north and a half-block west of the park.

STAYING SAFE: The center of the city is very safe, though it's a good idea to walk with a friend at night. The **police** can be reached at ☎ 311-3137 and the **fire department** at ☎ 311-2323.

MARKETS: There is a very good, centrally located **La Union** supermarket on the same block as the movie theater. Open Mon-Sat 7:30 am-8 pm and Sun 8 am-6 pm. Not as comprehensive but convenient if you're staying on the west side of town, **Supermercado Salman** is three blocks west of Iglesia La Merced. The city has several **markets**, though there isn't much for tourists; the most convenient and interesting is the *Mercado Central*. The market is behind the cathedral. Other markets include **La Terminal** (at the main bus station) and **El Mercadito** in Subtiava.

■ SIGHTSEEING

Every listing in this book is recommended and considered above average in its category. Listings with one star (☆) are highly recommended. Those earning two stars (☆☆) are considered worthy of a detour. A few places have three stars (☆☆☆), which means you should make every effort to see them.

León is packed with beautiful churches, most of them an easy, if hot, walk from the center of town. Try to plan

Opposite: Doorway, León

León

N
HUNTER PUBLISHING

1. Bigfoot Hostel
2. Hotel Posada del Doctor
3. Hotel San Juan de León
4. Hotel Colonial
5. Hotel Flor de Sacuanjoche
6. Hotel El Convento
7. Hotel Los Balcones
8. Hotel America
9. Hotel Austria
10. Museo de Leyendas Y Tradiciones
11. Casa Museo Rubén Darío
12. Heroes Y Matires Monument
13. Ruinas de San Sebástian
14. Viajes Mundiales
15. La Union
16. El Sesteo
17. Quetzal Trekkers
18. Tip Top
19. Panaderia El Leoncito
20. El Divino Castigo
21. Eskimo
22. Subway

© 2007 HUNTER PUBLISHING, INC

AVENIDA CENTRAL

Iglesia de San Juan
Old Train Station
Market
Park
Comedor Lucia
Internet
Iglesia El Calvari
Iglesia La Recolección
Cámara de Turismo
Catedral de León
Iglesia de La Merced
Park Central
Iglesia San Francisco
Parque Rubén Darío
Cyberfast
Kodak
Cyber Link
Supermercado Salman
TO SUBTIAVA AND PONELOYA BUSES
Iglesia El Labario
Rio Chinandeca
Not to Scale

1 Av. NO
4 CALLE NO
2 Av. NO
3 CALLE NO
2 CALLE NO
1 CALLE NO
3 Av. NO
4 Av. NO
5 Av. NO
6 Av. SO
CALLE CENTRAL
CALLE JOSE DE MARCOLETA
2 CALLE SO
3 Av. SO
4 Av. SO
3 CALLE SO
1 CALLE SE
2 CALLE SE
3 CALLE SE
H

your sightseeing for the morning or late afternoon to avoid the stifling mid-afternoon heat.

A WALKING TOUR

Everything can feasibly be viewed in an afternoon if you're pressed for time, but you'll likely want to take more time to explore.

Crowds milling around Parque Central, dominated by the cathedral.

The Pacific Lowlands

Parque Central is an attractive, well-loved gathering spot where you can enjoy views of the gorgeous **cathedral** ☆☆☆, Central America's largest. It was not the city's first. The current structure replaced the original diminutive cathedral, which was burned to the ground in 1685 by bandits. With León's proximity to seismic activity, building a sturdy structure was essential. An architect and two friars from Guatemala, also a hotbed of earthquake activity, designed the new one. The vast size and interior attention to detail meant that it took many years to build and, though the first stone was laid in 1747, it was not completed until 1860 (though Mass was held regularly at the construction site after 40 years of building had taken place). The bell tower was

added in 1905. Don't miss the chance to view the interior of the church as it represents some of Nicaragua's

finest design. Seventeenth-century paintings adorn the walls, and there is a statue of Christ carved from ivory along with the 12 apostles. The cathedral is the burial place of renowned poet **Rubén Darío** (1867-1916). Two other poets are also buried here, **Alfonso Cortés** and **Saloman de la Selva**. Heading back outside, you'll see the house of the **archbishop**, which faces the south side of the cathedral.

> **TIP:** *While León's churches are fascinating to visit any time of year, the best time to see them is during* **Semana Santa***, or Holy Week, which occurs annually during the week preceding Easter.* **Processions** *fill the streets, culminating in more than a dozen solemn groups of the faithful parading through the streets on Sunday. Each procession carries a* **paso***, a sculpture that depicts one of the most important events in the life of Jesus, from his arrival in Jerusalem until his resurrection. While March and April, the months during which Semana Santa occurs, are hot and dry in León, visiting at this time is worth it.*

Across the street from the north side of the cathedral you'll see a monument to the **Heróes y Mátires**, the Heroes and Martyrs. The monument is surrounded by murals. More **murals** can be seen across the street and slightly north (the artist certainly had a sense of humor: one of the murals depicts Sandino stomping on the heads of Somoza and Uncle Sam).

Walk a block north of here to see the home of León's patron saint, the Virgen de las Mercedes: **Iglesia La Merced**. An original La Merced church was built in León Viejo; when the town moved, the church was rebuilt in 1615. It didn't last long, however; it was burned to the ground in 1685 and twice rebuilt. The church is currently in need of restoration, but take a look at the ornate interior.

From here you can walk two blocks west to the **Casa de Cultura**, an artistic and cultural space. Stop in to find out about any upcoming events and peruse the permanent display of political paintings. Open Mon-Fri 8 am-noon and 2-6 pm.

Go south at the next corner (to the left) and on your left you'll see **Hotel El Convento**, the city's finest lodging, shown below. Stop in to see the historic common areas, and consider getting lunch at the restaurant there. Details about the history of the building can be found in *Where to Stay*, p 292.

A half-block south and a half-block west of the hotel you'll come upon **Casa Museo Rubén Darío** (☎ 311-2388), a museum that commemorates the life of Nicaragua's most revered poet. Darío lived in the house with his aunt and uncle until he was a teenager and some of his original works and mementos are on display. After Darío's family moved out, another poet, **Alfonso Cortés**, lived here. He experienced a mental breakdown while living in the house. He died in the house in 1969 and was buried in the cathedral. Even if you don't have a particular interest in poetry, the house is still worth a visit to see what an average home of a fairly comfortable family looked like during the 1800s. The museum is open Tues-Sat 8 am-noon and 2-5 pm; Sun 8 am-noon. A donation of $1 is suggested.

Backtrack from here a half-block, then head south a half-block to reach **Centro de Arte Ortiz-Guardián** (centrodearte@hotelelconvento.com.ni), a beautiful space that houses nicely-presented local and international paintings and other artwork. Open Tues-Sat 11:30 am-6:30 pm and Sun 11 am-7 pm.

From here it's a block south and a block east to see **El Teatro Municipal** (☎ 311-1788). Check the performance schedule at the theater or take a tour of the refurbished building, open 8 am-12:30 pm and 2-5 pm.

Two blocks south and 1½ blocks east of the theater are the **Museo de Leyendas y Tradiciones** ☆☆ and the **Ruinas de San Sebastián**. The museum details the legends and traditions of Nicaragua. Eerily, the building

The Pacific Lowlands

Mosaics at the Museo de Leyendas y Tradiciones.

itself was a **jail** with torture equipment. Even if the museum isn't open when you are touring, stop by to see the mosaics that depict Nicaraguan stories in the courtyard, which is accessible even when the museum is closed. Open daily 8 am-noon and 2 to 5 pm.

Directly across the street are the **Ruinas de San Sebastián**, the ruins of San Sebastián church. Built in 1742, the church was bombed in 1979 during Somoza's attempts to quell the city's Sandinista struggles. The ruins can be accessed at any time.

From here, you can walk several blocks north back to the center of town or, if time and energy permit, there are still several sights around the city that you shouldn't miss. The 18th-century **Iglesia El Calvario**, four blocks east of the cathedral, is one of León's most-photographed sights. The brightly-painted church is a blend of French and Spanish architecture and the building was restored six years ago.

© Va Pues Tours

Though León doesn't have a particularly strong economy, **Universidad Nacional Autónoma de Nicaragua**, the country's first university, is the city's lifeblood. The only building really worth seeing is the original structure two blocks north of the park. The rest of UNAN's buildings are dispersed throughout the city and many are downright unattractive.

Two blocks east of UNAN is **Iglesia La Recolección**, recognizable by its bright yellow paint. This Baroque-style church was built in 1786 and has a beautiful interior.

Take a taxi or a 20-minute walk to **Barrio Subtiava**, a traditionally indigenous neighborhood that was once a separate town. Though the area today doesn't look markedly different from the rest of León, there are ruins and a cathedral. **La Catedral de Subtiava** was finished in 1710. The polytheistic locals were not especially interested in attending church, much to the consternation of the Spanish. In an effort to increase church attendance, several symbols considered religious by the local community were added to the church interior, including a **sun carving**. While these additions did increase attendance, they did not necessary succeed in creating belief in a single god.

Across the street you'll find the **Museo Adiact** (☎ 311-5371), a homely little place that houses ancient artifacts from the area. The museum is open Mon-Fri 8 am-noon and 2-5 pm; Sat 8 am-noon. A donation of $1 is suggested. Another related sight is **El Tamarindón**, a tamarind tree three blocks south and two blocks west of the church. This 310-year-old tree is where **Adiac**, a well-respected Subtiavan chief, was hanged. The tree is an object of community pride representing the spirit of independence embodied by Adiac. Near here you'll also pass the **ruins** (*ruinas*) of Subtiava's first church, built in the 16th century.

■ ADVENTURES

ADVENTURES ON FOOT

Volcano Climbing & Boarding

The stark black **Volcán Cerro Negro** is simultaneously eerie and beautiful. The volcano, born in 1850, is the newest in Nicaragua. It is an easy half-hour ride from León and is one of the area's most accessible climbs. **Va Pues Tours** (on the north side of Iglesia El Laborío, ☎ 606-2276, www.vapues.com, info@vapues.com) and **Bigfoot Hostel** (a block east and a block south of

Iglesia La Recolección, ☎ 645-8552) run **volcano boarding** ☆☆ trips as well as **hiking excursions**. **Quetzaltrekkers** (☎ 311-6695, 1½ blocks east of Iglesia La Recolección, www. quetzaltrekkers.com), a non-profit organization started in Guatemala, also runs good **hiking trips** staffed by international volunteers, and their profits go toward supporting a

© Va Pues Tours

home for needy children. Cerro Negro is covered in loose volcanic rock. Though the hike is short, it can be slippery and there is no shade. Wear long pants if you are going volcano boarding, and bring water with you; there are no services near the volcano.

Adventures, including overnight **camping trips**, can be arranged to other nearby volcanoes, including **Telica**, **Mombotombo**, and **San Cristóbal**, through **Va Pues** and **Quetzaltrekkers**.

The Pacific Lowlands

VOLCANO CAUTIONS

The Los Maribios range, which includes all of the area's volcanoes, is highly active. As a result, visiting the volcanoes via a tour instead of independently is highly recommended. While visiting any active volcano carries some risk, a knowledgeable guide is strongly recommended for safety purposes. Volcán Cerro Negro, which last erupted in 1999, is predicted to erupt again at any time. It erupted three times in the 1990s, generally giving ample advance warning in the form of rumbling and shaking. If you experience these signs during your visit, leave the area immediately.

CULTURAL ADVENTURES

Metropolitana Spanish School (a half-block west of Iglesia El Calvario, ☎ 311-1235, www.metropolitana-ss.com), offers 20 hours of class plus a week-long homestay for $195. Optional afternoon activities include dance classes, visits to local organizations, and beach excursions. If you prefer a private teacher, **Ileana Vargas** (☎ 827-4626, www.clases-de-espanol.com) gets good reviews from students. If it's **French**, not Spanish, you're after, **Alianza Francesa** (☎ 311-0126, afleón@ibw.com.ni) is a half-block north of Iglesia La Recolección; 11 weeks of classes cost $375.

Quetzaltrekkers (☎ 311-6695, 1½ blocks east of Iglesia La Recolección, www.quetzaltrekkers.com) seeks volunteers to staff their office and to lead volcano hikes. Volunteers have the option of living in their convivial

© Quetzaltrekkers

on-site volunteer house for $75/month. **Las Tías**, affiliated with Quetzaltrekkers, accepts Spanish-speaking volunteers for a minimum of two months to work with underprivileged children.

■ SHOPPING

The streets surrounding the movie theater are dotted with small **clothing boutiques**; due to the number of students seeking up-to-date fashions, this area is one of the better places in Nicaragua to buy clothes. **Café Ben Linder** (☎ 311-0548) sells a few handicrafts and coffee two blocks north of the northwest corner of the park. **Cocinarte** (☎ 311-8784), facing the north side of Iglesia, also sells crafts. There are many bookstores around town (most with more office supplies than books), but very few have reading selections in English. The best of the bunch is **Librería Don Quixote** (1½ blocks west of the northwest corner of the park), which has a few books in English. Open Mon-Sat 8 am-7 pm. **Kodak** is a block south of Intur.

■ ENTERTAINMENT & NIGHTLIFE

Catch a **baseball game** with 8,000 of your closest friends at **Estadio Heróes y Mátires de Septiembre** on the northwest edge of town (take a taxi). The baseball season runs Oct-Jan and admission costs $1.75-$4. If you'd rather play than watch, practice your Spanish by joining one of the impromptu games of **basketball** that happen most nights at Parque Ruben Dario. If you'd rather escape the heat and catch a movie, the air-conditioned **movie theater** is on the east side of La Union supermarket. Movies, usually American flicks with Spanish subtitles, cost $3.60. The current schedule can be found at www.leónonline.net/top/cine.html. **El Teatro Municipal** (☎ 311-1788) has occasional performances. Even if you can't see a show, stop by for a tour of the theater, which is a block south of the southwest corner of the park.

When night falls, dancers head to **Dilectus** ☆ (☎ 341-1836), at the southern entrance to the city at Km 130 of the Pan American Highway. This disco attracts a well-heeled local crowd as well as a smattering of tourists willing to pay for its expensive drinks and $5.50 cover charge. Parking is available, and the disco is open Wed-Sun until the wee hours; there is sometimes live music. Closer to the center, **El Divino Castigo**, a block north of the main UNAN building, is a bar with good atmosphere. The house the bar is in has an interesting history; find the table that tells the story through old newspaper articles. If you can't get enough of the city's history, dance at **Las Ruinas**, in the ruins of a bombed building that overlooks Parque Ruben Dario. Neighboring **Bar El Alamo** has better views than any bar in town (if the creaky building doesn't scare you away, that is).

If you're craving conversation in English, **Vía Vía** (a half-block east and a half-block north of the movie theater) plies travelers with drinks and music daily until midnight. If you want a ride to your nightlife destination of choice, or just want to enjoy the atmosphere, hop on the **party bus** that leaves from the west side of the park on Sat and Sun evenings until around 9:30 pm; the train makes a loop around town, to the delight of the multitudes of families riding it.

■ WHERE TO STAY

León has a good selection of quality accommodations for the traveler. Be advised that it's worth splurging for air-conditioning in March, April, and early May.

HOTEL PRICE CHART	
Cost per night for two people, before tax	
$	Up to $15
$$	$16-$30
$$$	$31-$60
$$$$	Over $60

> **IMPORTANT:** *Multiple hotels and restaurants accept credit cards. However, as most of them are independent establishments with limited communications systems, many of which are serviced by generators only, traveling without enough cash for a few days' food and hotel is strongly discouraged as sometimes credit card service isn't available.*

Every listing in this book is recommended and considered above average in its category. Listings with one star (☆) are highly recommended, those earning two stars (☆☆) are considered to be exceptional. A few resorts and restaurants rate three stars (☆☆☆), which means they are worthy of a special occasion splurge.

☆☆ **Hotel El Convento** ($$$$, two blocks west and a half-block north of the northwest corner of the park, ☎ 311-7052, www.hotelelconvento.com.ni, informacion@hotelelconvento.com.ni). León's most luxurious hotel is a step back in time in the best possible way: the rooms and common areas have been painstakingly restored to create a colonial ambience to match the origi-nal building, a con-

© Hotel El Convento

vent completed in 1693. After religious groups were expelled from Nicaragua in 1830 the building changed hands and was eventually destroyed in 1960. Since that time, the building has been reconstructed to its original splendor. Rooms are well-priced and come with Saltillo tile floors, private bath with hot water, a/c, in-room phone, and cable TV. Singles cost $68.50, dou-bles $87, and suites $111. Rates include breakfast. The only thing missing at El Convento is a pool. Even if you don't stay here, stop by to admire the antiques in the common areas and to take advantage of the restaurant ($$-$$$$), which has a European flair and indoor and outdoor seating areas.

© Hotel Los Balcones

☆☆ **Hotel Los Balcones** ($$$, two blocks east and a block north of the cathedral, ☎ 311-0250, www.hotelbal cones.com, balcones@ibw. com.ni). The 20 rooms at the quaint colonial-style Los Balcones are attractively furnished and have dark wood accents and mosaic til-ing. The property has an at-tractive garden and colorful bar and restaurant with well-prepared Nicaraguan and international dishes. Each room has private bath with hot water, a/c, and cable TV. Breakfast is included and tours are available.

☆☆ **Hotel La Posada del Doctór** ($$$, 1½ blocks west of Iglesia San Juan, ☎ 311-4343). This cozy oasis has 10 impeccably clean rooms with small private baths, and good mattresses in some rooms and foam mattresses in others (check before selecting a room). Doubles cost $45 with fan or $55 with a/c. Check your

email in the beautiful, spacious garden area using the hotel's free wireless Internet. Private parking is available, and an attractive conference room is frequently used for weddings and banquets. Breakfast is included; cook lunch or dinner in the colorful kitchen.

Casa Colonial ($, 1½ blocks west of Iglesia San Juan, ☎ 311-3178). Tiny Casa Colonial represents excellent value and is popular with Peace Corps volunteers. The tidy garden area is lush and there is communal TV with cable. The five small rooms are quiet and have fan and private bath with hot water. Singles cost $10, doubles $15. Make a reservation; the guesthouse is often full.

Hostal La Casa Leonesa ($$$, a block north and a half-block east of Iglesia La Merced, ☎ 311-0551, www.

lacasaleonesa. com). This family-run property has small, cozy rooms with Old World furnishings, hot or cold water private bath, a/c or fan, and cable TV. The doors on some bathrooms are saloon-type swinging doors; ask for another room if you want additional privacy. The three rooms downstairs that edge the courtyard are nicer and more spacious than the rooms upstairs. Doubles cost $45 ($55 with hot water and a/c). There is a small pool and a pleasant sitting room.

Hotel Austria ($$$, a block south and a half-block west of the cathedral, ☎ 311-1206, www.hotelaustria.com. ni, haustria@ibw.com.ni). Austria is impeccably clean and well-maintained even though the furnishings are on the frumpy side. Rooms have private bath with hot shower, a/c, in-room phone, and cable TV. Wireless Internet is available for an additional fee. Suites sleep up to three guests and have minibars and tubs. The 24 rooms ($55 double) and two suites ($65 double) are often booked, so make a reservation in advance. **Car rental** and laundry service are available.

Solo travelers may want to consider staying in a hostel **dorm**. **Vía Vía** (☎ 311-6142) and **Bigfoot Hostel** (☎ 45-8552, www.bigfoot adventure.com) both have dorm beds for $4. Also, the folks at Hostel Oasis in Granada

© www.BigFootAdventure.com

Looking down on the garden at Bigfoot Hostel.

have opened a new hostel in a colonial building across from La Union supermarket. It's called **Lazy Bones** (☎ 311-3472, www.lazybonesleon.com) and has the same superb amenities as the Granada branch. The beds at Vía Vía and Bigfoot are basic, so if you want to stay in a dorm, check into Lazy Bones.

■ WHERE TO EAT

☆☆ **Restaurante El Sesteo** ($$$-$$$$, on the north side of Parque Central, ☎ 311-5327). This historic restaurant has some of the best people-watching in town and good upscale, traditional food to boot. The thick, fruity *licuados* are some of the best in the city. Diners can sit indoors or in the small park-side seating area. Open daily 8 am-9:30 pm.

DINING PRICE CHART	
Price per person for an entrée, not including beverage, tax or tip	
$	Up to $3
$$	$3-$6
$$$	$6-$10
$$$$	Over $10

☆☆ **Restaurante Taquezal** ($$$-$$$$, a half-block west of the southwest corner of the park, ☎ 311-2282). This upscale, dinner-only place has some of the best steak in town and also prepares delicious seafood. Main courses run $6-10. There is often live local music on weekends. Open Mon-Sat 6 pm-2 am.

You won't find better Nica food at any price than at **El Buen Gusto** ☆ ($), a scrappy *fritanga* 2½ blocks west of the southwest corner of the park. Just point to what you want from the steaming pots. Veggie options are always available and a filling meal will set you back less than $3. Open Mon-Sat for lunch and dinner.

Cocinarte ($$, facing the north side of Iglesia El Laborío, ☎ 311-8784). This new place has good international food and a variety of veggie options. Give the watery cocktails a miss. Open daily 11 am-10 pm.

Restaurante Italian Pizza ($$$, a half-block north of the northeastern corner of the park, ☎ 311-0657). This restaurant does quite good pizza, but if you need a change of pace, come here for the **Middle Eastern** dishes, a particularly good option for vegetarians. Service is good and meals average $8. Open Mon-Sat 9 am-9 pm.

Puerto Café Benjamin Linder ($, a block north of the northwest corner of the park, ☎ 311-0548). This relaxed, socially-conscious spot has simple fare like healthy sandwiches and organic coffee. Open daily 8 am-midnight.

Restaurante Flor de Sacuanjoche ($$-$$$, two blocks north and a half-block west of the park, ☎ 311-1121).

Your food will be there before you can figure out how to pronounce the name of this restaurant, but the atmosphere is pleasant and the service good. International and Nicaraguan food is served, along with several veggie options. Open daily 10 am-midnight.

There are a couple of fast food places in town if you're in the mood for a quick bite. **Tip Top** ($-$$, next to the movie theater, ☎ 311-7086) is a clean, efficient chicken joint that has surprisingly good food. **Subway** ($-$$), just north of Hotel El Convento, makes American-style sandwiches daily from 10 am-10 pm.

Laid-back and perpetually popular **Vía Vía** ($$, two blocks west and 1½ blocks north of the park, ☎ 311-6142, www.viaviacafe.com) has remarkably slow service but good international food, including pasta and sandwiches. If you get tired of waiting, head across the street to **Comedor Lucía** ($, ☎ 311-4932), which is primarily frequented for its inexpensive *comida corriente* and breakfasts.

White House Pizza ($$, facing Iglesia La Recolección, ☎ 311-7010). One of the few places open until late evening, White House has nine types of mediocre pizza in five sizes, including by the slice. There is a small playground for kids, and free delivery is available. Open daily 10 am-10 pm.

For **snacking**, **Panadería El Leoncito** (☎ 311-1270, two blocks west of the southwest corner of the cathedral) has a good selection of **pastries** for 40¢. There is an **Eskimo** ice cream shop two blocks east of the cathedral and another in the La Union supermarket, neither of which have seating.

■ DAY-TRIPS FROM LEÓN

LEÓN VIEJO

This UNESCO World Heritage Site encompasses the **ruins** of the original town of León, established in 1526. Abandoned by the villagers after a series of earthquakes, the site was covered in ash, which helped pre-

The Pacific Lowlands

serve it until it was first excavated in 1966. International and local researchers have since explored the site and reconstructed some of the buildings' foundations, giving an interesting look back in history. Entry costs $2 plus an additional $1.50 to take photographs. ☎ 886-2087.

Reaching the site on your own is inconvenient as there are only a couple of buses per day; a tour from León is a better option. If you want to go on your own, take a bus to the town of La Paz Centro. There are two morning buses from there to the ruins; the last bus leaves the ruins in mid-afternoon. Guides, some of whom speak basic English, are available at the ruins.

LOS HERVIDEROS DE SAN JACINTO

Deep within Volcán Telica, air and moisture are heated and they escape through the earth's surface at the village of San Jacinto. The resulting boiling mud pots are worth the effort of getting here, but watch your step,

particularly during the rainy season when the ground becomes spongy. Hiring one of the pint-sized guides for around 35¢ is a smart idea as they will point out routes that will keep you from becoming the main ingredient in a pot of mud soup.

The easiest way to reach the site is to take a **tour** from León. Alternatively, you can take a northbound **bus** from León headed to Estelí or Malpaisillo and get off after 45 minutes at the village of San Jacinto (there is a sign on the highway for Los Hervideros de San Jacinto).

For the return trip, buses pass every half-hour or so until early evening. Driving is also a convenient option.

PONELOYA & LAS PEÑITAS

These two adjacent **beach** towns 12 miles from León are normally quiet except during holidays. Though both have **dangerous currents** and are largely useless for swimming, if you want to spend a day on the sand you could do worse: the crashing waves and wide strip of yellow sand are clean and attractive, but there is no shade, so bring lots of sunscreen and water. **Las Peñitas** is slowly gaining popularity with the backpacking crowd, but it's

Las Peñitas beach

still a quiet village of 1,000. Poneloya's beach is lined with summer houses belonging to the élite of Managua and León and there are few hotels in either town, so a day-trip from León is a good option. If you do want to spend the night, Las Peñitas has cleaner, more comfortable options. **Hotel Supaya** ($$-$$$, ☎ 854-2699, www.hotelsupaya.com) has 22 rooms with private bath, warm water, a/c, a mini-pool, and a good **restaurant**. Doubles cost $29-$35 (the price depends on room size) and rooms sleeping up to five people are available. Some rooms have ocean views. Credit cards are accepted. **Tours** are available to Isla San Juan Venado. **Hostal La Montana** ($$$, ☎ 882-9816) has several quality rooms with private bath and a/c for $40 each. There is also a bar/restaurant. Make reservations during holidays (when prices double) and during the **sand castle festival**, which takes place in March.

> **TIP:** *Follow the local families to La Bocana de Poneloya, an inlet edging the beach that provides a more protected area for swimming. Caution is still essential as just a few feet away from shore there is still a current.*

Local families swim at La Bocana de Poneloya.

Buses serve both beaches from León's El Mercadito and leave at least once per hour until late afternoon (45 minutes/60¢). It's a straight shot west of León by private car; you'll be on the beach in 20 minutes. **Taxis** are a good deal if you have a group and cost around $8.50 each way.

RESERVA NATURAL ISLA JUAN VENADO

Just south of Las Peñitas lies Isla San Juan Venado, a barrier island and estuary. Best known for its **birdwatching** and **mangrove forests**, the island is 13 miles in length. More than 180 species have been documented on the island, including 109 types of birds and three kinds of **sea turtle**. Arrange a trip through a tour operator in León; alternatively, guesthouses in Poneloya or Las Peñitas.

CHINANDEGA

Surrounded by fertile volcanic soil, Chinandega is the most important agricultural area in the country, and trade is facilitated by the newly-paved road leading north toward the border with Honduras. Modest Chinandega is the capital of the department and has a population of almost 500,000, but sees few tourists. Anyone visiting during the dry season can discern why: Chinandega is considered to be the hottest city in the country. Chinandega's transportation connections render it a convenient stopover, and most visitors are just here to spend the night before moving on.

Chinandega Highlights

■ Crocodiles in the park

■ *Fiestas patronales* (July 17-July 26)

■ Any place with air-conditioning

■ GETTING HERE & AWAY

BY BUS

The main entrance to the city is via Rotonda Los Encuentros. The adjacent main **bus station** is at **Mercado Bisne**. *Ordinario* buses leave from here to **León** every 15 minutes from 4:30 am-6 pm (1 hr 15 minutes/70¢); frequent **express** buses are also avaialable. *Ordinario* buses go to **Managua**'s Mercado Israel Lewites (aka Mercado Boer) every 40 minutes from 5 am-7:30 pm (2 hrs 40 minutes/$2.20). Beat the heat by taking an early bus. Buses also head to the Honduran border at **El Guasaule** every other hour (2 hrs/$2) and to **Corinto** every half-hour (45 minutes/$1).

A second minor **bus lot** at **El Mercadito** just north of the park sends buses to small towns north and west of Chinandega, including the beach communities in the **Jiquilillo** area, **Puerto Morazán**, and **Potosí**. Buses leave for Jiquilillo at 7, 10, 11:30 am, 3, and 4:30 pm.

International luxury coaches leave Chinandega daily for **San José**, **Panama City**, **San Salvador**, **Choluteca**, **Tegucigalpa**, **San Salvador**, **San Pedro Sula**, and **Tapachula**. Contact the local branches of **Transnica** (☎

The Pacific Lowlands

341-1584, www.transnica.com) and **Ticabus** (☎ 341-4331) for schedules.

BY CAR

If you plan to come by **private car**, most better hotels in Chinandega have private parking, and driving here is straightforward. The newly-paved road that leads toward the border of Honduras has made northbound travel from Chinandega much more pleasant.

Chinandega's economy is largely based on agriculture. Early in the 20th century citrus trees dominated the landscape, but from the 1940s through the 1960s, cotton was the most important crop. The fertilizers and insecticides used to cultivate the cotton caused substantial environmental damage (note the swirling dust) and led to poor soil quality. Today, the area's most important crops include bananas, sugarcane, soybeans, and peanuts. Keep an eye out for them as you drive into town.

Trucks haul mounds of sugarcane.

■ GETTING AROUND

Chinandega's layout is straightforward and the city is flat, but due to the heat you may rely on **taxis** here more than elsewhere. Fortunately, there are plenty cruising around. Rides within town cost 50¢ per person. There are also a few **carriages** pulled by parched-looking horses. There is a city bus system (30¢ per ride), but unless you are familiar with the city and speak Spanish it's much easier to take a taxi instead.

Avis **car rental** begins at $40/day and is available at Hotel **Cosigüina**.

■ SERVICES

TOURS & INFORMATION: Intur doesn't see much action here, but they have an office in the Centro Comercial Chinandega near the Costa Rican Consulate. Contact them at ☎ 341-1935 or chinandega@intur. gob.ni. **Hostal Los Maribios** (just outside of town at Km 132 on the Pan American Highway, ☎ 341-2040, maribios@hotmail.com) organizes tours, including **fishing**, **volcano hikes**, and **diving**. **Eco Expedition Tours** (☎ 278-1319) takes visitors to the **Flor de Caña rum factory** (see *Adventures*, p 306, for more information).

American citizens require visas to enter El Salvador, so if you need to apply for one, go to the **Consulate of El Salvador** (☎ 341-2049), two blocks north of the group of banks. A visa costs $30; bring dollars. Passports and applications need to be dropped off before 11 am. Open Mon-Fri 8 am-2 pm.

There is also a **Honduran consulate** (facing Enitel) and a **Costa Rican consulate** (just north of Banpro). The Honduran consulate (☎ 341-0949) is open Mon-Fri 8:30 am-4:30 pm. The Costa Rican consulate (☎ 341-1584) is open Mon-Fri 8:30 am-5 pm and Sat 8:30 am-noon.

MONEY: Chinandega's **banks** are clustered around a corner (*esquina de los bancos*) two blocks east of Parque Central. There is an **ATM** at **BAC**, which is in a different location than the other banks; find it two blocks south of Kodak. BAC is also the only bank in town that exchanges travelers' checks. There is another **ATM** at the Esso gas station next to the bus station. **Moneychangers** congregate at the Mercado Central (Central Market).

INTERNET, MAIL & TELEPHONE: There are a handful of places scattered through the center of town: choose one with air-conditioning. There is also a fast connection available at **Hotel Cosigüina**. The **post office** is three blocks east and a half-block north of Parque Central. **Enitel** is just east of Parque Central, or make international calls in air-conditioned bliss from Internet cafés.

MEDICAL: The **hospital** (☎ 341-4902) is a half-block south of Parque Central.

STAYING SAFE: The **police station** (☎ 341-3456) faces the west side of Parque Central.

MARKETS: Chinandega has a whopping three markets: **Bisne**, **Central**, and **El Mercadito**. There is also a **Pali** supermarket a block east of Parque Central, and **Supermercado Selecto** 3½ blocks east of the park.

■ SIGHTSEEING

At the end of the 19th century a violent earthquake triggered by nearby volcano activity devastated the city. Not a single house was left standing. As a result, Chinandega doesn't have the colonial architecture of other cities in the region. There isn't a lot to see in town, and everything appears a bit gritty. You may wish to beat the heat by doing your sightseeing via taxi. **Parque Central** houses what is perhaps the city's biggest tourist attraction: the **crocodiles** that reside fence-free in two grungy turtle-filled pools. The locals are quite blasé about their presence, but if you value your limbs you may not want to get too close.

Iglesia Santa Ana sits on the north side of the park. Take a peek inside, though the interior hasn't been well-maintained. This church was built in 1855 as an offering to the Virgin of Guadalupe with the hope that she would put an end to a cholera outbreak that was plaguing the city (yep, it worked). Chinandega's other major church, the brightly-painted **Iglesia El Calvario**, is on the other side of town. Built in 1874, it was destroyed just a few years later by earthquake activity and later rebuilt. Walk six blocks east of the park to check it

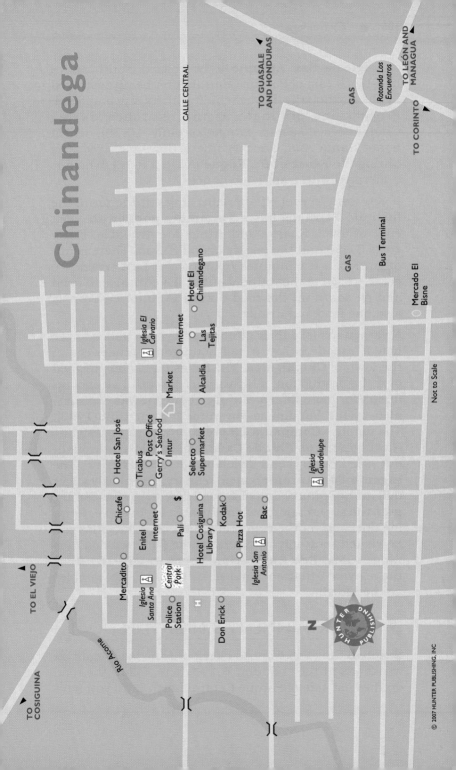

Chinandega

TO COSIGUINA

TO EL VIEJO

Río Acome

TO GUASALE
AND HONDURAS

CALLE CENTRAL

TO LEÓN AND
MANAGUA

Rotonda Los
Encuentros

GAS

TO CORINTO

Mercadito

Iglesia
Santa Ana

Police
Station

H

Don Erick

Chicafe

Enitel
Internet

Pali

$

Hotel Cosiguina
Library

Kodak

Pizza Hot

Iglesia San
Antonio

Bac

Central
Park

Hotel San José

Ticabus
Post Office
Gerry's Seafood

Intur

Selecto
Supermarket

Alcaldia

Market

Iglesia El
Calvario

Internet

Hotel El
Chinandegano

Las
Tejitas

Iglesia
Guadelupe

GAS

Bus Terminal

Mercado El
Bisne

N

Not to Scale

HUNTER PUBLISHING

© 2007 HUNTER PUBLISHING, INC

out. **Iglesia San Antonio** is two blocks south and a half-block east of Parque Central. After being destroyed by the earthquake, it was rebuilt with its size amplified. Processions originate at the churches during Chinandega's *fiestas patronales* (July 10-26), which honor Santa Ana. Another interesting time to visit is during the **Feast of St. Roque** (August 8-16), which is celebrated with traditional dances.

If you want to cool off after checking out the town, the Instituto San Luis has a **swimming pool** on the east edge of town. Snacks and drinks are available. Entry costs $1.50 and the pool is open Fri-Sun. There is another pool a few minutes from town at **La Terraza**. To get there, go to the roundabout at the entrance to town and go south on the road toward Corinto. La Terraza also has food and drinks.

Nicaraguans love their alcohol, and your chance to see how it's made is just a half-hour from Chinandega in the town of **Chichigalpa**. The Pellas family has reigned over the production of Nicaragua's powerful alcohol industry for more than a century (though it was expropriated by the Sandinista government from 1988-1992). The family's **Compania Licorera** produces the famous Nicaraguan rum **Flor de Caña**, which is loved throughout the country and available in 15 varieties. The **Ingenio San Antonio** sugar refinery, the oldest sugar mill in the country and also owned by the Pellas family, puts the sugarcane grown in the area to good use, forming the basis for the rum production. Both facilities can be visited, but only with a tour; the factories don't arrange visits. **Eco Expedition Tours** (☎ 278-1319) arranges visits that encompass both (sorry, no samples are included!).

■ ENTERTAINMENT & NIGHTLIFE

Baseball fans will want to check out the local team on weekends at the stadium. To get there, follow the road on the east side of Parque Central north until you have crossed the river. You can take a taxi there for around $2.

There isn't much in the way of nightlife in the center of town, but **Hotel Chinandegano** has a bar with a good drink selection. **Las Vegas Star City Casino** (☎ 341-1091) is a block north of the corner with the banks. Head to the roundabout and down the road toward León to get to the hopping **Dilectus Disco** (a quarter-mile south of town, ☎ 341-1836), the most popular spot for nightlife in the area. It's open until the wee hours.

*The **volcano** that towers over Chinandega is named **San Cristóbal** (Saint Christopher). It is instrumental in keeping the area's soil fertile and is responsible for the occasional ash that dusts the city.*

■ ADVENTURES

Hotel Cosigüina (☎ 341-3636, www.hotelcosiguina. com) organizes **kayaking** tours to El Realejo. Most hotels can arrange tours to Volcan Cosigüina.

■ SHOPPING

The best place to buy souvenirs is **Chicafe**, which carries the best variety of crafts in town and is run by a local NGO. You can also poke around in any of the city's three **markets**, though you won't find much in the way of crafts. If you need photo supplies or passport photos, **Kodak** is one block south and two blocks east of Parque Central.

■ WHERE TO STAY

Despite Chinandega's dearth of tourists, there are a surprising number of good places to stay in and around town. The city's hot climate renders air-conditioning a necessity.

> **NOTE:** *Few hotels and restaurants accept credit cards, so cash is the norm. Most travelers rely primarily on ATMs , which are popping up even in smaller towns, are generally reliable, and involve a minimum of fees.*

Hotel El Chinandegano ($$, 1½ blocks east of the Esso station, ☎ 341-4800). This clean and cozy place

has a central location. The 20 rooms are small but serviceable and offer cable TV, private bath with hot water, and a/c. Singles cost $25, doubles $30, and triples $35. There is private parking, a tiny gym and a bar/restaurant on-site. Breakfast is included in the room price.

© Hotel El Chinandegano

Hotel San José ($$$, 2½ blocks north of the corner with the banks, ☎ 341-2723). The eight rooms at

friendly San José have tiled floors, private baths with hot water, TV, a/c, and closets. There is a small, sparse patio. A good breakfast is included in the price, and credit cards are accepted.

© Hotel San José

Hotel Casa Grande ($, 4½ blocks west of Iglesia El Calvario, ☎ 341-0325). This centrally-located hotel's 10 rooms offer great value. Doubles cost only $10 ($17 with a/c) and include private bath and TV. Free laundry service is available.

Hotel Cosigüina ($$$, two blocks east and a half-block south of Parque Central, ☎ 341-3636, www.hotel cosiguina.com, reservaciones@hotelcosiguina.com). Cosigüina doesn't have much in the way of atmosphere, but it does offer all the amenities you'd expect from the most upscale place in town: a business center, gym, secure parking, and laundry service. The 20 rooms aren't anything special, but they are spacious

© Hotel Cosigüina

and comfortable; they come with private bath and hot water, cable TV, tiled floors, and a/c. Credit cards are accepted.

There are several good hotels outside of town along the highways. These places are often quieter than staying in town, but they're only practical if you have your own vehicle.

Hotel Los Volcanes ($$$, at Km 129.5 on the Pan American Highway, ☎ 341-1000, www.losvolcanesho tel.com, gerencia@losvolcaneshotel.com). This well-maintained hotel has attractive plant-filled corridors, a restaurant, and several conference rooms. Internet is

© Hotel Los Volcanes

available free of charge. Rooms are small but nicely furnished. Each room has private bath, cable TV, and a/c. Singles and doubles have double beds; suites are large and have two double beds.

Hostal Los Maribios ($$$, at Km 132 on the Pan American Highway, ☎ 341-2040, maribios@hotmail.com). This family-run place has 11 rooms and a country feel. Rooms have private baths, cable TV, and a/c. Singles cost $30 while doubles run $40. A suite has a walk-in closet, minibar, and a larger, more luxurious bathroom. The common areas are set up for socializing, and there is a billiards table, Internet access, and a children's pool. The hotel can arrange a variety of tours, including fishing trips and volcano hikes. Credit cards are accepted.

Villas del Cortijo ($$$$, at Km 134 on the highway toward Corinto, ☎ 340-3390). If you're planning to stay more than a few days, consider the apartments at Villas del Cortijo. They are in a group of pastel-colored buildings that share a gym, pool, lawn, and *ranchos* for

© Villas del Corjito

lounging. The surroundings feel a bit sterile, but the area is pleasant enough. Each apartment has a kitchen, living room, cable TV, a/c, a bath with hot water and marble detailing, and two bedrooms. Cortijo is also constructing additional suites and rooms for rental. Each apartment sleeps up to four and costs $69. Discounts are available for long-term stays. Credit cards are accepted and meals are available.

■ WHERE TO EAT

Las Fumarolas ($$$, two blocks east and a half-block south of Parque Central, ☎ 341-3636). Located at Hotel Cosigüina, this modern and spacious restaurant is a bit plain, but the paintings adorning the walls help brighten it up. Breakfast is their most popular meal; pancakes, French toast, or *gallo pinto* costs around $3. Nicaraguan food and foreign fare is available for lunch and dinner as well; try the shrimp. Las Fumarolas accepts credit cards and is open Mon-Sat 6 am-10 pm and Sun 6 am-6 pm.

Gerry's Seafood ($$-$$$, two blocks east of Parque Central) is the best option in town for seafood. Try the *ceviche*. Open Mon-Sat 10 am-10:30 pm.

The new **Chicafe** ($-$$, one block north and 1½ blocks east of Parque Central) has a good vibe and caters to foreign tastes with peanut butter sandwiches and other light meals you may not have seen in awhile. This is a good place to go with your journal and relax. Try the locally-made wine or the fruity *licuados*. Open Mon-Sat 8 am-6 pm.

A few minutes outside of town on the highway to León at Km 120 is **Los Vitrales** ($$-$$$, ☎ 341-1005), the restaurant at Hotel Los Volcanes. Nicaraguan food, including seafood, is served in the attractive dining room. The restaurant's specialty is *"filet a los volcanes,"* beef with mushrooms, asparagus, and mozzarella cheese. There is also a bar. Credit cards are accepted. Open Sun-Thurs 6 am-11 pm and Fri-Sat 11 am-11 pm.

Restaurante Buenos Aires ($$-$$$, 2½ blocks north of the roundabout at the entrance of town, ☎ 341-3764). If you are driving through town, this is a convenient lunch stop. They specialize in grilled meat. Credit cards are accepted, and the restaurant is open from 11 am-1 am.

Even travelers on a budget can eat well in Chinandega. Local volunteers give a big thumbs up to **Las Tejitas** ($), a *fritanga* that sets up shop evenings only two blocks east of the Mayor's Office. A full meal of excellent Nica food costs $3. **Don Erick** ($) is one of the best deals in town for *comida corriente*. This air-conditioned spot is one block south and one block west of Parque Central.

■ DAY-TRIPS FROM CHINANDEGA

EL VIEJO

El Viejo, originally an indigenous enclave, is a separate city of 35,000, but this farming community virtually blends into the sprawl on the west edge of Chinandega. Though the town is sleepy and not worth a detour, the **cathedral** is attractive and worth a look if you're driving through on your way to Volcan Cosigüina or the beaches. The cathedral is famous and dedicated to Maria Santisima en el Misterio de su Inmaculada Concepcion (try saying that three times fast!).

A particularly lively time to visit El Viejo is during the *fiestas patronales*, in the week of December 6. **Buses** go back and forth between Chinandega's El Mercadito at least every half-hour until 10:30 pm and arrive behind the cathedral in El Viejo. A large pillar marks the entrance to town.

El Viejo is known for its "Rosquillas Viejanas," a popular snack of handmade rings made from crunchy cornmeal. You can buy them at the entrance to El Viejo at Las Castillo or next to Iglesia Esquipulas at the house of Juana Ulloa.

There aren't any decent places to stay in town, but you can grab a bite at **Restaurante Piscina Olímpica** ($$$, two blocks north and a half-block east of the cathedral, ☎ 344-2263). This cavernous restaurant lives up to its name: restaurant patrons have complimentary use of the Olympic-sized pool, which is cleaned frequently. The menu is extensive, with lots of meat options, but vegetarians can be accommodated. Meals average $7. On weekends the restaurant turns into a bar and disco. The restaurant is open Mon, Wed, and Thurs 11 am-midnight and Fri, Sat, and Sun 11 am-2 am. Credit cards are accepted.

If you just can't tear yourself away from El Viejo, **Texoatega** is a nightlife hotspot just south of the cathe-

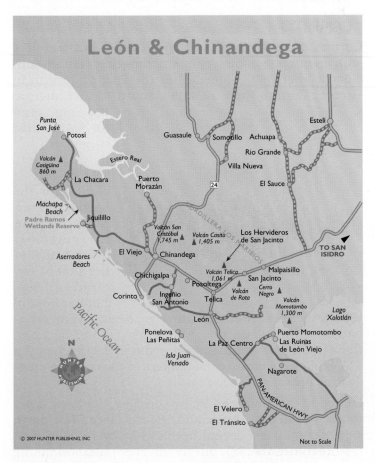

León & Chinandega

Punta San José
Potosí
Volcán Cosigüina 860 m
La Chacara
Estero Real
Machapa Beach
Padre Ramos Wetlands Reserve
Jiquilillo
Aserradores Beach
Corinto
Chichigalpa
El Viejo
Ingenio San Antonio
Puerto Morazán
Volcán San Cristóbal 1,745 m
Volcán Casita 1,405 m
Chinandega
Posoltega
Volcán Telica 1,061 m
Telica
Volcán de Rota
Cerro Negro
San Jacinto
Malpaisillo
Volcán Momotombo 1,300 m
Lago Xolotlán
León
Ponelova Las Peñitas
Isla Juan Venado
La Paz Centro
Puerto Momotombo
Las Ruinas de León Viejo
Nagarote
El Velero
El Tránsito
PAN-AMERICAN HWY
Guasaule
Somotillo
Achuapa
Estelí
Río Grande
Villa Nueva
El Sauce
Los Hervideros de San Jacinto
TO SAN ISIDRO
Pacific Ocean
CORDILLERA LOS MARIBIOS
N
24
© 2007 HUNTER PUBLISHING, INC
Not to Scale

The Pacific Lowlands

dral that also has food. There is live mariachi music on Thursday nights.

PUERTO MORAZÁN

A road leads 24 miles northeast from El Viejo to **Puerto Morazán**, an impoverished but friendly community on the edge of **Estero Real**, a 50,000-acre mangrove estuary that is home to a variety of bird species. There is not yet any tourist facilities in the area (though a community-based ecotourism project is in the works), but daily **buses** connect the town with El Viejo and Chinandega (1½ hrs/$1.75). Local fishermen can be hired to take you through the beautiful and natural estuary by boat.

CORINTO

Corinto doesn't have any major draws, but travelers with an interest in history or shipping may want to consider a brief visit. Named after the Port of Corinth in Greece, Corinto, just 13 miles south of Chinandega, has long been an important cargo port, but it wasn't until 1912 that it came into the spotlight internationally, and it certainly wasn't under the best of circumstances.

Marines landing in Corinto, 1926.

Thousands of US Marines descended on the town, beginning an occupation of Nicaragua that would last for two decades. Corinto became infamous yet again in 1983 when the CIA exploded a group of oil tankers in the port in a clandestine operation.

Linked to the mainland by two bridges, the town is actually situated on an island, Punto Icaco. The north side of town has a decent beach with several tasty seafood **restaurants** ($$), but the most popular swimming spot is **Playa Paso Caballo**, just outside of town on the road to Chinandega. There is a good restaurant, **El Español** ($$), just before you reach the beach. If you're beached out, the **Museo Santa Cruz**, in the former train station, is now a railroad museum, library, and auditorium (open daily 8 am-noon and 2-6 pm). The **port** is closed to tourists.

Ferry service to El Salvador may be available by the time you visit, and **buses** leave every half-hour from the Texaco station to the main bus station in **Chinandega** (45 minutes/$1). If you need to overnight in Corinto, the best option is **Hotel Central** ($$$, ☎ 341-0325), which faces the dock and has eight clean and decent rooms in a two-story house that offer private baths, cable TV, and a/c. Singles cost $25, doubles $35.

DID YOU KNOW? More than half-of Nicaragua's commerce passes through Corinta's port.

MARINA PUESTA DEL SOL

Marina Puesta del Sol (☎ 883-0781, www.marina puestadelsol.com, mpuestadelsol@yahoo.com). Located two hours from Chinandega, the opulence of this

© Marina Puesta del Sol

place, the only tourist marina in Nicaragua, contrasts starkly with the poverty of the surrounding area. The 600-acre project is fairly new, and the impact on the area remains to be seen. The project is the epitome of luxury and consists of a yacht club (there are 33 slips for boats), heliport, tennis courts, a pool, expansive grounds, a restaurant, and a **hotel** ($$$$). The hotel's luxury suites are plush, have all the amenities you'd expect from one of Nicaragua's most exclusive resorts,

© Marina Puesta del Sol

plus views of the ocean and mountains. Rooms cost $160-$540 and include breakfast. Beautiful and secluded **Playa Aposentillo** is a 15-min walk from the hotel. The road is newly paved and secure parking is available.

A **bus** leaves the marina for Chinandega daily at 5 am and makes the return trip at 12:30 pm. Another bus goes to **El Viejo** at 7:45 am, returning at 3 pm. A **taxi** from Managua costs around $100. To drive to the marina from Chinandega, take the road that leads to Cosigüina for 12 miles and turn at the sign for the marina. It's another five miles to the property.

The Pacific Lowlands

JIQUILILLO

Jiquilillo is a secluded beach village 24 miles west of El Viejo that until very recently received almost no visitors except during Semana Santa. **Rancho La Esperanza** ($, www.rancho.esperanza.bvg3.com), a rustic new guest-house and one-man community development project implemented less than a year ago, has begun drawing a steady trickle of visitors to Jiquilillo. The guesthouse is very basic (think no electricity or running water) and meals are simple Nica fare, but the guests like the friendly, convivial atmosphere and the focus on sustainability. The main reason that people come to this secluded guesthouse is to **volunteer** in the community, which yields a discount on accommodation. Current projects include teaching literacy, community gardening, and children's programs, but workshops designed by volunteers are encouraged. Short-term volunteers are welcome. Contact Nick at hospedaje_rancho_esperanza@yahoo.com. There is no Internet at the guesthouse, so a reply may take a few days.

ESTERO PADRE RAMOS

Estero Padre Ramos is an estuary just outside of Jiquilillo (stay on the bus a few minutes beyond Jiquilillo and ask to be let off at Padre Ramos). The estuary is named after Father Francisco Ramos, a parish priest from El Viejo who drowned here. Rancho La Esperanza can help set you up with a tour or, if you want to overnight here, there is a very simple, friendly place behind the school with rooms for just a few dollars. The bus can drop you off here (ask for "*la casa de Doña Reyna*"), or it's a 100-yard walk from the estuary. There is a good place to eat next to the Padre Ramos visitor center called **Elli's Rancho** ($) that serves Nicaraguan fare.

Buses leave El Mercadito in **Chinandega** for Jiquilillo at 7, 10, 11:30 am, 3 and 4:30 pm. For Rancho La Esperanza, ask the driver to let you off at "el rancho del chino."

RESERVA NATURAL VOLCAN COSIGÜINA & POTOSÍ

With a height of 2,860 feet, the summit of **Volcan Cosigüina** offers views of Honduras and El Salvador. This little-visited volcano has a crater lagoon that was formed after an eruption in 1835. Located at the end of a long and lonely road, the volcano is often accessed from the village of **Potosí**, a speck of a town on the edge of the Gulf of Fonseca. Only intrepid travelers make it as far as Potosí, a bone-crunching four-hour **bus** odyssey that departs Chinandega six times each day. There used to be a ferry to El Salvador from here, but service has ceased (upcoming passenger service to El Sal from Corinto farther south is rumored). If you've come this far, it's to visit the volcano. The easiest way to do so is by making arrangements for guides and transport through **Hostal Hacienda Cosigüina** (see *Where to Stay*). You can also hike the volcano on your own (hire a guide) either via the **Sendero El Jovo** trail that leaves from the edge of Potosí or from the other trail, **Sendero La Guacamaya**, which begins next to the ranger station in El Rosario. To arrange a **guide** for hiking the volcano (or even **horses** for climbing up it!), go to the **wildlife station** in El Rosario (nine miles beyond Potosí) or contact non-profit **Líder** in El Viejo, which manages the reserve, at ☎ 344-2381, lider@ibw.com.ni.

> **TIP:** *A three-day festival happens annually in mid-May (call the ranger station for this year's dates) on a nearby island belonging to El Salvador called Isla Meanguera. At this time only there are no immigration checks, so here is your big opportunity to visit El Salvador visa-free, at least for a few hours.*

The Pacific Lowlands

✩ **Hostal Hacienda Cosigüina** ($$$, at Reserva Natural Volcan Cosigüina, ☎ 341-2872, www.hacienda cosiguina.com.ni). This hotel is 39 miles from Chinandega at the south side of the crater on the road to Potosí. Located on a working farm that produces peanuts, sesame, cashews, and squash, it specializes in introducing guests to the local environment and arranges tours to nearby points of interest. Tour options include a horseback ride to (and through!) the wetlands on the property ($15), a trip to explore the cliffs at Playa Mechapa ($10), and an excursion to Volcán Cosigüina ($22 by either car or horse). The hotel is decorated with wood from the local area, and the rooms are simple but nicely furnished. There are five rooms with fans, plus a large room with seven beds. Singles cost $25, doubles $40, and the large room costs $20 pp. Extra beds are available for all rooms for an additional $20. Set meals cost $22 per day; let them know in advance if you have dietary restrictions. There is private parking.

If you want to rough it, the reserve's **ranger station** in El Rosario rents **tents** and rustic **bunk beds** ($4 pp for either). Let them know you are coming either by email (lider@ibw.com.ni) or by stopping at the **Líder office** in El Viejo (three blocks north of the market).

HONDURAS BORDER CROSSING: EL GUASUALE

El Guasale is the primary border crossing into Honduras from Nicaragua. Honduras does not require visas for citizens of the US, Canada, and most European countries. The border is open 24 hours, but delays are common. It costs $2 to leave Nicaragua and $7 to enter. Be sure to get your passport stamped. There is a small Bancentro **bank** here and a few snacks and drinks can be purchased. The town of **Somotillo**, three miles before the border, has food, fuel, and other services.

Buses head from the border to and from **Chinandega** every other hour (2 hrs/$2), and **Ticabus** and **Transnica** also ply this route. Buses on the Honduran side of the border shuffle passengers to Choluteca and Tegucigalpa.

Warning: If you are taking an international Ticabus or Transnica bus and the route passes through **El Salvador**, a Salvadoran **visa** is required in advance for American citizens even if you are just passing through. Acquire a visa (bring dollars) at the Consulate of El Salvador in Chinandega.

Bank door, León

The Pacific Lowlands

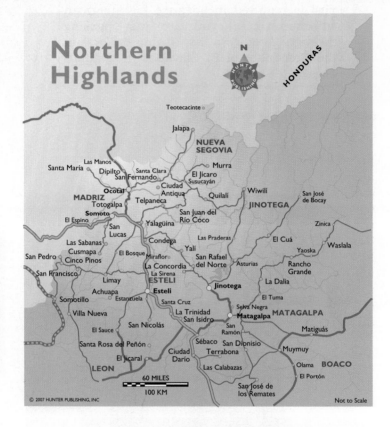

Northern
Highlands

N

HONDURAS

Teotecacinte

Jalapa

NUEVA
SEGOVIA

Santa María   Las Manos   Murra
        Dipilto   Santa Clara   El Jícaro
            San Fernando   Susucayán
        Ocotal   Ciudad   Quilalí   Wiwilí   San José
MADRIZ   Antiqua   de Bocay
    Totogalpa   Telpaneca   JINOTEGA
    Somoto
El Espino   San Juan del   Zinica
        San   Yalagüina   Río Coco
        Lucas   El Cuá
    Las Sabanas   Condega   Las Praderas   Waslala
    Cusmapa   El Bosque   Yalí   Yaoska
San Pedro   Cinco Pinos   Miraflor   San Rafael   Rancho
                La Concordia   del Norte   Asturias   Grande
San Francisco   La Sirena   La Dalia
        Limay   ESTELI
    Achuapa   Estelí   Jinotega   El Tuma
Somotillo   Estanzuela   Selva Negra
            Santa Cruz   Matagalpa   MATAGALPA
    Villa Nueva   La Trinidad   San
                San Isidro   Ramón   Matiguás
    El Sauce   San Nicolás   Sébaco   San Dionisio   Muymuy
    Santa Rosa del Peñón   Terrabona
        El Jícaral   Ciudad   Olama   BOACO
LEON   Darío   Las Calabazas   El Portón

60 MILES
100 KM
© 2007 HUNTER PUBLISHING, INC   San José de   Not to Scale
                los Remates

The Northwest Highlands

The Northwest Highlands are lush and mountainous and offer some of Nicaragua's finest ecotourism opportunities. **Finca Esperanza Verde** and **Selva Negra**, both of which are within easy reach from Matagalpa, give visitors the chance to experience life on a sustainable farm and to experience Nicaragua's nature at its finest. **Matagalpa** and **Jinotega** are centers of coffee production, while **Estelí** is home to the country's finest **cigar** industry. The Northwest Highlands' cool, crisp climate is a welcome change from the heat of lower elevations, and visitors won't be disappointed by the lush mountains, vibrant cities, and intriguing rural villages that this region has to offer.

ESTELÍ

Estelí, a center for tobacco production, is the north's major city. While visitors may initially be disappointed by the fairly unattractive city of 115,000 (and its lack of shade), a couple of days of exploring nearby attractions will pick up your spirits. Foreigners are not an uncommon sight in town: Estelí has numerous language schools and a history of receiving international volunteers, but the city retains its slow pace of life and agricultural heritage.

Estelí is rich in history, and its staunch Sandinista tradition is still evident in the city's murals and prominent use of black and red, the Sandinista colors. The city was destroyed in 1978-79 by Somoza's forces, which were intent upon quelling widespread support of the Sandinistas. Today the city is decidedly more peaceful, but it's smart to take taxis at night and refrain from displaying valuables.

Estelí Highlights

- La Galería de Heróes y Mátires
- An excursion to Salto Estanzuela

■ GETTING HERE

BY CAR

The excellent road from Managua makes driving here a cinch in just under two hours. In town, Budget **car rental** is available at **Agencia de Viajes Tisey** in Hotel El Mesón.

BY BUS

There are two **bus stations** in town, both of which are along the highway. Count on a 15-minute walk from the center of town to reach either one, or take a taxi. Buses leave from **Cotran Norte** (North) for destinations north of the city, including **Somoto** and **Ocotal**. Buses go from **Cotran Sur** (South) to points south, including **Managua**, **León**, and **Matagalpa**.

Express buses leave from **Managua**'s Mercado Mayoreo daily at 5:45, 8:15, 9:15, 10:45, 11:45 am, 12:20, 1:15, 1:45, 2:45, 3:15, 3:45, and 5:45 pm (2 hrs/$3.50). *Ordinario* buses leave every half-hour from Mayoreo from 4 am-5:30 pm (3 hrs/$2). Sit on the left side of the bus to Managua for prime views. There are two daily **express** buses to **León** at 5 am and 6:45 am (3 hrs/$4). Buses ply the roads between **Estelí** and **Matagalpa** every half-hour from 5:15 am-5:45 pm. **Ocotal**-bound buses depart every hour until 5 pm (2 hrs/$2). Buses also go to **Somoto** every hour (2½ hrs/$2.75).

International luxury coaches leave daily for **San José**, **Panama City**, **San Salvador**, **Choluteca**, **Tegucigalpa**, **San Salvador**, **San Pedro Sula**, and **Tapachula**. Contact the local branches of **Transnica** (☎ 713-6574, www.transnica.com) and **Ticabus** (☎ 713-7350, www.ticabus.com) for schedules.

GETTING AROUND

ON FOOT

The city is flat and the relatively cool climate makes walking pleasant. Take a taxi after dark for safety reasons.

BY TAXI

Taxis have fixed prices in town (50¢ per person during the day/$1 at night). When arriving at one of the bus stations in town, it's easy to hail a taxi on the adjacent highway.

SERVICES

TOURS & INFORMATION: Intur has limited information and little in the way of information, but give it a try (☎ 713-6799). Stop by in person (Hospital Viejo on Avenida Principal, open Mon-Fri 7 am-2 pm). **Agencia de Viajes Tisey** (☎ 713-3099) has a knowledgeable, English-speaking staff, though prices for plane tickets can be high. Credit cards are accepted. Their office is in Hotel El Mesón and is open Mon-Fri 8 am-5 pm and Sat 8 am-noon. **Careli Viajes** also offers tour services a block west and a half-block north of the park.

MONEY: The city's banks are clustered around *la esquina de los bancos*, a corner a block south and a block west of the park. You'll find **ATM**s there. **BAC** changes traveler's checks, as does **Agencia de Viajes Tisey**, just north of the cathedral.

INTERNET: CyberTown (☎ 713-2065) faces the east side of the church. Find **Soluciones Computarizadas** on the northwest corner of the park. If you're staying near the highway, a convenient, fast option is **Internet Express**, on the west side of the highway facing the Shell station (open daily 8 am-midnight). These places and most others charge 70¢/hr.

MAIL: The **post office** (☎ 713-2085) is a block south and a half-block west of the park (open Mon-Fri 7 am-8pm). **DHL** (☎ 713-7077) ships packages from its office a block west and a half-block north of the park.

TELEPHONE: Make calls from **Enitel**, which is a block south and a half-block east of the church (open Mon-Fri 8 am-8 pm and Sat 8 am-5 pm).

LAUNDRY: The expensive but speedy **Super Steam** (☎ 713-7681) is on the east side of the Pan American Highway. Dry cleaning and laundry take just a few hours; the latter is priced per piece.

MEDICAL: Hospital Regional (☎ 713-6300) is just south of town – take a taxi. **Pharmacies** and **private health clinics** are widely available on Avenida Principal.

STAYING SAFE: Though most visitors won't experience any problems, crime has increased in the city in the past few years. Locals warn against walking around after dark. Take a taxi instead. The **police station** is on the northern side of town on the Pan American Highway (☎ 713-2615).

MARKETS: The market consists primarily of produce and edges the southern end of Avenida Principal. Pick up groceries at **Pali**, 3½ blocks south of the park on Avenida Principal.

■ SIGHTSEEING

The **Parque Central** is nothing special, but it's a good spot to kick back with a *raspado* and watch the world go by. The city's cathedral, **Iglesia de San Francisco**, sits on the east side of the park. The church, built in 1823,

Iglesia de San Francisco

was refurbished and expanded in 1889 and again in 1929. The interior is airy and light and there are a number of carvings and statues.

Head a block south and a block west to see the mural-clad **Casa de Cultura**, a space dedicated to art displays. Classes are frequently on offer, so stop by to sign up for a painting, drawing, or music course if you plan to stay in town for awhile.

Estelí

TO SOMOTO, OCOTAL, AND HONDURAS
TO MIRAFLOR
GAS

Río Esteli

Uca Miraflor

Soccer Stadium

TO JINOTEGA

1. Hotel El Mesón/ Travel Agency
2. Hotel Los Arcos
3. Hotel Nicarao
4. Hotel Panorama/Licuados Ananda
5. Hotel Sacuanjoche
6. Hotel Esteli
7. Hotel Alameda
8. Hotel Panorama
9. Burger King
10. White House Pizza
11. Artesenía La Esquina
12. Movie Theater
13. La Esquina de Los Bancos
14. La Casa de Cultura
15. Artesenia Nicaraguense
16. Nica Cigars

La España
5 NE
4 NE
11   1
3 NE
2
Las Brasa
2 NE
Alcaldía   Central Park
Internet
Internet
Internet
1 NE
Post Office
13
12
Enitel   10
4 14
GAS
CALLE TRANSVERSAL
Library
15 9
3
1 SE
Rincon Pinareño
Ancentro
2 SE
3 SE
Funarte
Palí
5
6
4 SE
GAS
5 SE
6 SE
Parque Infantll
7 SE
8 SE
9 SE
GAS
10 SE
Cotran Norte
7
16
11 SE

AVENIDA 1 SO
AVENIDA PRINCIPAL
PAN-AMERICAN HIGHWAY
N

Market
8

TO BASEBALL STADIUM
TO COTRAN SUR
TO LA CASITA, HOSPITAL AND MANAGUA

Not to Scale
© 2007 HUNTER PUBLISHING, INC

In the same building there are two other museums. Be sure to see **La Galería de Heróes y Mátires** ☆☆ (☎ 713-3753), a museum created by an association of mothers that lost sons in the war. The gallery is sandwiched into a former Somoza jail and displays relics from the war along with newspaper articles and photographs. Some displays have explanations in English. Open daily 8 am-noon and 2-5 pm. Small donation requested. The other museum in this building is the **Museo de Historia y Arqueología**, which displays a handful of pre-Columbian pieces. Open 9 am-noon Mon, Tues, Thurs, and Fri.

If the lush tobacco fields surrounding Estelí have piqued your interest, head a few miles north of town (about 10 minutes) on the highway to visit **Estelí Cigar**. The factory doesn't formally have a tour or program, but give them a winning smile and keep your fingers crossed; you just may get a free tour (buy some cigars to thank them for their hospitality). Excellent *puros* (cigars) are produced here; the seeds from which the tobacco comes were brought over from Cuba when the 1959 revolution left growers searching for a new

Tobacco plants

place to call home when their farms were expropriated by the government. The Estelí area's soil proved ideal and the rest is history. Find the factory north of town at Km 155 on the Pan American Highway right next to **Rancho de Pancho** ($$-$$$), a fun stop for a meal or drink.

Parque de Ciencia Estelimar (☎ 713-7453) is a science park that could be just the thing to entice young travelers. Primarily visited by local schoolchildren, the

A "triceratops" at the park.

exhibit has an eclectic assortment of displays on agriculture, solar energy, and mechanics, the latter of which is explained through the use of puppet-like dinosaurs. A free one-hour tour is available in Spanish. Reach the park by private car or taxi; it's seven miles east of town (from the Monumento El Centenario take the highway toward Las Torres).

■ ADVENTURES

Many of Estelí's most interesting attractions are outside the city. See *Day-Trips from Estelí* (p 334) for ideas.

ADVENTURES ON WHEELS

Café Bar Vuela Vuela (☎ 713-6893) rents bicycles for a bargain $2 per day.

CULTURAL ADVENTURES

There are numerous places to **study Spanish** in town, and students will want to take advantage of afternoon excursions to nearby places of interest. You will see surprisingly few students out and about in town, but that makes it even easier to practice your new language skills! Schools open and close at a rapid pace, but these options have long-standing reputations. Prices listed below are for 20 hours of class and a week-long homestay; ask about discounts if you come with a group.

Sacuanjoche Spanish School, ☎ 713-7580, sacuanjoche spanishschool@yahoo.fr. This one-woman operation gets high marks for friendliness and competence. Owner Norma teaches students one-on-one for four hours each morning, and a homestay is available with her

Parque Central

family. Norma doesn't speak English, but she can round up a friend to translate if necessary. Norma is happy to show students around on weekends; just pay her bus fare. A week costs $145.

Escuela Horizonte Nica, ☎ 713-4117, horizont@ibw. com.ni. Escuela Horizonte is a well-established school that offers class, a homestay, and afternoon activities for $165. Students are enthusiastic about opportunities to volunteer and activities available after class, including excursions to local non-profit organizations.

CENAC Spanish School, ☎ 713-5437, www.ibw.com. ni/~cenac cenac@ibw.com.ni. This 15-year-old school has experienced teachers and costs $140. A portion of profits supports a local organization.

Students studying Spanish in town can often combine their courses with **volunteering**. Check with language schools for options. The Casa de Cultura may also be able to provide tips on opportunities. Bilingual visitors can offer to upgrade the English descriptions at local museums.

SHOPPING

There are two good shopping venues for **handicrafts** in town. **Artesanías La Esquina** (☎ 713-2229) is a block north of the church and has a wide selection of crafts from throughout Nicaragua, including pottery, leather-work, and soapstone carvings. MasterCard is accepted. **Artesanía Nicaragüense** (☎ 713-4456) has a similar selection a block south of the church.

Though the **market** doesn't offer much in the way of crafts, it does have some interesting leather shops where you can watch saddles and **boots** being made (a pair can be custom-made in five to six days for $50). **Clothing** shops can be found along Avenida Principal but, for something more personalized, stop by **Mano Mágica**, just north of Palí, where you can get custom-printed t-shirts and other items. Credit cards are accepted.

ENTERTAINMENT & NIGHTLIFE

The **movie theater** faces the south side of the park and shows mostly American flicks with English subtitles (weekend evenings only, $3). The center of town is quiet at night during the week, but dancing is the diversion of choice Thursday through Sunday. Just a block south of the southwest corner of the park, **Discotek Traksis** keeps things hopping with Latin American music and pop tunes. Cover $1.50, free for women on Thursday nights. **Discotek Cyber** is a gay and lesbian hotspot for dancing. It's in the old site of the Telcor Calvario. Cover $1. Take a taxi back to your hotel from any nightspots.

WHERE TO STAY

> **NOTE:** *Few hotels and restaurants accept credit cards, so cash is the norm. Most travelers rely primarily on ATMs, which are popping up even in smaller towns, are generally reliable, and involve a minimum of fees.*

☆☆☆ **Hotel Los Arcos** ($$$, a block north of the cathedral, ☎ 713-3830). This is the city's best option for convenience and comfort. Rest well here, knowing that profits benefit a local non-profit that helps local families. The

HOTEL PRICE CHART	
Cost per night for two people, before tax	
$	Up to $15
$$	$16-$30
$$$	$31-$60
$$$$	Over $60

18 rooms are in excellent condition, though you may find yourself wanting to spend your time on the rooftop balcony or in the courtyard garden instead. Rooms offer private bath with hot water, a/c, cable TV, tile floors, and comfy beds. Singles and doubles cost $42 and the only triple costs $60. There is free Internet access and a great on-site restaurant, Vuela Vuela.

Hotel Estelí ($-$$, four blocks south and 1½ blocks west of the southwest corner of the park, ☎ 713-2902, mejm78@yahoo.es). Housed in a bright, modern building, this hotel gets high marks for friendliness. Though the interior doesn't live up to the sparkling exterior, the 15 rooms are comfortable enough and have hot water and TV. Doubles with shared bath cost $8.50, while those with private bath cost $14.50. Triples (shared bath only) go for $11.50.

Hotel Panorama 2 ($$, next to Casa de Cultura, ☎ 713-5023). This centrally-located hotel has 15 good-value rooms. It is most attractive to visitors with cars, who can utilize the secure parking. On the downside, these cars are what you look out on from the rooms, and the staff isn't particularly friendly. If you can overlook those shortcomings, Panorama has very clean, modern singles for $15, doubles for $20, and triples for $25. All rooms have private bath with hot water and cable TV. There is a basic selection of food and drinks available.

Hospedaje Sacuanjoche ($, 3½ blocks south of the park, ☎ 713-2862). This budget favorite is quiet, secure, and well-priced. Rooms cost $6 per person and include tiny private baths with cold water. The rooms

The Northwest Highlands

surround a poinsettia-filled courtyard. Breakfast is available.

Hotel Nicarao ($, 1½ blocks south of the park, ☎ 713-2490). Another budget find, the Nicarao is one of the city's most sociable hotels, making it a good option for solo travelers. There is also an on-site restaurant that serves as a gathering spot. Rooms have sagging beds and private or shared baths. Knock at night to be let in.

Hotel El Mesón ($$-$$$, a block north of the cathedral, ☎ 713-2655). Though it's a bit dowdy, El Mesón is functional and boasts ample on-site amenities, including a restaurant, car rental, and a travel agency. The eight clean rooms come in singles, doubles, triples, and quads and look somewhat out of date, but they do have private bath with hot water and cable TV. Doubles cost $20 with fan, $30 with a/c. The rooms surround a quiet courtyard. Private parking is available and credit cards are accepted.

If you have a private car or are just passing through, **Hotel Alameda** (☎ 713-6292) has a highway location removed from the city center – convenient if you are driving, but give it a miss if you are taking public transport. The hotel is on the east side of the Pan American Highway behind the Shell station on the southern side of town. It is very close to the Cotran Sur station, so if you need to catch an early bus the Alameda is a good choice.

■ WHERE TO EAT

Estelí has a surprisingly small number of good restaurants for a city of its size. The fare is generally simple but filling.

☆☆ **Café Bar Vuela Vuela** ($$$-$$$$, ☎ 713-3830). This gem may be the city's best restaurant. Located inside Hotel Los

DINING PRICE CHART	
Price per person for an entrée, not including beverage, tax or tip	
$	Up to $3
$$	$3-$6
$$$	$6-$10
$$$$	Over $10

Arcos, Vuela Vuela cooks up great Nicaraguan food, along with a small assortment of European fare. Meals average $7-$12. Patrons rave about the beef dishes. The colonial-style space is tranquil and spotless. Open daily 7 am-11pm.

☆☆ **Rincon Pinareño** ($$-$$$, faces Hotel Panorama 2). This lunch and dinner spot is popular with good reason: it serves the best Cuban food in Northern Nicaragua. Cigars are also sold here. Open noon to 9 pm daily except Tues.

☆☆ **Las Brasas** ($$$, faces the northwest corner of the park, ☎ 713-4985). This popular spot overlooks Parque Central and is one of the city's see-and-be-seen hotspots. Better yet, the Nicaraguan specialties are well-prepared. Open Tues-Sun 11:30 am-midnight.

Though it's several miles south of town on the Pan American Highway, the food and atmosphere at **La Casita** ☆☆ ($$-$$$, ☎ 713-4917) makes it a worthwhile destination. The Scottish owner specializes in breakfasts; dig in to delicious granola with yogurt, or select one of the baked goods. You'll have a hard time tearing yourself away from the plant-filled eating area; consider bringing a book. There are also plants and crafts for sale. Open Tues-Sat 7 am-7 pm, Sun 9 am-7 pm, and Mon 1-7 pm. Closed the first Monday of every month.

Licuados Ananda ($, on the west side of the Casa de Cultura). Spanish students spend hours poring over their studies at this friendly spot. Ananda specializes in juices and *licuados* (fruit drinks blended with milk or water), but it's also a good place to relax with a snack or sandwich. This is the best option in town for vegetarians; there is a healthy plate of the day that wins over non-vegetarians as well. Ananda is set back from the street in a plant-filled courtyard (sorry, the swimming pool is empty). Open daily 8 am-6 pm.

Burger King ($-$$, faces Enitel, ☎ 713-2902). Not to be confused with the American chain, Burger King does little more than burgers but does them well. Sample one of the more than a dozen burger varieties.

For a light breakfast, stop by **España**, a bakery with goods that can't be beat. Find it 3½ blocks north of the northwest corner of the park. Open Mon-Fri 8 am-noon and 2-5 pm.

If you get a craving for pizza and are tempted to try **Pizza Hot**, resist that urge. Enough said. **White House Pizza** ($-$$) has passable pies, 2½ blocks east of the movie theater.

■ DAY-TRIPS FROM ESTELÍ

RESERVA NATURAL TISEY ESTANZUELA & SALTO ESTANZUELA

This **waterfall** and **nature reserve** are easily accessed from Estelí by 4WD or on foot. Many intrepid travelers choose to hike the 3.6 miles to the waterfall, which takes about two hours. To reach the waterfall on foot or in a vehicle, walk a half-mile south on the Pan American Highway, then turn west off the highway when you see a small sign indicating Estanzuela (the sign is on the right near a bus stop). From there, hike another three miles for a well-deserved dip.

> **Warning:** The waterfall is virtually nonexistent late in the dry season, so ask around locally about its status before making the trip there.

Continue down the same road from the waterfall to explore the Reserva Natural Tisey Estanzuela. Explore the hiking trails and, if you have the energy, climb to the top of the mountain, where you'll enjoy fantastic views. If you can't get enough of the reserve, **Ecoposada Tisey** ($, ☎ 713-6213) has dorms for $5 and double beds for $10, $4 for communal living, $9.50 for a double bed and some privacy, $1 per meal). Even if you don't plan to overnight, this is a good stop for information, to secure a **guide**, or to rent **horses**.

SAN JUAN DE LIMAY

A village 26 miles from Estelí along a grueling dirt road, this is known for its soapstone (*marmolina*) carvings. Originally conceived by priest as a job-creation strategy in this low-income area several decades ago, the craft is still practiced by a handful of carvers. Information is available in Spanish at ☎ 719-5115. **Buses** leave Estelí's Cotran Norte for San Juan de Limay at 8:45, 9:15 am, and 12:15 pm (two hrs/$3). The last bus back to Estelí is in mid-afternoon.

Local carver

RESERVA NATURAL MIRAFLOR

This decade-old nature reserve stretches into the department of Jinotega, but it's most accessible from Estelí. The reserve is privately managed and it is very much a community effort. Tourism is just getting started here, so don't expect much in the way of facilities. Hiking is a real pleasure in Miraflor; be sure to hike with a guide. The reserve boasts more than 300 species of **orchids** and wildlife abounds; see if you can spot the elusive **quetzal**. The startlingly blue **Laguna**

de Miraflor is an attractive spot for a picnic and birdwatching.

Arrange your trip before leaving Estelí by contacting UCA-Miraflor (this is a local association unaffiliated with the Managua university of the same name). Call them at ☎ 713-2971 or learn more at www.miraflor-uca.com (Spanish only). UCA can help arrange guides and visits to farms to see sustainable agriculture in practice. There is rustic accommodation and meals available, which can also be arranged through UCA. Also check out www.voluntaris-figueres.org/miraflor.

The reserve is 18 miles from Estelí. Drive north on the Pan American Highway until you reach the highway toward Yali; turn east there and keep an eye out for the reserve entrance beyond the village of Las Palmas. It is also possible to take a bus to the reserve, though this requires planning and probably an overnight. A **bus** leaves **Estelí**'s Cotran Norte at 8 am, while other buses leave Cotran Sur at noon, 2:15, and 3:45 pm. Buses return to Estelí at 7, 11 am, and 4 pm. An easier option is to arrange **private transport** through UCA. The reserve is open Thurs-Sun. Visits are possible Tues and Wed by appointment only.

CONDEGA

This sleepy agricultural village of less than 10,000 is 33 miles north of Estelí. Notable for its proximity to a well-regarded pottery cooperative and the Ecological Park of Cantagallo, both of which can be visited on a day-trip from Estelí. If you want to overnight in town on your way north, **Rincón Criollo La Gualca** ($, ☎ 715-2431) has simple, new doubles with shared ($6) or private ($15) bath. **Buses** headed from Estelí to Somoto, Ocotal, or Jalapa deposit you on the highway just a couple of blocks from the center of Condega. To return to Estelí, take any Estelí- or Managua-bound bus (go to the highway for **express** buses; catch *ordinarios* at the park).

Taller de Cerámica Ducualí Grande is a cooperative of a dozen women who use traditional methods to produce their renowned pottery. You can see them at work and purchase some of their wares, all of which cost less than $10. The workshop is a mile north of Condega and can be reached by bus or private car. Look for the sign from the highway and follow it west for another half-mile, at which point you will go through the town of Ducualí Grande. Turn left at the church and you'll see a sign for the workshop.

Parque Ecológico de Cantagallo (☎ 713-2468) is a worthwhile excursion for nature lovers, though the park is accessible only by private transport. Drive 13 miles east of Condega on the unpaved road to reach the local communities of **San Jerónimo** and **Venecia**. Tourism is in its infancy here, but in the village of

Venecia **guides** can be hired and **rooms** can be arranged in a community-managed guesthouse. Take one of the three **trails** from town and **hike** through pine and orchid-laden forests. One trail, known as Campamento Guerrillero, leads to a former Sandinista campsite.

OCOTAL

Though Ocotal is not generally a destination in itself, it's worth a brief stop if you're headed north to the Honduran border at Las Manos. The city was named after

the ocotl **pine trees** that used to enshroud the area (they have begun to meet their demise as development moves in). Ocotal is a quiet town of dirt roads, but it is the center of economic activity for the area's farmers.

Ocotal's main claim to fame is its venerable **Parque Central**, which was designed by a former mayor and tropical plant aficionado. The park is home to more than 100 species of plants and is an oasis in the rather unattractive town. The adjacent cathedral, **El Templo Parroquial de Ocotal**, is handsome and was built in 1869. The **Casa de Cultura** is just west of the park and has an exhibit about the US Marines' activity in the area (in fact, the Marines were housed in the building that the Casa de Cultura now occupies). Ocotal was bombed in a Marine air raid in 1927 in an effort to dispose of Sandino.

> **TIP:** *If you're in the area the week of August 15, don't miss the Ocotal's fiestas patronales, a flurry of parades and live music.*

Fruits for sale in the market.

If you need to pick up last-minute supplies before heading across the border to Honduras, the **market** is a block north and a block west of the park. There are a couple of good places in town for a meal. A half-block west of the park you'll find **Llamaradas del Bosque** ($$, ☎ 732-2643), which serves Nica favorites. A block west and 1½ blocks south of the park is **La Yunta** ($$$, ☎ 732-2180), another good choice for Nicaraguan food. Open daily from 11 am-11 pm.

There is one high-quality resting spot in town. **Hotel Frontera** ☆ ($$$, ☎ 732-2668, hofrosa@ibw.com.ni) has singles ($37), doubles ($47), and triples ($57) with private bath (enjoy the hot water!) and cable TV. Parking is available and there is a bar. The property has some luxuries as well: a pool, Internet, in-room phones, and balconies with mountain views. The hotel is behind the Shell station on the highway. Another decent hotel option is **Hotel Bel Rive** ($, ☎ 732-2146), which faces the Shell station on the highway. Rooms are more comfortable than other budget options. They cost $12 for a double and have private bath, fan, and secure parking.

Buses arrive and leave from the **bus station**, which is on the southeastern edge of town. **Express** buses leave **Managua**'s Mercado Mayoreo for Ocotal at 5:10, 6:10, 6:45, 7:45, 8:45, 10:15, 11:15 am, 12:15, 2:15, 4:15, and 5:15 pm. Buses also go back and forth to **Estelí** hourly until 5 pm (two hrs/$2). Buses head to the Honduran border at **Las Manos** every half-hour until 4:30 pm (45 minutes/$1). Somoto-bound buses leave every 45 minutes until 4 pm (2½ hrs/$2). A **taxi** to the border at **Las Manos** costs just under $10.

SOMOTO

This tiny (pop. 15,000) capital of the Madriz Department is the last town you'll reach before crossing the Honduran border at El Espino, nine miles distant (see p 342 for crossing details). There is little of note in Somoto, but there are a few things to see in this pretty town if you find yourself with an hour or two to spare. The town has a very low crime rate, and exploring on foot is a pleasure. The **Iglesia Santiago** cathedral is the centerpiece of town, and the church is more than 370 years old. There is a **religious procession** leaving from the church on the eighth day of each month that leads to a nearby village. A small **museum** (☎ 722-2210) in the Mayor's Office houses some pre-Columbian pottery and a few other items. Open Mon-Fri 1-4 pm.

SCORE!

During the dry season the most popular diversion in town is soccer, which is played in front of thousands of fans at Somoto's surprisingly large stadium. Tickets to see Real Madriz, the local professional team, cost less than $2.

Somoto has a few services, including a BDF **bank** that faces the Mayor's Office and can change traveler's checks. The **post office** (☎ 722-2437) is on the southeast corner of the park. **Enitel** (☎ 722-2374) is behind the cathedral.

> **TIP:** *Don't miss Somoto's snack specialty:* rosquillas, *crunchy rings cheese of cornmeal. The best place to sample them is two blocks west of the bus station, where Betty Espinoza (☎ 722-2173) has baked her treats for decades and visitors can watch the preparation process. Open Mon-Sat 5 am-10 am.*

Somoto has one good place for shopping: the **handicrafts shop** at the Hotel Panamericano. The owner knows the craftspeople and he can point you in the direction of their workshops (which are usually in their homes) if you'd like to see how your purchases were made. **Hotel Panamericano** ☆ ($-$$, ☎ 722-2355) is also a good place to spend the night. The hotel can be found on the north side of Parque Central; the location can't be beat. Rooms have private bath (double $17) or shared bath ($10) with hot water, fan, cable TV, and mini-fridges. Take a look at several rooms as they vary in quality. There is a restaurant on-site and parking is available. **Hotel Colonial** ☆ ($$, ☎ 722-2040) is another good option just south of the church. The rooms are very clean and offer private bath with hot water and cable TV. A simple breakfast is included. Singles cost $22, doubles $27.

Restaurante Somoteño ($$, ☎ 722-2518) offers the best dining experience in town in its open-air eating area. There is **karaoke** on Saturday evenings. **Restaurante Almendro** ($$, ☎ 712-2252) is just south of the church and is named after the giant tree that grows in the center of the restaurant. Almendro has good mid-priced meals; the beef dishes are particularly tasty here. Open daily 10 am-8:30 pm.

Somoto's **bus station** is several blocks from the center of town across the highway. **Express** buses leave **Managua**'s Mercado Mayoreo for Somoto at 7:15, 9:45 am, 12:45, 1:45, 3:45, and 4:45 pm. **Express** buses go to **Managua**'s Mayoreo at 3:45, 5, 6:15, 7:40, 2 pm, and 3:15 pm (3½ hrs/$4); you can also get off on the highway just outside of the center of Estelí by taking any of these buses. Buses bound for **Estelí** leave every hour until 5 pm (2½ hrs/$2.75), plus there are two **express** buses at 10 am and 4:30 pm, which shaves an hour off the journey. Buses go to the Honduran border at **El Espino** every hour (45 minutes/75¢).

Cañon de Somoto

The Somoto Canyon ☆☆ is a beautiful, peaceful retreat that has yet to be discovered by tourists. Located nine miles from Somoto, the

canyon is graced by three **rivers**, including the formidable Río Coco, Central America's longest river. Be careful while climbing over the rocks; many parts of the canyon, which is 1.8 miles in length, are very narrow. There are several calm places where it's possible to swim. There are no services at the canyon, and a guide is essential in this remote area. Stop by the mayor's office in Somoto, where you can hire a **guide** (one recent visitor was accompanied by the mayor himself!).

> **Caution:** The canyon should only be visited during the dry season due to a risk of flash floods.

To reach the canyon, take a bus (in the direction of the Honduran border at El Espino) or private transport west of Somoto until you reach the bridge. From there, walk 25 minutes into the canyon.

> **TIP:** *Cañon de Somoto is known locally as Namancambre.*

HONDURAS BORDER CROSSING: EL ESPINO & LAS MANOS

Crossing the border at either of these crossings is straightforward and the wait time is usually short. Both borders are open 24 hours per day. You will complete brief paperwork, pay $2 to leave Nicaragua ($4 if it's a night or weekend) and proceed on foot to the Honduran side (100 yards ahead at both crossings). Be sure to get an exit stamp in your passport when leaving Nicaragua. If you're coming into Nicaragua from Honduras, the fee is $7 (plus an additional $2 after hours).

> **NOTE:** *Buses shuttle passengers into Honduras from the Honduran side of the border until 4:30 pm; if you near the border in late afternoon and are traveling by public transport, overnight in Somoto or Ocotal and cross the border in the morning instead.*

ON THE ROAD FROM MANAGUA TO MATAGALPA

If you're driving to Matagalpa from the south on the Pan-American Highway, there are a few worthwhile stops along the way. These sights are also accessible by buses headed from Managua to Matagalpa or Esteli, but be sure to take an *ordinario* and not an express bus, which doesn't make stops.

La Casa-Hacienda San Jacinto, 21 miles north of Managua, is the site of a battle between William Walker's filibusters and Conservative fighters. A monument off the highways marks where a bout of fierce fighting left Conservative Andrés Castro out of ammunition. He threw a rock and killed one of the filibusters, rendering him a hero among Nicaraguan nationalists.

The *hacienda* itself is an easy 20-minute walk east of the highway, though the lack of building maintenance renders it a disappointment. There is a $1.50 entry fee to view the interior, which includes some musty displays of artifacts.

Continuing along the highways you'll come to El Madroño, 45 miles north of Managua. Though there is nothing of note to see in the town itself, keep an eye out on the highway in this area for colorful displays of carvings. It's worth a stop to see local artisan Asención Zeladón's **handicrafts** and furniture, which are made of local wood.

Poetry lovers shouldn't miss **Ciudad Darío**, home of Nicaragua's famous Ruben Darío. On the main street in town you'll find **Casa Natal Rubén Darío**, where the poet was born and lived for a short time before moving to Leon. The museum is open Mon-Fri 8 am-noon and 2-5 pm. A good lunch or dinner stop is **Doña Conchi's** ($-$$), a comfortable spot with good Nica food a block north of the Shell gas station.

Chaotic **Sébaco** is situated at the point where the highway splits and leads to Estelí and Matagalpa. The town's offerings are geared toward motorists and bus passengers,; you can buy virtually anything you might need (and many things you don't) through the windows of your bus or car. There's nothing of note to do in town, but this is the best place to pick up any supplies you may need for your onward journey, including great produce from the market. There are a few cheap, dingy places to stay, but continuing on to Matagalpa or Estelí to overnight is recommended. A surprisingly good restaurant, **El Sesteo** ($-$$), offers Nicaraguan favorites and air-conditioning.

MATAGALPA

The hills of Matagalpa are a welcome respite from the heat of the lowlands, and the city is a pleasant destination year-round. Misty Matagalpa sees surprisingly few tourists, but this coffee center of nearly 150,000 residents is a worthwhile destination for its cool climate, proximity to nearby places of interest, and the opportunity to experience an authentic highlands town. It's easy to spend a couple of days exploring the attractive center with its minor sights, and it is a good stopover before venturing farther into the highlands.

Coffee fresh from the farm.

Matagalpa's biggest draw for visitors is also the foundation of its livelihood: the region's justifiably famous coffee industry. Coffee growing in the area was initiated in the 1870s by German immigrants, and the areas near the city still hold Nicaragua's largest concentration of coffee *beneficios* (processing plants). Visitors can combine Matagalpa's urban pursuits with exploring nearby coffee farms Esperanza Verde and Selva Negra.

Matagalpa Highlights

- ■ Museo del Café
- ■ Spending a night or two at nearby coffee farms Finca Esperanza Verde or Selva Negra

> **TIP:** *If you're interested in seeing coffee production in full swing, visit the Matagalpa area from November to February. At other times you'll see little evidence of the importance of the industry, but you can find a great cup of joe throughout the year!*

Matagalpa viewed from a hill.

■ GETTING HERE & AWAY

By Car: The drive from Managua is scenic and the road is paved and in good condition. Parking options are few in the center of Matagalpa and streets are narrow; if you're driving, consider staying near the highway or outside of the center.

By Bus: Buses arrive at and leave from the terminal in the southwestern part of town next to the river. **Express** buses leave **Managua**'s Mercado Mayoreo for Matagalpa at 3:30, 5:30, 6, 7, 9, 11 am, 12:30, 1:30, 2:30, 3:30, 5 and 6 pm. *Ordinario* buses leave **Managua**'s Mercado Mayoreo every half-hour from 3:45 am to 6:45 pm. **Express** buses leave Matagalpa for **Managua**'s Mercado Mayoreo every one to two hours, while *ordinario* buses depart every half-hour from 3:35 am to 6:05 pm. **Jinotega**-bound *ordinario* buses leave every half-hour from 5 am to 7 pm. Buses also head to **Estelí** every half-hour 5:15 am-5:45 pm. There are **express** buses to **Chinandega** at 5 am and 2 pm.

GETTING AROUND

Though Matagalpa is surrounded by hills, the city center is fairly flat and readily walkable. For the sake of safety, take a taxi at night or if you're going to one of the barrios accessible by unpaved road outside of the city center.

Taxis are readily available and cost approximately 75¢ per person in town.

There is a **Budget** rental office at the Shell gas station at the southern end of town. Prices average $70/day. Note that there are many one-way streets in town.

SERVICES

TOURS & INFORMATION: Intur has an office a block south of the mayor's office. A better option is to contact **Matagalpa Tours** (a half-block east of Banpro, ☎ 772-4581, www.matagalpatours.com, info@matagalpa tours.com), which provides good local info as well as **tours** and **guides**. Tour options include a full day-trip to Jinotega, an excursion to the indigenous village of El Chile and a visit to a historic mining area. Custom multi-day-trips are also available. Spanish, Dutch and English are spoken.

Centro Girasol (☎ 772-6030), in a bright yellow building next to the southernmost bridge into town, is a non-profit organization that uses proceeds from its tourist services and on-site gift shop to support local children's projects. The Centro sells **maps** that outline local points of interest and they can arrange guides.

CANIMET (facing the post office, ☎ 772-6000), organized by local business owners, offers tour information and guides. **Homestays** can also be arranged here.

MONEY: Banks are clustered just north of the movie theater. Bancentro has an **ATM** (Visa/Plus only). A second **ATM** that accepts both Visa and Mastercard, is at **BAC**, a half-block east of the southeast corner of Parque Morazán. **Moneychangers** hang out in front of the Eskimo ice cream shop just south of the southeast corner of Parque Morazán.

INTERNET: Ciber Central is just south of Parque Morazán on the main street. Open 9 am-9 pm daily. **IBW Internet** has fast connections next to the post office. There are several other places along the main street south of Parque Morazán; 70¢/hr is standard.

Matagalpa street

PHOTOCOPIES: A half-block south of Parque Morazán on the main road you'll find **Centrocopiados** (open Mon-Sat 7:30 am-6 pm).

MAIL: The **post office** is a block south and a half-block east of Parque Morazán.

TELEPHONE: Enitel is just east of Parque Morazán and is recognizable by the building's large antenna. You can also make inexpensive international calls from Internet cafés.

BARBER: Barbería Telica (a block south of the movie theater, ☎ 612-3477) does a spiffy traditional straight-edge shave for $2.50.

MEDICAL: There is a hospital on the northern edge of town near the river, but the private **Clinica Maya Flores** is a better option. There are plenty of pharmacies in town, including **Farmacia San Benito** and neighboring **Farmacia Oziris #2**, a half-block south of the southeast corner of Parque Morazán. **Farmacia Alvarado** is on the northwest corner of Parque Darío (French and Spanish spoken).

Staying Safe: Matagalpa is generally a safe city, but it's a good idea to avoid walking in the *barrios* on the edges of town. Avoid the parks at night. Contact the **police** at ☎ 772-3870.

MARKETS: Matagalpa has two markets, both with bus stations, but neither is near the center of town. The main market is next to the river in the southwest part of the city; Guanuca market is north of the center a block before the river. A more convenient option for picking up groceries is to head to **Pali**, three blocks north of Parque Morazán (open Mon-Sat 8 am-8 pm, Sun 8 am-6 pm). On the other end of town, the slightly more expensive but centrally-located **Supermercado La Matagalpa** is 2½ blocks north of Parque Darío. Open Mon-Sat 8 am-9 pm and Sun 8 am-8 pm).

■ SIGHTSEEING

Museo del Café (1½ blocks south of Parque Morazán). Matagalpa's museum was initiated by the folks at City Hall, not only to spotlight the region's coffee industry, but also to introduce visitors to the history of Matagalpa. Displays in Spanish and Dutch describe the process of growing and harvesting coffee. Historical photos take viewers back to the early days of coffee production in the area. Old coffee-processing machinery is on display, as is a small selection of pre-Columbian artifacts found in the area. There is also a makeshift café in the museum where visitors can purchase steaming cups of local coffee. There is a limited selection of gifts, including packaged coffee. It's supposedly open Mon-

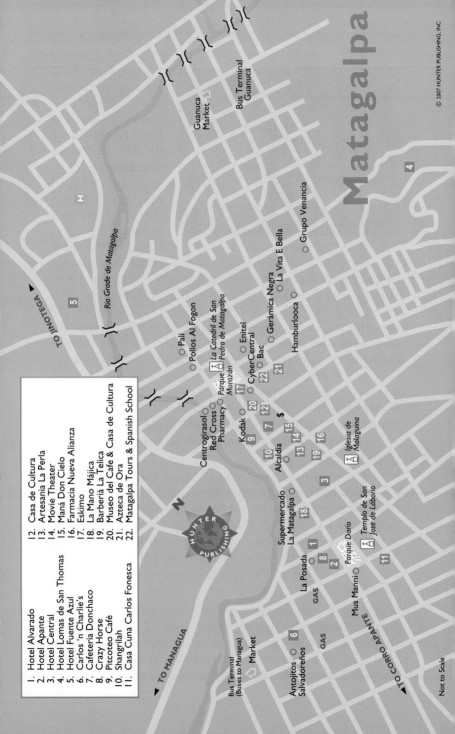

1. Hotel Alvarado
2. Hotel Apante
3. Hotel Central
4. Hotel Lomas de San Thomas
5. Hotel Fuente Azul
6. Carlos 'n Charlie's
7. Cafetería Donchaco
8. Crazy Horse
9. Pitcoteo Café
10. Shangrilah
11. Casa Cuna Carlos Fonesca
12. Casa de Cultura
13. Artesanía La Perla
14. Movie Theater
15. Maná Don Cielo
16. Farmacia Nueva Alianza
17. Eskimo
18. La Mano Májica
19. Barbería La Telica
20. Museo del Café & Casa de Cultura
21. Azteca de Ora
22. Matagalpa Tours & Spanish School

TO JINOTEGA ►

TO MANAGUA ►

Río Grande de Matagalpa

Guanuca Market

Bus Terminal Guanuca

Matagalpa

© 2007 HUNTER PUBLISHING, INC

N

HUNTER PUBLISHING

Palí
Pollos Al Fogon
La Catedril de San Pedro de Matagalpa
Parque Morazán
Enitel
CyberCentral
Bac
Gerámica Negra
La Vita E Bella
Hamburlooca
Grupo Venancia

Centrogirasol
Red Cross
Pharmacy
Kodak
Alcaldía
Iglesia de Molaguina

Supermercado La Matagalpa

La Posada
GAS
Mus Manni
Parque Darío
Templo de San Jose de Lóborio

Bus Terminal (Buses to Managua)
Market
Antojitos Salvadoreños
GAS
GAS

TO CORRO APANTE ►

Not to Scale

Sat from 8 am to 12:30 pm and 2-6 pm, but hours can vary. Free.

La Catedral de San Pedro de Matagalpa

Matagalpa has several noteworthy churches that are worth a look. **La Catedral de San Pedro de Matagalpa** towers over Parque Morazán. Completed at the end of the 19th century, the Baroque cathedral was the third-largest church in Nicaragua at the time, and it is still the most commanding structure in Matagalpa. The cavernous interior houses carvings and pain-tings. Mass takes place every evening at 6 pm. **El Templo de San José de Laborío** is on the eastern edge of Parque Darío. Originally constructed in the mid-18th century, the church was rebuilt in 1917. It is notable for housing an indigenous uprising in the 1881. **La Iglesia de Molagüina**, two blocks south of the movie theater, is Matagalpa's oldest church, though the year of construction is disputed. The church is now a school and convent.

The diminutive **Museo Casa Cuna Carlos Fonseca** (☎ 772-3665) is sandwiched on a corner one block east of the southeast corner of Parque Darío. This was the birthplace of Carlos Fonseca, the founder of the FSLN (Sandinista) party. The house has been kept largely in its original condition and displays memorabilia chronicling Fonseca's life. Open Mon-Fri 8 am-noon and 2-5 pm.

Matagalpa's two attractive parks are good for a stroll. **Parque Darío**, on the southern side of town, is well-shaded. Check out the ceramics for sale on the southern edge of the park. Seven blocks north of Parque Darío is **Parque Morazán**, a favorite haunt of the local shoe-shining crew. Both parks are popular places to relax during the day, but when the crowds clear out in the evening you should, too.

WALKING TOUR

The highlights of Matagalpa are easily accessible on foot; plan to spend approximately two hours to explore the sights on this itinerary. Begin on the northern side of town by exploring **La Catedral de San Pedro de Matagalpa**. Ven-

dors sell sliced mangoes (small bag 20¢) and other fruit near the front steps if you'd like a snack. Cross the street and take a walk through **Parque Morazán** before continuing south along the main road. Stop in at the **Museo del Café** to learn more about the region's history and coffee

Matagalpa Park

industry. This is also a good place to sample a cup of local coffee. Stop for a snack or a smoothie and a chat with the regulars at **Cafetería Don Chaco**, on your left just after the museum. Since you've just seen photographs of all of the mayors in the history of Matagalpa at the Museo del Café, take note of the **mayor's office**, two blocks ahead on the left.

Continue south for four blocks to reach Parque Darío. Take time to explore the **Templo de San Jose de Laborío** church on the east side of the park before walking one block east of the southeast corner of the park to **Museo Casa Cuna Carlos Fonseca** to learn more about the founder of the Sandinistas. If you're still

The Northwest Highlands

feeling energetic, this is a good jumping-off point to begin a **hike** in Reserva NacionalCerro Apante (see below).

Matagalpa is surrounded by lush hills that are particularly beautiful during the rainy season.

■ ADVENTURES

ON FOOT

© Matagalpa Tours

Reserva Nacional Cerro Apante, whose namesake mountain reaches 5,412 ft above sea level, offers hiking opportunities and great views of the surrounding area. The reserve has cool forests and bubbling creeks. It's a bit of a challenge to find on your own and there is no access to the top of the mountain – arranging a tour or guide is recommended. To strike out on your own, head south from the southwestern corner of Parque Darío (the mountain will be on your left) and ask locals to point you in the right direction along the way. Plan to spend about three hours round-trip, and bring water. To arrange a guided trip, contact Matagalpa Tours, which runs half-day excursions (see *Tours* on p 346).

© Matagalpa Tours

CULTURAL ADVENTURES

Matagalpa's brand new and only Spanish school is **Escuela de Español "Matagalpa"** (1½ blocks east of Banpro, ☎ 772-0108, www.matagalpa.info, escuela@matagalpatours.com). Matagalpa is a good place to study Spanish because there are few foreigners in town, which means you get a full-immersion experience. Classes at the school are one-on-one and cost $120/week for four hours of class per day. Homestays can be arranged. The school is run by the owner of Matagalpa Tours, so it's easy to arrange after-class excursions.

© Habitat for Humanity

Habitat for Humanity (☎ 772-6121, www.habitat.org) builds homes for area residents. Contact them in advance to find out about volunteering during your stay. **Grupo Venancia** (☎ 772-3562, venancia@ibw.com.ni) is a women's organization that has volunteer activities focused on arts, culture and activism. **Centro Girasol** (☎ 772-6030) supports programs for disabled children and sometimes offers volunteer opportunities.

■ SHOPPING

Black pottery, a specialty of the area, is made by a special firing process and is available in several shops in town, including **Ceramica Negra** (two blocks east of the northeast corner of Parque Morazán), **Artesanía La Perla** (next to the

Mayor's Office) and at **La Vita e Bella**, which also has jewelry (see *Where to Eat* on p 359).

Centro Girasol (☎ 772-6030), a local non-profit, sells handicrafts and local food products that make good gifts, including coffee and jam. It's in a bright yellow building next to the southernmost bridge into town. Another place to pick up local coffee is **Museo del Café** (1½ blocks south of Parque Morazán).

For **photo** supplies, **Kodak** (☎ 772-2065) is a block south of Parque Morazán. You can use the instant photo machine to make good-quality, expensive prints ($1 each). Open Mon-Sat 8 am-6 pm.

Piggy banks (around $1.50) and other ceramics are for sale along the southern edge of Parque Darío.

Make custom-designed t-shirts, banners, and other silkscreened items at **La Mano Mágica** (☎ 772-5863), a block south of Supermercado La Matagalpa. Open Sun-Fri 8 am-7 pm. Credit cards accepted.

■ ENTERTAINMENT & NIGHTLIFE

For a taste of local culture, join the cluster of *Matagalpinos* who congregate every evening to relax and chat on the steps of the cathedral.

Matagalpa's cathedral

☆ **Grupo Venancia** is a community artistic space run by a women's non-profit organization that offers an eclectic assortment of performance and visual art from Thursday to Saturday. Every Saturday evening there is a free event, showcasing anything from an independent film to a lecture on the environment. Contact the group to find out about upcoming events (☎ 772-3562, venancia@ibw.

com.ni), or stop by their difficult-to-find space just west of Hotel Lomas de San Tomás.

☆ **Crazy Horse** is a half-block west of the northwest corner of Parque Darío. The in-crowd has moved from La Posada to this stylish new neighbor, which has creative menus made of wood and an atmosphere resembling an upscale log cabin. Meals are also available and range from $6.50 to $10. Rum and Coke, $1.

Picoteo Café (two blocks south of Parque Morazán on the west side of the street, ☎ 772-6000). Matagalpa's upscale professionals head to Picoteo for evening snacks and drinks despite service that often leaves something to be desired. Make your way through the front room to the back of the restaurant to the fun, casual thatched bar. Picoteo also has hamburgers, *nacatamales* and snacks. Open daily 10 am-10 pm. Credit cards accepted.

La Casona (a half-block west of the northwest corner of Parque Darío) is a mainstay of Matagalpa's nightlife scene, with live music on Friday nights and decent meals available.

If you feel like parting with a few *córdobas*, there is a plethora of slot machine mini-casinos (*tragamonedas*) just southwest of Parque Darío that are immensely popular with locals.

■ WHERE TO STAY

Matagalpa has surprisingly few hotels for a town of its size. Select a hotel with hot water in this crisp climate.

> **NOTE:** *Matagalpa has a few places each that take credit cards. However, traveling without enough cash for a few days' food and hotel is strongly discouraged.*

☆ **Hotel Fuente Azul/Hotel Fountain Blue** ($-$$, just west of the bridge at the third highway entrance into Matagalpa, ☎ 772-2733). Fountain Blue is a traveler favorite for its good-value rooms and included extras, such as free coffee and secure parking. Ask to see several of the hotel's 12 rooms before selecting one; small, simple rooms cost $15 double, while more spacious digs with cable TV, private bath and hot water cost

HOTEL PRICE CHART	
Cost per night for two people, before tax	
$	Up to $15
$$	$16-$30
$$$	$31-$60
$$$$	Over $60

$26. It's an easy, if slightly hilly, walk into the center of town from the hotel. Fountain Blue is a good option if you're driving as it's a block and a half-from the highway that heads to Managua and Jinotega.

Hotel Lomas de San Tómas ($$$, on the east edge of town a quarter-mile east of Escuela Guanuca, ☎ 772-4201). The hotel's 25 rooms are the most upscale in town. The hotel largely caters to a business crowd with

© Hotel Santo Tómas

its three conference centers and secretarial services, but it's also a good option for leisure travelers, who can enjoy the tennis court and quiet setting. Rooms cost $35 single/$45 double plus tax and they come with private bath, hot water, cable TV and in-room phones. Spacious family rooms ($70) are good for groups. Take a taxi to the hotel ($1 per person from the center of town) as it's removed from the center of town and a bit hard to find. If you're driving, take the third (northernmost) exit into Matagalpa, then follow the signs to the hotel. Credit cards accepted.

Hotel Alvarado ($, across from the northeast corner of Parque Darío, ☎ 772-2830). Owned by a doctor and his wife, who run the

© Hotel Alvarado

pharmacy downstairs, Alvarado is a friendly, secure and conveniently-located option. The guesthouse's eight rooms have either shared or private cold water bath and cable TV. The rooms with private bath are larger; ask for one on the top floor for good views of the surrounding mountains. Rooms have mismatched but comfortable furniture, including real mattresses, and come complete with a rule list adorned with Bible verses. Singles with private bath cost $9/doubles $13. The owners speak French and Spanish.

Hotel Apante ($, facing the west side of Parque Darío, ☎ 772-6890). This simple place has a good location and simple but clean rooms. The guesthouse offers singles, *matrimoniales*, and triples (rooms for two people have one bed only; if you want two beds, get a triple). Singles and triples have private baths with hot water, while *matrimoniales* have shared cold water bath. Most rooms come with cable TV. Free coffee and bread is available, and triple rooms come with a small fridge. Single $6, *matrimonial* $10.50, triple $17.50.

© Hotel Apante

Hotel Central ($, 2½ blocks north of Parque Darío, ☎ 772-3140). True to its name, Central is right in the heart of town. This friendly place is a good budget option and has basic rooms with shared or private bath and hot or cold water. Be sure to choose a room with walls that reach the ceiling to keep away

© Hotel Central

mosquitoes and noise. A double with shared, cold water bath costs $10.

> **NOTE:** *Though you likely will not notice it (because most hotels have water tanks), Matagalpa has a limited and fluctuating water supply, which is exacerbated by deforestation on the hillsides around the city. Residents have access to running water in their homes only once per week, while others rely on community wells. Take short showers and conserve water whenever possible.*

■ WHERE TO EAT

Inexplicably in this coffee-producing area, you'll find that instant coffee is frequently served in Matagalpa's restaurants.

DINING PRICE CHART	
Price per person for an entrée, not including beverage, tax or tip	
$	Up to $3
$$	$3-$6
$$$	$6-$10
$$$$	Over $10

☆ **Cafetería Don Chaco** ($, 1½ blocks south of Parque Morazán, ☎ 772-2982). For a thoroughly local experience, Cafetería Don Chaco's food and prices can't be beat. This unassuming little place a half-block south of Parque Morazán has good-value *comida corriente* for $2; try the *pollo en salsa*. This is also a good place to try traditional drinks like *chicha* or *cacao con leche*, or, if you're really feeling brave, try one of the more creative options like the orange and spinach or pineapple and garlic smoothies. Open Sun-Thurs 7:30 am-5 pm, Fri 7:30 am-5 pm.

☆ **Pollos El Fogón** ($, 1½ blocks north of the northwest corner of Parque Morazán, ☎ 772-6004). Carlos and Sadhy roast some of the most delicious chicken in Nicaragua. This tiny place has only a couple of tables, but waiting for a spot is well worth it. Select the amount of chicken you'd like and pair it with side dishes. A quarter-chicken with rice and salad is $2.25.

☆ **La Vita e Bella** ($$-$$$, in the alley behind Hamburlooca, ☎ 772-5476). Serving up the best pasta and pizza in town, La Vita e Bella also has good desserts, an extensive wine list and reasonable prices. The restaurant is a bit hard to find; consider taking a taxi. Open 12:30-10:30 pm Tues-Sun.

Casual **Maná del Cielo** ☆ ($, ☎ 772-5686) is a good pre-movie dinner option: it's just north of the theater. Locals can't get enough of the high-quality Nicaraguan food – it's one of the best buffets in town. Vegetarian options are always available, and selection changes daily. Open Mon-Sat 7 am-9 pm.

Restaurante y Bar Sacuanjoche ($$-$$$, on the eastern edge of town a quarter-mile east of Escuela Guanuca, ☎ 772-4201). Located in Hotel Lomas de San Tomás, Sacuanjoche has Nicaraguan and international food in a pleasant setting. Finding the hotel on your own can be a bit tricky; a taxi from the center costs $1. Credit cards accepted.

Shangrilah ($, a half-block south of the mayor's office, ☎ 772-3074). Friendly and centrally-located Shangrilah offers buffet meals with a cozy indoor or courtyard seating. Meals run $1.50-$2.50 and vegetarian dishes are available. Open Mon-Sat 7 am-7 pm.

La Hora del Taco ($$-$$$, on the east side of the highway to Managua). A bit farther afield, this restaurant is worth seeking out if you've been craving good Mexican food. La Hora del Taco has indoor and outdoor seating from which to enjoy the views. This restaurant is a good option if you're just driving through Matagalpa: it's a few miles south of town on the east side of the highway toward Managua. Take a taxi if you're coming from central Matagalpa. Open daily 11 am-11 pm.

Restaurante Azteca de Oro ($$-$$$, facing BAC bank, ☎ 772-3122). This promising new Mexican place was just opening at press time – check it out. Open daily 11 am-11pm.

For pastries and other treats, **Panadería Mus Manni** is the best-stocked bakery in town; find it on the south-west corner of Parque Darío (open daily 6 am-8 pm).

Exploring the Matagalpa-Jinotega Highway

If you're driving from Matagalpa to Jinotega, there are a few stops you may want to consider making. You'll come first to **Mirador de La Chispa**, a viewpoint on the right side of the highway at Km 133 that has beautiful views of the city and surrounding mountains. At Km 143 you'll find **Restaurante Disparate de Potter** ($$-$$$), which has great views and good Nicaraguan food (open daily 8:30 am-8 pm). There is also a **platform** at the site that you can climb for 50¢ for panoramic views. If you're still hungry, a bit farther up the highway at Km 152 there are a handful of **produce stands** selling some of the freshest, juiciest fruits and vegetables you'll see in Nicaragua. If you're traveling by **bus** and you want to stop at any of these places, you'll have to wait until the next bus passes (about 30 minutes) to continue on your journey. You may find that it's worth it!

■ DAY-TRIPS FROM MATAGALPA

The Matagalpa area is famous for its java production, and there is no better way to experience Nicaragua's **coffee country** than by visiting **Finca Esperanza Verde** or **Selva Negra**. Most visitors choose one farm to visit but, if you have the time, spending a couple of days at both is worthwhile. If you're having difficulty deciding which to visit, your choice may come down to accessibility: both are easy to reach via private transport from Matagalpa but, if you plan to go by bus, Selva Negra is significantly easier to access. Another consideration may involve planning time: Finca Esperanza Verde requires reservations, usually well in advance, while Selva Negra virtually always has space for drop-ins. However, if you prefer to have sightseeing arrangements made for you or if you want to participate in a homestay, Finca Esperanza Verde is a better option. The choice is yours, but either farm is well worth a visit.

There are more than 30,000 coffee farms in Nicaragua, most of which are near Matagalpa and Jinotega.

FINCA ESPERANZA VERDE

Finca Esperanza Verde ☆☆☆ (Green Hope Farm) was initiated by two former Peace Corps Volunteers and is a component of a Sister City partnership between San Ramón, Nicaragua, and Durh am, North Carolina. The project has evolved into a community-based **nature preserve** and a 220-acre **coffee farm** and it's particularly popular with groups. The property  won the *Smithsonian Magazine* Sustainable Tourism Award for Conservation in 2004. The farm includes a butterfly breeding project, hiking trails and greenhouses. Tour profits fund community projects. Guides are available for birdwatching, horseback riding, hiking and other activities. Knowledgeable guides are from the local community and speak Spanish only; a translator is available for $50/day. Day-use entrance costs $1.50 for Nicaraguans, $3 for foreigners.

Getting Here

The Finca is not easy to access without costly private transport. To get here on your own, take a **bus** from Matagalpa's Guanuca station headed toward Pancasan/El Jobo. You'll pass through the village of San Ramon; get off at the Yucul stop a few miles later (40 minutes from Matagalpa). From here it's a 45-min-

The Northwest Highlands

ute uphill walk to the farm; follow the signs pointing toward Finca Esperanza Verde.

The farm can arrange **private transport** for groups of up to 12. From Managua, Leon, or Granada, transport by minivan costs $400; from Matagalpa by pickup truck it's $120. Needless to say, going with a group significantly reduces costs.

Where to Stay & Eat

Finca Esperanza Verde ($$-$$$$, ☎ 772-5003 in San Ramon, ☎ 919-489-1656 in the US, www.fincaesperanzaverde.org, herma@ibw.com.ni) has space for 26 guests in three types of accommodation. **Cabins** of wood and brick with large porches sleep up to six in bunk beds. Each has a private bath with solar hot water and flush toilets. A second option is to participate in a **homestay**. This is not the rustic experience you might expect: all homes have electricity and flush toilets. There is also **camping** available in a pleasant clearing on the farm.

Most guests visit Esperanza Verde through a **package** deal, with options outlined on the farm's website. Packages focus on either nature or *campesino* culture or a combination of both. They range from two to four nights and include accommodation, meals and activities.

Food at the farm's **restaurant** is, not surprisingly, fresh, delicious and grown right on the property. Dietary restrictions can be accommodated; let them know in advance.

Reservations are essential to visit Finca Esperanza Verde; two months in advance is recommended, though you can call about last-minute availability. Email in English can be answered from January through April; the rest of the year only Spanish speakers are available. Esperanza Verde has an **office** in San Ramon at Albergue Campestre, 1½ blocks east of the police station, if you want to make arrangements in person or find out more about the project.

SELVA NEGRA

Selva Negra ☆☆☆, a 1,500-acre farm, hotel, and spectacular natural area, is perfect for learning about coffee production as well as hiking or horseback riding. Selva Negra has been one of Nicaragua's most important coffee farms since its founding in the 1800s. The current owners of Selva Negra, Eddy and Mausi, are descendants of the original families that came to Nicaragua to grow coffee. They have slowly added amenities to the property, turning it into a model of environmental sustainability and a comfortable base for exploring the gorgeous mountains.

Selva Negra is a convenient day-trip from Matagalpa, but to really experience the surroundings, staying overnight is recommended. There is a C30 ($1.90) entrance fee to go beyond the guard gate near the hotel, which can be used as a credit at the hotel's restaurant. Even if you don't plan to stay overnight, take advantage of the hotel's hiking trails, tours and views of the surrounding mountains.

The old military tank that marks the entrance to Selva Negra wasn't placed here intentionally. A remnant from the war in the 1980s, the tank was abandoned when it became incapacitated and has been a well-known landmark ever since.

Getting Here

Selva Negra is a half-hour **bus** ride north of Matagalpa (75¢); take a Jinotega-bound bus from Matagalpa and look for the old **military tank** on the east side of the road that marks the entrance to Selva Negra. From here it's a half-hour mostly downhill walk to the hotel along a well-maintained unpaved road. The hotel can arrange for a taxi to meet you at the highway that will take you to the hotel if you contact them in advance. Otherwise, count on walking, which is not recommended if you have luggage. For the return trip, have the hotel arrange transportation for you to the highway; **buses** pass every half-hour in both directions.

If you prefer to go to Selva Negra by private transport, ask your guesthouse in Matagalpa to arrange a **taxi** to bring you directly to the hotel. If you have a rental car, it's an easy 25-minute drive from Matagalpa.

> **NOTE:** *If you're in the area in late October, be sure to head to Selva Negra for their annual* **Oktoberfest** *celebrations. Beer, clowns and German music are all part of the festivities, which take place on October 24 and 25.*

Adventures on Foot

The hotel maintains 14 trails that crisscross the upper portion of the property beyond the hotel. Pick up a free map at reception before exploring the area, but keep in mind that the map and posted signs can be confusing. Hike up into the **cloud forest** and try to spot one of the area's elusive **quetzals**, among the world's most beautiful birds. Hikes range from 30 minutes to several hours.

An interesting walk takes visitors behind the scenes to see daily life on the Selva Negra farm. Over 300 employees work on the farm, 70% of them living on the property. You can walk down the hill from the hotel (10 minutes) to see their village, which is complete with a schoolhouse and a laundry area. Not many guests come down here, but the residents are friendly and the scenery is beautiful.

- ■ Greenhouse Tour ☆: This is a must for visitors interested in the environment. Not just limited to the property's greenhouses, the tour shows visitors how the hotel makes good on its commitment to sustainability. Various sites around the property that involve production of food and electricity are visited, including the methane gas reservoir, which takes by-products from the washing and de-pulping of coffee beans and turns them into energy. Tours cost $2 on foot, $3 by minibus.

■ Coffee Production Tour: The hotel offers excursions to see its coffee production facilities accompanied by interesting explanations of the coffee growing and harvesting process in English, Spanish, or German. Per-person costs for the tours are $2 on foot, $3 by minibus.

Adventures on Horseback

The hotel offers guided rides on six trails – an excellent value at $2 for a half-hour.

Where to Stay & Eat

☆☆ **Hotel de la Montana Selva Negra** ($$$-$$$$, Km 140 on the highway between Matagalpa and Jinotega, ☎ 772-3883, www.selvanegra.com, resortinfo@ selvanegra.com). Most accommodation consists of private villas, each of which has a unique style reflecting the owners' German heritage. Prices vary by villa and average $25 per person. Owner Mausi recommends Villa #9, from which you can see monkeys and hear the creek trickling by. The villas, which have up to six

© www.SelvaNerga.com

bedrooms, are an excellent option for groups. Spacious and perfectly comfortable "backpacker rooms" have two double beds with private bath ($30 double). The only drawback is that they don't come with hot water, which is definitely preferable in this high-altitude location. Dorms are available for $10 per person.

> **NOTE:** *Email sent to the hotel often goes unanswered; give them a call instead. The hotel has space for 220 guests, so reservations are not essential.*

The on-site **restaurant** ☆☆ ($$-$$$$) puts the organic produce and livestock grown at Selva Negra to good use in its high quality German and Nicaraguan meals. It's a recommended stop even if you don't plan to overnight here. Vegetarian options are available, and meals are served either in the dining room or on the lakefront patio. Don't miss a cup of shade-grown coffee from the surrounding countryside!

If the romance of Selva Negra has inspired you, the hotel is adept at arranging weddings. This beautiful stone chapel on the property was built for the wedding of the owners' daughter.

There is a path leading from the restaurant around to the pond, which is made of a unique material: coffee bean hulls. The machine used to remove the hulls from the beans was designed by the ancestors of the current hotel owners. You can learn more about the history of the property and the four generations of the family that has lived here in the **mini-museum** located in a loft above the restaurant.

STRETCH YOUR LEGS

Reserva Natural El Arenal (Km 142.5 of the Matagalpa-to-Jinotega Highway) has walking trails through the forest and coffee fields; stop at the hotel for information.

Hotel Fuente Pura ($$, ☎ 876-5081) is just off the highway on the edge of the reserve one hour from

Matagalpa; look for signs at Km 142.5. Rooms have private bath with hot water and TV with DVD player (choose from the complimentary movie selection). Doubles cost $20, or $25 for a larger double. The dining room has nice views of the forest.

Across from Hotel Bosawas you'll find **Netcafe**, offering Internet. Centrally-located **Cyber Mundo** is another option two blocks east of the park's southeast corner. Both places are open daily 8 am-10 pm and cost 60¢/hr. **Photocopies** are also available at Cyber Mundo.

JINOTEGA

■ SIGHTSEEING

Built in 1805, Jinotega's **cathedral** is well-maintained and definitely worth a look. The cathedral faces **Parque Central**, which is a good spot from which to see the **La Cruz**, a cross on a nearby mountainside that is lit up at night (see *Adventures* below for information about hiking to the cross).

Jinotega's attractive **cemetery** is a good place for a stroll, particularly on Tues and Sun, when a well-known **medicine man** comes to cure the ills of local residents with homemade potions made primarily from plants. There is little shade in the cemetery, so wear sunscreen.

Visitors with an interest in war history may want to walk down to the river (locals can point the way) to see where Sandinista Commander German Pomares (known as **"El Danto"**) was killed. A marker shows where the battle took place against Somoza's troops.

> **TIP:** *If you're in the Jinotega area in late early May, don't miss the town's lively* ***fiestas patronales****, a lively week filled with crafts, music, horseshows, and dancing, culminating in a Catholic mass on May 3 at the top of the hill next to the cross.*

The Northwest Highlands

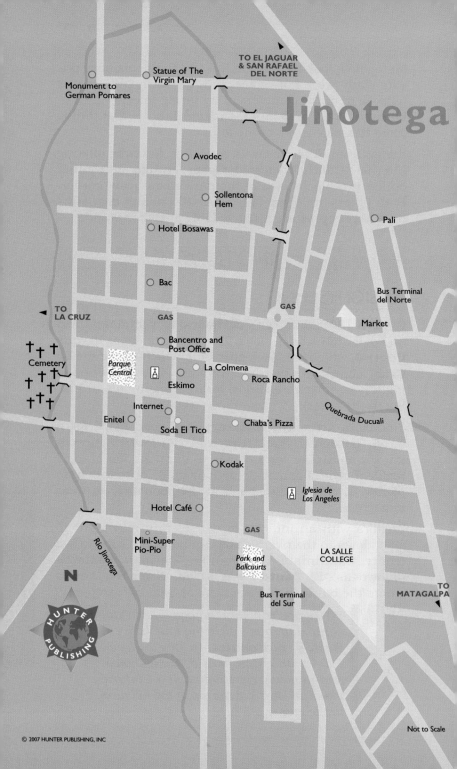

TO EL JAGUAR
& SAN RAFAEL
DEL NORTE

Jinotega

Statue of The
Virgin Mary

Monument to
German Pomares

Avodec

Sollentona
Hem

Pali

Hotel Bosawas

Bac

Bus Terminal
del Norte

TO
LA CRUZ

GAS

GAS

Market

Bancentro and
Post Office

Cemetery

Parque
Central

La Colmena

Eskimo

Roca Rancho

Internet

Quebrada Ducuali

Enitel

Chaba's Pizza

Soda El Tico

Kodak

Iglesia de
Los Angeles

Hotel Café

GAS

Mini-Super
Pio-Pio

LA SALLE
COLLEGE

Park and
Ballcourts

TO
MATAGALPA

N

Río Jinotega

Bus Terminal
del Sur

HUNTER
PUBLISHING

Not to Scale

© 2007 HUNTER PUBLISHING, INC

■ ADVENTURES

ADVENTURES ON FOOT

The most popular hike in the area leads up to the **cross** (*la cruz*) on the hillside west of town. It's said that the cross was placed on the mountain in order to stop incessant flooding, and locals consider the cross to have saved the city from destruction. The original cross has been replaced by a new one that is lit up at  night. To hike up to the cross, begin on the west side of town and cut through the cemetery. You'll see the trail on the northern side of the cemetery that leads up the mountain. The hike is fairly steep, but not long (about 90 minutes round-trip). Hikers are rewarded with beautiful views of Jinotega and the surrounding mountains. Bring water and sunscreen.

© www.Jinotega.com

ADVENTURES ON WATER

El Centro Recreativo de Tomatoya is a swimming area formed by a dammed stream, is outside of Jinotega on the highway that heads northwest to San Rafael del Norte. Refreshments are available. Entry is $1.30.

Lago de Apanas was formed in 1964 by the Mancotál Dam and is the largest man-made lake in Nicaragua. The lake is used to create hydropower and is also a good spot for swimming. You can reach the dam by taking a bus headed for Pantasma; get off at the town of Asturias (a little over an hour from Jinotega). Along the way you'll see a former military base from the 1980s that served to protect the dam from the Contras. Avoid

The Northwest Highlands

swimming near the spillway for safety reasons but, other than that, the lake is all yours – it's rarely visited.

CULTURAL ADVENTURES

AVODEC (Association of Volunteers for Community Development) 3½ blocks north of the Esso gas station, ☎ 782-6502. This is a local non-profit organization that focuses on development projects in rural communities near Jinotega. Volunteers are accepted for a variety of tasks both in the office (such as translating documents) and in the field (including building homes). AVODEC also accepts volunteering families, including kids. Most of the Nicaraguan families that AVODEC works with include young children, and volunteering is a great way for kids to meet local friends while performing meaningful service within the community. Families are advised to contact AVODEC in advance to find out about current needs. Spanish is helpful, but not essential.

Club Infantíl de Niños Trabajadores de Jinotega (☎ 782-3435) accepts volunteers to teach or assist with vocational workshops for street children. Spanish-speaking volunteers with practical skills are particularly needed.

■ ENTERTAINMENT

The movie theater is no longer in business and has turned into (not surprisingly) a church. **Baseball** games are a popular pastime and take place at the stadium, a 10-minute walk south along the highway. On Sundays semi-organized **basketball** games take place on the courts next to the south bus terminal.

Restaurante Borbón in Hotel Café is a relaxed place with an extensive foreign and national drink menu. **Roca Rancho**, south of the Shell Station, is a lively spot for a beer that is popular with affluent Jinotegans; take a taxi back at night (open Mon-Sat 10 am-midnight).

There are a few discos in town, mostly patronized by a young crowd. If you want to go dancing, try **Disco Monkey Jungle** (☎ 782-3605), just north of the Esso station and across the street. At the time of writing, an upscale bar was in the

Disco Monkey Jungle

© www.Jinotega.com

process of opening in a flurry of orange paint on a corner two blocks north of Disco Monkey Jungle. Check it out.

■ WHERE TO STAY

Jinotega's crisp climate means that you'll want hot water here. Remember to bring cash.

> *Every listing in this book is recommended and considered above average in its category. Listings with one star (☆) are highly recommended, those earning two stars (☆☆) are considered to be exceptional. A few resorts and restaurants rate three stars (☆☆☆), which means they are worthy of a special occasion splurge.*

☆☆ **Hotel Café** ($$$, one block north and one block west of the Texaco station, ☎ 782-2710). This is the most upscale hotel in the department of Jinotega and a welcome respite if you've been spending time in small mountain towns. The communal areas are immaculate,

© Hotel Café

with an attractive garden and tile work. The property has a business center, and Internet is available. Rooms are all decorated differently, so see several before you select one. Rooms include a/c, cable TV, private bath with hot water, and in-room phones. Singles cost $35, doubles $45, and suites $55 plus 15% tax. Continental breakfast is included. The friendly staff speaks English. Room service from the restaurant is available from 6 am to

HOTEL PRICE CHART	
Cost per night for two people, before tax	
$	Up to $15
$$	$16-$30
$$$	$31-$60
$$$$	Over $60

9 pm. Valet parking is available, as is laundry service.

☆ **Hotel Bosawas** ($, three blocks north of the northeast corner of the park, ☎ 856-6233). Offering excellent value, especially for solo travelers, the budget Bosawas has nine very clean rooms with shared or private bath and hot water. There isn't much common area in this guesthouse, but service is friendly, the place is brand is new and the location is central. A small single costs $5, a more spacious double, $15.

La Colmena ($$, 1½ blocks east of the park, ☎ 782-2017). Though primarily a restaurant, La Colmena has three quiet rooms available, each for $30. These clean rooms have fans and private baths with hot water. Each room sleeps up to three people.

Sollentuna Hem ($-$$, two blocks west and 2½ blocks north of the Shell station, ☎ 782-2334). A favorite with volunteers and church groups, friendly Sollentuna Hem is owned by a Nicaraguan woman who used to live in Sweden. Doubles cost $16; if you look the part, ask for a nearly identical "backpacker" room for $10 double, $15 triple. All rooms in the guesthouse are perfectly adequate if a bit worn and include private bath and good beds. All rooms have hot water. Breakfast is available, and there is a comfy sitting area with old magazines.

■ WHERE TO EAT

Jinotega has a good selection of restaurants for a town of its size.

DINING PRICE CHART	
Price per person for an entrée, not including beverage, tax or tip	
$	Up to $3
$$	$3-$6
$$$	$6-$10
$$$$	Over $10

☆ **Restaurante Borbón** ($$-$$$, in Hotel Café, ☎ 782-2710). Borbon has a refined ambience and serves Jinotega's most upscale food. Offering American, French and Nicraguan cuisine, Borbon has good service and an extensive foreign drink menu. Meals range from $5 to $10. Open daily 6 am-9 pm. Credit cards accepted.

☆ **Roca Rancho** ($-$$, South of the Shell Station, ☎ 782-3730). Roca Rancho dishes up hearty Nicaraguan specialties in a huge *rancho*. They specialize in grilled meats. Portions are large and the spicy jalapeño steak is particularly good. Open Mon-Sat 10 am-midnight. Credit cards are accepted.

☆ **Soda El Tico** ($-$$, a block east and a half-block south of the cathedral, ☎ 782-2059). El Tico has an extensive menu of Costa Rican favorites (which you'll have trouble distinguishing from Nicaraguan favorites), as well as a handful of well-prepared American staples, including hamburgers. The restaurant is very clean and popular with local families. There is a lunch buffet available (priced per-plate, so fill 'er up). Meals range from $1.50 to $5 and portions are generous. Papaya *refresco* 50¢, enormous ice cream sundae $1.25.

Restaurante La Colmena ($$-$$$, 1½ blocks east of the park, ☎ 782-2017). A longstanding favorite, La Colmena has a good reputation among the town's professionals, who come to toast business deals and enjoy the good food. While the atmosphere isn't notable, the restaurant's good service and quality beef and chicken dishes keep diners coming back. Meals average $8.

Chaba's Pizza ($$, 2½ blocks east of the park, ☎ 782-2692). If you're craving a pie, this is your best option in town. Decent thin-crust pizzas attract a loyal local following and delivery is available. Open Tues-Sun 11 am-10:30 pm.

The local **Eskimo** ice cream shop is the place where you're most likely to run into volunteers and other international types, especially on Sundays, when most places in town are closed. Service is lackluster, but the giggly teenaged couples sharing sundaes are too enamored with each other to notice. Eskimo is next to the old movie theater a block south of Soda El Tico.

DAY-TRIPS FROM JINOTEGA

EL JAGUAR CLOUD FOREST RESERVE

This private reserve and organic coffee farm has six trails through the forest and taking a hike along one of

the paths (from one to three hrs) is the best way to see the reserve's flora and fauna. The reserve is primarily visited by scientists and researchers, who come to investigate bromeliads, orchids, and birds. More than 200 bird species live in the reserve; early morning and late afternoon are the best times to spot them. Good coffee is grown here, and you can watch owners Georges and Lili roasting beans. Entry to the reserve costs $10 pp, which includes a guide. Bring a sweater; the high altitude keeps things cool, which is an excellent reason to visit during the dry season.

The only practical way to reach the reserve is

by 4WD; there are no buses. It's down a dirt road that leads from the Jinotega-San Rafael highway (look for the sign indicating the turnoff). Turn east off the highway, just past Lago de Apanas at the Empalme de San Gabriel and take the dirt road eight miles to the reserve. Contact the reserve in advance to let them know you're coming and get specific directions.

© www.jaguarreserve.org

If you'd like to overnight, there are two expensive **cabins** ($$$$), as well as 30 **dorm beds** ($) that are used primarily by researchers. Cabins (shown at left) have

© www.jaguarreserve.org

rustic baths, small kitchens, and can sleep four guests in two twin beds and two sofa beds. Reservations are mandatory. ☎ 279-9219, www.jaguarreserve. org, orion@ibw.com. ni.

> **TIP:** *If you can't make it to the reserve, coffee grown here is sold at most Whole Foods Markets in the US.*

SAN RAFAEL DEL NORTE

San Rafael del Norte is not typically a destination in itself, but it's a worthwhile stopover on the drive between Jinotega and Esteli. Populated by a few thousand farmers and ranchers, it sees few tourists, but there are several interesting sights in town that will keep you busy for an afternoon.

San Rafael del Norte Highlights
- La Catedral
- Fiestas patronales (last week of September)
- Sandino's Wedding Celebration (May 18)

GETTING HERE

BY CAR

The road from **Jinotega** to San Rafael del Norte is fairly good, but the dirt road from **Estelí** is in poor condition. The road leading to the villages north of San Rafael del Norte is not paved.

BY BUS

There is no bus station; buses leave from the main street just outside Casita San Payo Hotel y Cafetín. Locals are generally well-versed in the bus schedules. San Rafael del Norte is feasible as a day-trip from Jinotega or Esteli as the town is served multiple times daily by buses headed to and from **Jinotega**, **Estelí** and the village of **San Sebastián de Yalí** (usually referred to as Yalí). Times vary based on the day of the week; check locally for updates. There is one **express bus** to **Managua** leaving San Rafael del Norte at 4:30 am, stopping in **Jinotega** at 5:30 am and **Matagalpa** at 6:30 am. The same bus leaves **Managua** at 3 pm, drops passenger in Matagalpa and Jinotega and arrives in San Rafael del Norte at 7 pm.

SERVICES

Farmacia Guadalupe (☎ 652-2336) is on the main street and is open 24 hrs. There is a basic **health clinic** just east of the church, but supplies are very limited.

SIGHTSEEING

La Catedral. San Rafael del Norte's especially attractive church is a must-see for any visitor to town. Stained-glass windows light up the building, which was constructed in 1887. The church was renovated in 1961 under the tutelage of Italian Father Odorico, who passed away over a decade ago and is still revered by the community for his attention to local social projects.

The church is one of the most impressive village churches in the country.

Museo Sandino (*Casa Museo Ejército Defensor de la Soberanía Nacional*). Located on the main street next to the park, the Sandino museum is a testament to this small town's importance during the 1930s when it was a center of operations for the rebels during the occupation of the US Marines.

The museum was originally the house of the father-in-law of General Augusto César Sandino, who had married his typist, Blanca. The museum's simple collection includes paintings and artifacts from the time of the conflict. The museum's opening times are erratic; the caretaker can be found at his house behind the church.

The Tepac. The burial place of Father Odorico, a highly respected Italian priest who worked in San Rafael del Norte for 43 years, the Tepac is on a hill at the northeast side of town. Climb the stairs to Father Odorico's tomb for beautiful views of the peaceful surrounding hills.

The Northwest Highlands

ADVENTURES

ADVENTURES ON WATER

There are several spots near town that are good for swimming. The most convenient are less than 10 minutes from town on foot. Take the road that leads north of town toward Yalí until you reach Los Encuentros Restaurant. The two creeks that meet here are good for swimming, and you can relax afterward with a snack at the restaurant.

ENTERTAINMENT & NIGHTLIFE

San Rafael del Norte goes to sleep early, but you can shoot pool on the main street across from the hotel at **Billares El Chele**.

WHERE TO STAY & WHERE TO EAT

There is one good option in town.

Casita San Payo Hotel y Cafetín ($$, on the main street, ☎ 784-2327). Located on the west side of the main street where the bus stops, San Payo is a pleasant surprise in such a small town. The hotel's six rooms are very clean and have hot water, cable TV and a restaurant that opens early and stays open until the last customer leaves. Singles are $9, doubles are $14. The restaurant is small but pleasant and the food is satisfactory if you stick with the Nicaraguan options. The hotel is occasionally booked up with volunteer groups; make a reservation if possible.

BOSAWAS BIOSPHERE RESERVE

In the extreme northeast of Jinotega Department, Bosawas consists of 1.8 million acres of virtually unexplored territory. A visit to Bosawas is a serious adventure activity and should only be considered by visitors with extensive backcountry experience. Bosawas is sparsely populated by indigenous residents and no accommodation or food is available – visitors should bring anything they may need with them, including camping equip-ment, rain gear, emergency medicine supplies, a water filter and food. It is also required that visitors receive permission to enter the reserve before arranging a trip (contact the MARENA office in Managua, ☎ 233-1594). MARENA can help arrange guides, which are mandatory for the sake of safety and cost $8/day plus food.

The easiest way to reach Bosawas is to take a **flight** from **Managua** or **Puerto Cabezas** to Siuna in the Las Minas area. From here, **private transport** is recommended; contact Pedro Lopez, whose office is on the Parque Central in Siuna (☎ 794-2036). Pedro may be able to help arrange **guides**. It is also possible (but not recommended) to take a **bus** to Siuna, but the ride is long and uncomfortable regardless of where you begin the trip. From Siuna's northern bus station there are buses headed to Wasala at 5 am and 7:30 am ($2.50). Get off at the village of Wilí to begin your adventure.

The Northwest Highlands

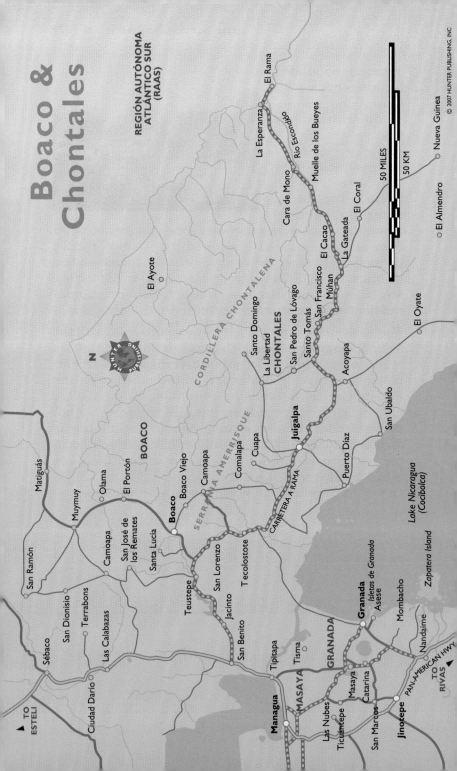

Boaco & Chontales

REGIÓN AUTÓNOMA ATLÁNTICO SUR (RAAS)

CORDILLERA CHONTALENA

CHONTALES

BOACO

SERRANÍA AMERRISQUE

CARRETERA A RAMA

Lake Nicaragua (Cocibolca)

Zapatera Island

GRANADA

MASAYA

PAN-AMERICAN HWY

TO RIVAS

TO ESTELÍ

El Rama
La Esperanza
Río Escondido
Muelle de los Bueyes
Cara de Mono
El Cacao
La Gateada
El Coral
San Francisco
Múhan
Santo Tomás
San Pedro de Lóvago
Santo Domingo
La Libertad
Acoyapa
El Oyate
San Ubaldo
Puerto Díaz
Juigalpa
Cuapa
Comalapa
Camoapa
Boaco Viejo
Boaco
El Portón
Olama
Muymuy
Matiguás
San Ramón
Camoapa
San José de los Remates
Santa Lucía
San Lorenzo
Tecolostote
Teustepe
Jacinto
San Benito
San Dionisio
Terrabons
Las Calabazas
Sébaco
Ciudad Darío
Tipitapa
Tisma
Managua
Las Nubes
Ticuantepe
San Marcos
Masaya
Catarina
Jinotepe
Nandaime
Mombacho
Granada
Isletas de Granada
Asese
El Ayote

Nueva Guinea
El Almendro

50 MILES
50 KM

© 2007 HUNTER PUBLISHING, INC.

Boaco & Chontales

T he gateway to Nicaragua's eastern and southern regions lies in Boaco and Chontales, ranching departments that adhere to a traditional lifestyle and a slower pace that's easy to adapt to. Known for their **cheese** industry, these departments receive few visitors. **Boaco**, capital of the department of the same name, and **Juigalpa**, capital of Chontales department, are small-scale commercial centers that hum with low-key activity as the area's ranchers come to take care of business. Juigalpa is home to several of the region's main sights, including a nationally-recognized **zoo** and a **museum** that displays some of the country's most important **pre-Columbian artifacts**. A few days in Boaco and Chontales gives visitors a chance to experience the pleasure of rural life in Nicaragua.

BOACO

At Km 74 of the road between Managua and El Rama, it splits and leads to Boaco, the capital of the department of the same name. Boaco is known as the "*Ciudad de Dos Pisos*," or City of Two Floors, because of the two tiers that developed as the city grew down the hill from its original location. Boaco is a ranching town and there is not much to draw in tourists, but it's a pleasant enough place to stop for lunch and take a poke around.

Boaca Highlight

■ *Fiestas patronales* (three weeks in July)

GETTING HERE

BY CAR

The road to Boaco is paved. North of Boaco at Muy Muy, the road turns to dirt and continues that way to Puerto Cabezas (Bilwi).

BY BUS

Ordinario buses leave from **Managua**'s Mercado Mayoreo every 45 minutes. **Express minibuses** go to **Managua** at 6:30 am and 12:30 pm ($3), and *ordinario* buses leave every 45 minutes from 5 am to 5:30 pm. For **Juigalpa** or **El Rama**, take a Managua-bound bus to the highway that leads to El Rama and then an east-bound bus from there (every 30 minutes to one hour).

> Boaco was the birthplace of numerous literary talents, including Nicaraguan Ruben DaRio prize for literature winners Julián Guerrero, Antonio Barquero, Diego Sequerira, and Hernán Robleto.

SERVICES

For **banking**, Banpro and Bancentro are both in the lower part of town. **Enitel** is on the northeast corner of the park, and slow **Internet** connections are available there for ridiculously high prices. The **post office** is a block east and a 1½ blocks north of the park. Next door is **Kodak** for all of your photo needs. The **market** is in the lower part of the town, while comprehensive **Minisuper La Dispensa** grocery store is in the upper area. There is a good **cheese shop** near the entrance to town.

Restaurant
Los Cocos

Restaurant
el Borbon

Monument
To Writers

Restaurant
Alpino

Minisuper La Dispensa

Post Office

Kodak

Fundación
Niebrowski

Parque
Cerro el
Faro

STAIRS

Enitel

Bailante
Statue

STAIRS

LA PARROQUIA
DE SANTIAGO
APOSTOL

Central
Park

Hotel
Sobalvarro

Bar / Disco La Cueva

Eskimo

STAIRS

Banpro

N

HUNTER
PUBLISHING

Capilla de La
Santisima

Bancentro

Boaco

Cemetery

Bus Terminal

© 2007 HUNTER PUBLISHING, INC

TO EMPALME
DE BOACO

Not to Scale

SIGHTSEEING

Boaco has two churches. **Capilla de la Santísima Sacramento** is in the lower part of town next to the cemetery. The church is filled with a mishmash of statues, some depicting the area's indigenous groups. **La Parroquia de Santiago Apostol** in the upper part of town, is more than 150 years old and retains its original look.

ADVENTURES

For a panoramic **view** of town, take a short hike up to the lighthouse of Cerro El Faro; locals can point the way. After all that walking, you'll want to soothe your muscles in the **hot springs** of Aguas Claras (see p 385).

ENTERTAINMENT & NIGHTLIFE

El Ranchón de Peter Carbonaro, a new disco, attracts a fairly mature crowd and is north of town on the road toward Muy Muy (take a taxi for less than $1 per person).

WHERE TO STAY

Most visitors choose to stay at **Aguas Claras**, and you should, too (see p 385). In a pinch, get a room at **Hotel Sobalvarro** ($), which has a dozen rooms (doubles $10) on the south side of the park. It's a simple place in a historic building that has seen better days, but there is a balcony overlooking town as well as a courtyard.

WHERE TO EAT

Boaco's restaurants are concentrated in the upper part of town. **Restaurante Borbón** ($, two blocks east and 1½ blocks north of the park) has Nica favorites and good views. **Restaurante Alpino** ($-$$) is also good value and has similarly-priced Nicaraguan food, along with a few American options. Beat the heat with an **Eskimo** ice cream on the south side of the park.

Typical Chontales countryside.

DAY-TRIPS FROM BOACO

Aguas Claras Hot Springs, ☎ 244-2916. Just a few miles west of the Empalme de Boaco, the hot springs of Aguas Claras (entry $1.75) are the area's main draw, with good reason. The complex includes five geothermally-heated pools, a good restaurant ($$-$$$), *ranchos* with hammocks, and the area's best **hotel** ($$), which has 20 rooms situated in a main building and in cabins. Doubles with a/c and private bath with hot water are good value at $29, while budget travelers have the option of two rooms with fan and shared bath at $17 for a double. Make reservations during holiday periods.

JUIGALPA

It's said that in Juigalpa the rivers are made of milk and the stones of cheese – a testament to the area's **dairy industry**. Juigalpa remains off the tourist radar, but this pleasant town's location as a crossroads on the

highways connecting the Southwest, the Río San Juan, and the Caribbean Coast make it a convenient stopping point, especially as Juigalpa's bus station is in the center of town within a couple of blocks of the main guesthouses. Juigalpa is perhaps best known in Nicaragua for its **zoo**, though visitors may cringe at the conditions. The town also boasts Nicaragua's best museum of pre-Columbian artifacts, as well as some of the nation's liveliest *fiestas patronales*. Perhaps most importantly, Juigalpa allows you to experience life in a typical friendly ranching town.

Juigalpa Highlights

■ Museo Arqueológico Gregorio Aguilar Barea

■ Views from Parque Palo Solo

FIESTAS PATRONALES

Juigalpa's *fiestas patronales* are celebrated with vigor during the third week of August in honor of the local patron saint. The bullring, where much of the action takes place, will likely have moved from its current central location to the north of town by the time you visit. Lively *chichero* music, a procession of cowboys and bulls carrying an image of Mary to the cathedral, and a never-ending flow of Victoria beer keep the locals hopping throughout the week.

GETTING HERE

Juigalpa's location makes it a transportation hub for buses to the east, south, and west.

Boaco & Chontales

BY CAR

The road from Managua is in good condition, and driving is a fine option. Consider staying on the highway if you have a car; parking can be a challenge at in-town guesthouses.

BY BUS

Express vans leave Mon-Sat from the north side of the cathedral to **Managua**'s Mercado Mayoreo – supposedly every hour from 7 am to 4 pm, but they are more likely to leave whenever they're full ($3.50/2½ hrs). All other buses leave from the station at the market. There is an information booth at the rear of the bus lot; double-check schedules, especially on Sunday when buses run less frequently. *Ordinario* bus service to **Managua**'s Mercado Mayoreo runs every half-hour from 5 am-5 pm (3½ hrs/$3). There is one bus to **Masaya** ($6/4½ hrs) Mon-Sat at 10 am (alternatively, catch a bus to Managua and change there for points south). For Boaco, take a bus headed to Managua and get off at the Empalme de Boaco intersection (1½ hrs/$2); buses continuing to Boaco are available there. Buses sail along the newly-repaved highway to **El Rama** (for continuing boat service to Bluefields) hourly from 4:30 am-1:30 pm (4½ hrs/$4.50). There is a bus to **Nueva Guinea** at 3:20 pm Mon-Sat. For the interminable ride to **San Carlos**, catch a bus at 8:15 am or 12:15 pm (seven hrs/$7).

GETTING AROUND

Juigalpa is fairly compact but, while the center of town is flat, the edges are very hilly. If you want to go farther afield, catch a **taxi** near the park. Taxis also pass frequently on the highway.

SERVICES

TOURS & INFORMATION: The location of **Intur** is in flux; at the time of writing it was on the south side of the park. If you can't find it, ask at the mayor's office. If you want to explore the nearby mountains by foot, horse, or vehicle, including a camping option, arrange a trip through Carlos Villanueva. He can be found at the museum or by phone, ☎ 512-0511.

If you need a **guide** to explore the area by foot or bus, including local hot springs, ask for Billy Matuz in the shoeshiners' pavilion in the park or email him at **billybobjamaica@yahoo.com**. Billy is personable, knows the area well, and speaks some English ($15/day, negotiable).

MONEY: Banpro and BDF are on the southwest corner of the park. Bancentro, which exchanges **travelers' checks**, and Banco ProCredit are a block north of the park. Banks are open 8:30 am-4:30 pm Mon-Fri and 8:30 am-noon Sat. Banpro and Bancentro have **ATMs**, but there are no ATMs in town that accept MasterCard.

MAIL & INTERNET: The **post office** is on the southeast corner of the park. Internet cafés with fast connections are opening at a rapid pace in Juigalpa; 60¢/hr is standard. Try **Bennet Cybercafe** (☎ 512-0101, open 9 am-10 pm) or **Cyber Speedyway** (open 8 am-10 pm) for air-conditioned bliss. Both cafés also burn photo CDs. If you're staying on the highway, there is an Internet place tucked right behind the Texaco station – look for the green Carnicería Espacio sign. Open daily 8:30 am until whenever the family decides to close.

TELEPHONE: Enitel is four blocks north of the park. Open 8 am-noon and 1:30-5:30 pm Mon-Sat. Internet cafés make international calls for around 10¢/minute.

> NOTE: *The prefix for Juigalpa's phone numbers recently changed from 812 to 512, with the remaining numbers staying the same. Signs at local businesses are often not up-to-date.*

RESTROOMS: The **public restrooms** (8¢) in the Parque Central are occasionally open; a better bet is to stop for a drink at a restaurant and use the restroom there.

MEDICAL: Hospital La Asunción is on the highway in the southeastern part of town, but better facilities and a more convenient location two blocks west of the park are available at the **private clinic Lab Lafayette and Salazar** (☎ 512-2292). Juigalpa has a large number of **pharmacies** (most are open daily 7 am-10 pm). **El Buen Pastor** (☎ 512-0079) is a block north and 1½ blocks west of the park and **Farmacia San José** (☎ 512-3195) is on the west side of the park.

MARKETS: There are two **supermarkets** in Juigalpa. Supermercado San Antonio has a good selection and is one block west of the park. Pali is one block north and one block east of the park. Stock up on snacks for the bus at the **market**, two blocks east of the park, surrounding the bus station. The market has a limited selection and is mostly outdoors. **La Casa del Queso** (facing the cathedral in the same building as 7/24) has a selection of Nicaraguan **cheeses**.

SIGHTSEEING

☆☆ **Museo Arqueológico Gregorio Aguilar Barea** (2½ blocks east of the park, ☎ 512-0784). Famous for its Chontal statues, dating back more than a thousand years, the museum has some of the best pre-Columbian pieces in the country. Many aspects of Chontal history are still unknown, and ancient statues are still occasionally being uncovered in the nearby Amerrisque Mountains, the Valley of the Mayales, and in Garrobo Grande. The museum also houses paintings, coins, and, oddly, a

© www.vianica.com

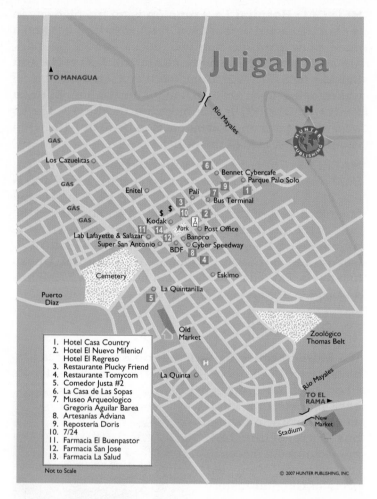

TO MANAGUA

Rio Mayales

N

GAS

Los Cazuelitas

Bennet Cybercafe
Parque Palo Solo

GAS

Enitel

Pali

Bus Terminal

GAS

GAS

Kodak

Post Office

Lab Lafayette & Salazar

Banpro

Super San Antonio

BDF

Cyber Speedway

Cemetery

Eskimo

Puerto
Diaz

La Quintanilla

Old
Market

Zoológico
Thomas Belt

1. Hotel Casa Country
2. Hotel El Nuevo Milenio/
Hotel El Regreso
3. Restaurante Plucky Friend
4. Restaurante Tomycom
5. Comedor Justa #2
6. La Casa de Las Sopas
7. Museo Arqueologico
Gregoria Aguilar Barea
8. Artesanías Adviana
9. Repostería Doris
10. 7/24
11. Farmacia El Buenpastor
12. Farmacia San Jose
13. Farmacia La Salud

La Quinta

Rio Mayales

TO EL
RAMA ►

New
Market

Stadium

Not to Scale

© 2007 HUNTER PUBLISHING, INC

stuffed animal collection. Curator Carlos Villanueva is an excellent source of information about the museum pieces and also leads guided excursions to see the region (see *Tours* above).

The private museum was created in 1952 by respected former town mayor Gregorio Aguilar Barea. Open Mon-Fri 9 am-noon and 2-4:30 pm, Sat 8-11:30 am. Entrance 75¢. Stop by even if the museum is closed; the statues can be seen from outside.

Catedral de Nuestra Senora de la Asuncion (facing Parque Central). Juigalpa's cathedral is a modern anomaly compared with other cathedrals in the region. Built in 1966 to replace the original deteriorating cathedral dating from 1648, the structure includes two bell towers and stained-glass symbols of both Christ and the local region, including cowboy images.

© www.vianica.com

Jardín Zoológico Thomas Belt (eight blocks south of the southwest corner of the park). Housing a fairly comprehensive collection of more than 60 species from all over Nicaragua, Juigalpa's zoo is popular with families on Sundays. There is an on-site cafeteria. Open daily 8 am-5:30 pm. Entrance 75¢.

SHOE SHINING

One thing every Parque Central in Nicaragua has in common is an army of shoe shiners. Identified by their ubiquitous wooden shoeshine boxes, which serve as a seat as well as a place to hold brushes and polish, they come in all ages. You will be amazed at the speed with which they spiff up a pair of shoes (or, in Juigalpa, more often boots) for a mere C5 (40¢); feel free to tip for a job well done. Juigalpa is a good place to start if your footwear needs some help: the shoe shiners are based in the Parque Central's shoeshine pavilion, and, if asked, they will regale you with the story of how one of them became Juigalpa's most respected mayor.

Parque Central. Juigalpa's park is best known for its **statue** of a shoe shiner, commissioned in 1994 by

Mayor Salvador de Leo Rivas, a much-revered figure in Juigalpa who died a year after the statue's completion. Rising from poverty as a shoe shiner, the mayor became a popular politician, considered one of Nicaragua's best.

There is often a mentally ill woman lecturing on the steps of the kiosk, and she really likes foreigners – be prepared. The park closes in early evening and the action shifts to Parque Palo Solo.

Parque Palo Solo. The well-tended Parque Palo Solo has excellent views of the Amerrisque Mountains. The fountain in the center of the park is decorated with ears of corn – a testament to Juigalpa's agricultural tradition. Enjoy the scenery with a drink or a meal at the good on-site restaurant. The park is a popular early evening spot for young local couples wanting to avoid the prying eyes of their parents.

Juigalpa's cemetery

Cemetery. Located on the west side of the highway four blocks from the park, Juigalpa's cemetery is particularly attractive and worth a stroll. Mornings or late afternoons are best – there is not much shade.

ADVENTURES

ADVENTURES ON WATER

Balneario El Salto, a mile from town just off the highway to Managua, is the area's most popular swimming spot. You can take a taxi, or it's easy to walk along the highway (turn off the highway when you see a blue sign on the northeast side of the road). There is a waterfall that cascades over a dam in the rainy season, but the large swimming hole is usable year-round. The surrounding tree-shaded banks are a good spot for a picnic. There are no facilities available – bring water. There is a $1 entrance fee during holidays.

It's easy to laze away an afternoon at **La Peñita**, a complex just off the highway toward Managua comprising three swimming pools and a large *rancho* complete meals, drinking, and dancing that is packed with Nicaraguan families when the weather is hot. To get there, take a bus from Juigalpa's station (15 minutes/30¢) or a taxi and ask to be let off at La Penita. You may be able to hitch a ride back into Juigalpa with a local family; exercise caution as many revelers have too much to drink before getting behind the wheel.

ADVENTURES ON HORSEBACK

Horses can be arranged for day or overnight trips through Carlos Villanueva (see *Tours* above). Intrepid travelers can make their own arrangements for day-trips by taking the pedestrian path next to the high school down into the rural village area south of town. Continue straight upon reaching the bottom until you reach the first large ranch (a 10-minute walk from the high school) where you can arrange horses – ask for Wilmer. To get a better sense of where you're headed, stop at Parque Palo Solo, where you'll get a clear view of the ranch below.

KIDS RUNNING THE SHOW

Juigalpa takes a unique approach to governance, for one week at least, when kids take over the mayor's office! In June, a special municipal election is held, and only kids below the age of 13 can participate. The children elect a mayor, vice mayor, and advisors, and, with some adult assistance, they take over town management for a week. It's not over when the real mayor returns: he implements the community projects initiated by the kids!

SHOPPING

For a **cowboy hat** of your own, hit the market; the area just north of the bus lot has lots of options. Your best bet for locally-produced **crafts**, including piggy banks, windchimes, and pottery, is the **artisan stand** on the southeast corner of the park next to the post office. **Artesanías Adriana** (☎ 512-2413), near Eskimo also has some handicrafts. The underground shop in the **kiosk** in the Parque Central has a decent selection of **handicrafts** (along with a disturbing number of cartoon character-embellished items). Boot-shaped cowhide keychain $1. Open daily 10 am-7:30 pm.

ENTERTAINMENT & NIGHTLIFE

Check out **www.bacanalchontales.com** for upcoming events (check again the next morning for photos of your adventures). **Baseball** games are played at the stadium on the south side of the highway on Sundays. **Cock-fights** take place at 6 pm on Sunday just outside of town on the road to La Libertad – look for the Brava beer signs.

Juigalpa is a hardwork-ing town, and there is not much in the way of nightlife. **La Quinta** (☎ 512-2485) is the place to go for drinking and dancing and is a popular venue for televised sports events ($1.50

© www.vianica.com

cover on Sat night). It's on the highway near the edge of town. Take a taxi at night. **Restaurante 7/24**, over-looking the cathedral, has an upstairs balcony and is Juigalpa's centrally-located see-and-be-seen bar. Juigalpa's old movie theater is now a Pali supermarket; check out what's playing at the movie room just west of the park, which shows one movie on Sunday evenings at 6 pm (followed by a showing of an, ahem, "adult" movie at 8 pm).

WHERE TO STAY

Juigalpa's hotel patrons are primarily ranchers from nearby villages ar-riving for a night to do business. Accommoda-tion is generally simple but comfortable, and your neighbors will likely be very early risers.

HOTEL PRICE CHART	
Cost per night for two people, before tax	
$	Up to $15
$$	$16-$30
$$$	$31-$60
$$$$	Over $60

NOTE: *Few hotels and restaurants ac-cept credit cards, so cash is the norm. Most travelers rely primarily on ATMs , which are popping up even in smaller towns, are generally reliable, and in-volve a minimum of fees.*

☆ **Hotel Casa Country** ($$, half-block west of Parque Palo Solo, ☎ 512-2546). The most comfortable place to stay in town, Casa Country has four good-value rooms (all with private bath, a/c, and cable TV) in a modern, well-maintained home across from Parque Palo Solo. Single $11.

Hotel El Nuevo Milenio ($, 1½ blocks east of the park, ☎ 512-0646). Simple but welcoming, El Nuevo Milenio has 16 small, spotless singles and doubles with good mattresses and shared or private bath and fan or a/c. Private baths are separated from the room by a flimsy curtain and aren't really worth the extra expense. Ask for a room near the back; those near the street aren't as quiet and the walls don't reach the ceiling. There is a shared balcony overlooking the street that is a pleasant spot for reading. Single with shared bath and fan $5.

Hotel El Regreso ($, ☎ 512-0646). Next door to El Nuevo Milenio and with similar quality and prices. This friendly place is a good option if you are arriving late or leaving early; the bus station is just around the corner. English is spoken.

La Quinta ($$, facing La Asuncion Hospital, ☎ 512-2574). Right on the highway, this is a convenient place to stay if you are driving through and just need a place to stop for the night. Saturday and Sunday nights bring revelers to the on-site disco: La Quinta is not a good weekend option unless you want to join them. There is an on-site restaurant.

WHERE TO EAT

Restaurante Palo Solo ($$-$$$, in Parque Palo Solo, ☎ 512-2735). This is Juigalpa's most up-scale restaurant (it's all relative). Palo Solo's open-air park setting and good food make it a big draw on pleasant

DINING PRICE CHART	
Price per person for an entrée, not including beverage, tax or tip	
$	Up to $3
$$	$3-$6
$$$	$6-$10
$$$$	Over $10

evenings. Open for lunch and dinner from 10 am-10 pm.

Restaurante Tomycom ($-$$, 2½ blocks south of the park, ☎ 512-4213). Tomycom's attentive waiters serve up *comida corriente* ($2) in a pleasant, relaxed atmosphere. Sandwiches and burgers are available for the homesick. Nica breakfast $1.10. Open daily 7 am-10 pm.

Restaurante Plucky Friend ($-$$, 1½ blocks north of the park, ☎ 512-2874). Worth a stop for the name alone, newly-opened Plucky Friend is one of the best centrally-located options for *comida corriente* ($2). There are a few vegetarian options, including potatoes and cheese served with salad and rice ($3). Housed in a cavernous, warehouse-style place, Plucky Friend is not big on atmosphere, but the extensive menu of juicy meats and fast service will keep you coming back.

Las Cazuelitas ($$, two blocks east of the Shell Station, ☎ 512-1986). Juigalpa's professionals can't get enough of the air-conditioning and the tasty meat dishes at modern Las Cazuelitas. This is one of Juigalpa's most upscale places, with good food to boot. Closed Mon.

7/24 ($$, facing the north side of the cathedral). A good option for dining late in the evening, 7/24 has Nicaraguan, Chinese, and nominally American fast food downstairs, but head upstairs for slightly overpriced but good Nicaraguan dishes. Open daily 11 am-midnight.

La Casa de las Sopas ($, northeast of the market, ☎ 812-2933). For a true local experience, try this unpretentious place known primarily for its soup selection. La Casa also has *comida corriente* (the jalapeño steak is particularly good). Bulls' balls soup $2.

There are several no frills budget eateries along the highway (no phones) that are very popular with local families for lunch. Try **La Quintanilla** ($), 1½ blocks south of the cemetery, or neighboring **Comedor Justa No. 2** ($) for good, simple food.

Tiny, family-run **Repostería Dora** ☆☆ ($, ☎ 512-1004), next to the museum, is the best **bakery** in town. Try the seriously tasty braided doughnut-like *trenza* (60¢). Takeaway only. Open from around 3 to 9 pm.

For ice cream, friendly **Eskimo** is four blocks south of the park. Unfortunately, it closes for lunch at the hottest part of the day when you need it most (reopens at 3 pm, closed Sun).

DAY-TRIPS FROM JUIGALPA

Though none of these towns have major sites, they offer a chance to see rural life in the area.

CUAPA

Steeped in history, tiny Cuapa is also offers a challenging **hiking** opportunity.

The war was not kind to Cuapa, which saw vicious fighting between the Sandinistas and Contras in the 1980s. Since that time, things have become decidedly more peaceful. A sign at the entrance to Cuapa proclaiming "*Bienvenido a la Tierra de María*" welcomes visitors to the land of Mary, so named due to a vision of the Virgin Mary that appeared before a local farmer in the early 1980s. Her message to the farmer was interpreted as a condemnation of the Sandinista government. Devout Catholics from throughout the country visit Cuapa annually on the May 8th anniversary of the appearance to visit the hillside monument. Visitors also flock to Cuapa during the *fiestas patronales* June 19-27.

At the entrance of the road to Cuapa behind the school there are some **ruins** of historic homes. Hikers can take advantage of the granite **El Monolito de Cuapa** (Cuapa Monolith), which offers a challenging three-hour **hike**, with several steep portions. Local guide Nicolas, who speaks English, can show you the way.

There is one very basic guesthouse/restaurant in town called **La Maravilla**, with rooms for $4, but your best option is to return to Juigalpa for accommodation.

Buses run between Juigalpa's bus station and Cuapa six times per day (less often on Sunday), beginning at 6 am; the last bus leaves at 6 pm. From Cuapa to Juigalpa, buses leave from the center of town at 6 am-4 pm.

The following villages are worth a look if you have some free time to poke around.

PUERTO DÍAZ

If you're curious to see a *vista* of Lago de Nicaragua from the eastern shore, Puerto Diaz is a small fishing village that is eas-
ily reached from Juigalpa. There are no facilities for travelers, but you may be able to ar-range a boat excur-sion with a local fisherman. Buses ply the bumpy dirt
road from Juigalpa with departures Mon-Sat at 5 am, 2, and 5 pm (30 minutes/75¢). Check upon arrival for re-turn times to ensure you don't miss the last bus back to Juigalpa.

LA LIBERTAD & SANTO DOMINGO

The villages of La Libertad and Santo Domingo have been minor **gold mining** centers for more than a cen-tury. La Libertad is known primarily as the birthplace of former president Daniel Ortega and Catholic arch-bishop Miguel Obando y Bravo. Englishman Thomas Belt wrote his definitive book, *A Naturalist in Nicaragua,* in the late 19th century in Santo Domingo. An enjoy-able way to see the area is to rent a **bike** in Juigalpa, then take one of the frequent daily buses up the road to Santo Domingo. Enjoy the downhill ride back to Juigalpa, which passes through La Libertad.

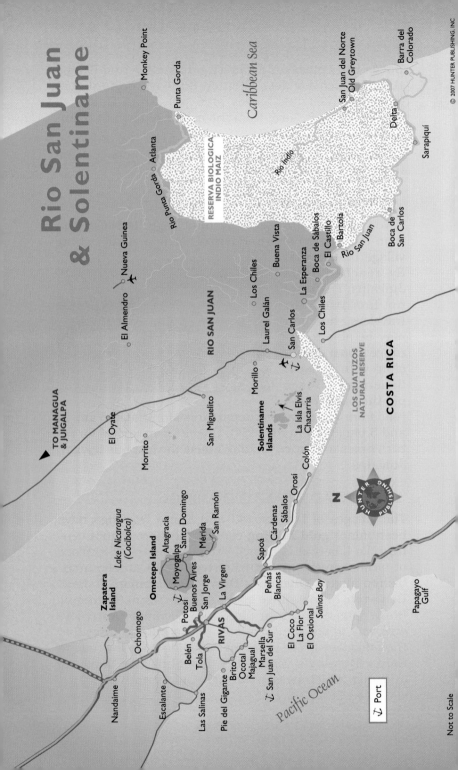

Rio San Juan
& Solentiname

© 2007 HUNTER PUBLISHING, INC

Caribbean Sea

Monkey Point

Punta Gorda

Barra del Colorado

San Juan del Norte
Old Greytown

Delta

Sarapiquí

Atlanta

Rio Punta Gorda

RESERVA BIOLOGICA
INDIO MAIZ

Rio Indio

Nueva Guinea

El Almendro

Los Chiles

Buena Vista

Boca de Sábalos

El Castillo

Bartola

Boca de
San Carlos

RIO SAN JUAN

Laurel Galán

La Esperanza

Rio San Juan

Los Chiles

San Carlos

Morillo

**TO MANAGUA
& JUIGALPA**

El Oyate

San Miguelito

Morrito

Solentiname
Islands

La Isla Elvis
Chacarría

LOS GUATUZOS
NATURAL RESERVE

COSTA RICA

Colón

Orosí

Lake Nicaragua
(Cocibolca)

Ometepe Island

Altagracia
Santo Domingo

Moyogalpa
Mérida

Buenos Aires

San Ramón

Sábalos

Cárdenas

N

**Zapatera
Island**

Potosí

San Jorge

La Virgen

Sapoá

Peñas
Blancas

Papagayo
Gulf

Ochomogo

Nandaime

Escalante

Belén

Tola

La Virgen

RIVAS

Marsella

El Coco
La Flor
El Ostional

Salinas Bay

Las Salinas

Pie del Gigante

Brito

Ocotal
Majagual

San Juan del Sur

Pacific Ocean

⚓ **Port**

Not to Scale

Río San Juan
& Solentiname

This secluded region, located in the southernmost section of Nicaragua and largely covered by dense **jungle**, offers some of Nicaragua's most interesting adventures, and the area's history was central to the development of Central America.

In 1524, conquistador Hernán Cortés wrote a letter to King Carlos I of Spain proclaiming, "He who possesses the San Juan River could be considered the owner of the World." Over the next three centuries, the river remained an important cross-isthmus route both for those with commercial interests and for insatiable adventurers: Mark Twain; William Walker in his quest to control Central America; and "69ers," giddy with gold fever and utilizing **Cornelius Vanderbilt**'s transit route to California. All traversed the waters of the Río San Juan.

Though the construction of the Panama Canal at the beginning of the 20th century relegated the Río San Juan to obscurity, its incredible potential as a tourist destination is just beginning to be discovered. Few travelers make it to the Río San Juan, but those that do are rewarded with lush scenery and a dizzying array of **wildlife**. There are few more enjoyable journeys in Nicaragua than a ride down the secluded Río San Juan. The river itself, the lifeblood of the entire region, starts at the southwest corner of Lago de Nicaragua at San Carlos and meanders 123 miles before reaching the Caribbean at Greytown. **Bird** life along the river is particularly plentiful, including toucans, harpy eagles, herons, egrets, and cormorants. Howler monkeys are a frequent sight and, in the evening, caimans sometimes make an appearance. Pack binoculars (and perhaps a good book) for the trip down the river, and enjoy the ride.

The **Solentiname Archipelago**, located in Lago de Nicaragua and accessible by boat from San Carlos, has a fascinating lifestyle and a beautiful natural environment. Famous for its **Primitivist paintings** and history of **liberation theology**, Solentiname has developed a unique culture due to its isolation.

The Río San Juan and the islands of Solentiname are a challenge to access, but visitors who make the effort to get here will be richly rewarded with incomparable adventure and cultural experiences.

SAN CARLOS

Though San Carlos has a population of only 8,000, it is the most economically important town in the region. In fact, San Carlos's strategic location has been its main draw for centuries. King Carlos V of Spain founded the town, then known as Nueva Jaén, in 1526. The town

was subsequently abandoned and later became known as San Carlos when it was repopulated in the 17th century and became a key port. The town fortress, built to support the Spanish at El Castillo against attacks by British and Dutch pirates, remains partially standing today despite damage sustained in 1670 from a pirate attack. The fortress also withstood occupation by **William Walker** during his bid to expropriate Vanderbilt's steamship company, along with the entire country of Nicaragua. In 1977 Sandinista guerillas from Solentiname briefly took over the fort but were then pushed over the border to Costa Rica.

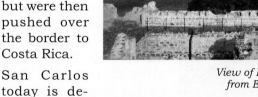

View of Rí San Juan from El Castillo.

San Carlos today is decidedly more peaceful, though it still has a transient feel to it: everyone seems to be coming from or going somewhere. Most visitors find that San Carlos has little to recommend it; the town burned to the ground in 1984 and rebuilding was haphazard. Recent years have seen a bit more effort to improve its ramshackle aesthetics, and the streets are looking cleaner. Nonetheless, there is little to do in town; consider making arrangements to arrive early in the day in order to avoid spending the night in one of the town's poor accommodation options. If you do find yourself with a few hours to spend in town, head up to the fortress for views of the town and river and take a walk along the waterfront to see the busy port in action.

■ An excursion to Los Guatuzos
  Wildlife Refuge

■ The international sport fishing tournament
  (September 14-15)

■ Views of the sunset from the port

■ Some may consider leaving town
  a highlight!

■ GETTING HERE

BY PLANE

Flying to San Carlos is strongly recommended over other options.

La Costeña (☎ 263-1228 in Managua or 263-2142 in San Carlos) has one daily flight to San Carlos from **Managua**. Mon, Tues, Wed, Thurs and Sat at 9 am; Fri

and Sun at noon (50 mins, $99 round-trip/ $69 one-way). The flight returns to **Managua** approximately 20 minutes after arrival. The San Carlos airstrip is a few miles north of town; grab a taxi for $1.

There is a La Costeña "**office**" (really a home) one block east of the bank. During the rainy season the road to Managua is sometimes impassable; at these times flights can be packed; be sure to book as far in advance as possible and reconfirm your flight.

BY CAR

Driving to San Carlos is strongly discouraged. The road is in serious disrepair, particularly in the rainy season, when it becomes a never-ending mud pit. The road is paved until you reach Acoyapa (a little more than an hour from Juigalpa), which is also the last significant village until you reach San Miguelito five hrs and 45 mins later. If you do attempt to drive to San Carlos, carry food, water, gasoline, and spare car parts. The journey takes about 7½ hrs from **Managua**.

BY BUS

This journey follows one of the most poorly maintained routes in the country; there are rumors that the road will be paved in the next couple of years, but don't hold your breath. The ride is bumpy, cramped, choked with dust in the dry season and with mud in the wet months. There are one to two stops at roadside restaurants with decent food available for takeaway, but bring snacks, water, and a lot of patience. Try to avoid this route during Semana Santa and Christmas; buses are packed and travelers sometimes have to ride on the roof. Keep in mind that during the rainy season the road sometimes becomes impassable. A flexible schedule is a must.

*The road to San Carlos is long and lonely,
with just a few tiny settlements along the way.*

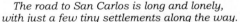

Río San Juan & Solentiname

Still determined to take the bus? There are at least two buses per day from **Managua**'s Mercado Mayoreo at 8 and 11:45 am; others may depart sporadically (nine hrs/$9). Buses leave **Juigalpa**'s station at 11:30 am and 3:15 pm (ask at the bus station about other buses that will pass by on the highway coming from Managua).

For your return trip, confirm bus times at San Carlos's bus station the day before your departure. Buses leave from San Carlos for **Managua** at 8, 11:45 am and 8 pm. Buses head to **Juigalpa** at team, 11 am, 12:40 and 1:30 pm. There is also a daily bus to **Nueva Guinea** and, sporadically, a bus to **El Rama**. Alternatively, to reach El Rama, take the Managua bus as far as the east-west highway (six hrs), then change to a bus for El Rama (one runs every hour).

BY BOAT

Many travelers prefer the boat journey (15 hrs/$9) over the option of taking a bus to San Carlos from the western side of the country. If you opt to take the boat, first class is recommended for its air-conditioning and less crowded conditions. Both first and second class offer deck passage only. Snacks are sold on board, but bring water, food, a hammock or sleep sack, and earplugs. Tickets can be purchased at the dock prior to departure; get there 90 minutes early for this route.

The boat leaves from **Granada** on Mon and Thurs at 3 pm, stopping in **Altagracia**, **Ometepe** four hours later, **San Miguelito** at 4:30 am, and arriving in **San Carlos** around 6 am.

The boat leaves San Carlos on Wed and Fri at 3 pm, stopping in **San Miguelito** and **Altagracia** and arriving in **Granada** the next morning at 6 am.

Night owls beware: the *lancha* from **Solentiname** to San Carlos (1½ hrs/$5) picks up sleepy passengers Tues and Fri (sometimes on Mon as well) at 4:15 am from **Isla Mancarrón**, stopping at **Isla Elvis Chavarría** at 4:30 am and **Isla Venado** at 4:45 am, arriving San

Río San Juan from Sabalos Lodge.

Carlos at 6 am. The public *lancha* leaves the dock next to Roman Lake Lines in the center of San Carlos for **Solentiname** on Tues and Fri at 1 pm (there is sometimes a Mon boat at 1 pm as well). The fare is paid on the boat.

From **Los Guatuzos** (Papaturro) there is a boat to San Carlos on Mon, Tues and Thurs at 7 am (four hrs/$6). From San Carlos to **Los Guatuzos** the boat leaves on Tues, Wed and Fri at 7 am.

Boats come up the Río San Juan from the center of **El Castillo** Mon-Sat at 5, 7 am and 2 pm; Sat 5 and 7 am; Sun 1 pm (three hrs/$3.50). Boats leave San Carlos headed for **El Castillo** Mon-Fri at 8 am, noon and 3 pm; Sun 1 pm. You can also stop at any of the hotels between San Carlos and El Castillo, or in the village of **Boca de Sábalos** using this boat. Boats leave down the Río San Juan from a dock just south of the bus station on the east side of the road. Look for a covered waiting area with benches, and purchase tickets at the cream-colored kiosk facing the road; arrive one hour in advance as boats do fill up. The attendant will ask for your destination when you purchase your ticket and the boat driver will drop you off at the correct dock.

Boats come to San Carlos from **San Juan del Norte** (also known as San Juan de Nicaragua) only twice per week (nine-10 hrs/$13) on Thurs and Sun at 4:30 am. From San Carlos to **San Juan del Norte** there are boats on Tues and Fri at 6 am (11 hrs). Bring plenty of water and sunscreen.

If you are coming from **Los Chiles**, **Costa Rica**, there are boats leaving for San Carlos Mon-Fri at 1:30, 3:30 and 4:30 pm, Sun 4 pm (1½ hrs/$7). Boats from San Carlos to **Los Chiles** leave from the dock next to the Immigration Office Mon-Sat at 10:30 am, 1:30 and 4 pm, Sun 12:30 pm.

> **NOTE:** *If weather conditions are unfavorable, particularly likely during windy late March and April, the boat that crosses Lago de Nicaragua between Granada and San Carlos may not stop at Ometepe.*

Costa Rica Border Crossing: Los Chiles

Before taking the boat to Los Chiles, you need to go to the blue and white Migracion (Immigration) Office on the waterfront road to get an exit stamp. The office opens at 8:30 am, but try to get there an hour before it opens to avoid an endless wait. You'll wait in one line to have your passport examined before being waved to a second line where you'll pay the $2 **departure tax** (US dollars only). The boat to Los Chiles leaves from just beyond the passport window.

Upon arrival in Los Chiles (1½ hrs later) walk up the road 200 yards, where your bags will be searched and you'll have to get in a second line to get your passport stamped ($8). There are daily buses from here to San Jose and La Fortuna.

If you are crossing the border from Costa Rica into Nicaragua, you'll need to get a **Cruz Roja (Red Cross) stamp** before you can cross the border. Acquire one for

$1.20 at either the Nicaragua Consulate (just north of the church; open Mon-Fri 8:30 am-noon and 2-4:30 pm) or at the office across from the Immigration Office. It costs $7 (US dollars only) to cross into Nicaragua from Costa Rica.

> NOTE: *There is a village north of the Río San Juan also named Los Chiles; if you're asking for information be sure to specify that you're referring to the Los Chiles in Costa Rica.*

CRUISING LAGO DE NICARAGUA

A businessman from Isla Ometepe has purchased an old Soviet ship that will soon offer the most luxurious and efficient means of getting around Lago de Nicaragua. Complete renovation of the ship is in progress, and passenger service is slated to begin in 2007 between Granada, Isla Ometepe, Solentiname, and San Carlos. The ship, which will offer comfortable passenger cabins as well as deck passage, will also transport vehicles.

SERVICES

TOURS & INFORMATION: The **Intur** office (just southwest of the post office across from Eskimo, ☎ 583-0301) is friendly and has some useful brochures. Some of the transport information is out of date; reconfirm at the dock. Open Mon-Fri 8 am-noon and 2-5 pm.

There is an agency in San Carlos that arranges day or overnight tours of the local area; **private boat transportation** can also be arranged with one of the numerous tour operators servicing this area.

See also the *Down the Río San Juan* (p 415) and *Solentiname* (p 429) sections for information about tours specifically for these areas.

MONEY: Banco de Finanzas is the only **bank** in town (one block east of the park, ☎ 583-0144). Open Mon-Fri 8:30 am-4 pm and Sat 8:30 am-noon. The bank exchanges dollars, but not other currencies nor traveler's checks. There is no ATM in town. The **money changers** at the bus station will find you before you find them. There is a Western Union southwest of the church.

INTERNET: Find speedy access and friendly service for 75¢/hr at the youth center on the east side of the park (look for the bright yellow building). Staff member Bernardo is friendly and a good source of information about San Carlos. A second Internet café just opened south of the park across from Hotel Carelhys.

MAIL & TELEPHONE: The **post office** is a block south of the park (☎ 583-0276). Open Mon-Fri 8 am-5 pm (closed for lunch) and Sat 8 am-1 pm. **Enitel** is on the highway near the hospital.

RESTROOMS: The best option in this compact town is to return to your hotel. There is a dingy **public restroom** just south of the bus lot (8¢) that also has **showers** for weary travelers, but afterward you may feel less clean than you did upon arrival.

MEDICAL: San Carlos has basic medical services. For a serious emergency, flying to Managua or chartering a boat (one hour) to Los Chiles, Costa Rica, is recommended. San Carlos's **Hospital Luís Felipe Moncada** is just north of town on the highway to Managua (☎ 583-0244 or 583-0238). The **Centro de Salud** can be reached at ☎ 583-0361.

STAYING SAFE: San Carlos has a bit of a rogue feel to it; walking around at night is not recommended. The **police station** (☎ 583-0350) is two miles north of town on the highway to Managua. The **fire department** can be reached at ☎ 583-2149.

MARKETS: San Carlos's unsightly market surrounds the bus station and is a good place to pick up supplies for onward journeys. *Comedores* line the north side of the bus lot. This is a decent spot to get a quick, inexpensive meal, though the food is nothing to write home about. Numerous *pulperías* surround the market; be sure to stock up on water if you are headed to Solentiname, Los Guatuzos, or down the Río San Juan. There are no supermarkets in town.

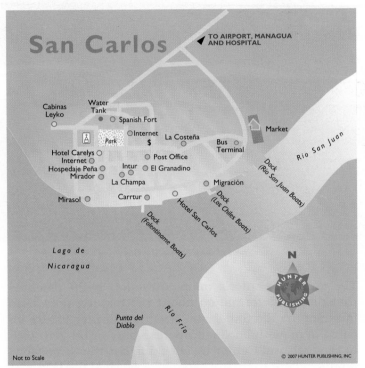

San Carlos

TO AIRPORT, MANAGUA AND HOSPITAL

Cabinas Leyko

Water Tank

Spanish Fort

Internet

La Costeña

Market

Park

$

Bus Terminal

Río San Juan

Hotel Carelys
Internet

Post Office

Dock (Río San Juan Boats)

Hospedaje Peña

Intur

El Granadino

Mirador

La Champa

Mirasol

Carrtur

Migración

Dock (Los Chiles Boats)

Dock (Solentiname Boats)

Hotel San Carlos

Lago de Nicaragua

N

HUNTER PUBLISHING

Punta del Diablo

Río Frío

Not to Scale

© 2007 HUNTER PUBLISHING, INC

Río San Juan & Solentiname

SIGHTSEEING

Most visitors don't stay long in San Carlos, but if you find yourself with some time to spare, head to the **Casa Cultural José Coronel Urtecho** in the old fortress (located up the steps on the north side of the park), named after a Nicaraguan poet. Though not much remains of the **fortress** today, it has been used for various purposes through the tumultuous history in the region: the Spanish built it to protect commercial interests, the Somoza family used it as a prison, and it was later used as a police station during the Sandinista regime.

The fortress overlooks the river.

The cultural center's main attraction is 29 placards that display information about the history, flora, and fauna of the Río San Juan. The town **library** is also located here (with books in Spanish only). End your visit to the Cultural Center by checking out the three viewpoints, where there are expansive views of the lake, the river, and the town.

ADVENTURES

San Carlos is primarily a jumping-off point for adventures in the surrounding areas. See *Tours* above, or the *Down the Río San Juan* (p 417), *Los Guatuzos* (p 415), and *Solentiname* (p 429) sections for adventures accessible from San Carlos.

CULTURAL ADVENTURES

San Juan Río Relief (☎ 337-988-3274, in Louisiana, US, www.sanjuanriorelief.org, sanjuanriorelief@cox.

net). Founded by an American traveling on the Río San Juan, non-profit San Juan Río Relief accepts donations of medical supplies; volunteers are also needed to work on its short-term medical missions in villages along the river.

SHOPPING

Shopping consists of little more than picking up provisions for journeys into the surrounding areas. Consider acquiring rubber Wellington **boots** ($8-$9) in one of the shops around town, especially during rainy season.

ENTERTAINMENT & NIGHTLIFE

You can have a drink at one of the restaurants, but your best option is probably to turn in early. Going out alone at night is not recommended.

WHERE TO STAY

San Carlos has a very limited selection of accommodations, and rodent roommates are common. Cabinas Leyko and Hotel Carelhys are by far your best options (everything is relative). If you've ever considered opening a hotel in Nicaragua, San Carlos would be an excellent option! Remember to bring cash.

Cabinas Leyko ($$$, two blocks west of the church, ☎ 583-0354, leyko@ibw.com.ni). The best choice in town, Cabinas Leyko has rooms with shared or private bath, cable TV, a/c or fan, and views of the lake. A double with a/c is $55.

Hotel Carelhys ($$, a half-block south of the park, ☎ 583-0389), also a good option, is a narrow, clean 10-room guesthouse offering singles, doubles, and triples with private baths and fans.

Hotel Costa Sur ($$, 50 yards north of the bus station, ☎ 583-0224). If you've just stumbled out of the bus after a long ride from Managua, you may be tempted to stop at the closest guesthouse to the bus station. Resist that urge. Costa Sur has dark, dingy singles and doubles with shared or private bath and an unfriendly staff. Use it only if you're desperate.

■ WHERE TO EAT

Not surprisingly, San Carlos's restaurants specialize in fish, though other Nicaraguan favorites are available as well. Bring a book and be prepared to wait awhile for your food. If you just need to grab a fast bite while you're waiting for a bus or boat, the *comedores* at the market has the quickest service in town.

El Mirador ($$-$$$, 1½ blocks south of the church, ☎ 583-0377) is the best option in town for good food and views of the lake all the way to Solentiname. The specialty is freshwater fish filet, but there are chicken and beef options as well. Choose from an enclosed space or an open covered terrace. Open Mon-Sat 7 am-10 pm.

Mirasól ($$-$$$, on the waterfront below the cannons). Don't let the fact that it looks like the raised building could topple over at any moment deter you. Mirasól has tasty food and even better views. The food isn't quite as good as at El Mirador, but it's a good spot to watch the action at the dock. And it's good for a beer in the evening.

El Granadino ($$, just east of the post office, ☎ 839-2880) has slow service but good chicken, beef, and fish dishes for $2-$7.

■ DAY-TRIPS FROM SAN CARLOS

LOS GUATUZOS WILDLIFE REFUGE

The reserve, founded a decade ago to preserve the area's pristine tropical wetlands, makes for an easy day-trip from San Carlos but is a world away from the grime of urban life. The refuge of over 100,000 acres contains 12 rivers. A unique aspect of these waters is that they are home to fish from the Jurassic era called *gaspar (Actractoseus tropius)*, which devour their prey with their large fangs.

Within the refuge there are a dozen small communities populated by Guatuzo and Zapote indigenous people who eke out a living by farming and fishing. But overall the environment is virtually untouched. A particularly interesting time to visit the area is in March and April when the birds are nesting.

There are two options for visiting the refuge, depending on the amount of time you have and your level of interest. The quickest way to see it is by visiting **Esperanza Verde**, 15 minutes from San Carlos and accessible by any of the **public boats** that go to Los Chiles, Costa Rica (you can also arrange for a private boat in San Carlos). Ask to be let out at the dock at the Centro de Interpretación Ambiental Konrad Lorenz. Here you can get information about the reserve or stay the night at the rustic **guesthouse** (each of the six rooms costs $10 per person plus $13 for three meals). To make a reservation, contact Leonel at Cabinas Leyko in San Carlos or call ☎ 583-0080. Though there isn't anything of interest near the guesthouse, a 45-minute walk takes you

 into the pristine jungle. Be sure to wear long pants and sturdy shoes to protect you from underbrush and the occasional snake.

For a more in-depth look at Los Guatuzos, head to the **Centro Ecológico**, 24 miles up the Río Papaturro from San Carlos. Public boats leave San Carlos for Papaturro on Tues, Wed and Fri at 7 am (four hrs/$3). Return to San Carlos on Mon, Tues and Thurs at 7 am. Unless you arrange for a private boat, you will need to stay overnight at the Centro Ecológico, which has simple dorms with shared bath housing up to 16 people ($11). Be sure to make a reservation, as it does sometimes fill up with groups (☎ 270-5434, www.fundar.org.ni, centro.ecologico@fundar.org.ni). It is also possible to **camp** on the grounds, and tent rental is available. The primary purpose of the Centro Ecológico is to support research, but visitors are welcome. There is a meeting space for groups, a small library, an **orchid display**, **butterfly sanctuary**, and a few handicrafts for sale that are produced by local artisans. There are plenty of tours available to keep you busy during your time at the Centro, including boat trips, night **hikes** to see the caimans, and visits to local villages. It's also possible to arrange a day excursion or overnight trip to Solentiname (12 miles away by boat).

SAN MIGUELITO

There isn't anything of note to do in San Miguelito, the only real town along the desolate Managua-bound road north, until you reach Acoyapa, but there is a guesthouse if you want to overnight here on your way to or from San Carlos. **Hotel Cocibola** ($) has 16 rooms with shared bath and views of the lake for $7. Local fishermen can provide trips by private boat to nearby rivers or to Solentiname.

To reach San Miguelito by **bus** from **San Carlos** (1½ hrs/$1), take a Managua-bound bus and get off at the road that leads into San Carlos. Vans shuttle passengers the final four miles into town. To reach San Miguelito from Managua, take a bus from Mercado Mayoreo bound for San Carlos and get off at the road leading into San Miguelito. Alternatively, there is one daily direct bus to San Miguelito from Mercado Mayoreo at 7 am. To get to San Miguelito by **boat**, the ferry that plies Lago de Nicaragua between San Carlos and Granada stops here in each direction.

SOMETHING FISHY GOING ON

Along the Río San Juan visitors will frequently see a large shimmering fin emerge from the waters. One of Nicaragua's storied freshwater sharks? Nope, the graceful fins belong to the **tarpon** (*sábalo real*), a big draw for visiting sport fishermen, mainstay of the local fishing economy, and the namesake of a local river (the Río Sábalos and a town on its banks, Boca de Sábalos). The area's tarpons can reach six feet and 200 pounds. Hooking a tarpon is notoriously difficult, but there are plenty of tour operators out there waiting for you to give it a try!

ALONG THE RÍO SAN JUAN

A boat trip down the Río San Juan is an experience not to be missed if you've come this far. The public boat schedule is quite reliable, if sparse; travelers on a tight schedule should seriously consider hiring a private boat, an expensive option without a group. If you have sufficient time, opting to use the public boat offers a more meaningful glimpse into rural life on the river as you make periodic but quick stops along the banks of the river for passengers to embark and disembark. Foreigners are still not a common sight on the public boats, and other passengers, many of whom have never been beyond the reaches of the Río San Juan, are often eager to chat. Local residents provide for their families through cattle ranching, farming, and fishing, and, increasingly, tourism, which many see as a bright spot in what is basically a subsistence economy.

Public lanchas *take passengers down the Río San Juan.*

■ PREPARING FOR YOUR JOURNEY

The rugged and isolated nature of travel on the Río San Juan brings special packing considerations. Malaria prophylaxes are generally recommended for the region; consult your physician; treatment generally begins two weeks prior to arrival in the endemic area. Mosquito repellent and sunscreen are essential, and neither is readily available in the region. Bring at least one pair of long pants – snakes sometimes inhabit underbrush and there is little in the way of medical care in the region. Nights can be chilly throughout the year; long sleeves protect you from insects as well as cool temperatures. Bring a raincoat even if you're visiting during the dry season. You'll rarely see locals out and about without their Wellington boots, a particularly good purchase during the rainy season; try the shops in San Carlos.

While most guesthouses have generators, a flashlight or headlamp is a must for evenings. Binoculars are useful for anyone serious about seeing wildlife. If you plan to spend time hiking or kayaking, consider purchasing a water filter (available at camping stores) and a durable water bottle (such as a Nalgene bottle) before leaving home. Most guesthouses have bottled water available, but stocking up in San Carlos before heading out is a good idea as supplies sometimes run low.

As a final precaution, bring more money than you think you'll need. Most guesthouses along the river geared toward foreigners accept dollars but, beyond San Carlos, banks are non-existent and flashing a credit card or traveler's checks will incite laughter (or just plain confusion).

Traveling in the Río San Juan takes some advance preparation, but the unique experience is worth the extra effort!

Birdlife on the Río San Juan.

■ TOURS

Tours of the area are quite expensive but definitely worth considering, especially if your time is limited. Tour operators are generally very flexible and can ac-

commodate specific requests or recommend itineraries. The following operators have significant experience organizing trips in the area:

Careli Tours, ☎ 278-6919 in Managua, www.careli tours.com, info@carelitours.com.

Tours Nicaragua, ☎ 270-8417 in Managua, www.tours nicaragua.com, info@toursnicaragua.com.

Sabalos Lodge, ☎ 278-1405 (Managua), 583-0046 (Río San Juan), www.sabalos lodge. com, sabalos lodge@ibw.com.ni.

Sabalos Lodge Cabin

Nicaragua Adventures, ☎ 883-7161, www.nica-adventures.com, info@nica-adventures.com.

Río Indio Lodge, ☎ 866-593-3176 toll free in the US, ☎ 506-381-1549 in Costa Rica, www.Ríoindiolodge.com, info@ríoindiolodge.com.

Monte Cristo River Resort, ☎ 583-0197, www.montecristoriver.com, mcrr@cablenet.com.

WEATHER ON THE RÍO SAN JUAN

Southeast Nicaragua's weather can be intense and often changes at the drop of a hat. The long rainy season begins in May and ends in late January, but downpours occur frequently throughout the year. In general, the farther down the river you go, the more rainfall you'll encounter: San Juan del Norte is one of the wettest spots in the hemisphere. There are few paved roads in the region, and you'll likely be

Opposite: Exploring on horseback.

slip-sliding your way through plenty of mud. Pick up a pair of Wellington boots in San Carlos before setting off into the interior. Strong sun shines between rainfalls, which is compounded by the reflection from the water on the river. Sunscreen is indispensable. When the rains cease near the end of January, the region's abundant plant life bursts into bloom, and this is a great time for birdwatching.

Solentiname Archipelago

Solentiname's secluded location and infrequent public transportation renders it a challenge to visitors, but the lucky few who make it here are rewarded with beautiful views, a unique artistic culture, and possibly the friendliest people in all of Nicaragua.

Solentiname is most famous for its unique **Primitivist-style painting**, and over 50 painters and artisans to

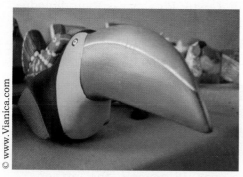
© www.Vianica.com

live and work on the islands. The Primitivist style incorporates elements of fantasy and draws from the beauty of the islands' natural surroundings as seen through the eyes of the artists.

Visitors can see artists at work on Isla Mancarrón and Isla Elvis Chavarría, and the painters are generally pleased to tell travelers about their work. Solentiname's Primitivist movement was inspired by Ernesto

Solentiname

N

Isla Santa Elena

Isla Santa Rose

Isla Cigüeña

Punta de Caña

ISLA LA JUANN

ISLA MANCARRÓN

Cerro Las Cuevas

Communidad de Solentiname

Hotel Mancarrón
Village

Isla El
Padre

Punta
el Gorro

ISLA ELVIS CHAVARRÍA

Albergue Celentiname
Mireestrellas
Cabinas Paraíso
Isla   Museo
Limón   Musas

Isla El
Encanto

Isla
Atravesada

ISLA DONALD GUEVARA

(1.5 KM/10 MILES)

ISLA ZAPOTE

ISLA ZAPOTILLO

Isla La
Sevilla

Punta
Santa Ana

(40 KM)

ISLA ZANATA

ISLA MANCARRONCITO

Punta
Los Jocotes

▲ Public Boat Dock

▲ Public Boat Dock

Lago Cocibolca

3 MILES

3 KM

© 2007 HUNTER PUBLISHING, INC

Cardenal, who is still a revered figure in the islands (for more on Cardenal, see p 8).

In addition to its artistic tradition, Solentiname is also a nature lover's paradise, with abundant bird life, white-tailed deer, iguanas, caimans, howler monkeys, and, less commonly seen, boa constrictors. The beauty of the islands is at its peak when the end of the rainy season brings lush foliage, but the archipelago is pleasant to visit year-round. Another draw of the archipelago is the **petroglyphs** and carvings that remain undisturbed in their natural setting; locals can offer directions.

THE LEGEND OF EL VIEJO DEL MONTE

Folktales are a tradition in Solentiname, and the legend of the fictitious El Viejo del Monte (the Old Man of the Mountain) has been well-known among island residents for generations.

El Viejo del Monte was a ruthless character known for shooting animals with abandon, not even bothering to utilize them for food. In order to punish him and to teach him a lesson, the gods transformed him into a creature that was part man and part monkey, a *sisimico*. They also put him in charge of Solentiname's fauna and fragile ecosystem. He continues to hold responsibility for instilling respect for the environment in the islands' people and for protecting the abundant wildlife of the archipelago against irresponsible hunters.

The moral of the story? Leave nature untouched – a good thing to keep in mind for locals and visitors alike.

ISLA MANCARRÓN

Of the 36 islands here, only two, Isla Mancarrón and Isla Elvis Chavarría, have facilities for tourists. If you have a limited amount of time to explore, consider arranging a tour, as public transportation runs infrequently.

Isla Mancarrón Highlights

- Musas Museum
- Shopping for paintings or handicrafts at Casa de Taller
- Meeting local painters.

Internet Resources: www.solentiname.com.

■ GETTING HERE

BY BOAT

There is a public *lancha* that leaves the dock in the center of **San Carlos** for Solentiname on Mon, Tues and Fri at 1 pm, stopping at **Isla Donald Guevara** (also known as Isla La Venada), **Isla Elvis Chavarría** and **Isla Mancarrón** (2½ hrs/$5). The boat returns to **San Carlos** from Solentiname on Mon, Tues and Fri from **Isla Mancarrón** (4 am), **Isla Elvis Chavarría** from the dock at Hotel Cabinas Paraiso (4:30 am) and **Isla Donald Guevara** (4:45 am). The boat has a sunshade and generally is not overly crowded. The friendly captain lives just behind the dock at Hotel Cabinas Paraiso; stop by if you have any questions about schedules. **Mar Dulce**, a ferry company that ostensibly runs a large boat between **Granada, Ometepe**, **San Carlos** and Solentiname. It leaves San Carlos at 11 am on Sun, arriving in Solentiname at 11:45 am, then returning Fri at 10:45 am and arriving in San Carlos at 11:30 am. But this boat was not running at the time of printing. Get an update at ☎ 254-5430 or mardulce@cablenet.com.ni.

■ GETTING AROUND

There are no roads on the islands. There is no public inter-island transportation other than the boat from San Carlos, so if you take the public boat, you'll need to stay a few days. To arrange a private boat, talk to the public *lancha* driver or ask at any of the guesthouses. Boats cost around $100 between **San Carlos** and Solentiname, depending on your negotiating skills. It is also possible, but expensive, to arrange for a boat to **Los Guatuzos Wildlife Refuge**, **Isla Ometepe** or even as far as **San Jorge**.

> NOTE: *Some maps label Isla Elvis Chavarría as Isla San Fernando and Isla Donald Guevara as Isla La Venada; the islands were renamed after local martyrs that were killed fighting in the war. Both names are still in use, but locals use the latter.*

SERVICES

Isla Mancarrón and Isla Elvis Chavarría are the only islands with facilities for tourists. There is no **phone** service in Solentiname other than Costa Rican cell phone service. **Bottled water** is usually available at hotels and guesthouses, but bring your own from San Carlos if possible as supplies do sometimes run low. The nearest **hospital** is in San Carlos, though, for higher-quality care, charter a boat to Los Chiles, Costa Rica.

TOURS & INFORMATION: There is no Intur office in Solentiname, but the guesthouse owners are good resources for local tourism info. Companies with extensive tour experience in Solentiname include:

Fundacion Musas (☎ 583-0095 in San Carlos or ☎ 249-6176 in Managua, musasni@yahoo.com). The foundation, which runs the museum in Solentiname, also offers a comprehensive tour of the archipelago. The trip lasts four days and includes visits to all of the sites of interest in Solentiname as well as a visit to Los Guatuzos. The trip includes transportation from San Carlos, four days and three nights of lodging and meals. For five people the trip costs $150-$200, depending on your choice of guesthouse.

Careli Tours (☎ 278-2572 2572, www.carelitours.com, info@carelitours.com) and **Tours Nicaragua** (☎ 228-7063, www.toursnicaragua.com, nicatour@nic.gbm.net), both based in Managua, have professional comprehensive trips through the region. Tours can be customized based on guests' interests. **Albergue Celentiname** (☎ 377-4229 in Nicaragua, ☎ 877-720-3034 toll-free in the US) arranges tours of local attractions, including Los Guatuzos Wildlife Refuge, artists' studios, and the islands of Solentiname. Trips can be combined with accommodation and meals at their guesthouse to create multi-day tours of the whole region.

MONEY: There are no banks in Solentiname. Bring more money than you think you'll need; the islands are one of the most expensive places in Nicaragua. Dollars are generally accepted at guesthouses; credit cards are virtually unheard of.

■ SIGHTSEEING

☆☆☆ **Musas Museum** (Isla Elvis Chavarría, ☎ 283-0095 in San Carlos or ☎ 249-6176 in Managua). The Musas Museum is justifiably a source of community pride and provides an excellent and colorful introduction to the flora, fauna, and culture of Solentiname. There are displays about life on the islands from the pre-Columbian era to the present, a small turtle hatchery, and a labeled garden behind the museum that displays medicinal plants. If the museum is closed when you arrive, ask the neighbors who has the key. Entry $2. Open daily 7:30 am-12:30 pm and 2:30-5:30 pm.

☆☆☆ **Casa de Taller** (Isla Elvis Chavarría). A showcase for the 50 artists in the **Unión de Pintores y Artesanos de Solentiname** (Union of Painters and Craftspeople), Casa de Taller displays paintings, handicrafts, and information about the artists' partnership with the Friends of Solentiname in Massachusetts. It also offers painting workshops for local children. The friendly caretaker, Luis, is a good source of information about

artisans in the area. Donations accepted, or you can support the project by making a purchase of artwork.

ADVENTURES

ADVENTURES ON WATER

Islands other than Mancarrón and Elvis Chavarría can be visited for day-trips by private boat. It's not cheap ($50-$100, depending on where you want to go), so try to gather a group to lower costs. Ask at your guesthouse for suggestions on hiring boats and captains, or try the public *lancha* driver, who lives just behind the dock at Hotel Cabinas Paraiso on Isla Elvis Chavarría. Bring everything with you that you may need; there are no services on these islands. **Isla Mancarroncito** has the archipelago's only old growth forest. The terrain is hilly and good for **hiking**, though the jungle is thick and you should bring a guide with you. There are two islands next to Isla Elvis Chavarría: **Isla El Padre** has a large **howler monkey** population, and **Isla La Atravesada** is home to many crocodiles. Don't swim there!

If you want to go solo, canoes can be rented at Albergue Celentiname. It takes about three hours to circle Isla Elvis Chavarría.

> **Warning to Swimmers:** The waters of Solentiname are clean and generally good for swimming. Ask the locals before taking a dip to be sure you haven't chosen a spot inhabited by crocodiles.

Anglers may be able to rent equipment and fish off the dock at Albergue Celentiname on Isla Elvis Chavarría. Rainbow bass and guapote are the most commonly caught fish around the islands. A fishing trip by boat costs between $60 and $120, depending on the length of the trip. Mornings and evenings are best, as the water can get rough at midday. Ask at your guesthouse for recommendations on boat hire, or try the helpful Daniel

Opposite: The setting sun signals fishermen to return home

Río San Juan & Solentiname

and Maria at Albergue Celentiname. You can ask your guesthouse to cook up your catch for dinner.

ADVENTURES ON FOOT

Perhaps the most interesting option (due to visibility) if you're visiting the islands in March or April is taking a trip to see the **petroglyphs** in La Cueva del Duende (**Elf's Cave**), so named because of the tiny unexplainable footprints frequently found near the entrance to the cave. Located on a private island, the cave's ancient carvings are hidden in a crevice that runs beneath the island. Due to a collapse of the cave's roof, the petroglyphs were discovered. Unique albino bats also inhabit the depths of the cave. The climb to see the petroglyphs is a bit challenging; wear good walking shoes.

Isla Mancarrón and **Isla Elvis Chavarría** offer pleasant paths where you will undoubtedly meet friendly locals along the way, particularly as the path cuts right through residents' gardens! Ask at guesthouses for walking suggestions based on your interests. On Isla Elvis Chavarría, don't miss the so-called "Artists' Path," which winds along the shore. Chances are good that you will come across a painter at work. Another walk, leaving from Albergue Celentiname, takes you to the highest point on the island and some petroglyphs. Circling the island takes about three hours. Finish your walk at the Musas Museum for great sunset views.

SHOPPING

Primitivist paintings ($30-$250), **colorful balsa wood carvings** ($1.20), and postcard reproductions of paintings are available at the Casa Taller. Prices for paintings are similar to those in Masaya. Local painters may also have paintings available, or you can commission a painting if you plan to return to Solentiname.

ERNESTO CARDENAL

Ernesto Cardenal Martínez, who became one of the most famous **liberation theologians** of the Nicaraguan Revolution and the founder of the **Primitivist painting movement** in Solentiname, was born in 1925 to a wealthy family in Granada. He studied literature in Managua, Mexico, and the US. After traveling in Europe, he returned to Nicaragua in 1950 and took part in the "April Revolution" against Anastasio Somoza's regime. The coup failed, and Cardenal retreated to a monastery in Kentucky. A few years later he left to study theology in Mexico, later returning to Nicaragua, where he was ordained a **Catholic priest** in 1965. He encountered the Christian, close-knit nature of Solentiname, and remained there for the next decade. While there, Cardenal wrote his most famous book, *El Evangelio de Solentiname* (The Gospel of Solentiname) and, in collaboration with Roger Perez de la Rocha, a painter from Managua, taught locals to paint.

Cardenal collaborated closely with Sandinistas, fighting against Somoza. On July 19, 1979, the day of victory in the Nicaraguan Revolution, the new Sandinista government named Cardenal the Minister of Culture. He held this post until the position was eliminated in 1987. When Pope John Paul II visited in 1983, he scolded Cardenal for defying his order to resign from the government as Cardenal knelt before him.

Cardenal left the FSLN in 1994 protesting of what he perceived to be the authoritarian direction that Ortega was heading in. Today he is a member in the board of advisers of the television station Telesur. In May 2005 he was nominated for a **Nobel Prize** in Literature.

The residents of Solentiname hold Cardenal in the highest esteem, and he maintains a home on Isla Mancarrón.

■ WHERE TO STAY & WHERE TO EAT

There are few restaurants in the archipelago. Solentiname's guesthouses and hotels provide meals to guests and non-guests alike. Let them know several hours in advance if you plan to eat. Hotel Cabinas Paraíso and Hotel Mancarrón are recommended for consistently good food.

HOTEL PRICE CHART	
Cost per night for two people, before tax	
$	Up to $15
$$	$16-$30
$$$	$31-$60
$$$$	Over $60

NOTE: *Few hotels and restaurants accept credit cards, so cash is the norm. Most travelers rely primarily on ATMs , which are popping up even in smaller towns, are generally reliable, and involve a minimum of fees.*

Every listing in this book is recommended and considered above average in its category. Listings with one star (☆) are highly recommended, those earning two stars (☆☆) are considered to be exceptional. A few resorts and restaurants rate three stars (☆☆☆), which means they are worthy of a special occasion splurge.

ISLA MANCARRÓN

☆ **Hotel Mancarrum** ($$$$, up the hill from the dock, ☎ 583-0083 in San Carlos, ☎ 267-0304 in Managua). Sometimes referred to as Hotel Mancarrón, Mancarrum has 15 comfortable rooms with screened windows, mosquito nets, and private baths. Guests can use the hammocks in the garden area. The friendly managers can recommend walks in the area, including to the

Ducklings, Solentiname residents.

nearby artisan village and to see wildlife. There is a generator for nighttime electricity. Rooms cost $40 per person, including all meals.

Hospedaje Reynaldo Ucarte ($$, in the main village area). The four rooms at this friendly place are basic with shared baths and a homestay atmosphere. Meals are available.

ISLA ELVIS CHAVARRÍA

☆☆ **Hotel Cabinas Paraíso** ($$$, directly above the public dock, ☎ 506-301-8809 in Costa Rica, gsolentiname@ifxnw.com.ni). Run by a genial family of painters, Cabinas Paraíso is spotless and comfortable. Rooms have good mattresses, the whitest sheets you'll have seen in weeks, and private cold water baths. The tiled patio is a great spot to watch the sunset. Panoramic views, hammocks, and good food. There is a generator for nighttime electricity. Rooms cost $30 per person, including all meals.

Albergue Celentiname ($$$, 10-minute walk left from the public dock, ☎ 506-377-4229 Costa Rican cell in Solentiname, ☎ 276-1910 in Managua, ☎ 583-0083 in San Carlos. Celentiname has been in business for 25 years. The hotel has five rooms with cold water shared or private bath, and balconies overlooking the water. Rooms cost $20 per person with shared bath, $25 per person with private bath, including all meals.

Hospedaje Mire Estrellas ($$, a five-minute walk left from the public dock) has simple, rustic rooms with a homestay atmosphere. The family that owns the place is friendly ($10 per person, negotiable.

The Caribbean Coast

The country's Caribbean Coast has an atmosphere all its own and visitors arriving from elsewhere in Nicaragua will encounter a remarkably different culture and language. The Caribbean Coast has

the country's most linguistically and culturally diverse population, and it's not uncommon to be surrounded by conversations in **Miskito**, **Spanish**, and **English**. The region encompasses the **RAAN** (the Northern Atlantic Autonomous Region) and the **RAAS** (the Southern Atlantic Autonomous Region), areas that have historically marched to their own drummer. Many residents feel disconnected from Nicaragua's capital and economic centers, and the region is in fact physically disconnected from the rest of the country as well. These challenges are compounded by widespread poverty. **Bluefields**, the Caribbean Coast's largest city, is not accessible by road, and **Puerto Cabezas**, the other main town, is even more secluded.

The pristine white sands of the **Corn Islands**, a 20-minute flight or a six-hour boat ride, are just beginning to receive attention from international visitors. Get there to see it for yourself before the crowds discover this unique and pristine region.

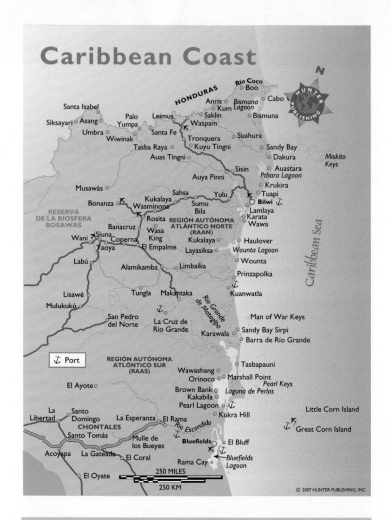

Caribbean Coast

HONDURAS

Río Coco
Boo
Anris Bismuna Cabo
Kum Lagoon
Santa Isabel Saklin Bismuna
Siksayari Asang Palo Leimus
Yumpa Waspam
Umbra Santa Fe
Wiwinak Tronquera Suahura
Tasba Raya Kuyu Tingni Sandy Bay
Auas Tingni Dakura Miskito
Keys
Sisin Auastara
Auya Pinni Pthara Lagoon
Musawás Krukira
Sahsa Yulu Tuapi
Bonanza Kukalaya Sumu Bilwi
Wasminona Bila Lamlaya
RESERVA Rosita Karata
DE LA BIOSFERA REGIÓN AUTÓNOMA Wawa
BOSAWAS Banacruz Wasa ATLÁNTICO NORTE
Siuna King (RAAN)
Wani Coperna Kukalaya Haulover
Yaoya El Empalme Layasiksa Wounta Lagoon
Labú Wounta
Alamikamba Limbaika
Prinzapolka
Lisawé Tungla Makantaka Kuanwatla
Mulukukú
Río Grande
San Pedro de Matagalpa Man of War Keys
del Norte La Cruz de
Río Grande Sandy Bay Sirpi
Karawala Barra de Río Grande
Port REGIÓN AUTÓNOMA
ATLÁNTICO SUR Tasbapauni
(RAAS) Wawashang
Orinoco Marshall Point
El Ayote Pearl Keys
Brown Bank Laguna de Perlas
Kakabila
La Santo Pearl Lagoon Little Corn Island
Libertad Domingo La Esperanza El Rama Kukra Hill
CHONTALES Río Escondido Great Corn Island
Santo Tomás Mulle de Bluefields El Bluff
los Bueyes
Acoyapa La Gateada El Coral Rama Cay Bluefields
Lagoon
El Oyate 250 MILES

250 KM

© 2007 HUNTER PUBLISHING, INC

Caribbean Sea

EL RAMA

Used almost solely by travelers as a transit point between the west of Nicaragua and Bluefields to the east,
hardscrabble El Rama doesn't have much to recommend it. That said, the bus ride between Managua and
El Rama and the boat ride between El Rama and
Bluefields are a good way to see the changing land-
scapes and attractive scenery as you move between

these significantly different regions of the country. Many travelers choose to take an overnight bus to avoid a long day of travel. Regardless of your method of transport, you'll thank yourself if you arrive early enough to avoid an overnight in town.

Originally a trading village of the indigenous **Rama** people, the town is now inhabited by an eclectic mix of Mestizos from the west and Creoles from the Caribbean Coast. El Rama has the dubious distinction of being integrally  tied to water. While the river is the mainstay of the local economy, the town has been flooded three times by hurricanes in the past two decades, with the water reaching 50 feet. The town now has an adequate flood warning system in place to alert residents to evacuate, but El Rama will continue to struggle with the flooding problem, which has been worsened by deforestation further upstream.

El Rama Highlight

■ Enjoying the scenery on your journey to El Rama by boat or bus.

■ GETTING HERE

BY CAR

The highway between **Managua** and El Rama is in good condition but, since El Rama is unlikely to be your destination, driving is not a good option unless you want to bring your car on the boat to Bluefields (not recommended). There is a very poor road that leads to **Puerto Cabezas** (Bilwi) and is only passable at the height of the dry season.

The Caribbean Coast

BY BUS

Road leading out of El Rama, into the wild.

The road between Managua and El Rama was recently repaved, significantly reducing travel time. Buses leave from **Managua**'s Mercado Mayoreo every two hours from 4 am to 10 pm (eight hrs/$7.25). **Transporte Aguilar** (☎ 248-3005) leaves Mayoreo at 9 pm and 10 pm, arriving in El Rama at 4 and 5 am. **Transporte Vargas Peñas** (☎ 280-4561 in Managua, ☎ 572-1510 in Bluefields) leaves from **Managua**'s Mercado Ivan Montenegro at 9 pm, arriving in El Rama around 5 am. The same company owns the *pangas* that continue on to Bluefields and can sell you a ticket. Buses (many of them fairly upscale) leave **Juigalpa** for El Rama every hour on the hour from 9 am to 1 pm, less often on Sun ($6).

One long block up from El Rama's boat dock is a string of buses hugging the side of the road. There is no bus station to speak of, but the bus *ayudantes* will likely find you before you find the buses anyway. Buses leave El Rama for **Managua**'s Mercado Mayoreo every two hours from 4 am to 8 pm (eight hrs/$7). **Express buses** leave one

block east of Hotel Amy at noon, 7 and 10 pm on Tues, Sat and Sun (six hrs/$8). Each of the Managua buses stops in **Juigalpa**, though the express buses drop you off on the highway (a five-minute walk to the center of town), not at the bus station.

BY BOAT

There are two options for getting to **Bluefields**: the hulking **slow boat** offers a better chance to enjoy the scenery and leaves Tues and Sat at noon (five hrs/$6.50). There is a second large blue and white ferry that leaves El Rama for **Bluefields** Mon, Wed, and Fri at 8 am, arriving 4 pm. It continues on from Bluefields to El Bluff and Corn Island. Cars can be shipped on the ferry ($22 from El Rama to Bluefields). The times of this ferry are prone to change; get an update on schedules from the company (☎ 228-1069) and make a reservation if you plan to bring a vehicle. *Pangas* are more expensive and more crowded, but significantly faster and depart more frequently, approximately every hour from 5 am-4 pm (2½ hrs, $11). There is a port fee of 33¢. To catch the slow boat, head directly into the port area. To purchase *panga* tickets, go to the small office (☎ 572-1010) just outside the port (look for the white benches). Purchase a ticket and wait there; you'll be called when the boat is ready. Waits can last up to two hours in the afternoon when there are fewer passengers. *Pangas* aren't covered, so wear plenty of sunscreen. Try to sit near the sides of the boat: if it rains (which occurs frequently even in the dry season), the driver will throw a huge plastic tarp over the boat and all its passengers and the air can be stifling toward the center of the boat.

■ SERVICES

There is nothing of note to see in town, but if you need to pick up provisions, head down the road perpendicular to the dock for a long block to reach the **market** area. The **post office** and the **Enitel** (open 7 am-9 pm,

Mon-Sat) face each other. **Farmacia El Carmen** is open 8 am-1 pm and 2-6:30 pm.

■ WHERE TO STAY & WHERE TO EAT

Accommodation in El Rama is typically austere and geared toward traders passing through town. Avoid the guesthouses down by the port area. The best option in town is **Hospedaje Garcia** ($), which has rooms on the second story that offer a/c and river views for $12. It also has more basic rooms downstairs ($6). The other guesthouses in town average $3 per person, but cleanliness is dubious. **Restaurante El Expreso** ($) has

plentiful options and good food, including all of the Nicaraguan standards. It's also the best restaurant in town, though if you're trying to catch the next boat, keep in mind that the restaurant's name is not exactly accurate – be prepared to wait awhile for your food. **Eskimo** ($) has sandwiches you can take away as well as ice cream. If you're waiting for a *panga*, there is a good **fritanga** ($) in the waiting area with *comida corriente* for less than $1.

BLUEFIELDS

The energy of Bluefields is inescapable: the sounds of reggae waft through open windows, and there is a distinct Caribbean influence in everything from food to architecture. Bluefields, the capital of the RAAS department, has a population of 50,000, rendering it the most important city on Nicaragua's Caribbean Coast. Though culturally and linguistically tied to other towns in the region, Bluefields' lack of road connections means that it has developed a personality all its own.

Unfortunately, despite its vibrant way of life, Bluefields struggles with crime and unemployment and the city has a somewhat seedy feel to it, especially after the sun goes down. Bluefields is best used as a jumping-off point for adventures farther afield.

Though Bluefields is not a typical stop on most visitors' itineraries, a night in town gives an inside look at the rhythms of life on the urban Caribbean Coast.

Internet Resources: www.bluefieldspulse.com.

Bluefields Highlights

- Mayo Ya festival in late May
- Excursions to Pearl Lagoon and Rama Key

■ GETTING HERE

There is no road access to Bluefields, but boats and flights are plentiful. The boat schedule to the Corn Islands from Bluefields is erratic; flying is recommended.

BY PLANE

The minuscule Bluefields **airport** is less than 10 minutes from town. Taxis wait at the airport for the flights to come in. The most convenient place to get an updated flight schedule is at **Hotel South Atlantic II**, just south of the Moravian church. If you're flying from **Managua** to **Corn Island** you can stop over in Bluefields for an additional $60.

Flights leave from Bluefields to **Corn Island** daily at 7:40 am and 3:10 pm (20 minutes/$99 round-trip or $65 one-way). From **Corn Island** to Bluefields, **La Costeña** flights leave daily at 8:10 am and 3:40 pm. **Atlantic Airlines** (☎ 222-3037, reservaciones@atlantic airlines.com.ni) flies the same route with similar times and prices.

La Costeña (☎ 263-2142) whisks passengers to **Managua** daily at 7:40, 8:40 am, and 4:10 pm (one hr 10 minutes/$127 round-trip). From **Managua** flights head to Bluefields daily at 6:30 and 10 am on **La**

Costeña. **Atlantic** flies at the same times, plus an additional flight from **Managua** at 2:10 pm.

From Bluefields to **Puerto Cabezas** La Costena has flights on Mon, Wed and Fri at 12:10 pm. Flights go from **Puerto Cabezas** to Bluefields on Mon, Wed and Fri at 11:10 am ($148 round-trip/$96 one-way). The flight takes 50 minutes.

BY BOAT

All boats leave from Bluefields' cramped port. Purchase tickets and get information on times at the booth in the port. There is a 33¢ departure tax. **_Pangas_** to and from **El Rama** are speedy but crowded. They depart frequently, approximately every hour from 5 am-4 pm (2½ hrs/$11). _Pangas_ aren't covered, so wear plenty of sunscreen. The **slow boat** to El Rama offers a better chance to enjoy the scenery and leaves Tues and Sat at noon (5 hrs/$6.50). There is a second large blue and

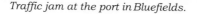

Traffic jam at the port in Bluefields.

white ferry that leaves **El Rama** for Bluefields Mon, Wed, and Fri at 8 am, arriving 4 pm. It continues on from Bluefields to **El Bluff** and **Corn Island**. The trip to Corn Island averages five hours. Cars can be shipped on the ferry, but a car is more of a hindrance than a help in this water-bound region. The times of this ferry are particularly prone to change; get an update on schedules from the company at ☎ 228-1069.

> **NOTE:** *The days and times of the ferry to Corn Island seem to operate on the whims of the captain. If you are pressed for time, flying is by far the best option.*

■ GETTING AROUND

ON FOOT

Bluefields can be confusing to navigate, but the city is fairly flat and walking is a good option when the heat and humidity aren't overpowering. Downpours are common, even during the dry season, so put an umbrella in your day pack. Take a taxi after dark, even for short distances.

BY TAXI

Taxis are plentiful and inexpensive in town. A taxi to the airport costs less than $1 per person, while rides in the center of town run less than 75¢. The streets in the commercial center (where most hotels are found) are cramped and crowded, so if you're only going a few blocks, walking is probably a better option.

■ SERVICES

TOURS & INFORMATION: Intur (bluefields@intur. gob.ni) faces the mayor's office and can help with guides and maps. **CIDCA** (just north of the police station) is affiliated with a local university and offers the area's most comprehensive selection of books and pamphlets about the region's culture. The office is just

north of the police station and is open Mon-Fri 8 am-
noon and 1-5 pm. **Atlantic Adventures** (200 yards
north of the port, ☎ 572-0367) arranges guides, fishing
trips, private boat transport, and rents bikes and snorkeling equipment.

> *Virtually everyone in Bluefields speaks*
> ***English****, but it may be far different from the*
> *English that you are accustomed to! Locals*
> *often switch to a more standard form of*
> *English when speaking with foreigners, but*
> *keep your ears open on the street to hear*
> *the unique Caribbean Coast way of speaking.*

MONEY: Stocking up on cash is smart if you'll be taking
excursions to nearby locales. Use the **ATM** on the east
side of the park, or go to **Banco Caley Dagnall**, which
faces the Moravian church. **Bancentro** faces the Mini
Hotel Central.

INTERNET & MAIL: The main commercial area has a
host of Internet options for around 60¢/hr – take your
pick. The **post office** is a block south of Loteria
Nacional (☎ 822-1784).

TELEPHONE: Enitel is next door to Mini Hotel Central
and is open Mon-Fri 8 am-5 pm and Sat 8 am-noon.

MEDICAL: Hospital Ernesto Sequeira (☎ 572-2391) is
on the southeastern side of town.

STAYING SAFE: Bluefields has a bit of a rogue feel to it,
and after dark it's a smart idea to take a taxi. Keep an
eye on your belongings in the port area. The **police station** (☎ 572-2333) is 1½ blocks south of Hotel Caribbean Dream. The **fire department** (☎ 572-2050) is on
the north side of the Moravian church.

MARKETS: The market is along the water in the commercial center. The road leading down to the port also
has a handful of market stalls. There are no large supermarkets in town; purchase water and supplies at
shops in the commercial center.

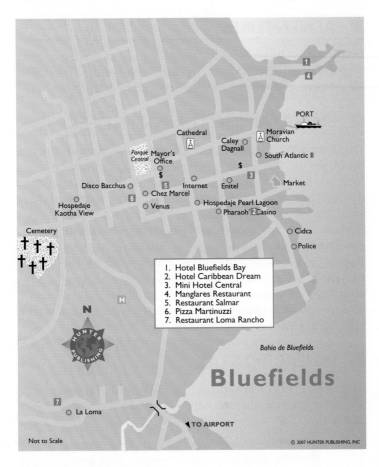

1. Hotel Bluefields Bay
2. Hotel Caribbean Dream
3. Mini Hotel Central
4. Manglares Restaurant
5. Restaurant Salmar
6. Pizza Martinuzzi
7. Restaurant Loma Rancho

Bahia de Bluefields

Bluefields

Not to Scale

© 2007 HUNTER PUBLISHING, INC

■ SIGHTSEEING

There are few sights in town. Take a walk to soak up the
Caribbean-tinged atmosphere. The dilapidated park is
well-used but is desperate for a makeover. It is not safe
after dark. Two churches are worth a look: the wood
Moravian church overlooks the port and the Catholic
cathedral is 1½ blocks east of the park.

The Caribbean Coast

■ ADVENTURES

Guides post notices in the waiting area at the Bluefields port offering excursions by **boat**. See *Day-Trips from Bluefields*, p 448, for adventure ideas in the area.

■ ENTERTAINMENT & NIGHTLIFE

The **Mayo Ya** festival takes place in late May and is the highlight of the year, showcasing Caribbean culture, food, dancing, and music. Bluefields has a handful of discos, but some are rough around the edges; ask at your guesthouse for updates. The most convenient options for dancing to a mix of Caribbean and Latin tunes are **Disco Bacchus** (a half-block south of the park) or **Venus** (a block south and a block west of the park). **Pharaoh's Casino** (a half-block east and two blocks south of the cathedral) is remarkably popular. Even if you're not into the gambling scene, it may be worth a visit for its Arctic air-conditioning.

■ WHERE TO STAY

In general, accommodation in Bluefields is overpriced and in need of maintenance. These are the best options in town.

> NOTE: *Bluefields has a few places each that take credit cards. However, traveling without enough cash for a few days' food and hotel is strongly discouraged.*

☆☆ **Hospedaje Kaorha View** ($$, two blocks west of the north side of the park and a half-block south, ☎ 572-0488). A bright light on the disappointing accommodation horizon, Kaorha View is spotless and reasonably

HOTEL PRICE CHART	
Cost per night for two people, before tax	
$	Up to $15
$$	$16-$30
$$$	$31-$60
$$$$	Over $60

priced. Singles cost $11, doubles $15, and triples $23. All rooms have tiled floors, good mattresses, TV, big windows with sturdy screens, and shared baths. There is a balcony upstairs. The hotel is in a residential area; take a taxi after dark.

☆ **Hotel Caribbean Dream** ($$, 2½ blocks south of the Moravian church, ☎ 572-0107). Another good option with a central location, Caribbean Dream has clean doubles with private bath and a/c for $25.

☆ **Hotel Bluefields Bay** ($$$, two blocks north and a block east of the dock, ☎ 572-0120) has nice rooms and a quiet location on the water's edge. The on-site Manglares Restaurant has great food. Doubles run $37.

Hotel South Atlantic II ($$$, a half-block south of the Moravian church, ☎ 572-1022) has a convenient location but is overpriced at $35 for a single. Nonetheless, its small rooms are fairly comfortable, with private bath and a/c. The hotel can help arrange domestic plane tickets and there is a bar/restaurant.

Mini Hotel Central ($$, Facing Bancentro, ☎ 572-2362). The best centrally-located budget option in town, Central is in the heart of the commercial district. Rooms are clean if plain and have TV and a/c. There is an on-site restaurant.

■ WHERE TO EAT

Bluefields has a number of good restaurants. Be sure to try some of the local **seafood** and **rondon**, a stew made of meat, veggies, and coconut milk that is a specialty of the region.

DINING PRICE CHART	
Price per person for an entrée, not including beverage, tax or tip	
$	Up to $3
$$	$3-$6
$$$	$6-$10
$$$$	Over $10

☆☆ **Chez Marcel** ($$$$, a block south of the park, ☎ 572-2347). Bluefields' finest dining takes place in comfortable, air-conditioned bliss.

The Caribbean Coast

The attentive staff serves up delicious seafood and Caribbean-style specialties for around $13. There is also an extensive selection of international drinks. Credit cards are accepted. Open daily 11:30 am-3 pm and 5:30-10 pm.

☆☆ **Manglares Restaurant** ($$$-$$$$, in Hotel Bluefields Bay, northeast of the port). This restaurant's name means "mangroves" and, with its over-water location, it's easy to see why. Manglares has good seafood and Nicaraguan dishes, with nice views. Take a taxi at night.

Restaurante Salmar ($$-$$$, a block south of the mayor's office, ☎ 572-2128). Offering a wide selection of seafood and local favorites, Salmar makes for a good dinner stop. The staff is friendly. Open daily 4:30 pm until late.

Pizza Martinuzzi ($$-$$$, a block south of the park) has surprisingly good pizza, though personal-sized pizzas are on the small side. Try the seafood pizza ($6). Chicken, burgers, fries, and salads are also available. Credit cards are accepted. Open daily 11 am-2 pm and 4:30 pm until late.

■ DAY-TRIPS FROM BLUEFIELDS

GREENFIELDS NATURE RESERVE

This privately-run reserve is a world away from the hustle and bustle of Bluefields, 18 miles distant. The reserve has a plethora of wildlife and is best explored in a

canoe or by hiking the numerous nature trails, which you will likely have all to yourself. Day visits to the reserve cost $15 per person. Overnights don't come cheap, at $140 per couple, including meals. Private transport by *panga* is available for $70 each way per group, and public boats cost around $8 per person. Reservations are mandatory; ask them for updates on public boat schedules. ☎ 268-1897, near Kukra Hill, www.greenfields.com.ni, info@greenfields.com.ni.

PEARL LAGOON

This tiny fishermen's community offers a relaxing excursion from Bluefields. Though there isn't much to see, you can check out the local **Moravian church** and the town's centerpiece: a **cannon** from 1803. **Casa Blanca Hotelito y Restaurante** (☎ 572-0508) is a one-stop shop for organizing your visit to Pearl Lagoon. You can arrange **boat trips**, **horseback riding**, **snorkeling**, and **fishing** here. When you need a place to rest your tired bones, Casa Blanca has clean rooms ($$-$$$) and a good on-site restaurant. Another accommodation option is **Hospedaje Estrella** ($), which has rooms with shared bath and fan for $12 double.

The town's Moravian church.

Day excursions to Pearl Lagoon can be tricky without private transport. **Atlantic Adventures** in Bluefields (200 yards north of the port, ☎ 572-0367) can arrange a trip with private transport that includes visits to nearby indigenous villages as well as time for relaxing. If you want to do it on your own, *pangas* leave daily from the dock in Bluefields when full (early morning offers the shortest wait times), but the last *panga* generally returns to Bluefields in the early afternoon, so be prepared to overnight. The ride takes an hour and costs around $7 each way.

The Caribbean Coast

RAMA CAY

Rama Cay is populated by a community of approximately 1,000 Rama indigenous people. Miskitos, supported by the British during colonial times, overtook much of the land that was originally Rama, and Rama Cay is one of the few Rama communities in existence today. The Ramas here subsist on fishing and are largely uninfluenced by events beyond their island. An exception to the tranquility of the area was in 1984, when Sandinistas in search of Contra loyalists attacked the island. The islanders were tipped off in advance to leave the island, so no one was harmed.

Rama Cay is a half-hour by *panga* from the Bluefields dock ($6). Check at the dock for the schedule of returning *pangas* as there is no accommodation on the island.

PUERTO CABEZAS (BILWI)

Puerto Cabezas is culturally linked to the other towns on the Caribbean Coast, but its isolation means that it has a character of its own. Referred to throughout Nicaragua as Puerto Cabezas, or "Puerto," the town is now officially known by its indigenous name, "Bilwi." The name comes from the indigenous Mayangna language and stems from the plethora of "bil" (snakes) and "wi" (leaves) in the area. While many of the original indigenous groups remain in the area today, Puerto is also populated by Creoles and Mestizos. The town's indigenous population soared in the 1980s during the war as residents of villages along the Río Coco were forced to leave their homes and migrate to the city. The region was supportive of Somoza, who allowed the area's communities to live fairly autonomously. As a result of their communities' sympathies for Somoza, they were treated harshly by the Sandinistas. Most of the indigenous people have since returned to their villages.

Today Puerto Cabezas has a population of 40,000 and is the capital of the RAAN (North Atlantic Autonomous Region) department as well as its largest town. Though poverty permeates Puerto Cabezas and many buildings are in disrepair, Puerto was until recent times a thriving center of trade in lumber and minerals, including gold from the Las Minas area that was shipped from Puerto's port. The economy declined as the 20th century progressed, and today Puerto Cabezas is a humble commercial center that retains its importance to surrounding indigenous communities.

There isn't much to see or do in Puerto, but it is the main base for intrepid travelers intent upon exploring the Mosquitía. Keep in mind that Puerto Cabezas is one of the most remote towns in Nicaragua. The town sees the occasional business person or volunteer, but the area isn't a tourist destination by any stretch of the imagination. Arranging excursions to nearby areas is a challenge, but with perseverance it's possible to see local indigenous villages and remote forests that few outsiders ever experience.

Internet Resources: www.pto-cabezas.com (Spanish only)

Puerto Cabezas Highlights

- *Fiestas patronales* (June 29)
- Semana Santa
- Visiting nearby indigenous communities

■ GETTING HERE

BY PLANE

Flying is by far the best option for getting to Puerto Cabezas. The only airline that flies here is **La Costeña**. The airport is open 6 am-6 pm daily (☎ 282-2601). To get into town from the airport (half a miles), take a taxi (90¢ per person).

Flights are available from Managua to Puerto Cabezas Mon-Sat at 6:30, 10:30 am and 2:30 pm. On Sun there are flights at 6:30 am and 10:30 am ($149 round-trip/$97 one-way). The flight takes 90 minutes. Flights return to Managua Mon-Sat at 8:20 am, 12:20, 4:10 pm, Sun 8:20 am and 12:20 pm.

Flights go from Puerto Cabezas to **Bluefields** on Mon, Wed and Fri at 11:10 am ($148 round-trip/$96 one-way). The flight takes 50 minutes. A connecting flight is available from there to **Corn Island** ($159 round-trip/ $103 one-way). From **Bluefields** to Puerto Cabezas there are flights on Mon, Wed and Fri at 12:10 pm.

Fly from Puerto Cabezas to **Las Minas** (Bonanza/ Siuna/Rosita) daily except Sun at 1:15 pm ($107 round-trip/$70 one-way). The flight takes 30 minutes. The return flight from **Las Minas** to Puerto Cabezas is Mon, Wed and Fri at 10:30 am.

BY BUS

Puerto Cabezas is marginally connected by bus from Managua, though it's really not an option in the rainy season when the road disintegrates into mud. Buses leave **Managua**'s Mercado Mayoreo daily at noon and 5 pm, arriving 24 hrs later ($17.75). It's also possible to reach Puerto Cabezas from **Matagalpa**. Take a bus to Siuna and change there for Puerto Cabezas. The trip takes at least 20 hrs. The Puerto Cabezas bus station is southeast from the center of town; a taxi into town costs 90¢ per person.

BY BOAT

There is one interminable boat per month from **Corn Island** (three days, $30). There are no other public boats, but you may be able to arrange private transport to nearby communities at the dock.

■ GETTING AROUND

ON FOOT

Puerto is small and quite walkable, though roads are in poor condition. Take a taxi at night due to safety concerns.

BY TAXI

There are an abundance of taxis in town. Fares are fixed at 70¢ to go anywhere within town (90¢ for the bus station or the airport).

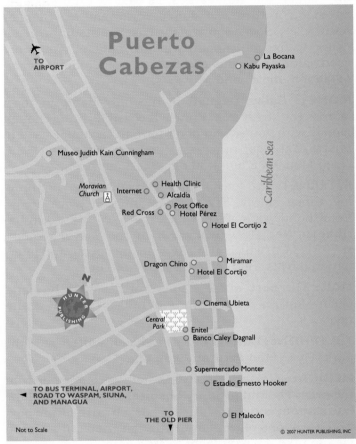

■ SERVICES

TOURS & INFORMATION: There is no **Intur** office in town. The **mayor** is a good person to talk to for tourist information (his office is just north of the post office).

AMICA (The Association of Atlantic Coast Indigenous Women), ☎ 792-2219, amicaenlace@nicarao.org.ni).

This local development organization arranges personalized tours that focus on the area's indigenous people. The tours visit nearby villages (Haulover, Karata and Wawa Bar) and offer an assortment of activities, including comfortable **homestays**, as well as excursions focused on **nature** and **dance** performances. Stop by AMICA, 2½ blocks south of the baseball stadium, in advance to find out about available options. Tours are good value and average $25 per day, including accommodation, meals and activities.

MONEY: Caley Dagnall is the only **bank** in town (across the street from Enitel). If possible, bring enough money with you so you don't have to exchange cash in Puerto Cabezas; otherwise, prepare for a long wait. Open Mon-Fri 8 am-4:30 pm, Sat 8 am-noon.

INTERNET: The town's Internet availability is improving, albeit slowly. Try the new Internet place across from the mayor's office, which has a/c, or head to **Caribbean Net** (150 feet north of the mayor's office, ☎ 792-2343), which also offers photocopying and international calls. Both places cost $1.50/hr.

MAIL: The **post office** is just northeast of the park. Open Mon-Fri 8 am-noon and 1:30-5 pm, Sat 8 am-noon.

TELEPHONE: Enitel's office is a block southeast of the park. Open Mon-Fri 7 am-9:30 pm.

MEDICAL: Malaria prophylaxes are recommended for the area. The rudimentary **hospital** is a block from the bus station, and there is a very basic **health clinic** next to the mayor's office. For anything serious, it's a good idea to take the next flight to Managua.

STAYING SAFE: Puerto has a very high rate of unemployment, and it pays to be cautious; taking a taxi at night is a smart idea. Avoid the port area after dark.

MARKETS & SHOPPING: Supermercado Monter has the best selection of groceries and dry goods in town. There are a few other small stores along Calle Comercio. Handicrafts are hard to come by.

■ SIGHTSEEING

There are few things to see in town. You can check out **Museo Judith Kain Cunningham** (☎ 282-2225), situated in a house built in 1955 and diplaying 62 of the artist's paintings. Kain Cunningham moved here in 1981 from Wampám when her family was displaced by the war, and she lived here until her death in 2001. Entry $1. You should also check out the **dock**, built to handle a bustling lumber and mineral trade that has since tapered off. If you're here in late November, the Moravian Church (Iglesia Morava) has a **Thanksgiving** celebration in honor of the American holiday. Puerto's *fiestas patronales* honoring St. Peter (San Pedro) and St. Paul (San Pablo) are celebrated in style the week of June 29 and, if you're here during **Semana Santa**, head to La Bocana.

■ ADVENTURES

ADVENTURES ON WATER

La Bocana is a beach on the northern end of town that is a focus for tourism development in the town. It is particularly popular during Semana Santa. A few minutes' walk north is an old shipwreck.

A bit farther afield, **Tuapi**, a town nine miles northwest of Puerto Cabezas, has a popular swimming area on the banks of the **Río Tuapi**. You can also bring a picnic to enjoy on the forested riverbank. To get there, take a bus from the station in Puerto Cabezas.

You'll need to make arrangements at Puerto's dock if you'd like to take a boat excursion. Consider visiting some of the indigenous communities along the coast. You can also explore the Rio Tuapi by boat.

CULTURAL ADVENTURES

Stop by **AMICA** (The Association of Atlantic Coast Indigenous Women, ☎ 792-2219, amicaenlace@nicarao. org.ni) for suggestions. The **hospital** is always in need

The Caribbean Coast

of even the most basic medical supplies, so if you can bring anything in it will be most appreciated.

ENTERTAINMENT & NIGHTLIFE

Baseball is a popular pastime in Puerto, and games are played almost every weekend at the **Estadio Ernesto Hooker**. Schedules can be found at www.pto-cabezas. com. Catch a movie ($2.20) at **Cinema Ubieta** on the north corner of the park. There is another movie theater, also next to the park, but it shows, ahem, adult films only. On weekends both **Miramar** (also called Hongo Jack) and **The Malecón** have drinking and dancing next to the ocean. Solo women should not go out at night unaccompanied.

> **TIP:** *For a bit of local culture, talk shows and music in the Miskito language can be found on the radio at 104.1 FM.*

WHERE TO STAY

> **NOTE:** *Few hotels and restaurants accept credit cards, so cash is the norm. Most travelers rely primarily on ATMs, which are popping up even in smaller towns, are generally reliable, and involve a minimum of fees.*

The best option in town is **Hotel El Cortijo 2** ($$), which overlooks the beach just north of the town center. The hotel has a communal terrace and six attractive rooms with a/c, private bath and cable TV. Doubles cost $25. Breakfast is available. **Hotel El Cortijo** ($$, ☎ 792-2340) isn't as nice as its successor, but it's still a good option. Located a block south of the mayor's office, El Cortijo has rooms with a/c, private bath, and cable TV. Doubles go for $25. A third option is the fading wooden **Hotel Peréz** ($$, ☎ 792-2362) on Calle Comercio just south of the post office. There is an upstairs terrace and meals are available. Doubles cost $21 and include private bath; some have a/c.

■ WHERE TO EAT

Seafood is a great option in this oceanfront town.

Miramar ($$-$$$, northeast of Hotel El Cortijo) has great seafood and views, as does **Restaurante Kabu Payaska** ($$-$$$, ☎ 282-2318) on the northeast edge of town – take a taxi in the evening. Kabu Payaska has *ranchos* on an attractive seaside lawn. Open daily, except Wed, 10:30 am-midnight. More good seafood can be had at **El Malecón**, another beachfront restaurant with good views just south of the stadium. If you'd like to follow your dinner with a drink, Miramar and El Malecon are also two of Puerto's nightlife mainstays. If you're looking for a bit of Asia (albeit Nicaraguan-style), try **Dragón Chino** (next to Hotel El Cortijo, ☎ 792-2332).

LAS MINAS

The area referred to as Las Minas includes the towns of **Siuna**, **Rosita** and **Bonanza**. The name Las Minas (The Mines) refers to the long-time mainstay of the local economy, silver and gold mining. Unemployment is a devastating problem in the region and the continued lack of legitimate employment opportunities has added to the insecurity of the region. Guns are common and there is little law enforcement: avoid the area if possible. There is little reason to visit Las Minas unless you are undertaking a trip to Bosawas Biosphere Reserve (p 378). **Bus** travel in the region is not recommended due to safety concerns and discomfort. Buses leave Managua's Mercado Mayoreo every two hours from 4 am-8 pm (seven hrs/$7). A better option is to fly. **La Costeña** flies from **Puerto Cabezas** to Las Minas (stopping in Bonanza, Siuna and Rosita) daily except Sun at 1:15 pm ($107 round-trip/$70 one-way). The flight returns from Las Minas to **Puerto Cabezas** Mon, Wed and Fri at 10:30 am. It takes 30 minutes. From **Managua** to Las Minas there is a flight daily at 9 am. To return from Las Minas to **Managua**, there are flights daily at

10:30 am, plus another one Mon, Wed and Fri at 2:15 pm. The flight takes one hour and costs $127 round-trip/$83 one-way to Siuna, $10 more to Rosita or Bonanza.

WAMPÁM

An indigenous community of 4,900, Wampám hugs the banks of the Rio Coco on the Honduran border. Wampám is the most significant town in the Mosquitía and a regional trading center for approximately 120 tiny communities. Most of the traders come to Wampám by dugout canoe (*cayuco*). Wampám doesn't have much to see, and most people that come here do so for a specific reason (Wampám receives a fair number of missionary groups and medical teams). Some Spanish is spoken in town, though you'll most often hear Miskito. English is virtually nonexistent; if you don't speak Spanish, bring a guide or at least a good phrasebook with you.

Wampám has had a difficult recent history. The government saw the community and its neighbors along the Río Coco as a threat due to their allegiance to the Contras. As a result, the government burned their crops and homes, forcing residents to leave. Many residents fled to Puerto Cabezas, though a significant number have since returned to Wampám. Another blow came with the devastation of **Hurricane Mitch**, which destroyed crops and homes when it flooded the area in 1998. Deforestation continues to be a problem in the area as an effect of the hurricane as well as logging in the region.

■ GETTING HERE

By Air: Flights ply the route between **Managua** and Wampám on Tues, Thurs and Sat at 10 am. The flight takes 90 minutes. The flight returns to **Managua** on Tues, Thurs and Sat at 11:40 am and costs $160 round-trip/$104 one-way.

By Bus: It is feasible to drive to Wampám from Puerto Cabezas in the dry season, a journey that takes three to four hrs. There are one to three **buses** per day during the dry season from Puerto Cabezas to Wampám; the trip takes about five hrs. There are few to no buses in the rainy season when the road is usually impassable.

*The **Río Coco** is known locally as the **Wangki**.*

By Boat: There is no scheduled passenger service, but you can try arranging a ride at the dock in Puerto Cabezas, as the journey between the towns is a common trading route. You'll have the most luck in the mornings when the port is at its busiest.

> **Warning:** Landmines are still present in the area and it is essential that you do not stray from paths. The landmines are left over from the war, when they were used by both sides of the conflict, and they still kill approximately 50 people per year in Nicaragua.

■ SERVICES

TELEPHONE & MAIL: There is an **Enitel** office that is open Mon-Fri 8 am-noon and 1-5 pm, Sat 8 am-noon. There is no **Internet** service. The **post office** is next to the airstrip.

MEDICAL: Malaria prophylaxes are essential in this particularly malaria-prone area. There are two very basic **clinics** in town: one is a government health center and the other is Catholic, slightly better, and has an English-speaking doctor on staff.

MARKETS: There are a few small shops in town. Bottled water is not always available, so bring some with you, along with a water filter if possible.

> **NOTE:** *Mosquitos can be fierce in the area; be sure to bring plenty of repellent and a mosquito net (mosquitero) with you.*

The Caribbean Coast

■ WHERE TO STAY & EAT

Water and electricity can be unreliable in town.

El Piloto ($$), on the main road, has rooms with a/c and private bath for $25. Meals are available. **Hospedaje Rose** ($) is situated across from the airstrip and has rooms with private bath and a generator. Movies are sometimes shown. A third option is **Las Cabañas** ($), which has huts with basic private bath and fan for $4.

> **TIP:** *Fresh fruits and vegetables can be difficult to come by in this remote town; if you find any they are likely imported from elsewhere in Nicaragua. If you're planning to stay a few days, consider bringing some fruit or veggies with you from Puerto Cabezas.*

El Ranchito has Nicaraguan plates for $3, and **Restaurante Funés** has good food, including fish from the river and great views.

■ HEADING OUT FROM WAMPÁM

EXPLORING DEEP

Delving farther into the Mosquitía is a major challenge and only advisable for true adventurers. Little Spanish is spoken in the villages and transport is difficult. Your best (and probably only) option is to arrange a guide in Puerto Cabezas (or possibly Wampám) that can speak Miskito and provide all transportation. Note that there is little to no accommodation or restaurants in the villages; your guide may know families that can provide a place to sleep and meals.

BORDER CROSSING: HONDURAS

While the border at **Leimus** is an official crossing point, the reality is uncertain and this route is not recommended. The border is a one-hour *panga* ride west of Wampám and you'll need to hire a private boat. This area of Nicaragua is very remote and the Honduran side is similar: plan on a five-hour journey to reach the nearest town, Puerto Lempira. If you plan to cross here, it's essential to get an exit stamp from the Immigration Office in Puerto Cabezas (open Mon-Fri, ☎ 792-2258) – there are no other immigration offices in the the area, including at the border.

The Corn Islands

If you've been fantasizing about spending part of your time in Nicaragua on a quintessential tropical beach, there is no better place than the Corn Islands. With an

average year-round temperature of 85°F, the Corns are ideal for swimming, snorkeling, diving, fishing, or just lazing on the beach. It was a haven for pirates in the 17th century; a couple of shipwrecks still remain and are ripe for exploration.

Centuries ago pirates came to the islands to stock their boats with the abundant wild game available on the island. "Carne" (meat) sounded similar to "Corn" to the British sailors, and the name Corn Islands stuck.

The Corn Islands were formed by a volcanic eruption and are fringed by coral reefs. The islands were originally inhabited by the indigenous Kukra and today are populated by Creole people descended from British slaves, as well as a smattering of Mestizos, mostly living on Corn Island, who came to work as laborers.

Keep in mind that the Corn Islands are far off the beaten path; services and facilities are not up to the standards of many other Caribbean locales, but, then again, neither are the prices! The Corn Islands' isolation has kept visitors from discovering their beautiful beaches and unique culture. In fact, on Little Corn, you will likely have met virtually every traveler on the island within a day or two (and many of the 700 locals, too!). Even on Big Corn, there are not likely to be more than a dozen travelers at any given time. In general, most visitors tend to prefer the atmosphere on Little Corn Island, which is eminently walkable, with little development and more opportunities to interact with locals. Corn Island, however, has more upscale accommodation available and allows you to skip the additional bumpy boat ride.

TIP: *The islands are decidedly casual, so you won't need much in the way of clothing. The airlines have a **weight limit** for luggage of 40 lbs per person. Consider leaving extra at a hotel in Managua to collect upon your return.*

■ SUGGESTED ITINERARY

Many people have difficulty deciding how to split their time between the islands, and the following is what I would recommend. If you have only a few days, take the morning flight from Managua to Corn Island. Wear your bathing suit under your clothes (this is both so you can take advantage of the fantastic beaches, and in anticipation of the upcoming wet boat ride). Hire a taxi at the airport to take you around the island (individual fares will probably be less expensive than negotiating an hourly rate), stopping to spend time at places that interest you. Don't miss a stop at **Picnic Center Beach** ✰✰✰, the most beautiful on the island. A few hours is plenty of time to see the entire island. Have a leisurely lunch at a beachfront restaurant before taking the afternoon boat to Little Corn Island.

Little Corn Island

The boats on the return trip from Little Corn to Corn Island match up with the airline schedule, so you can end your visit to the islands without spending additional time on Corn Island or, if you'd like to explore further, you can plan for a night or two on Corn Island before catching your flight back. Domestic flights in Nicaragua have no set dates and no fees for date changes, so if you want to extend your time in the islands, it's simple to change your flight. English is widely spoken on both islands.

Internet Resources: www.bigcornisland.com.

Corn Island Highlights

- Snorkeling or diving at the reefs
- Eating fresh seafood at a beachfront restaurant
- Lazing away an afternoon on Corn Island's Picnic Center Beach.

MONEY MATTERS

Bring plenty of dollars in small dominations with you to the islands; there are no ATMs available, and dollars are commonly accepted. However, be certain that the bills you have are immaculate: bills with even the slightest tear or mark will not be accepted.

CORN ISLAND

The larger of the two islands, Corn Island has everything you need for an island vacation: beaches, water activities, good restaurants, and quality accommodation. Corn Island has a wider availability of services than Little Corn Island and is a good option for visitors seeking a bit more comfort.

> **TIP:** *Try to take care of any communication needs before heading to the islands; phones are not widely available and Internet is unreliable and expensive, though plans are in place to improve service in the coming year.*

■ GETTING HERE

BY PLANE

Plane tickets to Corn Island have risen substantially in price recently, but flying to Corn Island is highly recommended due to the erratic boat schedule. Every flight to or from Managua makes a stop in Bluefields; if you want to explore the

Corn Island airport

area, stopovers are available for an additional $60. Hold on to your baggage claim ticket; even if there are only two or three people on the plane, they are fastidious about this. There is a $2.50 departure tax in each direction. Upon arrival on Corn Island be sure to confirm your return flight. The airport is less than 15 minutes by taxi from anywhere on the island and is a 10-minute walk from the commercial area of Brig Bay.

> **NOTE:** *If you are flying from the US and want to go directly to the Corn Islands, you can make perfect connections to a flight to Big Corn Island if you take the 11 am American Airlines flight from Miami to Managua and return on the 1 pm flight to Miami.*

La Costeña (☎ 263-1228) flies daily from **Managua** to Corn Island at 6:30 am and 2 pm (1½ hrs, $164 round-trip/$78 one-way). Flights leave from **Bluefields** at 7:40 am and 3:10 pm (20 minutes, $99 round-trip/$65

The Caribbean Coast

one-way). **Atlantic Airlines** (☎ 222-3037, reservacio
nes@atlanticairlines.com.ni) flies the same routes. Taxis
wait at the airport for the flights to come in.

From Corn Island to **Managua**, La Costeña flights leave
daily at 8:10 am and 3:40 pm; passengers headed to
Bluefields take the same flight. It is possible to connect
to **Puerto Cabezas** via Bluefields. If you haven't done so
already, make a reservation in advance by phone or in
person at the airport. For the best views, sit on the right
side of the plane on the trip to Bluefields.

> NOTE: *When inquiring about transpor-
> tation, you will find that locals often re-
> fer to Little Corn Island as "La Islita."*

BY BOAT

Boat travel between El Bluff in Bluefields and Corn Island is possibly the most sporadic of any route in the
country. The official boat schedule is **Bluefields** to
Corn Island on Wed, returning from **Corn Island** to
Bluefields on Sun, but this frequently changes, often
at the last minute. One-way takes at least five hrs and
costs $11. Reach El Bluff, which is actually just across
the harbor from Bluefields, by *panga*. They leave frequently from Bluefields' port until around 3:30 pm.
Double- and triple-check the schedule at the dock in
Bluefields, and make an alternate plan – you may very
well need it.

*Before Hurricane Joan devastated the
area, El Bluff was connected to Bluefields
by a sandbar. Today, El Bluff is
accessible only by boat.*

The boat schedule between **Corn Island** and **Little
Corn Island** is generally reliable and it coincides with
the flight schedule for Managua. The trip takes 40 minutes and costs $7 (pay on the boat). There is a 20¢ port
tax. You and your luggage will likely get wet during the
ride to Little Corn, which is consistently bumpy. The
boat has plenty of life preservers; sitting on one can do

wonders for your comfort level. Try to get a spot at the back of the boat for a smoother ride. To protect your luggage, you can buy large plastic trash-style bags for less than $1 in the shop directly across from the port on Corn Island. Boats depart **Corn Island** for **Little Corn** from the town dock (that's the one next to Fisher's Cave Restaurant) at 10 am and 4:30 pm. Boats go from **Little Corn** to **Corn Island** at 7 am and 2 pm.

There is also a boat once per month (check locally for departure day and time as the schedule changes) to **Puerto Cabezas (Bilwi)** that takes three days ($30), though obviously flying to Managua and then on to Bilwi is a much more comfortable option.

■ GETTING AROUND

ON FOOT

Corn Island is good for walking, though you will see surprisingly few locals walking, other than in the commercial area of Brig Bay. There is a paved road that circles the island, though there are no sidewalks. Cars often speed and are unprepared to encounter pedestrians – stay aware. Walking at night is not a good idea; take a taxi instead. It takes two hours to circle the island on foot if you stay on the main road; ask at your guesthouse for updates on safety before venturing off the beaten path.

BY TAXI

Taxis are your best option for getting around on the island, and they pass frequently on the road that circles the island. Taxis cost C15 (90¢) per person during the day, C20 ($1.15) at night. If you need to make any stops, the full fare is charged for the ongoing journey. Taxis on the island are communal: the driver picks up as many people as will fit.

BY BUS

There is a bus that circles the island, supposedly running every 30 minutes, but the schedule seems to follow the whims of the driver. A ride costs 40¢. Doing a complete circle of the island takes less than an hour and is a good way to acquaint yourself with the area, giving you a chance to meet locals.

BY MOTORBIKE OR GOLF CART

Hotel Cesar Beach at Picnic Center has motorbikes ($18 for a half-day) and golf carts that can fit up to six people ($24 for a half-day). Drivers on the island have the tendency to speed – be careful!

CORN ISLAND FAST FACTS

- The island is 42 miles from the mainland.
- Corn Island has a population of 10,000.
- The highest point on the island is Mount Pleasant (295 feet).

■ SERVICES

TOURS & INFORMATION: There is an **Intur** "office" at the airport with limited information. Guesthouses can arrange guides based on your interests. See the *Adventures* section, p 472, for excursion ideas.

MONEY: There is one **bank** on the island, Caley Dagnall, across from the airport. There is no ATM and cash advances are not available. Dollars are readily accepted by most businesses on the island. Credit cards are rarely if ever accepted.

The term "bucks" as used on the Corn Islands refers to cordobas.

INTERNET & MAIL: The only connection on the island is north of the dock after the road curves to the right; look for it on the right side. The **post office** is 50 yards south of the airport.

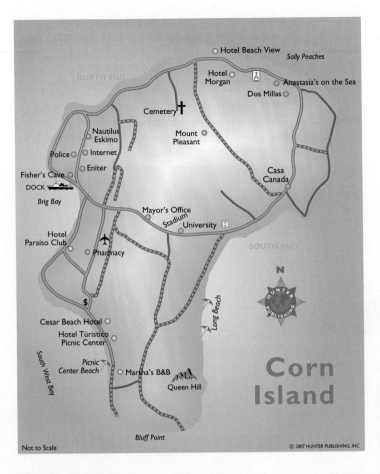

Not to Scale
© 2007 HUNTER PUBLISHING, INC

The Caribbean Coast

TELEPHONE: There are land lines and cellular signals on Big Corn. **Enitel** is north of the town dock just as the road curves to the right.

MEDICAL: For anything serious, catch the next flight to Managua. The island's **hospital** (☎ 285-5236) is on the road that cuts through the center of the island; there is also a **pharmacy** inside.

STAYING SAFE: The **police station** (☎ 285-5201) is just north of the dock on the left side as the road curves right. Safety has improved on the island the past couple of years, but be sure that the guesthouse you choose has secure locks. Even during the day it's not safe to walk on the **southern end of Long Bay Beach**, **Bluff Point**, or **Quinn Hill**. Ask at your guesthouse for updates. Solo women should avoid walking alone in areas where there are few people around. **Taxis** are recommended at night.

MARKETS: The largest concentration of shops is in Brig Bay along the road facing the dock. Prices are about 30% higher than on the mainland.

Picnic Center Beach is ideal for swimming and sunbathing.

■ SIGHTSEEING

There are no major sights. Walking is a perfect way to explore this 1.8- by 3.6-mile island. A road circles it, but be careful, as the cars often speed, particularly precarious on the many curves. The nicest **beach** on the island is Picnic Center in the south. See the *Adventures* section for suggestions about ways to spend your time.

WEATHER IN THE CORN ISLANDS

Though the Corn Islands follow the same general weather conditions as most of the Caribbean Coast of Nicaragua, the adventure activities available may motivate you to pay closer attention. Mid-January through mid-May tend to be the drier months and the best time to visit, though afternoons in April and May before the rains begin can be quite hot. Divers and snorkelers will want to keep in mind that water is best in late March and April. June, July and November tend to be the wettest months of the year, though the rains are often brief and the sun is usually shining a couple of hours later. November through March are often punctuated by strong north winds that can last for several days, which isn't great for boating, but it does keep the temperatures down and the mosquitoes away. Mid-August through mid-October are often the calmest months, with little rain and light breezes.

■ SHOPPING

Handicrafts are hard to come by on Corn Island (then again, so is pretty much anything else). **Nautilus** has a small selection of locally-made pieces.

■ ENTERTAINMENT & NIGHTLIFE

Baseball games are played on Sundays at the stadium on the road that crosses the center of the island. The **Crab Soup Festival**, celebrating the islanders' freedom from British slavery in 1841, takes place August 27-28. Keep an eye out for pageants like the selection of "Miss Coconut." Though most of the island is quiet in the evening, nightlife centers around rum and reggae. **Reggae Palace**, south of the dock in the large concrete building, and **Island Style**, on Long Beach, draw in the locals for

The Caribbean Coast

dancing on Sunday nights. A good spot to catch the sunset is the over-water bar at **Anastasia's on the Sea**. Ask around for occasional **live music**; local musicians sometimes play at **Nautilus Restaurant** (☎ 575-5077) in Brig Bay or at **Myers Bar** near the dock. Take a taxi back to your hotel after an evening out.

> **Caution:** Note that the bars in the dock area can be rowdy at night.

The over-water bar at Anastasids on the Sea is an excellent option for sunset views.

■ ADVENTURES

ADVENTURES ON WATER

The best beach for **swimming** is **Picnic Center Beach**, which also has a wide swath of picture-perfect sand for soaking up the sun. The area has several restaurant/ bars. **Long Beach** is also good for swimming, though it's more remote.

Snorkel equipment can be rented at Nautilus in the North End or Hotel Paraíso Club for $15/day. The best

Typical home on Corn Island.

snorkeling on the island is at **Anastasia's on the Sea Hotel**, which has a designated snorkel area complete with maps (free). Relax after your snorkel adventure with a snack at the over-water restaurant there.

Nautilus Dive Center (☎ 575-5077, www.divebigcorn. com, divechema@yahoo.com) offers snorkeling and diving trips as well as PADI certification (Open Water $250). Snorkel trips to Little Corn cost $35. Dives start at $35, or 10 for $250. There is a **night dive** for $60.

> **NOTE:** *The nearest hyperbaric chamber is at Puerto Cabezas.*

Bodyboarders should try the waves at Long Beach and Waula Point. Nautilus rents boards.

ADVENTURES ON FOOT

Though Corn Island is primarily flat, there are some areas with great views. Though you are unlikely to get lost, a guide is recommended for safety (your guesthouse can provide one, or Nautilus will arrange one for $15/day). For island views, head to **El Bluff** at the

The Caribbean Coast

southern part of the island. This excursion involves climbing over rocks but overall is an easy hike. In the South End near the soccer field a **tower** offers good island views. There is also a wooden bridge that allows you to walk over **swamps**. Keep an eye out for local wildlife.

ADVENTURES ON WHEELS

Nautilus in the North End rents **bikes** for $10 per day.

ADVENTURES ON HORSEBACK

The major hotels can arrange for horses at $12 per day.

■ WHERE TO STAY

With the exception of the Picnic Center Beach area and Casa Canada, many of the hotels on Corn Island are starting to look a bit frayed around the edges. Most places are family-run, and service is not up to international standards in many cases. All of the hotels listed below have running water and electricity, though electricity is not always available 24 hours a day (most hotels do, however, have generators for nighttime electricity). One of the best ways to choose a place is to simply drive around and take a look; almost every hotel is on the road that circles the island and they are seldom full (reservations are recommended during Easter and Christmas, however). Before exploring the area on foot, ask at your hotel about updated safety recommendations. Corn Island has a plethora of accommodations and not enough travelers to fill the rooms; in fact, it is common to have the entire place to yourself!

HOTEL PRICE CHART	
Cost per night for two people, before tax	
$	Up to $15
$$	$16-$30
$$$	$31-$60
$$$$	Over $60

Every listing in this book is recommended and considered above average in its category. Listings with one star (☆) are highly recommended, those earning two stars (☆☆) are considered to be exceptional. A few resorts and restaurants rate three stars (☆☆☆), which means they are worthy of a special occasion splurge.

> **NOTE:** *Few hotels and restaurants accept credit cards, so cash is the norm. Most travelers rely primarily on ATMs , which are popping up even in smaller towns, are generally reliable, and involve a minimum of fees.*

☆☆ **Hotel Cesar Beach** ($$$-$$$$, ☎ 575-5223, www.cesarbeachhotel.com, info@cesarbeachotel.com). A bright yellow and green place at gorgeous Picnic Center Beach, Cesar has new, tasteful rooms with terraces overlooking the sand. Doubles with private bath, a/c and cable TV cost $50. Live in luxury in a suite complete with a Jacuzzi and stocked fridge ($100). If you're with a group,

© Hotel Cesar Beach

rent a cabana, which is similar to a suite but without the Jacuzzi ($50 for one-three guests, $80 for four-seven guests). Cesar's restaurant specializes in seafood, and the bar is housed in a boat resting on the sand.

☆☆ **Centro Turístico Picnic Center** ($$$-$$$$, Picnic Center Beach, ☎ 575-5204). Housed in an attractive island-style complex, Centro Turistico has amenities not found most places on the island: queen-sized beds, a/c, and cable TV. All rooms are sparkling clean, with private bath and overlooking the ocean. There is a good on-site restaurant/bar. Single $35, double $45.

Casa Canada ($$$$, South End, ☎ 644-0925, www.casa-canada.com, casacanada@canada.com). Located on the eastern side of the island, Casa Canada is an upscale new place run by (who else?) Canadians. Rooms are situated in modern stucco and tile oceanfront cabins that have a/c, TV with DVD player and private bath with hot water. There is an infinity pool and a restaurant serving local and Canadian cuisine. Double $75, triple $80, quad $85. Casa Canada accepts Visa credit cards, and all-inclusive packages are available.

Hotel Morgan (North End near the church, ☎ 575-5052). Located in a secluded area on the north side of the island, Hotel Morgan is a family-run place with renovated rooms. There is a very good restaurant on-site, but the beach here isn't very good for swimming (there is a nice beach 120 feet north of the hotel). Doubles with two beds, TV, a/c, refrigerator and private bath go for $35 ($30 without a/c). Ask for an upstairs room on the beach side for the best views.

Martha's Bed and Breakfast (Picnic Center Beach, ☎ 835-5930). Occupying a large, modern home set back a bit from the beach in a tranquil garden, Martha's eight quality rooms are clean and cozy, with a/c and ca-

ble TV. There is a nice upstairs terrace overlooking the ocean. Meals are offered, and free guides are available for guests who want to go hiking. Doubles are $55, including breakfast. Packages available.

Hotel Paraíso Club ($$$, Brig Bay, ☎ 285-5111). With an in-town location, Paraiso Club isn't on the beach (it's a half-block away), but the hotel's thatched-roof *cabinas* are in a peaceful and attractive compound. *Cabinas* have a/c, cable TV and private bath. Visa and

Mastercard are accepted. Doubles range from $35-$46. The restaurant is overpriced, and walking around at night in the area isn't recommended.

Sunset on the Corn Islands.

Anastasia's on the Sea ($$, North End, ☎ 575-5001). Formerly Bayside Hotel, Anastasia's has decent but slightly tired rooms, each with two double beds and weak a/c. Ask for a room on the ocean side. They have tiny terraces with steps that go right down into the ocean. This place can be loud on weekend evenings due to its popular over-water bar, which also serves decent food. Single $20, double $30.

Hotel Beach View ($-$$, North End). The bright green hotel has seen better days, but it's one of the best budget options and offers good value. The hotel consists of two buildings and is set on the beach. Rooms in one of the buildings overlook the water and are less expensive ($12 double), but rooms in the inland building are nicer. An inland double with two double beds, private bath and refrigerator is $20; single $15. Meals are available; request them several hours in advance, or you can walk to one of the other nearby guesthouses for a meal.

The Caribbean Coast

Hotel Best View ($$, North End, ☎ 575-5082, www.bestviewci.com, mkaico@hotmail.com). Another budget option near the Beach View, you'll recognize the Best View from its location on a point jutting out into the ocean – you can't miss the green and yellow building. The quality and offerings are similar to the Beach View. Doubles, some of which have a/c, TV and fridge, go for $30, singles $25 (prices are a bit high; try negotiating). Meals are available. Free transportation from the airport if you reserve in advance.

> **DON'T MISS:** *During your stay on the island, be sure to try* **rondon***, the official meal of Corn Island. Derived from the words "run down," rondon is a stew comprised of seafood (or sometimes meat) and "bread kind" (breadfruit, cassava, plantains, coco, banana, sweet potato, or sometimes vegetables). The concoction is cooked in coconut milk and makes a hearty meal.*

■ WHERE TO EAT

As meal preparation time averages one hour, it's a good idea to order in advance and come back for your meal. Not surprisingly, **seafood** is an excellent option. Try it island-style, cooked in coconut milk. Another local favorite is **coco bread** (which really doesn't have much of a coconut flavor). Find homemade coco bread, and occasionally the island's excellent **plantain pastries** ☆, at private homes with small signs in front advertising their wares. Look for hand-painted signs on houses advertising *"pan de coco."*

DINING PRICE CHART	
Price per person for an entrée, not including beverage, tax or tip	
$	Up to $3
$$	$3-$6
$$$	$6-$10
$$$$	Over $10

☆ **Hotel Turístico Picnic Center** ($$$, Picnic Center Beach, ☎ 575-5204). Restaurant settings don't get much more beautiful than this! Meals are served in an enormous *rancho* overlooking the ocean, and service is professional. Order up some great seafood with organic vegetables and enjoy the view.

☆ **Nautilus** ($$$, Brig Bay, ☎ 575-5077). Serving the most international cuisine on the island, you won't find diners eating *gallo pinto* at funky and casual Nautilus. Have granola topped with yogurt and fruit for breakfast or delicious seafood curry for dessert. You'll also find those little details that you've been missing: real butter for your bread and fresh-brewed coffee. This is also the best choice on the island for vegetarians. Top off your meals with a dessert such as tiramisu. Open daily 7 am-9 pm.

☆ **Hotel Morgan** ($$-$$$, North End near the church, ☎ 575-5052). Served in an enclosed dining room across the road from the beach, the setting isn't particularly special at this restaurant, but the food is very good. The fish in garlic sauce or in coconut sauce are particularly tasty, and service is friendly. Meals average $8. Open 7 am-9 pm.

☆ **Dos Millas** ($$$, North End, ☎ 575-5058). Often referred to as "Seva's," this restaurant looks nondescript from the outside, but offers some of the island's best food. The restaurant overlooks the ocean.

Cesar Beach Hotel ($$$, Picnic Center Beach, ☎ 575-52230). Seafood, pasta, hamburgers, and more are served in this pleasant open-air restaurant facing the beach.

Fisher's Cave Restaurant ($$-$$$, in Brig Bay next to the dock). This is the place to go if you're waiting for a boat; it's right next to the dock. The food is decent, if nothing special. Seating is outdoor or indoor, and the restaurant serves breakfast, lunch and dinner. Take a look at the shark and other marine life in the pool below the restaurant's balcony.

The Caribbean Coast

LITTLE CORN ISLAND

An idyllic speck of palm-fringed bliss, Little Corn Island is still largely undiscovered. Visitors often find themselves spending more time on the island than originally intended, enjoying the warm weather and wealth of adventure activities. Though services on the island are minimal, most visitors are too busy swimming, diving, walking, and relaxing to notice.

GETTING HERE

The only way to reach Little Corn is by boat from Corn Island, which serves to keep the crowds away. The boat schedule conveniently matches up with the flight schedule, so it's entirely feasible to skip Corn Island

and head straight to Little Corn if you so desire (see the *Corn Islands*, p 466, for the boat schedule). If you're staying on the north side of the island, consider negotiating with the *panga* driver who brings you over from Corn Island to drop you off at your guesthouse; otherwise, it's a 20-minute walk.

GETTING AROUND

On this 1,100-acre island there is no need for motorized vehicles or even roads. Locals and visitors alike get around the island by using jungle paths and the single paved walkway that runs along the beachfront in the village area. If you need someone to help you carry your

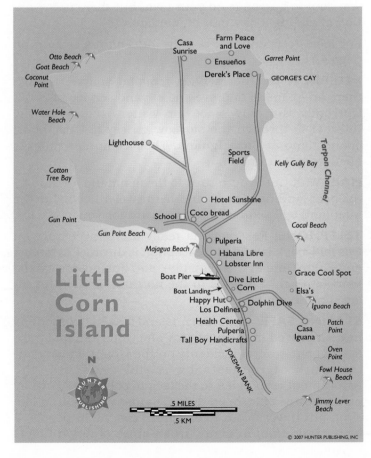

© 2007 HUNTER PUBLISHING, INC

luggage, teenaged boys can be rounded up to haul it in a wheelbarrow, normally used for collecting tropical fruit from the island's trees.

SERVICES

TOURS & INFORMATION: There is no Intur office on the island, but the expats that live here are good sources of info, as are the dive shops. **Casa Iguana** (www.casaiguana.net) offers good-value packages, with an assortment of activities focused on diving. See their website for options. **GAP Adventures** (www.gapadventures.com) offers a Little Corn Island package based at Casa Iguana. This package doesn't include anything you couldn't arrange on your own, but there is the option of adding a city tour of Managua.

For local tour options, see the *Adventures* section on page 484.

INTERNET: Internet service remains sparse, though there are plans to improve and expand service in 2007. Currently the only place for visitors to access the Internet is through the sloooow, pricey ($4 per hour) connections at **Casa Iguana**. Their computer room is open from 9 am-noon.

MAIL: Wait until you return to the mainland, or stop by the boat landing to see if another traveler headed to the mainland will send off your postcard for you.

TELEPHONE: Reservations really aren't necessary on this laid-back island (the exception is during Christmas and Easter and at Casa Iguana), and businesses can be hard to reach. **Enitel** is in the northern end of the village on the right.

STAYING SAFE: Little Corn Island's safety conditions have improved in the past year after international publicity about several incidents on the island. Finally, after years of requests by island residents, the government responded to the lack of police presence by placing three officers on duty. That may not sound like a lot, but it works out to officer for every 250 people, a better ratio than in many urban areas of North Amer-

School children walking home.

ica. Nonetheless, it never hurts to be cautious. Avoid the upper west side of the island beyond the village, an area that is home to many migrant workers from the mainland. Walking alone at night on the jungle paths isn't a good idea. Overall, however, Little Corn has a low crime rate.

MEDICAL: Hire a boat to Corn Island if you need a pharmacy or hospital. For anything serious, catch the next flight to Managua from Corn Island. For minor injuries or illness, ask at the dive shops for suggestions on where to procure supplies.

MARKETS: Little Corn Island doesn't have a central market, though the island is dotted with small *pulperías*. The best-equipped **shop** is just north of Habana Libre. About 50 feet north of Habana Libre is also a a good spot to buy the islands' famous **coco bread**; look for the bright pink house on the right.

WATER: The **well water** on the island is potable, and drinking tap water from local restaurants is safe; if in doubt (for example, after a storm), ask the expats. **Bottled water** is expensive by mainland standards and can be purchased at most of the shops in the village.

■ SIGHTSEEING

Little Corn Island doesn't have any must-see sights but, on an island so beautiful, who needs them? You can walk up to the **lighthouse** (an unattractive steel structure), which is also the highest point on the island, offering good views.

■ ADVENTURES

ADVENTURES ON FOOT

Rocky outcrops make a walk around the entire perimeter of the island unfeasible, but, for a beautiful walk, take a stroll along the eastern side of the island. Total walking time is about 30 minutes, but undoubtedly you'll want to stop for a **swim** along the way, so plan accordingly. Be sure to wear sunscreen and sandals you can wear in the water (such as Tevas), and bring water along. Start from the southern edge of the island next to Casa Iguana and walk north along the beach. You'll eventually reach a rocky outcropping which is dry at low tide, but if it's high tide you'll have to wade up to your knees.

ADVENTURES ON WATER

Both dive shops take **snorkelers** along on their dive trips ($20 for two hours including equipment). The shops also rent equipment for $15. If you want to snorkel from the beach, the North side of the island is the best option, though you can also snorkel on the east side.

The **diving** around Little Corn gets a big thumbs up. There are two dive shops on the island, both run by enthusiastic expats. See their websites for complete offerings.

Boats on Little Corn island.

The Caribbean Coast

Dolphin Dive (next to Hotel Delfin in the village, www.cornislandsscubadiving.com, dolphindivelci@hotmail.com). The new Dolphin Dive has PADI Open Water courses for $275, Advanced Open Water $195. Dives are $35 for one tank, $60 for two. The staff is friendly, Internet is free for customers, and their office has the best a/c on the island.

© Dolphin Dive

Dive Little Corn (at the boat landing in the village, www.divelittlecorn.com). Run by the Casa Iguana folks, this shop offers rental kayaks for $15/day or $6/hour, as well as PADI Open Water courses for $315, Advanced Open Water for $220. A night dive costs $45. Ask about dive/accommodation packages. They also offer two-hr **fishing** trips (open water trolling) at $45 for one person, $10 for each additional person. Their fishing *panga* is equipped with GPS, down rigger, and high-speed planer. Bait and tackle is included. Kingfish, barracuda, dolphin, jack and mackerel are the most common catches in the area.

Next door to Dive Little Corn, **Mario Allen** offers **fishing**, **snorkeling** and **beach trips** by boat.

ADVENTURES ON HORSEBACK

Farm Peace and Love gives tours of the island on horseback (1½ hrs, $25 per person).

■ ENTERTAINMENT & NIGHTLIFE

There isn't much in the way of nightlife on Little Corn. **The Happy Hut**, a lively, tiny thatched-roof, is the best place in town to get a beer. It attracts locals, expats, and travelers alike. Avoid Skinfits, a bar that attracts more than its fair share of fights.

■ WHERE TO STAY

The whole island is beautiful, so take your pick!

> **NOTE:** *Few hotels and restaurants accept credit cards, so cash is the norm. Most travelers rely primarily on ATMs, which are popping up even in smaller towns, are generally reliable, and involve a minimum of fees.*

EAST (WINDWARD) SIDE

Peppered with a few rustic backpacker places and, on the south end, Casa Iguana, the windward side has beautiful, secluded beaches. One of the draws of staying on this side is the breezes, which keep away both heat and mosquitoes.

HOTEL PRICE CHART	
Cost per night for two people, before tax	
$	Up to $15
$$	$16-$30
$$$	$31-$60
$$$$	Over $60

View from Casa Iguana.

☆☆ **Casa Iguana** ($$-$$$$, www.casaiguana.net). A Little Corn institution, Casa Iguana is run by an American couple and set on a bluff overlooking the ocean. Accommodation consists of cabins that dot a hillside; some have views, others are in a garden setting. Cabins are basic (some very basic) and range in price from $25 (small, rustic, outdoor shower) to $80 (queen-sized bed, CD player, solar hot water heater). Even if you're not staying here, stop in for a meal or to peruse the book exchange/magazine collection in the cozy communal room, which is a magnet for guests. The food here is very good and most of it comes straight from the sea or the garden on the grounds.

© Casa Iguana

Casa Iguana's Grand Casita.

There are also several **budget places** along the beach on the windward side for travelers wanting waterfront accommodation and very simple, colorful **huts** ($) with rustic private or shared bath and mosquito nets. Water and electricity here are sporadic, though most places have a generator for nighttime electricity. Options include **Elsa's, Curly Toes Sunrise Paradise** and **Grace Cool Spot** (which has kitchen use available for $2/day). These backpacker haunts are all near one another, so if you'd like to stay at one, take a look at the others before making a choice. Huts average $7 double. To get here from the village/boat landing, take the cross-island path and make a left down the slope when you've almost reached the beach (10 minutes).

WEST (LEEWARD) SIDE

Located next to the boat landing, the leeward side is a good option if you want to stay in the village area. Most of the places on this side are beachfront, and they are the most comfortable options on the island with block construction. Keep in mind that this side of the island is quite hot in April and May.

© Hotel Los Delfines

☆ **Hotel Los Delfines** ($$$, a few steps from the boat landing in the village, ☎ 892-0186 or 285-5239). With a look straight out of Miami, Los Delfines offers comfort in the heart of the village area. Doubles cost $40-55. Next door is Dolphin Dive, reviewed above.

☆ **Sunshine Hotel** ($$$, north end of the village, ☎ 883-9870). With the look of a large, modern house, the Sunshine is set back a bit from the main path and has clean, comfortable rooms. The bright yellow building is new, quiet and has a nice communal patio downstairs. Be sure to ask for a room away from the noise of the generator. Doubles are $45, including private bath and a/c.

☆ **Lobster Inn** (☎ 847-1736). Located in the heart of the village, this cheerful hotel represents good value.

Each of the 12 rooms is small but very clean with fan and private bath. Doubles are $20. There is a good restaurant downstairs.

NORTH END

The North End has arguably the island's most beautiful beaches and is a good option for travelers seeking a private, secluded stay. Note that it takes 40 minutes to walk to the village where the nearest restaurants are located; kitchens are generally available to guests who want to cook for themselves, which means that some visitors who plan an extended stay on the island opt for the North End. The area's accommodation is typically rustic and similar to the backpacker places on the windward side, though the North End generally attracts an older crowd. All accommodation is along a beach, which is great for **swimming** and **snorkeling**. To get there, pay the *panga* driver to take you to the North End

The North End has some of the island's most spectacular beaches.

when you come over from Corn Island, or take the path that goes through the center of the island, which is slightly uphill.

Derek's Place ($-$$). Run by an American expat and his young family, Derek's has an eclectic mix of creative, rustic huts, many on stilts, set in an attractive garden that faces the ocean. All rooms have shared bath. Derek's Place has the most creatively decorated bathroom on the island, so be sure to check it out.

Derek's Place

Meals are sometimes available (breakfast $3, lunch $6, dinner $8-$10), but ask before planning your evening.

Farm Peace and Love ($$$, www.farmpeacelove.com, paola@farmpeacelove.com). A good option if you want to stay awhile, Peace and Love has one guest room and

a cottage situated 60 feet from the beach. Each can hold up to three people. The room costs $40 for two guests ($50 for three guests using the double bed plus a futon). The room is very clean, with wooden floors, a good mattress, screened windows, and an outdoor shower. The cottage rents for a minimum of five nights for $65/night. Each has a similar setup along with a terrace, kitchen, washer and drier.

Casa Sunrise ($-$$, www.casasunrise.de, pasenic@ stratosnet.com). Owned by a friendly German Buddhist, this guesthouse is truly a back-to-nature experience: there is no running water or electricity on the property. There is, however, a beautiful beach and a peaceful setting. Kitchen use is available, and the property has trees with

© Casa Sunrise

fruit that the owner shares with his guests. Rooms range from $4 per person for a backpacker-style hut to $20 for a double in a rustic cabin. Camping is $6 per tent. **Ensuenos** ($-$$) is right next door and has a property and rustic cabins that are similar to Casa Sunrise.

■ WHERE TO EAT

Most guesthouses also have meals; give them a heads-up in advance if you plan to eat. Service is generally slow, but who's going to complain when virtually every restaurant has beautiful ocean views.

☆ **Lobster Inn** ($$-$$$, in the village center) has the option of eating inside its sparkling clean and bright interior restaurant or at its shaded tables along the waterfront. The restaurant offers one of the best-value *comida corrientes* on the island, which usually includes a chicken or fish option, at $5.50. The rolled tacos ($2) are also good.

© Habana Libre

☆ **Barra Intel Habana Libre** ($$-$$$, at the northern end of the village, ☎ 848-5412). Owned by a Cuban who married an islander, Habana Libre is a stylish, casual place overlooking the water. It also has some of the best food on the island, including juicy roasted pork sandwiches.

Habana Libre is particularly popular for its mojitos. Open daily 10 am-10 pm.

☆ **Casa Iguana** ($$$-$$$$, southern end of the island on the windward side, www.casaiguana.net). With the ingredients for most meals coming straight out of the

guesthouse's garden, you can be assured that the food at Casa Iguana is fresh and plentiful. Casa Iguana serves breakfast and lunch only and dinner is at a set time (7 pm). The communal nature of the meals here pro-

Meals are served in this lodge.

vides a good way to meet other travelers while enjoying the view of the ocean. Dinners range in price from $9 to $15. Vegetarians should advise the restaurant a day in advance.

Farm Peace and Love ($$$$, North End, www.farm peacelove.com) A real Italian meal in the islands? Owner Paola, originally from Italy, serves authentic three-course meals ($12) tailored to your preferences; vegetarians can be accommodated. Have one of the dive shops radio Paola a day in advance to reserve.

There are several additional good places for *comida corriente* in the village, including **First Stop Comedor** and **Grace's** (not to be confused with the restaurant at Grace Cool Spot on the windward side of the island, which is not recom-

mended). **Curly Toes Sunrise Paradise** has the best food of the back-packer places on the windward side and is a colorful open-air eating area on the sand; **Elsa's** is also good.

Esla's beachside eatery.

Appendix

USEFUL WORDS & PHRASES

Nicaraguans are patient and appreciate if you try a few phrases in Spanish. Remember to stress letters that have an accent mark!

ARRIVAL ESSENTIALS

passport	el pasaporte
ticket	el boleto
flight	el vuelo
schedule	el horario
backpack	la mochila
suitcase	la maleta
drugs	las drogas
plane	el avión
car	el carro
taxi driver	el taxista
truck	el camión
road intersection	empalme
speed bump	tope
dock	el muelle
neighborhood	el barrio
city	la ciudad
equivalent to a state or province	departamento

FINDING A PLACE TO STAY

hotel	el hotel
guesthouse	el hospedaje/el hostal
single room	sencillo
double room	doble
matrimonial	double or queen-sized bed for two people
one night	una noche
two nights	dos noches
private bathroom	bano privado
shared bath	bano compartido
air-conditioning	aire acondicionado
fan	abanico
available/free	libre
free of charge	gratis

■ GREETINGS & CONVERSATION

Good morning . . . . Buenos días
Good afternoon . . . . Buenas tardes
Good evening or good night . . . . Buenas noches
Hello . . . . hola
Goodbye . . . . adios
See you later. . . . . hasta luego
Please. . . . . por favor
Thank you. . . . . gracias
How are you? . . . . ¿Como estás?
Nice to meet you. . . . . Mucho gusto
Greetings to/say hello to. . . . . Saludos a. . . .
I don't understand . . . . No entiendo
Do you speak English?. . . . . ¿Habla inglés?
I don't speak Spanish. . . . . No hablo español.
Excuse me (to get by someone) . . . . Con permiso.
Excuse me (to ask for something). . . . . Discúlpeme
Excuse me (as an apology). . . . . perdón
large . . . . grande
small. . . . . pequeño, chico
fast . . . . rapido
slow . . . . despacio, lento

■ FAMILY & FRIENDS

Mrs or madam . . . . Señora (abbreviated to Sra)
Mr or sir . . . . Señor (abbreviated to Sr)
Miss or young lady . . . . Señorita (abbreviated to Srta)
you (formal). . . . . usted
you (familiar) . . . . tú
he . . . . él
she. . . . . ella
them . . ellos (males or males and females), ellas (all females)
we or us . . . . nosotros
family. . . . . la familia
mother . . . . mamá, madre
father. . . . . papá, padre
grandmother . . . . abuela
grandfather . . . . abuelo
sister . . . . hermana
brother. . . . . hermano
son. . . . . hijo
daughter . . . . hija
children. . . . . niños
husband . . . . esposo
wife . . . . esposa

```
friend . . . . . . . . . . . . . . . . . .amigo (male), amiga (female)
boyfriend . . . . . . . . . . . . . . . . . . . . . . . . . . . . . novio
girlfriend . . . . . . . . . . . . . . . . . . . . . . . . . . . . . novia
older . . . . . . . . . . . . . . . . . . . . . . . . . . . . más viejo
younger . . . . . . . . . . . . . . . . . . . . . . . . . . más joven
```

■ MONEY MATTERS

```
How much does it cost? . . . . . . . . . . . . . . ¿Cuánto cuesta?
money . . . . . . . . . . . . . . . . . . . . . . . . . . . . . . . . dinero
bank. . . . . . . . . . . . . . . . . . . . . . . . . . . . . . . . . banco
to pay . . . . . . . . . . . . . . . . . . . . . . . . . . . . . . . pagar
to change money. . . . . . . . . . . . . . . . . cambiar dinero
ATM . . . . . . . . . . . . . . . . . . . . . . . cajero automático
traveler's checks. . . . . . . . . . . . . . . . .cheques de viajero
credit card . . . . . . . . . . . . . . . . . . . .tarjeta de crédito
dollars . . . . . . . . . . . . . . . . . . . . . . . . . . . . dólares
price. . . . . . . . . . . . . . . . . . . . . . . . . . . . . . . precio
That's expensive. . . . . . . . . . . . . . . . . . .Es muy caro.
more . . . . . . . . . . . . . . . . . . . . . . . . . . . . . . . . más
less . . . . . . . . . . . . . . . . . . . . . . . . . . . . . . . menos
```

■ NUMBERS

```
zero. . . . . . . . . . . . . . . . . . . . . . . . . . . . . . . . . cero
one . . . . . . . . . . . . . . . . . . . . . . . . . . . . . . . . . uno
two. . . . . . . . . . . . . . . . . . . . . . . . . . . . . . . . . . dos
three . . . . . . . . . . . . . . . . . . . . . . . . . . . . . . . . tres
four . . . . . . . . . . . . . . . . . . . . . . . . . . . . . . cuatro
five. . . . . . . . . . . . . . . . . . . . . . . . . . . . . . . cinco
six . . . . . . . . . . . . . . . . . . . . . . . . . . . . . . . . . seis
seven . . . . . . . . . . . . . . . . . . . . . . . . . . . . . siete
eight. . . . . . . . . . . . . . . . . . . . . . . . . . . . . . . ocho
nine . . . . . . . . . . . . . . . . . . . . . . . . . . . . . nueve
ten. . . . . . . . . . . . . . . . . . . . . . . . . . . . . . . . diez
fifteen . . . . . . . . . . . . . . . . . . . . . . . . . . . quince
twenty . . . . . . . . . . . . . . . . . . . . . . . . . . . veinte
thirty. . . . . . . . . . . . . . . . . . . . . . . . . . . . treinta
forty. . . . . . . . . . . . . . . . . . . . . . . . . . . cuarenta
fifty. . . . . . . . . . . . . . . . . . . . . . . . . . . cincuenta
sixty. . . . . . . . . . . . . . . . . . . . . . . . . . . sesenta
seventy . . . . . . . . . . . . . . . . . . . . . . . . . . setenta
eighty . . . . . . . . . . . . . . . . . . . . . . . . . . ochenta
ninety . . . . . . . . . . . . . . . . . . . . . . . . . . noventa
one hundred . . . . . . . . . . . . . . . . . . . . . . . . cien
one thousand . . . . . . . . . . . . . . . . . . . . . . . . mil
one million . . . . . . . . . . . . . . . . . . . . un millón
```

■ TIMES & DATES

What time is it?	¿qué hora es?
today	hoy
tomorrow	mañana
day after tomorrow	pasado mañana
yesterday	ayer
last night	anoche
day	el día
month	el mes
year	el año
date	la fecha
in the morning	por la mañana
in the afternoon	por la tarde
in the evening/night	por la noche
Monday	el lunes
Tuesday	el martes
Wednesday	el miércoles
Thursday	el jueves
Friday	el viernes
Saturday	el sábado
Sunday	el domingo

■ ADVENTURE VOCABULARY

to study Spanish	estudiar español
to climb	subir
to swim	nadar
to walk	caminar, pasear
to dance	bailar
to cook	cocinar
volcano	el volcán
forest	el bosque
jungle	la selva
estuary	estero
river	río
lake	el lago
boat	la lancha
sea	la mar
beach	la playa
kayak	el kayak
snorkel	el esnorkel
scuba diving	el buceo
lagoon or lake	laguna
crocodile	cocodrilo
caiman	caiman
bird	ave

snake. . . . . .culebra or serpiente
agouti . . . . guatusa
parrot. . . . . loro
butterfly . . . . mariposa
white-faced monkey . . . . .mono cara blanca
howler monkey . . . . mono congo
pelican . . . . pelícano
sloth. . . . . perezoso
frog. . . . . rana
toad . . . . sapo
turtle . . . . tortuga
opossum . . . . zorro
deer . . . . venado
dangerous . . . . peligroso
mosquito . . . . el sancudo
repellent . . . . repelente

■ SHOPPING

market . . . . mercado
supermarket . . . . supermercado
bag. . . . . la bolsa
handicrafts . . . . artesanía
hammock. . . . . la hamaca
expensive . . . . caro
cheap. . . . . barato
long . . . . largo
short . . . . corto
How much does this cost? . . . . ¿Cuánto cuesta?
Can I see? . . . . ¿Puedo ver?
I'd like. . . . . Quisiera
too expensive . . . . demasiado caro

■ DIRECTIONS & TRANSPORTATION

to the left. . . . . .a la izquierda
to the right. . . . . .a la derecha
straight . . . . derecho
north. . . . . norte
south . . . . sur
east . . . . este
west. . . . . oeste
here, please . . . . .aquí, por favor
traffic circle/roundabout . . . . rotonda
slow down, please . . . . más despacio, por favor
bus . . . . bus
bus stop . . . . la parada

Appendix

bus station . . . . .terminal de buses
round-trip. . . . . .ida y vuelta
here . . . . aquí
there . . . . allá
where? . . . . ¿dónde?
I want to get off at_____ . . . . quiero bajar en_____
Can you tell me . . . . ¿me puede avisar cuando
when to get off?   debo bajar?

■ EATING

food . . . . comida
plate of the day. . . . . comida corriente
local food . . . . comida típica
breakfast . . . . el desayuno
lunch . . . . el almuerzo
dinner. . . . . la cena
fork. . . . . el tenedor
spoon. . . . . la cuchara
knife. . . . . el cuchillo
napkin . . . . la servilleta
meat (refers to red meat) . . . . carne
steak. . . . . bistec
cubed beef. . . . . salpicón
shredded beef . . . . desmenuzada
chicken. . . . . pollo
fish . . . . pescado
shrimp . . . . camarones
seafood. . . . . mariscos
I'm vegetarian. . . . . Soy vegetariano/a
without meat . . . . sin carne
eggs . . . . huevos
scrambled eggs. . . . . huevos revueltos
bread . . . . pan
toast . . . . pan tostado
fruit. . . . . fruit
salad . . . . ensalada
rice . . . . arroz
beans . . . . frijoles
beans and rice . . . . gallo pinto
fried. . . . . frito
roasted . . . . asado
barbecued . . . . a la parilla
cooked . . . . cocido
raw . . . . crudo
the bill or check . . . . la cuenta

■ DRINKING

water	agua
drinking water	agua potable, agua purificada
tap water	agua del grifo
juice	jugo
coffee	café
tea	té
sugar	azúcar
soda/soft drink	gaseosa
beer	cerveza
rum	ron
wine	vino
milk	leche

■ STAYING HEALTHY

I'm sick	Estoy enfermo/a
My_____ hurts	me duele_____.
stomach	el estómago
shroat	la garganta
leg	la pierna
arm	el brazo
head	la cabeza
fever	la fiebre
diarrhea	diarrea
to vomit	vomitar
condom	el condón, el preservativo
medicine	la medicina
pill	pastilla
pharmacy	la farmacia
hospital	el hospital
doctor	el médico

FURTHER READING

■ POETRY

Riverbed of Memory (Daisy Zamora)

Ruben's Orphans (Marco Morelli)

The Revolution

Blood of Brothers (Stephen Kinzer)

The Country Under My Skin (Giaconda Belli)

Fire From the Mountain (Omar Cabezas)

Washington's War on Nicaragua (Holly Sklar)

The Gospel in Solentiname (Ernesto Cardenal)

With the Contras (Christopher Dickey)

The Jaguar Smile (Salman Rushdie)

Daily Life in Nicaragua

My Car in Managua (Forrest D. Colburn)

■ NATURE & WILDLIFE

Naturalist in Nicaragua (Thomas Belt)

Savage Shore (Edward Marriott)

The Sharks of Lake Nicaragua: True Tales of Adventure, Travel, and Fishing (Randy Wayne White)

The Savage Shore: Life and Death with Nicaragua's Last Shark Hunters (Edward Marriott)

■ CHILDREN'S LITERATURE

Uncle Nacho's Hat: El Sombrero Del Tío Nacho (Harriet Rohmer and Veg Reisberg)

Mother Scorpion Country; A Legend from the Miskito Indians of Nicaragua (Harriet Rohmer)

The Invisible Hunters: A Legend of the Miskito Indians of Nicaragua (Harriet Rohmer, Octavia Chow, and Morris Vidaure)

Nicaragua (Jennifer Kott)

FILMS

Walker (1987)

The World Stopped Watching (2003)

Carla's Song (1996)

Index